Nicholas Atkin and **Frank Tallett** are Senior Lecturers in History at the University of Reading. They are the authors of *Priests, Prelates and People: A History of European Catholicism, 1750 to the Present* (I.B.Tauris).

THE RIGHT IN FRANCE

From Revolution to Le Pen

NICHOLAS ATKIN
&
FRANK TALLETT

I.B. TAURIS

LONDON · NEW YORK

FOR OUR PARENTS

Published in 2003 by I.B.Tauris & Co Ltd
6 Salem Road, London W2 4BU
175 Fifth Avenue, New York NY 10010
www.ibtauris.com

In the United States of America and in Canada distributed by
Palgrave Macmillan, a division of St Martin's Press
175 Fifth Avenue, New York NY 10010

ISBN 1 86064 916 5

A full CIP record for this book is available from the British Library
A full CIP record for this book is available from the Library of Congress

Library of Congress catalog card: available

Printed and bound in Great Britain by MPG Books Ltd, Bodmin

Contents

Maps and Tables

Preface

Many of the essays presented here were originally delivered as papers at a two-day conference on 'The Right in France' organized by the Department of History at the University of Reading in July 1996. The editors wish to thank all those who read papers as well as the delegates, who provided a lively forum for discussion. Thanks also extend to those authors who prepared specially commissioned chapters, often working to particularly tight deadlines. The Conference would not have been possible without financial support from the Department of History and the administrative talents of Mrs Liz Griffiths who undertook much of the practical organization.

We are indebted to Dr Lester Crook of I.B.Tauris for his enthusiasm and editorial advice, and to Professor Edward James of the University of Reading who has been unstinting in his help in preparing the manuscript for publication.

It is appropriate that we acknowledge the contribution of two distinguished French scholars who are now sadly deceased but who made, in different ways, crucial contributions to this book. Professor Peter Morris of the University of Aston spoke at the conference and was preparing an essay for inclusion here at the time of his death. His paper was delivered with his customary grace, humour and perception, and this volume and French studies in this country are much impoverished by his loss. We are particularly grateful to Professor Charles Hauss of George Mason University who, at short notice, provided a replacement chapter for the one that Peter was to have written.

Second, the editors owe an enormous debt of gratitude to Dr Ralph Gibson of the University of Lancaster. Ralph was a crucial in inspiring a series of conferences on French history organized by the Department of History at the University of Reading, and spoke at the first two of these. His intention was to be present at the third such gathering, but his untimely death robbed both the conference and the academic community of his scholarly talents. His influence, like Peter's, upon French studies will be sorely missed.

Nicholas Atkin and Frank Tallett

Preface to the Second Edition

We are delighted to produce a second edition of the *Right in France* which first appeared in 1997. In his closing chapter to the original edition, the American political scientist Chip Hauss remarked that 'it never makes sense to say that x will never happen.' The presidential elections in April 2002 underscored that very point when the Front National leader Jean-Marie Le Pen unexpectedly outscored the Socialist candidate Lionel Jospin to enter the second round face-off against the incumbent President Jacques Chirac. To reflect this significant and depressing event, this revised edition includes an additional chapter on what the election results mean for politics in France. While it may be that the Front National has reached a plateau in its support, the health of the Fifth Republic is in some doubt. This new edition has also allowed us to correct small errors which appeared earlier. The editors remain grateful to all those contributors who provided such a stimulating and lively collection of essays which tackle the French right in its many guises.

List Of Contributors

Martin S. Alexander is Professor of Contemporary History and Politics at the University of Salford, and was a Visiting Professor of Strategy at the US Naval War College in 1991-92. He is author of *The Republic in Danger. General Maurice Gamelin and the Politics of French Defence, 1933-40* (Cambridge, 1993) and is co-editor, with Helen Graham, of *The French and Spanish Popular Fronts* (Cambridge, 1989). He is currently working on the French experiences of war in Algeria, 1954-62.

Nicholas Atkin is Senior Lecturer in History at the University of Reading. He is author of *Church and Schools in Vichy France, 1940-44* (New York, 1991) and *Pétain* (London, 1997), and is co-editor, with Frank Tallett, of *Religion, Society and Politics in France Since 1789* (1991) and *Catholicism in Britain and France since 1789* (London, 1996). He is currently preparing a book on French exiles in Britain during the Second World War.

Michael Biddiss is Professor of Modern History at the University of Reading. He was President of the Historical Association, 1991-94, and since 1995 has been joint Vice-President of the Royal Historical Society. His books include *Father of Racist Ideology. The Social and Political Thought of Count Gobineau* (London, 1970), *The Age of the Masses. Ideas and Society in Europe Since 1870* (London, 1977) and *The Nuremberg Trial and the Third Reich* (London, 1992).

Michael Broers is Lecturer in History at the University of Leeds. He is the author of *Europe Under Napoleon, 1799-1815* (London, 1996), *Europe After Napoleon. Revolution, Revolution and Romanticism, 1814-48* (Manchester, 1996) and *Napoleonic Imperialism and the Savoyard Monarchy, 1773-1821. State-Building in Piedmont* (Lampeter, 1997).

Kay Chadwick is Lecturer in French Studies at the University of Liverpool. She has published in *French Historical Studies* and *Modern and Contemporary France*. She is editor of *Catholicism in Twentieth-Century France* (Liverpool, forthcoming).

LIST OF CONTRIBUTORS

Geoffrey Cubitt is Lecturer in History at the University of York. He is the author of *The Jesuit Myth. Conspiracy Theory and Politics in Nineteenth-Century France* (Oxford, 1993) and of several articles on French religious history.

Richard Griffiths is Professor of French at King's College, London. His many books include *The Reactionary Revolution. The Catholic Revival in French Literature, 1870-1914* (London, 1966), *Marshal Pétain* (London, 1970), *Fellow Travellers of the Right. British Enthusiasts for Nazi Germany, 1933-39* (London, 1983) and *The Use of Abuse. The Polemics of the Dreyfus Affair and its Aftermath* (London, 1991).

Charles Hauss is Adjunct Professor in the Department of Public and International Affairs at George Mason University, Fairfax, Virginia. He is spending 1995-98 as Visiting Research Fellow and Professor in the Department of Politics at the University of Reading. He is the author of five books, including two on French politics, and is currently working on a non-academic book on revitalizing the left , based on recent events in the USA and the United Kingdom, with occasional intellectual forays to France.

Michael Heffernan is Lecturer in Geography at the University of Loughborough. He has published numerous articles on the French imperial experience, and is co-editor of *Geography and Imperialism, 1820-1920* (Manchester, 1995).

David Parry was a Junior Research Fellow of Hertford College, Oxford. His Ph.D is on 'Conspiracy Theory and the French Third Republic'. He has published in *Contemporary European History* and *Intelligence and National Security*, and is currently working on a study of the city of Orléans, 1870-1914.

Kevin Passmore is Lecturer in History at the University of Wales at Cardiff. He is the author of *From Liberalism to Fascism. The Right in a French Province, 1928-39* (Cambridge, 1997) as well as articles in *French History*, *French Historical Studies* and *The Historical Journal*. He is currently working on a history of the French right since 1870.

THE RIGHT IN FRANCE

Pamela Pilbeam is Professor of History at Royal Holloway and Bedford New College, London. Her publications include *the Middle Classes in Europe, 1789-1914. France, Germany, Italy and Russia* (London, 1990), *The 1830 Revolution in France* (London, 1991) and *Republicanism in Nineteenth-Century France* (London, 1994). She is also editor of *Themes in Modern European History, 1780-1830* (London, 1995).

Miranda Pollard is Associate Professor of History and Women's Studies at the University of Georgia, Athens. She is the author of *The Reign of Virtue. Mobilizing Gender in Vichy France, 1940-44* (Chicago, forthcoming).

Frank Tallett is Senior Lecturer in History at the University of Reading. He is author of *War and Society in Early Modern Europe, 1495-1715* (London, 1992), and is co-editor, with Nicholas Atkin, of *Religion, Society and Politics in France* (London, 1991) and *Catholicism in Britain and France since 1789* (London, 1996).

Jonathan Watson is currently undertaking research for an Oxford D.Phil on Gaullism between 1958 and 1969. He recently held a Fellowship at the Institute of Historical Research, London.

Jim Wolfreys is Lecturer in French Studies at King's College, London. He is the author of several articles on contemporary French politics and is currently preparing a book on the Front National.

Abbreviations

ADR	Archives Départementales du Rhône
AF	Action Française
ALN	Armée de Libération Nationale
AN	Archives Nationales
APEL	Association des Parents des Ecoles Libres
APP	Archives de la Préfecture de Police
BDIC	Bibliothèque de Documentataion Internationale Contemporaine
CDU	Christlich-Demokratische Union
CGQJ	Commissariat Général aux Questions Juives
CGT	Confédération Générale du Travail
CGTSR	Confédération Générale du Travail Syndicaliste et Révolutionnaire
CJR	Cour de Justice du Rhône
CJS	Cour de Justice de la Seine
CNC	Cercle National des Combattants
CNGA	Cercle National des Gens d'Armes
CRAS	Comité du Rassemblement Anti-Soviétique
CSG	Conseil Supérieur de la Guerre
FFI	Forces Françaises de l'Intérieur
FLN	Front de Libération Nationale
FN	Front National
FNC	Fédération Nationale Catholique
JO	*Journal Officiel*
LVF	Légion des Volontaires Français contre le Bolchevisme
MPR	Mouvement Républicain Populaire
OAS	Organisation de l'Armée Secrète
OFC	*Les Origines de la France Contemporaine*
OSARN	Organisation Secrète d'Action Révolutionnaire Nationale
PCF	Parti Communiste Français
PDP	Parti Démocrate Populaire
PNF	Partito Nazionale Fascista
PPF	Parti Populaire Français
PRNS	Parti Républicain National et Social
PS	Parti Socialiste

PSF	Parti Social Français
RHDGM	*Revue d'Histoire de la Deuxième Guerre Mondiale*
RPF	Rassemblement du Peuple Français
RPR	Rassemblement pour la République
SFIO	Section Française de l'Internationale Ouvrière
SHAT	Service Historique de l'Armée de Terre
SR	Service Central de Renseignements
UCAD	Union des Comités d'Action Défensive
UDP	Union Démocratique du Travail
UFCS	Union Féminine Civique et Sociale
UNR	Union pour la Nouvelle République
VC	*Hippolyte Taine. Sa Vie et sa Correspondance*

1. INTRODUCTION: LES DROITES COMMENÇENT ICI, 1789-94?

Nicholas Atkin and Frank Tallett

Writing the Right

In 1954 René Rémond published his seminal study, *La droite en France de 1815 à nos jours,* which has remained the essential starting point for subsequent analysis.[1] His basic thesis was that the history of the right was a continuum made up of three constituent parts—Legitimism, Orleanism and Bonapartism—which manifested themselves in various guises throughout the nineteenth and twentieth centuries.[2] As several historians and political scientists have pointed out, the obvious drawback of this approach lies in its determinism, focusing attention on the survival of past attitudes and ignoring the advent of fresh ones. This is why, for example, Rémond provoked such a storm of debate over the issue of whether a French fascism ever existed.[3] In his view, movements such as Colonel de la Rocque's Croix de Feu were merely interwar manifestations of the Bonapartist tradition. To be fair, Rémond did accept that Doriot's Parti Populaire Français (PPF) probably represented an indigenous French fascism,[4] and in the 1982 edition of his volume, significantly entitled *Les droites en France*, he acknowledged the diversity of the right, while maintaining the basic tenets of his original thesis.

Although the debates about fascism in particular have been heavily influenced by English and American scholars, it is fair to say that until recently Anglophone historians of France have generally shied away from an all-embracing study of the right.[5] Obviously this would be a gargantuan undertaking, yet the neglect remains odd for a number of reasons. After all, the right, along with the centre, has been in power in France for most of the last two hundred years. Moreover, it was the French Revolution of 1789 that invented the very terms 'left' and 'right', and bequeathed them to

European political discourse: they were adopted by some of the German states by 1848; Denmark in 1870; Norway in 1882; Sweden in 1910; and Luxembourg in 1914.[6] Admittedly, an embryonic two-party system was developing in Britain from the 1760s, but Whig/Tory and Court/Country divisions could be hardly be characterized by the terms 'left' and 'right'.[7]

The reasons why Anglophone historians have overlooked the right are unclear. It may be, as Richard Vinen has suggested, that British and American scholars have been 'led astray by a fruitless search for a reformist or social-democratic left that would correspond to their own political sympathies', a comment which probably has more force when applied to the nineteenth rather than the twentieth century.[8] More contentious is his assertion that this quest was doomed to failure since the French left always looked either to a Jacobin past or to a Bolshevik future.[9] A more probable explanation for the neglect of the right may lie in the traditions of English historical writing on France. Historians on both sides of the Atlantic have been heavily influenced by the approaches of Alfred Cobban and Richard Cobb. Even though the two men rejected the grand theories of the Annales school of history, which marginalized politics by its stress upon the underlying socio-economic structures, they nevertheless shared with the annalistes a common concern with socio-economic matters to the relative neglect of politics.[10] In their opinion, the French Revolution is best understood through a social interpretation.

This is not in any way to suggest that the history of the French right has been wholly ignored by Anglo-American scholars, including Cobban and Cobb. As already implied, much important work has been done on the twentieth century where contemporary events merge with history,[11] and recently there has been a clear resurgence of interest in the political history of France, especially during the eighteenth century.[12] It is against this background that the editors brought together a number of British and American scholars from different disciplines to contribute to a volume on the French right. The objective was not to provide a comprehensive overview such as that offered in the monumental study directed by Jean-François Sirinelli.[13] Rather, it was to illuminate particular facets of the right on which anglophone historians have a distinctive contribution to offer. Many of these aspects—gender, empire and ethnicity, for example—have been partly or wholly overlooked. In addition, the contributors provide new insights into familiar territory: Legitimism; Orleanism; Bonapartism; political Catholicism; and Gaullism, to name but a few. Gaps inevitably remain, yet what all the chapters have in common is a concern with the right as it manifested itself after 1789.

Diverse though the interests of the contributors are, their essays share a concern with a number of questions. How does the right express itself in terms of political organization? What is its social constituency? What issues has it concerned itself with, and appropriated? What political influence has it exerted, and are we now, in the 1990s, witnessing the demise of the terms 'left' and 'right' as useful indicators of political allegiance? The picture that emerges from this volume is of a right which is always fluid, diverse and adaptable.The right depended on no fixed political organization expressing itself, at various times, through parties, pressure groups, leagues, coups d'états, *journées*, and conspiracies. Likewise, the right's social composition has been eclectic in the extreme; its support has been drawn from the top to the bottom of society, and has included powerful groups and institutions such as the Church, the army, the *patronat,* intellectuals and regionalists. Inevitably, the issues the right has addressed, and the influence which it has commanded, have fluctuated. Indeed, some political commentators have recently pronounced the funeral rites of the French right as parties from all over the political spectrum compete for control of the centre ground.[14]

The one thing which the contributors have not addressed is the question of when the right begins. The purpose of this essay is to provide a backdrop to the remainder of the volume by scrutinizing the genesis of the French right which, it will be argued, is found in the early years of the French Revolution. The chapter suggests that the right is best understood as a collection of ideologies, developed in response to the traumas of the 1790s, rather than as a social movement or as an organized political force. Such an analysis helps explain why, in the nineteenth and twentieth centuries, the right has proved to be so enduring, retaining an ability to reinvent itself in response to changing circumstances.

The Genesis of the Right

When does the right begin? While acknowledging the formative influence of the Revolution, Rémond dates its emergence from the Restoration of 1815, as it was only then that the doctrines of Legitimism, Orléanism and Bonapartism began to take on a life of their own.[15] A similar opinion is offered by Michel Denis in the opening chapter of Sirinelli's *Les droites françaises*: 'C'est en 1815, lors des Cent-Jours puis dans les premiers mois de la seconde Restauration, qu'on voit se dessiner de façon durable les contours d'une droite organisée.'[16] Alternatively, it has been suggested that the right's origins may be traced back to the politics of pre-revolutionary

France, in particular to the conflicts between crown and parlements and the debates in the Assembly of Notables.[17] There is some force to this argument. Although the men of 1789 were conscious that they were creating something new, in the formulation of policy and ideology they drew constantly upon the idioms and experiences of the old regime.

Surely, however, 1789 must be the real *point de départ*. One obvious reason for this is that the very terms 'left' and 'right' were products of the Revolution, stemming from what Mirabeau termed 'the geography of the Assembly'.[18] At the mass held on 4 May to inaugurate the Estates General, the deputies from the Third refused to restrict themselves to the benches allocated, showing a prescient appreciation of the significance of seating as an indicator of political sympathies,[19] though it was not until the debates of July to September, when the Assembly dealt with the vexed issue of the royal veto, that seating patterns began to reflect political divisions. To the right of the president's desk sat those constituents who favoured providing the monarch with an unrestricted veto; to the left were arranged deputies hostile to the king exercising such authority. Thereafter, where one sat in the assemblies—left, right or centre—provided some indicator of political affiliation. The arrangement of seating in a tiered and semi-circular shape further facilitated this, and the architecture of the French revolutionary assemblies provided a template for the representative institutions of several other countries, including the Congress in Washington.[20] The French Revolution thus invented the labels 'left' and 'right', together with the whole notion of a political spectrum, and firmly established these in the vocabulary of western political discourse.

Yet a study of seating plans takes us only a little way towards determining the nature of the right. After all, political power was widely diffused throughout France and bodies such as the Paris Commune and Sections, departments and district administrations all presented themselves as alternative focii to the national assemblies. The historian must also be cautious in using the labels of the period—patriots, noirs, monarchiens, Brissotins and Montagnards—to identify left-right sympathies. These groupings were not disciplined political parties of the modern type. Such parties simply did not exist, and would not emerge in France until the late nineteenth century.[21] The associations and clubs which flourished during the 1790s were loose gatherings of deputies and others, brought together as much by personal loyalties and common geographical origins as by shared ideological concerns. Members moved easily from one camp to another. This was especially true of the early stages of the Revolution when deputies, summoned from all over the country to the Estates General, floundered in a sea of unfamiliar names and faces.[22] With the advent of the Legislative in September 1791 and the Convention in September the following year, deputies were better disciplined, reflecting the emergence of a strata of society which had become accustomed to taking part in the polititical process.[23] Yet these men remained wary of organized parties which were deemed to represent sectional interest, thus flouting the associated notions of national sovereignty and the general will that were central to the Revolution.[24] It is significant that the term 'faction' or 'party' figured, alongside 'aristocratic', as one of the most damning indictments to level against an opponent.

Social analysis as a means of identifying the right also has its limitations. All that may be proffered by way of generalization is that the right drew its membership from all ranks of society. Admittedly, support for the right came predominantly from the princes of the blood, the lesser nobility and the higher clergy, yet the lower clergy and the newly emerging bourgeoisie were strongly represented. Even artisans and peasants may be legitimately counted among the right. For example, Suzanne Desan has argued that the peasantry appropriated the discourse and ideology of the Revolution in a conservative defence of their interests, though most historians do not see this section of society as being self-conscious members of the right.[25]

The right's social eclecticism is hardly surprising. It reflected the growing heterogeneity of French society. Even before 1789, wealth rather than birth was emerging as the key determinant of status,[26] and the Revolution, through the reforms of 4 August, the abolition of noble status in June 1790 and the promotion of careers open to talent, further eroded the corporatist farmework of the old regime. More importantly, the right's social diversity sprang from the fact that no group or individual was unaffected by the events of the 1790s. The scale of the changes brought about by the administrative, judicial and economic reforms of the Constituent was enormous, and the intrusion of the French state into the lives of its citizens became even more pervasive with the advent of war and its corollary, the Terror. French men and women were perforce obliged to take a stand for or against the Revolution; they could not be *attentiste*.[27]

Sovereignty and the Right

It was ideology that provided the right in the 1790s with an identity. In this context, the initial and overriding issue was that of sovereignty. Between 1787, the gathering of the Assembly of Notables, and the summer of 1789, the old regime monarchy in France collapsed and a revolution ensued. Political power slipped away from the crown, not least of all thanks to the ineptitude of Louis XVI and his ministers, and fell into the hands of the National Assembly. This presented the deputies with a problem: what was the basis of their authority? In an echo of Montesquieu, Rousseau and Saige's more recent *Catéchisme du citoyen*, they responded almost unanimously by asserting the notion of the sovereignty of the nation.[28] The *arrêté* of 17 June made clear that a constitutional revolution had happened by declaring that the Assembly alone possessed the right to formulate and interpret the general will of the nation,[29] a sentiment restated in Article 3 of the *Declaration of the Rights of Man and the Citizen* of August 1789.[30] Consequently, a majority of deputies accepted that there should be a constitution which defined the parameters of royal power.

If there was general agreement about the need for a constitution, the assertion of national sovereignty nevertheless raised as many problems as it solved. Who comprised the nation? What was the nature of sovereignty and how was it to be expressed? These issues caused less difficulty than building the king into the new constitution. Should the monarch have a suspensive or absolute veto over legislation, or no veto at all? Should he operate alongside a unicameral legislature or a bicameral one, a solution favoured by those who admired the British political system? Should he or his ministers be answerable to parliament? Should he have the right to nominate ministers, or should parliament have a say in this matter? Should he possess the power to dissolve the assembly? Should he enjoy the authority to declare war and make peace?

The debates on the position of the king were long and bitter, cutting across social strata and polarizing political opinion. A right emerged or, more accurately, several rights emerged. Some unreconstructed royalists, often referred to as the noirs and represented by orators such as Cazalès and the abbé Maury, comprised what might be termed the far right. They never accepted that a transfer of sovereignty away from the monarchy had taken place and many of them ultimately opted for emigration.[31] A more numerous body, led initially by Mounier, Bergasse and Lally-Tollendal and known collectively as the monarchiens, favoured granting the king a large measure of delegated authority, including an absolute veto.[32] However, they envisaged limitations on royal powers, notably through the establishment of a bicameral legislature, one house of which would be hereditary. In other words, they were seeking a redefinition of the old regime balance of power. The Assembly's vote for a unicameral system and the October Days effectively ended the monarchiens' influence.

Mounier returned to the Dauphiné and could not be tempted back into active politics.

In 1789-90 majority opinion, both inside and outside of the Assembly, favoured the creation of a constitutional monarchy in which the social order of the old regime would play no part. Men as diverse as Lafayette, Mirabeau and the Lameth brothers all sought to embody the king within a legal framework in which his function would be chiefly executive, but in which he would also enjoy a representative function. His exercise of a suspensive veto would delay legislation from the assembly to ensure that it was in accordance with the national will. Although there were inherent inconsistencies in this political conception—how, for example, could the king enjoy a measure of sovereignty if this was indivisible from and exclusive to the nation—it was nonetheless embodied in the Constitution of 1791. However, the efforts of the constitutional monarchists were torpedoed by the actions of Louis himself. Unwilling to cooperate with the Assembly, he opted in June to flee the country, leaving behind a document in which he explicitly repudiated all that he had previously appeared to endorse.[33] His obduracy ensured that the Constitution of 1791 would never be implemented.

Sovereignty and the role of the king had thus provided a defining issue for the right. Whatever precise role accorded to the monarch, the right remained attached to some form of kingship. Accordingly, many who had so far supported the principles of 1789, however unenthusiastically, broke with the Revolution when Louis' intransigeance led to the creation of a Republic in September 1792 by the newly elected Convention. There were few deputies with monarchist sympathies in this fresh assembly. Not only were they out of tune with the Convention's republicanism, changed voting procedures had in any case effectively excluded them from putting up for election.

Its membership drawn largely from the bourgeoisie, the Convention was dominated by bitter fighting between two principal factions: the Montagnards and the Girondins. Although the former may be characterized as the left, it would be unfair to regard their opponents as being on the right since the policies of both groups were essentially identical. Their factional disputes represented conflicts within the left wing.[34] A 'new' right, however, distinct from that which had existed in the two previous assemblies, did exist, located in that part of the Convention designated the 'plain', or 'swamp' by its detractors.[35] Once again, its emergence was evidenced in the debates over the future of the king. The new right, unlike the old, accepted the Republic but was uncomfortable with proposals for the trial of Louis XVI. As a matter of principle, this new right considered that the Assembly ought not to act as accuser, judge and executioner. The verdict on and fate of Louis should instead be subject to an 'appel au peuple'.[36]

Numerically, the deputies of the plain were a majority yet, lacking the zeal and sense of purpose of the radical left, they struggled to make their influence felt. These unaligned conventionnels acquiesced reluctantly in the purge of the Girondins of 31 May-2 June 1793 and, desperate to turn the tide of war and crush counter revolution, agreed to vote for the establishment of emergency powers which culminated in the Terror and the concentration of authority in the hands of the Committee of Public Safety. During the debates over these issues, differences between left and right over sovereignty crystallized still further. The Montagnard left increasingly regarded itself, rather than the whole assembly, as the embodiment of the general will of the nation although, when it suited them, members of the Mountain were prepared to espouse the doctrine of popular sovereignty—this was how they justified the involvement of the Sections in the attack on the Girondins, for example. While the right accepted the need to consult the people from time to time, direct democracy was an anathema, as were the dictatorial pretensions of the left. The will of the nation was represented by the whole of the assembly.[37] Only at Thermidor did the right assert itself and check the radical impulses of the Montagnards, the Jacobins and the popular movement. The new constitution that was framed in 1795 provided for a bicameral chamber and a weak executive, as well as enshrining several of the entitlements, notably the inviolability of property, that had been first formulated in the *Declaration of the Rights of Man and the Citizen*.

Entitlements and Duties

If sovereignty and monarchy were above all central to the identity of the right, the issue of entitlements and duties offers a further defining characteristic. From the outset, unreconstructed elements on the right, notably princes of the blood and many representatives of the clergy, adopted a corporatist position in which rights and obligations interlocked with social status. Such people, largely drawn from the extreme, focused upon the old corporatist institutions—family, region, community—as a counter-weight to the growing power of the state.[38] Accordingly, they never came to terms with the disappearance of the world of privilege, symbolized by the night of 4 August. Most deputies did, although they failed to resolve the conundrum of whether entitlements were inborn, as Montesquieu had argued, or were socially derived, as Rousseau had suggested.[39] The formulation of the *Declaration of the Rights of Man and the Citizen* owed as much to the propertied origins of the deputies and their wish to renounce the worst abuses of the old regime as to the musings of the *philosophes*. Hence the inviolability of property figured prominently in the *Declaration*. Small wonder that, during the Revolution, the ability to participate actively, and at any given level in the political process, always hinged upon the fulfilment of property qualifications.[40]

On property, at least, deputies of all shades of opinion were initially in accord. There was additionally widespread agreement upon equality before the law, careers open to talent, and the operation of laissez-faire principles. Consensus evaporated as the Revolution came under pressure from two directions. First, a popular movement outside of the assemblies, which reached its peak in 1793 with the *enragés* movement led by Jacques Roux, pushed for a redistribution of wealth and the imposition of economic controls both as a matter of social justice and as a reward for Parisian support during the purge of the Girondins. These demands were taken up by the Montagnard left which corralled a reluctant Assembly to introduce limited price controls in the form of the *maximum*. In this way, the deputies temporarily abandoned their deeply held commitment to laissez-faire principles.[41] Second, and more importantly, mounting internal and external problems led the *conventionnels* to suspend the freedoms guaranteed by the Constitution and inaugurate the Terror. By spring 1794, this dictatorial form of government had dramatically reversed France's fortunes both at home and abroad, but had provoked fresh divisions in the chamber. The right now argued for the reestablishment of those legal and constitutional entitlements which had only been abandoned reluctantly and provisionally. By contrast, the left, represented by a diminishing but powerful group, centring on Robespierre and Saint Just in the Comité du Salut Public, sought an intensification of the Terror. Although Robespierre and his associates remained ill at ease with the social and economic egalitarianism of the popular movement, they favoured a policy of terror as being essential to the purification and regeneration of France.[42]

Regionalism

Throughout the 1790s, a fear of social disorder bound all deputies together. Yet, ironically, the left was not wholly wrong in seeing much resistance to the Revolution as inspired by principles which came to be the preserve of the right, in particular a commitment to regional identity. Old-regime regionalism, which had focused upon the province and which in 1787-88 produced the demand for provincial assemblies, was overtaken by the events of 1789. Two contradictory impulses then came into play: the desire to create an indivisible nation and the wish to devolve authority as a means of countering the centralization which, the revolutionaries believed, had characterized absolute monarchy. The reforms of the Constituent Assembly were initially driven more by the latter impulse than by the first. A new and uniform administrative system, based on 83 departments, was established which put a premium on the dispersal of power and participation of local citizens. Inevitably, there was occasional local resentment, particularly when a town did not receive the coveted status of *chef-lieu*, but on the whole the new system was well received and functioned smoothly, partly because members of the privileged orders generally failed to get elected to the new positions.

The defects of this novel system of decentralized administration became apparent with the outbreak of war. The need to focus the energies of the nation obliged Parisian politicians to override local autonomy. The growth of central control, coupled with resentment of the capital's pretensions, were significant factors in generating counter revolution in the Vendée and elsewhere in 1793. Thereafter, the left was associated with moves to suppress regional and linguistic cultural identity.[43] By contrast, the counter-revolutionary right became increasingly identified with the defence of regionalism.[44] Writing in the immediate aftermath of the Revolution, right-wing intellectuals such as de Maistre, Barruel and Le Play, came to espouse a roseate view of the old regime as the golden age of provincial liberties.[45] In addition, they championed organic units such as the family and community in their denunciation of the universalism of the Revolution. In their view, the outlook of the revolutionaries in perceiving individuals as equals—and, therefore, as identical with one another—was fundamentally flawed. As Paul Farmer comments in the context of Vichy's attempts to revive the virtues of *travail, famille, patrie*, such an individualistic conception

> strips a man of all those attachments to his fellows which alone give him individuality. Instead of real persons, whose distinctive attributes are defined by their position within a family and their role in a business, profession, or trade, the liberal state recognizes only shapeless abstractions who, as citizens, are neither fathers nor sons, peasants nor landlords, workmen nor patrons.[46]

From de Maistre to Barrès, from Barrès to Pétain, from Pétain to Le Pen, such an organicist view of the world has remained a characteristic of the discourse and ideology of a traditional right.[47]

Religion

The final issue that provided the right with an identity was religion. Initially, there was no connection between the right and a defence of religion. The Second Estate had few friends of any political complexion in the Assembly. Indeed, the anticlerical jibes which punctuated debates from an early stage were most likely to come from the right, and it was the nobility, the clergy's 'natural allies', who led the attack on tithes on the night of 4 August. The abolition of the tithe and the nationalization of ecclesiastical property in November 1789 made the Church economically dependent on the state and implied its complete reorganization so as to make it cost-effective. This was achieved with the Civil Constitution of the Clergy. It was during the debates over this and closely related matters, including the abolition of monastic vows, whether Catholicism should be the state religion and whether clerics should swear an oath to the Civil Constitution, that a polarity between left and right over the issue of religion clearly emerged.

These unruly and acrimonious debates, beginning in the autumn of 1789 and running through the following year, shattered the veneer of harmony and common purpose which the deputies had hitherto sought to create.[48] Not wholly without justice, the left accused the bishops of blocking change in order to preserve their old-regime life styles and accused its opponents, more generally, of using religion as a pretext to thwart wider social, economic and political reforms. For its part, the right accused the left of attacking religion. This charge, which some on the right believed to be true, was undoubtedly used by others to whip up popular hostility to the Revolution. More perspicacious than the left, in this respect at least, the right was quick to perceive just how emotive an issue religion might be. Its leading representative in the Assembly, the abbé Maury, had already begun to practise the *politique du pire* by the end of 1790, encouraging the adoption of extreme policies in order to inflame passions. Caught between the extremes of left and right were those deputies, many of them clerics, who sought some reform of the Church and believed this could only be brought about by state action. In the event, the Civil Constitution of the Clergy proved too radical for their tastes, and its implementation sparked off a chain of events, culminating in the dechristianizing campaign of the year II, which alienated whole sections of society from the Revolution. Faith, along with fidelity to the king, moved into the camp of counter revolution.

Political calculation had thus played no small part in the right's defence of Catholicism. However, the debates in the Assembly in 1789 and 1790 also revealed a fundamental divergence between the perceptions of left and right in respect of the position of the Church within the state, and society more generally. The former, drawing upon predominant Enlightenment attitudes, wanted to establish the clergy as state-salaried and state-directed functionaries with responsibility for the teaching of morals and the maintenance of social order.[49] The right wished to maintain the Church as a separate order, free of government tutelage. Ironically, the imposition of state control, formalized in the Concordat of 1801, drove the nineteenth-century Church towards an ultramontane position. Rome offered an escape from state interference. The eighteenth-century Church could afford to be Gallican; its successor could not.

The Moving Frontier: Towards an Understanding of the Right

What conclusions may be drawn from this necessarily brief overview? To begin with, it was during the Revolution that the contours of the right emerged. These were delineated more by reference to ideology than to social origins or party organization. The emerging philosophical pre-occupations of the right were shaped by the events of the Revolution which threw up randomly a series of issues around which the right would coalesce: religion; regionalism; entitlements; and, most importantly, sovereignty, in particular the role of the monarch. One may therefore think of the right as being defined in relation to a 'moving frontier'. As the Revolution's centre of gravity moved leftwards, the right constantly reevaluated its position and added to its support.

An extreme right never abandoned its attachment to monarchy as the embodiment of sovereignty, and never relinquished its adherence to the values and structures of the *ancien régime*.[50] As the self-proclaimed standard bearers of traditional French values, right-wing fundamentalists believed themselves to be above politics in the sense that they rejected the wheeling and dealing, the corruption and compromises innate to the business of a modern mass politics which was born during the French Revolution. As Richard Griffiths has observed, the claim to be non-political has remained an enduring trait of a certain kind of right.[51] A conservative right also emerged in the 1790s, susbsequently dominated by the Orleanists, prepared to adopt a more modern view of the world in which sovereignty lay with the nation, church and state existed separately but in harmony, and entitlements and duties were inextricably bound up with the social order.[52] The failure to bring the Revolution to an end and establish a lasting settlement led to another variety of the right, a liberal right, prepared to accept a Republic, but rejecting the social and economic egalitarianism of the left. The Napoleonic regime would draw upon this liberal right's concern for social order and the protection of property as well as the Jacobin legacy of a nation in arms.[53]

Do we see here the origins of Rémond's tripartite division of the right into Legitimists, Orleanists and Bonapartists? The answer can only be a qualified 'yes'. We should be cautious in insisting upon any linear development between the right as it emerged in the 1790s and its later manifestations. The Revolution did not predetermine the subsequent development of the right. The form and nature of the right was always to be shaped by contingent circumstances: the Restoration; the 1848 Revolution; the collapse of the Second Empire; the Dreyfus Affair; the Stavisky Scandal; the disaster of 1940; Algeria and the end of empire. Nevertheless, the 1790s were important. Many of the issues which continue to confront the modern world—including the role of the state, individual liberties, the position of religion, regionalism, social and economic reform—had their roots in the Revolution. The 1790s thus constituted a treasure trove into which the nineteenth- and twentieth-century rights could delve for ideological and experiential trinkets to assist in their adaptation to new situations. The right possesses a continuous history yet, as Malcolm Anderson has suggested and as many of the essays in this volume demonstrate, it is a history of discontiniuities.[54]

Notes

1. Rémond, René: *La droite en France* (Paris, 1954)
2. As Robert Anderson observes, Rémond's thesis is an application of Siegfried's theory of political temperaments. See Anderson, Robert D.: *France, 1870-1914* (London, 1977) p 100
3. For a good introduction to the extensive literature on French fascism, see Sweets, John F.: 'Hold that Pendulum! Redefining Fascism, Collaborationism and Resistance in France', *French Historical Studies* 15/4 (1988), pp 731-58, and Jenkins, Brian: 'Robert Soucy and the "Second Wave" of French Fascism', *Modern and Contemporary France* 4/2 (1996), pp 193-208
4. For a contribution to the debate on the 'fascist' character of the PPF, see

Kevin Passmore's essay in this volume: 'Class, Gender and Populism: The Parti Populaire Français in Lyon, 1936-40'

5.   There is a wealth of studies in English on detailed aspects of the French right, but few are wide-ranging. Of those available, see Anderson, Malcolm: *Conservative Politics in France* (London, 1974) and Shapiro, David, ed: *The Right in France* (London, 1962). This paucity contrasts with the extensive general literature in French. In addition to Rémond, see Brigouleix, Bernard: *L'extrême droite en France* (Paris, 1977); Chebel d'Appollonia, Ariane: *L'extrême droite en France. De Maurras à Le Pen* (Brussells, 1988); Milza, Pierre,: *Fascisme française. Passé et présent* (Paris, 1987); Petitfils, Jean-Christian: *L'extrême droite en France* (Paris, 1983); and Sirinelli, Jean-François, ed: *Histoire des droites en France* (3 vols, Paris, 1992).

6.   Sirinell, Jean-François and Vigne, Eric: 'Des droites et du politique', in Sirinelli, ed: *Histoire des droites*, p *xiv*

7.   On this matter, see Colley, Linda: *Britons. The Forging of the Nation, 1707-1837* (London, 1992) and O'Gorman, Frank: *The Emergence of the British Two Party System, 1760-1832* (London, 1982).

8.   Vinen, Richard: *France, 1934-1970* (London, 1996), p *xii*. For recent Anglophone studies on the nineteenth century, see Pilbeam, Pamela M.: *Republicanism in Nineteenth-Century France* (London, 1995) and Magraw, Roger: *A History of the French Working Class* (2 vols, Oxford, 1992).

9.   Vinen: *France, 1934-1970*, p *xii*

10.   See especially, Cobb, Richard: *The Police and the People. French Popular Protest, 1789-1820* (Oxford, 1970); Cobb, Richard: *The People's Armies* (New Haven, 1987); and Cobban, Alfred: *The Social Interpretation of the French Revolution* (Cambridge, 1974). On 'writing French history', see Gildea, Robert D.: *The Past in French History* (New Haven, 1994), pp 1-12.

11.   On the twentieth century, the writing is both voluminous and unwieldy. Among very recent studies see, for example, Knapp, Andrew: *Gaullism since de Gaulle* (Aldershot, 1994); Marcus, Jonathan: *The National Front and French Politics* (London, 1995); Soucy, Robert: *French Fascism. The Second Wave, 1933-1939* (Yale, 1995); and Vinen, Richard: *Bourgeois Politics in France, 1945-1951* (Cambridge, 1995). Vichy particularly has been extensively studied by anglophone historians, too numerous to list here, and whose contibution has arguably been more significant than that of French scholars who have found this a delicate topic to address. Recently, however, the French academic community has been 'catching up'. See, for instance, the essays in J.-P.Azéma and F.Bédarida, eds: *Vichy et les français* (Paris, 1991).

12.   On the eighteenth century, for example, see the recent studies of 'high politics' by Swann, Julian: *Politics and the Parlement of Paris under Louis XV, 1754-1774* (Cambridge, 1995); Price, Munroe: *Preserving the Monarchy. The Comte de Vergennes, 1774-1787* (Cambridge, 1995);

Rogister, John: *Louis XV and the Parlement of Paris, 1737-1754* (Cambridge, 1995); and Campell, Peter R.: *Power and Politics in Old Regime France, 1720-1745* (London, 1996).

13. Sirinelli, ed: *Histoire des droites*

14. *L'Express* of November 1989 captured the *zeitgeist* when it announced that, 'Droite-gauche: c'est dépassé'. On the 'demise' of the right in France, see the essay in this volume by Charles Hauss: 'You *Can* Pour New Wine into Old Bottles: The French Right Since 1958'.

15. Rémond: *La droite en France*

16. Denis, Michel: 'Que faire de la révolution française', in Sirinelli, ed: *Histoire des droites*, p 13

17. Roberts, John M.: 'The French Origins of the "Right"', *Transactions of the Royal Historical Society* 5th series 23 (1973), pp 27-53; Baker, Keith: *Inventing the French Revolution* (Cambridge, 1990)

18. Roberts: 'The French Origins of the "Right"', p 33

19. Bombelles, marquis de: *Journal* ed J.Grassion and F.Durif (Paris, 1978-82), vol 2, pp 304-306

20. Young, Ronald: *The American Congress* (New York, 1958), pp 53-4

21. Weill, Georges: *Histoire du parti républicain en France de 1815 à 1870* (Paris, 1900)

22. Tackett, Timothy: *Becoming a Revolutionary. The Deputies of the French National Assembly and the Emergence of a Revolutionary Culture, 1789-1790* (Princeton, 1996), pp 119-148

23. Richet, Denis: 'Revolutionary Assemblies', in F.Furet and M.Ozouf, eds: *A Critical Dictionary of the French Revolution* (Cambridge, Mass., 1989), pp 534-5

24. See Hunt, Lynn: *Politics, Culture and Class in the French Revolution* (London, 1986); Furet, François: *Interpreting the French Revolution* (Cambridge, 1981), esp. pp 30 ff.

25. Dezan, Suzanne: *Reclaiming the Sacred. Lay Religion and Popular Politics in Revolutionary France* (Ithaca, 1990), esp. chap 4

26. See especially Lucas, Colin: 'Nobles, Bourgeois and the Origins of the French Revolution', *Past and Present* 60 (1973), pp 84-126, and Chaussinand-Nogaret, Guy: *The French Nobility in the Eighteenth Century. From Feudalism to Enlightenment* (Cambridge, 1985).

27. Hampson, Norman: 'The French Revolution and its Historians', in G.Best, ed: *The Permanent Revolution. The French Revolution and its Legacy, 1789-1989* (London, 1988), p 232

28. Baker, Keith: *Inventing the French Revolution* (London, 1996), pp 128-52 and Hampson, Norman: *Will and Circumstance. Montesquieu, Rousseau and the French Revolution* (London, 1983)

29. Cited in J.M.Roberts and R.C.Cobb, eds: *French Revolution Documents* (Oxford, 1966), vol 1, p 107

30. Cited in Roberts and Cobb, eds: *French Revolution Documents*, vol 1, p 172

31. Greer, Donald: *The Incidence of the Emigration during the French Revolution* (Cambridge, Mass., 1951); Vidalenc, Jean: *Les emigrés français, 1789-1825* (Caen, 1963)

32. Halévi, Ran: 'Monarchiens', in Furet and Ozouf, eds: *A Critical Dictionary*, pp 370-9

33. *Archives Parlementaires*, vol 27, pp 378-83

34. See Patrick, Alison: *The Men of the First French Republic. Political Alignments in the National Convention of 1792* (Baltimore, 1972); Sydenham, Maurice: *The Girondins* (London, 1961); and Sydenham, Maurice: *The First French Republic, 1792-1804* (London, 1974).

35. Much information on the Convention is to be found in Thibaudeau, Antoine: *Mémoires sur la convention* (2 vols, Paris, 1824).

36. Walzer, Michael: 'The King's Trial and the Political Culture of the Revolution', in C.Lucas, ed: *The French Revolution and the Creation of Modern Political Culture* (Oxford, 1988), vol 2, pp 183-92; Jordon, David P.: *The King's Trial. The French Revolution versus Louis XVI* (Berkeley, 1979)

37. Gueniffey, Patrice: 'Les assemblées et la repésentation', in Lucas, ed: *The French Revolution*, vol 2, pp 233-57

38. It is worth noting that although family was an issue for the right, gender was not. Neither left nor right adopted the cause of women. On this point, see Hufton, Olwen: *Women and the Limits of Citizenship in the French Revolution* (Toronto, 1992). For how the twentieth-century right has addressed gender issues, see the essay in this volume by Miranda Pollard: 'Sexing theSubject: Women and the French Right, 1939-58'.

39. Cranston, Maurice: 'The Sovereignty of the Nation', in Lucas, ed: *The French Revolution*, vol 2, pp 97-104 and Hunt, Lynn: *The French Revolution and Human Rights. A Brief Documentary History* (Boston and New York, 1996) provide a good introduction to the issue of entitlements.

40. Crook, Malcolm: *Elections in the French Revolution. An Apprenticeship in Democracy, 1789-1799* (Cambridge, 1996) is the most recent study on electoral procedures.

41. Richet, Denis: 'Les enragés', in Furet and Ozouf, eds: *A Critical Dictionary*, pp 337-42 and Bruguière, Michel: *Gestionnaires et profiteurs de la révolution* (Paris, 1986) on the *maximum*.

42. Tallett, Frank: 'Robespierre's Religious Views', in W.Doyle and C.Hadyn, eds: *Robespierre. History, Myth and Literature* (Cambridge, forthcoming); Hampson, Norman: *The Life and Opinions of Maximilien Robespierre* (London, 1974); and his *Saint-Just* (Oxford, 1991).

43. Bell, David A.: 'Lingua Populi, Lingua Dei: Language, Religion and the Origins of French Revolutionary Nationalism', *American Historical Review* 100 (1995), pp 1403-37; Lyons, Martin: 'Regionalism and Linguistic Conformity in the French Revolution', in A.Forrest and P.Jones, eds: *Reshaping France. Town, Country and Region during the French*

Revolution (Manchester, 1991), pp 179-192

44. On the complex variables which shaped revolutionary and post-revolutionary identities, see Vovelle, Michel: *La découverte de la politique: géopolitique de la révolution française* (Paris, 1993).

45. Gildea: *The Past in French History*, p 170

46. Farmer, Paul: *Vichy. Political Dilemma* (New York, 1955), p 218. See too Dezan, Suzanne: 'The Family as Cultural Battleground: Religion versus Republic under the Terror', in K.Baker, ed: *The French Revolution and the Creation of Modern Political Culture*, vol 4, pp 177-93; and Dupâquier, Jacques and Fauve-Chamoux, Antoinette: 'La famille', in Sirenelli, ed: *Histoire des droites*, vol 3, pp 15-48.

47. On Le Pen, see the the essay in this volume by Wolfreys, Jim: 'Neither Right nor Left? Towards an Integrated Analysis of the Front National'.

48. The defeat in 1789 of a motion by the reforming Dom Gerle declaring Catholicism the state religion revealed some of the splits over religion which were to become increasingly apparent. McManners, John: *The French Revolution and the Church* (London, 1969) remains the best short study.

49. In the nineteenth century, education was to become a key area of division between Republicans and the Church. Ozouf, Mona: *L'école, l'église et la république, 1871-1914* (Paris, 1963) is a good introduction to these squabbles.

50. Griffiths, Richard: *Marshal Pétain* (London, 1970) ,p 158

51. See the essay in this volume by Cubitt, Geoffrey: 'Legitimism and the Cult of Bourbon Royalty'. See, too, Locke: Robert R.: *French Legitimists and the Politics of Moral Order in the Early Third Republic* (Princeton, 1974) and Kale, Stephen: *Legitimacy and Reconstruction* (1994)

52. On Orleanism, see the essay in this volume by Pilbeam, Pamela M.: 'Orleanism: A Doctrine of the Right?'

53. On this issue, see the essay in this volume by Broers, Michael: 'The First Napoleonic Regime, 1789-1815: The Origins of the Positivist Right or the Zenith of Jacobinsim?'

54. Anderson: *Conservative Politics*, pp 339-40

2. THE FIRST NAPOLEONIC REGIME, 1799-1815: THE ORIGINS OF THE POSITIVIST RIGHT OR THE ZENITH OF JACOBINISM?

Michael Broers

The French Revolution invented the ideological concepts of 'left' and 'right', and the Napoleonic regime was created specifically to do away with them. Whatever particular stamp Napoleon or his officials put on their government in the years after Brumaire, the founding principle of the Consulate was that of a regime 'above faction'. This goal remained central to the regime and found active expression in the twin policies of *amalgame* and *ralliement*.[1] A regime whose raison d'être was to surmount the divisions of the Revolution had, perforce, to appear as neither 'left' nor 'right'. If it also had to incorporate partisans of both, this was to be on terms dictated by neither. Essentially, *ralliement* to the regime was meant to cleanse the *amalgamés* of their original ideological allegiances.

Nor did the aversion to the divisions of the 1790s end here. A marked, if relatively ignored, aspect of the Napoleonic regime was its continuous renewal from within. Just as a considerable number of 'new men' were present in the ranks of the Directorial assemblies between the coups of Fructidor and Brumaire,[2] so too the regime always sought to renew itself by recruiting and promoting younger men to its ranks,[3] who replaced former revolutionaries and counter revolutionaries.

Contemporaries sensed the opening up of this abyss between the new order and the immediate political past. Their reaction to this policy of abnegation is probably the most impressive evidence for seeing the Napoleonic regime as divorced from the divisions 'left' and 'right', as they had been conceived during the Revolution. By 1804, Chateaubriand had stormed out of the diplomatic service, and then out of the country. It was the execution of the duc d'Enghien that stirred Chateaubriand to this defiance, and his words underline contemporary perceptions of the ideological colouring of the regime:

> Cette mort, dans le premier moment, glaça d'effroi tous les coeurs; on apprehenda le revenir du règne de Robespierre. Paris crut revoir un de ces jours qu'on ne voit qu'une fois, le jour de l'exécution de Louis XVI. Les serviteurs, les amis, les parents de Bonaparte étaient consternés. Ce ne fut pas de but en blanc et sans précaution que l'on arrêta le duc d'Enghien; Bonaparte s'était fait rendre compte du nombre des Bourbons en Europe.[4]

Clearly, any early hopes raised by the Concordat, which may have given impulse to the completion of Chateaubriand's *Le génie du christianisme* were dashed by this *cause célèbre*. The execution of d'Enghien induced a profound response from contemporaries, and did more to shape contemporary perceptions of the regime than any other single event save, perhaps, the proclamation of the hereditary empire.

Set beside the collective response of the provincial nobility to the entreaties of the regime, even so abortive a case of *ralliement* as Chateaubriand's appears as a relative success. If the regime was truly of the 'right', it did not appear so to counter revolutionaries or, more importantly, to the less politically active elements of the *ancien régime* elite. Throughout the life of the First Empire, the old aristocratic families were notable by their absence from public life.[5] By and large, *amalgame* was stillborn, and where it did make some appreciable impact, it would appear to have been among a younger generation of nobles, who had come to maturity under the Napoleonic regime.[6] Neither the pomp and circumstance of the imperial coronation, nor the conclusion of the Concordat, still less the creation of an imperial nobility, convinced the elites of the *ancien régime* that this was a regime of the 'right', as both they and the revolutionaries had understood the term.

The counter revolution was not the only faction above which the regime sought to rise. The Consulate was equally successful in freeing itself from what might most usefully be termed the liberal, moderate revolutionaries. Despite his claims to favour the men and measures of 1789, Napoleon had only the shortest of political honeymoons with the ex-Feuillants. Madame De Staël was their answer—in word and deed—to Chateaubriand, on the 'right'. Perhaps she acknowledged more than she meant in the opening remarks of *Dix années d'exil*:

Le plus grand grief de l'empereur Napoléon contre moi, c'est le respect dont j'ai toujours été transmis comme un héritage; et je les ai adoptés dès que j'ai pu réfléchir sur les hautes pensées dont ils dérivent, et sur les belles actions qu'ils inspirent.[7]

Her political ideology had been inherited. It was more than politically inconvenient for the power-hungry First Consul to adopt. It ran against the ethos of all the Brumairiens, precisely because de Staël's *véritable liberté* carried in its wake the whole history of faction and division they regarded as the defining characteristic of the revolutionary decade. To resurrect it was to sanction the hounding of the monarchiens from the National Assembly and the narrowing spiral that led to the Champs de Mars. Although the new regime was anxious to laud the achievements of the early years of the Revolution, and to build on them in practical ways, it could not revivify the political process which had brought them about. The dangers of any such reversion were implicit in the history of the Directory itself.

The relationship of the Jacobin heritage to the Napoleonic regime was almost the mirror image of that of the liberals. Whereas the Consulate eulogized the achievements of the men of 1789-91, albeit refusing to bestow on them the kind of power they desired, it continued to denounce the Terror, while staffing the Ministry of Police with its veterans and cultivating its spirit in the armies. At the risk of exaggeration, certain events of the coup of Brumaire itself point to the fundamental, if hardly prominent, place of the Jacobin legacy in the life of the Napoleonic regime. Bonaparte, along with every other general considered as a candidate for the leadership of the coup, was chosen for his republican credentials, just as only those with explicitly royalist connections were discarded. At the height of the coup, when he had been driven from the chambers by a handful of determined deputies, Napoleon and Lucien appealed to the troops to carry out the coup. When they did so, it was in the language of the Terror:

Je vous déclare que ces audacieux brigands, sans doute soldés par l'Angleterre, se sont mis en rébellion contre le conseil des Anciens. Je confie aux guerriers le soin de délivrer la majorité de leurs représentants.[8]

It worked in these desperate circumstances and would continue to do so. In the army and the police, where it counted most, the regime chose to rely on men with Terrorist pasts, Hébertist as often as Montagnard. They were truly silent partners in the Napoleonic state. The fabricated purges after the 'infernal machine' hid this reality. Nevertheless, the deportations of 1801 also show the relationship between the regime and the Jacobin legacy to be a marriage of convenience, and a secret one at that.

In the context of the search for a Napoleonic ideology, what matters most is the fact of opposition from both the reactionary Chateaubriand and the liberal de Staël, rather than the reasons for this. De Staël perceived the outward nature of the regime, in its early phase, with cool clarity:

> Pendant que M de Talleyrand dirigeait les affaires étrangères, Fouché à la police s'était chargé de la partie révolutionnaire du gouvernement de Bonaparte, et tandis qu'on a vu les rois chrétiens prendre deux confesseurs pour faire examiner de plus près leur conscience, Bonaparte s'était choisi deux ministres, l'un de l'ancien et l'autre du nouveau régime, dont la mission était de mettre à sa disposition les moyens machiavéliques des deux systèmes contraires. Bonaparte suivait, dans toutes ses nominations, à peu près la même règle, de prendre, pour ainsi dire, tantôt à droite, tantôt à gauche ... le parti mitoyen, celui des amis de la liberté, lui plaisait moins que tous les autres, parce qu'il était composé du petit nombre d'hommes qui, en France, avaient une opinion.[9]

Writing in 1811-12, from outside France, de Staël grasped the workings behind the regime, but mistook these for its true character. In its final years, the regime began to dispense with the concept of balancing the factions, introducing new and younger men. *Ralliement* and *amalgame* were only stopgaps, for Napoleon and those closest to him were capable of thinking in terms which were broader and longer term than de Staël believed possible. Napoleon's expanding ambitions were not confined to the battlefield or the map. He looked beyond the political inheritance of the 1790s, as well as into it.

The Napoleonic regime sought initially to create an ideological void. The key to understanding the nature of its ideology lies in the way in which the regime filled that void. It attempted to do so with the new generation of administrators, trained in its own educational system, who began to emerge from 1807. When they did so, the regime also had new space for them to occupy. The 'Napoleonic generation' stepped into an imperial, not merely a French, role. Their circumstances were very different from those of the revolutionary politicians, whose positions they were usurping. Their relative estrangement from the factionalism of the 1790s and the imperial mission they served were the essential conditions in which the Napoleonic regime came closest to formulating an ideology of its own. The new generation was both its embodiment and its creator. They filled the void created in the early years of the regime, and they did so with their own ideas, not merely those of their master. Napoleon is quoted as saying of his political creation, 'All this may last my lifetime, but my son will have to govern very differently.'[10] There were many signs, as early as 1807, that he was already preparing the way.

La Grande Nation: Forging the French Nation

Napoleon's was the first regime since 1789 to recognize that the Revolution had, indeed, been a 'Machiavellian moment' to which there was no return.[11] This led to the realization that, although the French past could not be restored, something of it had to be salvaged, if only to sustain the Revolution when it could no longer sustain itself. Over half a century before de Tocqueville declared that the French had failed in their bold attempt to bring nothing from the old order into the new, Napoleon and his collaborators were already constructing their regime on precisely this assumption.

The history manuals written under the Consulate and the First Empire are an interesting guide to how the regime saw itself in the context of the French past and consequently they offer an insight into its ideology. The history of France was conceived of in almost Chinese terms, centred on the rise and fall of four dynasties—the Merovingian, Carolingian, Valois, and Capetian—in which the Revolution became a necessary interregnum leading to the emergence of a fifth, the Bonapartes, with a new mandate for a new era. The nature of this mandate was made clear by the treatment of the reigns of Louis XV and Louis XVI in these official histories. The last two Bourbon kings were depicted as well meaning reformers, unable to adapt to the new ideas and society taking shape around them. They proved incapable of mastering the Enlightenment, the manifestation of the new age, and so were swept away. The 'mandate of heaven' was exhausted when the ruling dynasty could not reform the French state in accordance with the spirit of the age. The old monarchy was doomed less because the Revolution willed it so, than by its failure to make the Revolution its own. Accordingly, the Revolution foreshadowed a new age, under a new dynasty, but it did not wholly embody that new age. The new dynasty, alone, could carry the Revolution forward, and this could be done only by reference to the French past, for that past had created the Enlightenment. It was a matter of looking back, rather than going back; of reference, not restoration.[12]

In this way, the *grand siècle* was rehabilitated, if in a particular context.

Its glories belonged firmly to the past, but it was a past that could be celebrated and drawn upon, for Louis XIV emerges as the last successful ruler of the old regime. With his passing, the old began to give way to the new. The essence of the Napoleonic interpretation of French history was Voltaire's *The Age of Louis XIV*, embellished by hindsight. The Enlightenment and the Revolution were the products of a long cultural evolution; they were not rooted in the *grand siècle*, but they would have been impossible without it. France had both a past and a future, neither of which need impede or deny the other, an attitude which set the Napoleonic regime apart from the reactionary right and the millenarian left. In the hard world of practical politics, the Napoleonic regime sought to rise above faction, especially in the early, testing years of the Consulate, but its ultimate goal was to move on, following the grand course of French history, leaving behind the factions of the 1790s, just as the four preceding dynasties had fallen by the wayside.

All of this represented an appeal to destiny, resting on the supposition that strong monarchy was the touchstone of French history. However, that monarchy could only be strong, and therefore valid, if it corresponded to the spirit of the age. There was no point in imitating Louis XIV, still less Clovis, in anything save the knowledge that France could only be ruled effectively by a centralized monarchy. The methods and spirit of the old monarchy were outmoded, but the aspirations of *frondeurs* and parlementaires—the true forerunners of the counter revolution—were irrelevant, and always had been.

The *longue durée* dictated absolutism, whose ethos now had to be the Enlightenment. Only if the concept of enlightened absolutism is categorized as of the right, can the Napoleonic regime also be called right wing. Although enlightened absolutism might be a problematic term when applied in its classic eighteenth-century sense, there is little doubt that it was the deliberately cultivated ethos of the First Empire. The new century, that of *Napoléon le Grand*, was also to be 'the century of light'. The whole point of the new dynasty was its modernity. The representative institutions of the Revolution could only open the way; they could never hope to secure the destiny of France as the heartland of the Enlightenment. Only the new dynasty —absolute, centralist and bereft of a past of its own— could hope to guide France to its proper role in the world, and that role was to oppose the forces of reaction, and to spread light.

The process began at home in the first months of the Consulate. In 1800, the new regime initiated the *Statistique des préfets*, for every department. The recent work of Marie-Noëlle Bourguet has pointed to ideology as the driving force behind this project:

> Le progrès serait donc la marche vers une société de plus en plus homogène, triomphe de l'homme sur la nature, de l'uniforme sur le divers. La philosophie des lumières et la révolution française forgèrent cet idéal d'une société rationnelle.[13]

The struggle against *patois*, against what Judith Devlin has termed 'the superstitious mind',[14] the process of turning 'peasants into Frenchmen'[15] was now under way. It would be driven first by prefects who were men of the Enlightenment—Thibaudeau, Fauchet and Bonnaire in Provence; Labretonnière and Borie in the west—and then by the new generation of *auditeurs*. The collapse of the Concordat by 1810, and the increasing influence of a police that was probably more Hébertist than Montagnard, ensured that the 'project' had lost none of its revolutionary bitterness by the end of the Empire. The pattern which so characterized the inner life of the Third Republic had already emerged by 1800. Put another way, if the First Empire is of the right, then so must be Jules Ferry, Clemenceau and Waldeck-Rousseau.

By the mid-nineteenth century, the drive for cultural uniformity, identified by Bourguet, had spawned its idealized stereotypes—one populist, the other elitist—both of which were rooted in the Napoleonic era. From the depths of *la France profonde*, emerged the vaudeville stock-character of Jean Chauvin, the *soldat-laboureur*, imbued with the spirit of the Enlightenment through military service, which reinforced the innate, natural good sense of the French peasant. Salient among his virtues, equated easily with Enlightened values by his creators in the nineteenth century, were French patriotism and martial spirit. He began life as a Napoleonic *grondeur*.[16] This blend was the secret of French identity, as conceived by the Napoleonic regime. It was nationalistic and militaristic as well as thoroughly enlightened and progressive, at least by its own standards, and by the standards of those who created and gloried in the figure of Chauvin in later decades. For most of the nineteenth century, these were hardly the hallmarks of the right. For Chauvin's upper class equivalents, one need look no further than the works or, indeed, the person, of Stendhal.

The search for unity and uniformity meant that French nationality replaced all other identities. Rationalism was at its core, yet so was bellicosity. The army was to become the school of the entire nation: Jean Chauvin and Julien Sorel were both willing volunteers, and their living counterparts would be conscripted, if necessary. They still are. Herein lies a paradox, at the very heart of the ideology of the regime, which was bequeathed to the Third and Fourth Republics, as well as to the Second Empire and the Fifth Republic. In the context of the 1800s, the *soldat-laboureur* epitomized the dangers of democracy to the powers of the Coalitions raised against Napoleon. His use and glorification of such troops branded him a Jacobin and a republican among his enemies. The cult of the warrior belonged to the left, as defined by the Revolution. That was how everyone wanted it. To the reactionary right, Chauvin was the mob-in-arms; to revolutionaries of all shades, he was republican virtue personified.

Any discussion of Jean Chauvin and Julien Sorel is a traffic in ideals. The reality of the army was a shift from the revolutionary ideals of civic service to older notions of honour, as John Lynn has revealed.[17] There are strong indications that old regime *mores* were taking root in the Napoleonic armies, above all, a sense of caste, of privilege and isolation from society as a whole, best epitomized by the Imperial Guard. However, even here, the whole truth cannot be found by seeing a return to the *ancien régime* in the Napoleonic *esprit de corps*.

Napoleon's regime attempted to confront directly one of the most profound traumas of the Revolution, the disintegration of community, not only by fostering a uniform national culture, but by what might be termed a culture of *esprit de corps*, which was military in origin and character but which extended to civil society. This ethos sought to displace traditional corporatism, but had to incorporate liberal individualism, social mobility and the career open to talent. The disintegration of collective identity and the desperate search to reconstruct it within the framework of the reforms of the Revolution, has been analyzed imaginatively by Lynn Hunt,[18] and Peter Gay has advanced a variation on her theme in the context of the Napoleonic period.[19] The *ancien régime* ended in parricide, to be replaced, unsuccessfully, by the myth of the nation as a 'band of brothers'. Hunt has indicated the two deep dilemmas which arose from the destruction of the paternalist state. First, 'If the father was now absent, should one or more of the sons be imagined as taking his place, or would they remain brothers?' Second, in practice, 'revolutionary legislation took power away from the father and ultimately vested a large portion of it in the state.' This, in turn, risked creating a moral void between the state and the citizen, 'this authority of affection that the laws cannot command.'[20] The Napoleonic regime grasped, with remarkable sensitivity, the need to square all this, and to do so in favour of the state. The iconography of the empire depicts the ruler in three guises, none of which correspond to the *ancien régime* patriarch: the heroic military leader, the hard working professional and the austere, remote representative of an abstract sovereign authority.

A great deal is made of the reassertion of the power of the father and husband under the Code Napoléon, and this is frequently held up as proof of the essentially right-wing, anti-revolutionary character of the regime. This is not only to forget the deeply masculine character of Jacobinism, but is also to lose sight of the wider contemporary context of the family. Napoleon never broke with the most radical Jacobin assertions, that the family was essentially at the service of the state, and of the General Will. He followed Danton in a belief that children belonged to society and to the state before they belonged to their families, whoever was in charge 'at home'. The regime created state boarding schools and military academies for its elites and a residential school for the sons of artisans at La Flèche. The armies became *l'école de la nation*. A father could dominate his family only as and when it was not requisitioned by the state. It was solely within this context that the state restored his familial powers. The demands of the *patrie*, which entailed the loss of sons to the state, either as bureaucrats or soldiers, were the greatest concerns of parents of both sexes, rather than their power relationships with each other. This assertion of state power had far more to do with Jacobin ideology than with the paternal authority of the old order. The patriarchs created by the Code were the masters of increasingly empty castles, as their former subjects swelled the ranks of the brotherhood of the Napoleonic state.

The new dynasty did not turn its back on the myth of brotherhood, even as it strove to reassert absolutism. Napoleon did, indeed, become the single brother who replaced that murdered father, but he never forgot that he was a brother, the first among equals, and not a new patriarch. This is obviously the heritage of the Revolution, for the new monarchy could not be like the old. Napoleon's claim to leadership arose because he emerged as the most able of the brothers and nothing more. Respect was fraternal; it rested on success in fulfilling the needs of those around him rather than on the automatic obedience owed to the paternal will. Indeed, the closer Napoleon got to his real sources of power and support, the clearer becomes the fraternal nature of the bond: the Marshalate, the Légion d'honneur, the Guard, even the office of the *auditeurs*, all reflect a society of brotherhood, more than of paternalism. His old comrades— from the Prince-Marshals to the veterans of Austerlitz and the Old Guard—were festooned with honours, both symbolic and venal, in a manner more reminiscent of the wary condescension of an older brother than of the measured, cautious approval won from a stern father. Napoleon worked on the assumption that he owed his brothers something; a true patriarch is owed blind devotion. The First Empire was the first revolutionary regime wholly to embrace 'fraternity', and to set it above liberty and equality.

However, embedded in this 'sibling state', produced by the regicide of the revolutionaries, are, perhaps, some of the few clear signs that the Napoleonic regime shared the sensibilities of the reactionary right, if not its ultimate goals. The perceived need to imbue the new order with 'this authority of affection that the laws cannot command' was more central to the reactionary right of 'Church and King' than to republicans, at least after 1794, and until the rise of the 'social question' from the 1830s onwards. Even here, caution is needed when attempting to associate the First Empire with the right, for the bonds of brotherhood it strove to forge were always linked to professionalism and to success. Above all, they were associated with youth and this, too, derived from the preoccupations of the Revolution. Napoleon's was the only regime spawned by the Revolution to last any length of time, and even it survived only fifteen years. Nonetheless, within this short period, it became obsessed by renewal through youth. Few states in European history have advanced, with such determination, the cause of youth in its service. Lynn Hunt is correct when she writes that, 'In the new family romance of fraternity, the revolutionaries seemed to hope that they would remain perpetually youthful, as the heroes of romances always were; they wanted to be permanently brothers and not founding fathers.'[21] Napoleon helped them perpetuate that hope.

As a visual example of this, Hunt has taken the transition from David's *Oath of the Horatii*, in which the father still dominates the brothers, to the engraving of revolutionary soldiers, made in 1793, *Mathey, Worker of Lille*, where the father figure is absent, and the emphasis on the martial, brotherly bond now occupies sole place.[22] The theme can be taken further, chronologically and symbolically, in David's *The Distribution of the Eagle Standard*, completed in 1810. Napoleon, his marshals and troops, are all young and eager for war; the impression is of a young, dynamic leader of youthful, enthused warriors. The immediate result of loyalty is reward: the batons, to the marshals; the eagles to the army; glory, for all. In many respects, this imagery reflected Napoleonic policy. The ranks of the imperial administration had become more youthful by the last years of the regime, as the *auditeurs* rose, with increasing rapidity, to become prefects or middle-grade administrators, often in their early twenties.[23] The judiciary, too, was purged, first in 1807 and again in 1810. This was less an attempt to reintroduce royalists into its ranks than to leaven them with youth. The ravages of war dictated that the armies would remain young, and become younger, but this need not have been the case within the Imperial Guard itself. Nevertheless, Napoleon took care that youth had pride of place, alongside experience, in the elite cadres of the army. Beside the Old Guard stood the Middle and Young Guards, as if to emphasize the process of renewal. Excellence was not confined to the oldest veterans. Nor was Napoleon even their 'father', but *le petit caporale*, ever the young general who had led them from the beginning, their brother.

As the transition of generations was made, between 1804 and 1814, loyalty to the Emperor or, indeed, to the nation, evolved into something more complex, and arguably still further removed from the ethos of the old monarchy than the ideal of the revolutionary citizen. Dynastic and national loyalty became entwined—almost seamlessly for contemporaries—with professionalism and, above all, with a belief in the 'civilizing mission' of France. The binding tie between professionalism and this sense of mission was a profound sense of cultural confidence and superiority among all those who served the regime.

The Civilizing Mission: French Nationalism and the Imperial Experience

De Tocqueville, a commentator never given to rash generalization, remarked on the French penchant for pedagogy, specifically on the national propensity to evangelize others: '... qu'on prêche aussi ardemment aux étrangers qu'on l'accomplit avec passion chez soi.'[24] The military expansion of the Napoleonic wars provided an unsurpassed opportunity to do so; the cultural hegemony fostered by the Napoleonic regime provided a clear curriculum to teach the rest of Europe. Above all, the experience of ruling and educating Europe sharpened the national identity of those French administrators and soldiers who dealt directly with their foreign charges. Essentially, the imperial experience heightened their sense of having a particular French identity, and that identity was defined, first and foremost, by a sense of superiority.

As French administrators came into immediate contact with the subject peoples of Spain, Italy and Germany, they felt themselves amid backward, ignorant, fundamentally retarded societies. This is not to deny, in any way, the objective similarities between their reactions to these cultures and those of their colleagues in the departments of the west or the Midi in the same years. However, because these encounters took place outside France, their impact on the French administrators acquired a wider dimension, in so far as they increased the bureaucrats' vision of France as an island of rationality and civilization. More importantly, the intensity of their confrontation with resistance to their own culture in these regions drove them to extreme positions. Counter revolution had been tamed within France, sometimes to the point where Napoleonic officials might tolerate rustic particularism.[25] Internal conquest ensured that it was harmless. Matters were very different in Italy and Spain, and even in Germany, after the Tyrolean revolt of 1809.

Whatever the complexities of the historical reality, Napoleonic officials blamed resistance to French rule, and the rejection of French culture, on religious fanaticism. As they abolished the Spanish Inquisition and supervised the removal of the Pope from Rome, the French drew increasingly on the tradition of the radical, Voltairian Enlightenment. Besieged by a superstitious *canaille*, numbered in thousands, if not in millions, and bedevilled by a determined, traditionalist clergy, this intellectual response was wholly predictable, but it places the regime more in the cadre of enlightened absolutism than of modern, right-wing Caesarism. In these circumstances, the regime rejected traditional authoritarianism, not just because it was impossible to establish, but because such a scheme did not correspond to the regime's conception of itself as an agent of modern civilization. Whatever the nuances, ambiguities and contradictions of its ideological coloration in a purely French context, when the Napoleonic regime looked south and east, it saw itself as the agent of enlightened progress. This is to say that, by the standards of the times, it set itself firmly on the left. Napoleon did not content himself with hébertist dechristianization, he struck at the heart of the Universal Church, the papacy. He dismantled the greatest living feudal edifice in Europe, the Holy Roman Empire. He translated the anticlerical rage of Voltaire's support for Calas into the destruction of the Spanish Inquisition; Llorente chose to defect, with his archives and his pen, to the Napoleonic regime.

Seen in this European context, the regime emerges as anything but right wing. Not only the subjective attitudes of its imperial bureaucrats, but the concrete actions of imperial policy, reveal Napoleon as the forbear of Jules Ferry, rather than Boulanger, de Gaulle, or even his own nephew. Under Napoleon I, monasteries and convents were closed in their thousands across Catholic Europe; two popes and a whole College of Cardinals were incarcerated; the see of Assisi was abolished, its shrine closed by police order; the cathedral of Zaragoza became a stable for Lannes' cavalry. The list is endless.

The Voltairian character of the Empire can be seen as clearly in its attempts to build as in its efforts to suppress. Even at the height of the war in Spain, in areas where the *chef-lieux* themselves were exposed to guerrilla raids, idealistic young prefects, drawn from the *auditeurs*, strove to improve public sanitation, to build parks, schools and hospitals for those who were trying to bushwhack them.[26] In his memoirs, Beugnot, a seasoned imperial administrator, recalled with pride his works of urban renewal in the Grand Duchy of Berg, and how he had improved the material lot of his German *administrés*; it was the retreating French troops, in 1813, who undid much of his careful work.[27] In Rome, Tournon, the youthful prefect of aristocratic family, dreamed of the economic potential of his department, and of the need to rebuild Rome on modern lines. In one of his first letters home, Tournon told his mother, of his new department, 'Il y a beaucoup à faire pour son bonheur: puisse-je en jeter du moins les premières semences.' To his father, a few days later, he wrote of his practical hopes for the local economy:

> Quand on voit cette terre d'une fertilité prodigieuse abandonnée aux joncs et aux roseaux, on ne peut s'empêcher de désirer vivement qu'elle soit, quoi qu'il en coûte, rendue à l'agriculture.[28]

Administrators such as Tournon carried the Enlightenment in their saddle bags, even as they taxed and conscripted their hapless charges. Only through membership of the Napoleonic Empire and by participation in its civilizing mission, could the peoples of Europe hope to enter the mainstream of modernity.

If the authoritarian aspects of the regime occlude, or even blight, the enlightened aura of the regime in the sweep of French history, this is not the case abroad. Beside the tightening of censorship in France, to the point of strangulation, must be set the abolition of the Inquisition in those states where it remained most powerful; beside the trappings of monarchy and the wooing of the Second Estate, must be set the ferocious assault on the feudal barons of southern Italy and north-central Germany. Napoleon's soldiers waged remorseless war against the greatest Vendée of all, the Spanish guerrilla, and the triumphs of his generals over the armies of the eastern autocracies were hailed, even by his most inveterate enemies, as the victory of meritocracy over a caste-bound society of orders. In the wake of Wagram in 1809, the *Edinburgh Review* declared, 'The diadem of Bonaparte has dimmed the lustre of all the ancient crowns of Europe; and her nobles have been outshone and out-generalled, and out-negotiated, by men raised by their own exertions from the common level of the populace.'[29] This perception may not have been wholly accurate, but it reveals the genuine contrast between the nature of the Napoleonic regime and its rivals. Unlike them, the Napoleonic monarchy was rooted in the Revolution and the 'career open to talent', even if it did not reflect the most radical aspirations of the Revolution at its height.

The Heritage: France and Europe, Left and Right

Few regimes were as much a response to contemporary circumstances as the First Empire, thus making its ideological character difficult to gauge. If we look beyond 1815, even as far as the Second Empire, it would seem more prudent to speak in terms of influences created than of precedents set, and these influences often serve to denature the true character of the regime, rather than to illuminate it.

Napoleon did, indeed, initiate the Caesarist tradition in French politics, but he was more a Caesar of the left than any of his future imitators. Nor did his Caesarism bring the army into politics. Even the Guard was kept strictly away from affairs of state, and none of the marshals dared intrude on the Conseil d'Etat, its workings or subordinate bodies. In a purely French context, Napoleon's immediate legacy was to the left; he became the 'Prestor John' of a marginalized revolutionary tradition between 1814 and 1851. Indeed, it took the brutal seizure of power by his nephew, in 1851, finally to dispel this imagery. Nor was the vision of Stendhal entirely fanciful for, as the *Edinburgh Review* evidenced in 1809, the Napoleonic regime did appear a regime of the left in the climate of the Restoration. In the wake of the Second Empire, perceptions of the First Empire changed profoundly; with the coming of the Fifth Republic, they have made the Napoleonic regime irrevocably of the right. Yet when its historical reality is approached in terms of its own times and, above all, from a wider, genuinely European perspective, it is the radical, positivist, almost Voltairian character of the First Empire that is most evident. The methods may have been Gaullist, but the essence of its policies and activities had more to do with the Third Republic. Its empire anticipated that of Jules Ferry, more than that of Napoleon III.

Notes

1.   Bluche, Fernand: *Le Bonapartisme. Aux origines de la droite autoritaire, 1800-1850* (Paris, 1980); Whitcomb, Edward A.: 'Napoleon's Prefects',

American Historical Review 79 (1974), pp 1089-1118

2. Hunt, Lynn *et al*: 'The Failure of the Liberal Republic in France, 1795-1799: The Road to Brumaire', *Journal of Modern History* 51 (1979), pp 734-59

3. Durand, Charles: *Les auditeurs au conseil d'état napoléonien* (Paris, 1954); Panagiatopoulos, Basile: 'Les structures d'âge du personnel de l'empire', *Revue d'histoire moderne et contemporaine* 17 (1970), pp 442-46

4. Chateaubriand: *Napoléon* ed C. Melchior-Bonnet (Paris, 1969), pp 144-5

5. Ellis, Geoffrey: 'Rhine & Loire: Napoleonic Elites and Social Order,' in G. Lewis and C. Lucas, eds: *Beyond the Terror* (Cambridge, 1983) p 266

6. Durand: *Les auditeurs*; Whitcomb: 'Napoleon's Prefects'; Nicloas, Jean: 'Le ralliement des notables au régime impérial dans le département de Mont Blanc', *Revue d'histoire moderne et contemporaine* 19 (1972), pp 92-127, for a local example. For a contemporary participant in this process see J. Moulard, ed: *Lettres inédites du Comte Camille de Tournon, préfet de Rome, 1809-1814* (Paris, 1914), part 1.

7. Staël, Mme de: *Dix années d'exil* (Paris, 1966 edn) p 2

8. Cited in Bertaud, Jean-Paul: *Bonaparte prend le pouvoir* (Paris, 1987) p 54

9. De Staël: *Dix années d'exil*, p 12

10. Quoted most notably by Felix Markham in *Napoleon* (London, 1963) p 264

11. For the concept, see Pocock, John Greville Agard: *The Machiavellian Moment. Florentine Political Thought and the Atlantic Republican Tradition* (Princeton, 1975).

12. For a general discussion on this topic see Burton, June K.: *Napoleon and Clio. Historical Writing, Teaching and Thinking during the First Empire* (Durham, 1979); and her, 'L'enseignement de l'histoire dans les lycées et les écoles primaires sous le première empire', *Annales historiques de la révolution française* 44 (1972), pp 98-109, for a more direct discussion.

13. Bourguet, Marie-Noëlle: 'Race et folklore: l'image de la France en 1800', *Annales E.S.C.* 13/4 (1976), p 812

14. Devlin, Judith: *The Superstitious Mind. French Peasants and the Supernatural in the Nineteenth Century* (New Haven, 1987)

15. Weber, Eugen: *Peasants into Frenchmen. The Modernization of Rural France, 1870-1914* (Stanford, 1976)

16. Puymège, G. de: *De Chauvin, le soldat-laboureur. Contribution à l'étude des nationalismes* (Paris, 1993)

17. Lynn, John: 'Toward an Army of Honor: The Moral Evolution of the French Army, 1789-1815', *French Historical Studies* 16 (1989), pp 152-73

18. Hunt, Lynn: *The Romance of the French Revolution* (Berkeley and Los Angeles, 1992)

19. Gay, Peter: *The Cultivation of Hatred. The Bourgeois Experience, Victoria to Freud* (London, 1993), vol 3, pp 235-43

20. Hunt: *Romance*, pp 67, 65

21. Hunt: *Romance*, p 69

22.   Hunt: *Romance*, pp 67-69
23.   Durand: *Auditeurs*
24.   Tocqueville, Alexis de: *L'ancien régime et la révolution* (Paris, 1979 edn)
25.   Bourguet: 'Race et folklore', pp 819-20
26.   Riba, J. Mercader: *Puigcerda, capital del department del Serge* (Barcelona, 1971) for the experiences of the young French prefect, the *auditeur* Viefville des Essars, in this tenuously held Catalan department, 1812-14.
27.   *Mémoires du comte Beugnot* (Paris, 1868 edn), pp 42-51
28.   *Lettres inédites du comte Camille de Tournon*, Tournon to his mother, 23 January, 1810; Tournon to his father, 25 January, 1810, pp 12-13, 22
29.   Cited in Colley, Linda: *Britons. Forging the Nation, 1707-1837* (New Haven, 1992), p 150

3. ORLEANISM: A DOCTRINE OF THE RIGHT?

Pamela Pilbeam

The Orleanist regime (1830-48) was founded on revolution and foundered by the same means. Its motto, 'Liberty and Order', echoed the ambiguity of its status. Observers have even questioned whether there is a doctrine to disentangle. In 1932, Thibaudet asserted that Orleanism was merely a hotch-potch of negatives.[1] In his 1963 voyage through the different manifestations of the right, Rémond included Orleanism in the text, but left it out of the bibliography, perhaps in sympathy with Thibaudet's dismissive summary.[2] We shall consider the case for and against a right-wing orientation using visual and written evidence.

Left- and right-wing designations in French politics began with seating arrangements in the National Assembly and indicated the individual's response to the 1789 Revolution. The conflicts of the 1790s must have made such definitions problematical. By 1814 one could not simply identify 'right' as those hostile and 'left' those in favour of the Revolution. The Restoration itself was a compromise with the previous quarter century and the Bourbons ruled a state whose institutions and codes of law had been drawn up over the revolutionary and imperial years and whose parliamentary constitution had been invented in 1814. For a variety of reasons, few Legitimists would have wanted to turn the clock back. Thus the majority of the Bourbon right, both ultra and more moderate royalist, accepted the Charter of 1814, although with varying degrees of enthusiasm.

Did the replacement of Charles X by his cousin, Louis-Philippe, duke of Orleans, undertaken reluctantly by the parliamentary liberal opposition, add a further slant to the 'right' after the 1830 Revolution? The high level of continuity between the two regimes would support this claim. Louis-Philippe, the head of the younger branch of the Bourbon family, was also a descendant of Louis XIII. He would probably have been regent had Charles X died while his grandson Henri, the 'miracle child', was still a minor. He joined the Bourbon brothers in emigration in 1800 and was their loyal supporter before 1830, and was closer to Charles X than to his predecessor, Louis XVIII.[3] Louis-Philippe's father had seen himself as a *frondeur* head of a reversionary interest and the Revolution swept him into a more radical role than suited him. It has been suggested that the Orleanism of the July Monarchy originates with the opposition of Louis-Philippe's father to his cousin in the 1780s.[4] In actuality, Louis-Philippe preferred to forget his own, and especially his father's, revolutionary past and to play down the reversionary aspect of his role during the Restoration.

Conservative Orleanists stressed that Louis-Philippe was made king 'parceque Bourbon', because of his family connections, rather than 'quoique Bourbon', despite them. The duc de Broglie, one of the founders of the new regime, suggested that the hereditary element should be emphasized by calling the new king Philippe VII.[5] Although this particular title was not acceptable to most liberals, in 1830 none quarrelled with the retention of a member of the Bourbon family as hereditary monarch. It might also reasonably be claimed that the confirmation of the 1814 constitutional charter after the July Days, modestly and rapidly revised in one brief sitting of the Assembly, could be considered conservative. The new regime was at least as repressive as the old in its treatment of opposition clubs and the press. The Orleanists only tinkered with the size of the ruling elite and their social policies echoed those of the Bourbons in the protection of the rights and property of the wealthy.

In all these respects, Orleanism merits inclusion in an account of the French right. However, the liberal parliamentarians who challenged Charles X's constitutional authority to decree changes to the Charter in 1830 were only united in their criticism of the king. The uneasy harnessing of 'Liberty with Order' was symptomatic of a power struggle between liberal factions labelled by contemporaries, *résistance* and *mouvement*. It was the triumph of the former, with the appointment of Casimir Périer as chief minister, in March 1831, which made Orleanism right-wing, otherwise, as Rémond observes, the French 'rights' might have been reduced by one. Is it possible to go further and to identify Orleanism as, in part, the heir of 1789?

Orleanism was invented in and through revolution, and for many supporters signalled the resurrection or continuation of 1789. The most vivid and best known contemporary representation of the 1830 Revolution was Daumier's *Liberty Guiding the People*. The buxom proletarian female champion of revolution sports a *bonnet rouge* (a very radical symbol of revolution from the 1790s), waves a large *tricolore* and thus proclaims the popular character of the revolution. There are no kings or well manicured *notables* in sight. The painting was bought by the Ministry of the Interior after it had been shown at the Salon in 1831 and immediately displayed at the Luxembourg Palace.[6] It is interesting that Casimir Périer, leading figure among the *résistance* and head of government and Minister of the Interior in September 1831 when the picture was bought, should have acquired and immediately put on show such a radical interpretation of the July Days. It underlines the fact that the basis of the new monarchy was different. The duke of Orleans was made king by the deputies, with a few peers in tow. He was 'king of the French people' and took his oath in the Chamber of Deputies. The contrast between his oath-taking and the medieval religious splendour of Charles X's coronation six years earlier was as striking to contemporaries as it is to historians.

This was to be an hereditary monarchy, but divine right, royal grace and favour and the dispensing power were gone. This was a kingship vested in popular rebellion. There were many contemporary illustrations of the July Days, showing barricades and people fighting the royal army. A revolutionary provisional government at the Hôtel de Ville was set up, recalling the turbulent 1790s, in which leading republicans were led by the veteran revolutionary, Lafayette. The 'heroes of July' were rewarded with medals and pensions. The revolutionary flag, the *tricolore*, was restored as the symbol of the nation, replacing the white or *fleur de lys* standards of the Bourbons. An equally potent symbol of the 1790s, the civil militia, or National Guard, abolished because of its radicalism by Charles X in 1827, was revived under Lafayette. Its officers were habitually ex-Napoleonic army men or left-wing liberals. All members were to take part in the election of officers, which created the potential for a massive electorate, limited only by the individual's ability to buy his uniform and arm himself. Louis-Philippe was careful to honour this institution. He wore his National Guard commander's uniform, and legion of honour, in all of his full-length portraits, in sharp contrast to Charles X's eighteenth-century finery.

Although the parliamentary electorate was nearly doubled by reducing the voter's tax qualification from 300 to 200 francs, elections were introduced at all levels of local assembly, enfranchising about 2 millions, just under a quarter of all adult males. The Roman Catholic Church lost its official status and, until the spring of 1831, repeated popular and violent anticlerical demonstrations and riots were encouraged by the more radical Orleanist officials. Charles X was allowed to leave for exile, but his ex-ministers were put on trial, accused of causing the July Days, and were given jail sentences. The composition of the Chamber of Peers was radically changed by the abolition of hereditary right of membership. Future members were to be appointed for life by the king. Finally, Guizot's Education Act of 1833 encouraged communes to set up lay-run primary schools from local taxation.

This impeccable revolutionary pedigree is usually discounted. Why? The culprits are legion, in particular the more conservative liberals themselves. They were enthusiastic participants in the political, and later the myth-making, manoeuvres. Two main considerations drove them apart from their former allies among the more radical liberals. First, their own hold on power was always tenuous. There were nearly as many changes of government between 1830 and 1840 as there were years in Louis-Philippe's reign. Although the Guizot-Soult government was in office from 1840 until the revolution of 1848, Guizot had the personal allegiance of a mere 23 deputies at the outset. Contemporaries shunned the idea of permanent political parties as treasonably divisive. Clinging to power in a regime born of revolution, the *résistance* liberals were terrified of popular unrest, which drove them to try to control critics by declaring their ideas and organizations illegal. The republican clubs of the early 1830s, Blanqui's revolutionary societies and attempts to take power, added to an unprecedented seven assassination attempts on the king and ensured that the political ethos of the ruling elite would be conservative. In addition, economic change made artisans opponents of an unsympathetic laissez-faire regime and susceptible to the ideas of socialists like Etienne Cabet. Thus while Orleanists might claim to be the heirs of the Great Revolution, they were determined to smother criticism and demands for further change and found the king an eager ally.

If Orleanists were eager to slough off their own revolutionary origins, their opponents were keen to deny their revolutionary credibility and assert themselves as the sole heirs of the traditions of 1789. The revolutionary years were painted in republican colours with some Bonapartist overtones. With the demise of Louis-Philippe in 1848 the revolutionary tradition was up for grabs, although it was not until the Third Republic that republicans established monopoly control. At this stage Orleanism underwent another of its chameleon changes, one that was to produce the image which survives to this day.

Until the Third Republic, the story of the July Monarchy was told by its servants, notably Guizot[7] and critics, such as Louis Blanc.[8] It was in the 1870s and 80s that the image of Orleanism as entirely right-wing was established in the prolific work of Paul Thureau-Dangin who relied heavily upon Guizot for both his information and his interpretation.[9] Curiously,

Michael Marrinan in his ground-breaking study of the official art of the July Monarchy used Thureau-Dangin as one of his main guides to the ideology of the regime. The history of past glories aside, Orleanists contributed much to the establishment of the conservative Third Republic. Thiers and de Broglie were merely two of the leading Orleanists to shape the new regime. Orleanism as an elitist parliamentary idea was vindicated, as a monarchist creed it was left stranded. After the comte de Chambord died in 1886 without a Bourbon heir, the Orleanist comte de Paris was left to pretend alone and those with monarchist predilections had no choice but to make common cause.

Orleanism took on a far more right-wing aura as a mythology than it had possessed as a reality, particularly when Charles Maurras's Action Française sashayed into view. A major exponent of monarchism as memory, nostalgia and wistful thoughts for the future, Maurras excoriated parliaments and constitutions.[10] In 1936 Henri, comte de Paris, urged 'the French race' to recognize the corrupt and threadbare nature of the Republic and restore him to the throne 'of St Louis' and 'a thousand years of history'.[11] De Gaulle's rejection of monarchy did nothing to improve the pretender's parliamentary credentials. Myth, linked to contemporary *résistance* ambitions, seems to confirm Orleanism as a doctrine of the right long since stripped of its association with written constitutions and elected assemblies. Since 1958 the successful creation of a presidential republic has made Orleanism superfluous as a constitutional alternative to the Republic.

On the other hand, the collapse of the millenarian Marxist-republican explanation of 1789 and subsequent revolutions permits a less rigid perspective of the Great Revolution, and, possibly, of the little revolution of 1830 and Orleanism. With 1789 reclaimed as a political accident, the earlier years of the Revolution are being examined more constructively. The moderate constitutional monarchist phase of the Revolution now gains serious attention from historians, although even today it is dismissed as transient and unworkable.[12] Is there space to restore Orleanism into a moderate, constitutional monarchist revolutionary tradition?

At the time of the July Days, there was a brief consensus in written and visual accounts that the Great Revolution had been re-born. All shades of opinion, from ultra-royalist to socialist, were united in seeing the 1830 Revolution as a continuation of 1789. However, the July Days were not made by Orleanists. Undoubtedly there were a few discontented radical liberals, particularly those who made the wrong choice in the 100 Days and had spent the Second Restoration unemployed, who nursed alternative aspirations in the 1820s. It became a popular journalists' device to compare Louis XVIII with Charles II of England, Charles X with James II and speculate on Louis-Philippe as the equivalent of William and Mary. Louis-Philippe's banker, Jacques Laffitte, founded the liberal paper *Le National* in January 1830, and lost no opportunity to observe that France had a choice of ruler. However, in the 1820s, the Orleanist alternative was much less substantial than Bonnie Prince Charlie's chance of regaining the British throne in 1746.

The duke of Orleans did little to nurture Orleanism even though his radical credentials were impressive. He was the son of a regicide and himself joined the Jacobin club in November 1791. As an officer in the French army he fought on the revolutionary side until his defection to the Austrians, along with Dumouriez, in March 1793. He never fought with the *émigré* armies. Much was made of this in Thiers' advertising campaign at the climax of the July Days. After Napoleon's triumphant return in March 1815, Louis-Philippe did not join Louis XVIII in exile, but travelled extensively, venturing to North America, and did not return to France until 1817. Such a past left the duke of Orleans under a cloud on his return and Louis XVIII never forgave him. Louis-Philippe concentrated on rebuilding his fortune from the 74 million livres of debt his father had accumulated at the time of his execution in November 1793. His father's estates had been equal to about three modern departments and Louis-Philippe recovered his fortune to become the biggest property-owner and richest man in France next to the king. In addition, he was careful after 1817, despite snubs at court, to stay as close as possible to his royal cousin. He practically holds hands with the king in the paintings of all major state occasions.

The accession of Charles X strengthened the links. Charles was a frequent visitor to the Palais-Royal, Louis-Philippe's home in central Paris, and Neuilly, his rural retreat. Louis-Philippe and his sister were the biggest beneficiaries of the 1825 compensation fund for former *émigrés*. It was in the interests of the duke of Orleans to support his cousin and there is no evidence that he shared the reversionary ambitions of some of his friends. The Orleanism of 1830 owes very little to its eighteenth-century or revolutionary antecedents. Philippe-Egalité's willingness to vote for his cousin's death and his subsequent similar demise went somewhat beyond traditional *frondeur* reversionary tactics. Louis-Philippe attempted to inter a memory that was a liability, not an asset. In his memoirs of the 1789 Revolution, begun during the emigration, he never denied his support for the Revolution and his Jacobin links, but used terms such as 'lamentable' in describing aspects of the period.[13]

1830 was an accidental, but popular, revolt in Paris, taken over by opportunistic parliamentary liberals. The Orleanism of the 1830s was invented and manufactured by the liberals and their new king after the event. Orleanism was a doctrine 'du lendemain', not 'de la veille'. The July Monarchy was concocted as a stop-gap compromise and Orleanism was made to measure. Thiers was an eloquent weaver of myth but his impressionistic sketch of Louis-Philippe's revolutionary origins deserves as much serious attention in the search for reality as do the numerous portraits of the new king. This was a two-step monarchy; the hesitant liberal deputies first invited the duke to be lieutenant-general and only when they concluded that Charles was no good for more than the odd game of whist did they change the invitation to include a throne. The duke himself was genuinely reluctant, pushed along by sister and wife. The liberal deputies, a convincing majority in parliament since early July, would have preferred to retain a quiescent Charles. They were too divided and frightened of popular unrest to risk a republic and had no Bonapartist candidate to hand. They made some fuss about the need to avoid civil war and invasion by the Allied Powers and saw Louis-Philippe as a safe pair of hands. The duke of Orleans was the choice of eighty-odd deputies who were in Paris at the beginning of August.

Having invented a king and short-circuited a potentially threatening artisan rising in central Paris, the liberals created the myth that Orleans was a—whatever you will—a 'citizen-king', a 'bourgeois' monarch, a king 'surrounded by republican institutions', even the 'king of the barricades'. Such epithets may have been taken seriously by some observers at the outset, but their irony soon became apparent. The king himself was an enthusiastic self-publicist. As Marrinan has so eloquently demonstrated, Louis-Philippe organized the reinvention of both the 1789 and the 1830 revolutions to place himself centre-stage and push the artisan revolution to the wings and beyond. He commissioned a series of paintings recording his view of both revolutions planned initially for display in the Tuileries, but actually housed in a wing of Versailles which he revamped as a museum of the history of France. A huge room was created to recall the 1830 revolution. There are no barricades, no semi-naked heroines, no courageous youthful insurrectionaries. Two massive paintings document the duke's arrival at the Hôtel de Ville on 31 July 1830 to be embraced by Lafayette as 'the best of republics' and welcomed by a few well-washed tame post-revolutionary artisans. In reality, he was nearly lynched and Lafayette rescued the situation, rather as Garibaldi saved Victor Emmanuel's reputation in Naples in 1860. Another painting displays the almost theatrical aspect of his oath as king. A further huge canvas shows the king presenting battalion standards to the National Guard in which he is centre-stage and their commander, Lafayette, is almost hidden by one of the flags. In these, as in all full-length portraits, the king of the French wore his National Guard uniform.

The desire of this prince of the blood to be accepted as a man with bourgeois moral family standards was genuine. It was no wonder that Hugo's play, *Le roi s'amuse,* in which the king is shown as a philanderer, achieved only one performance before it was banned by the censor in 1832. Early portraits play on his citizenship. No crown, impressive throne, staff of office, symbol of justice are present. In Hersent's portrait, exhibited at the Salon of 1831, the recently-readopted revolutionary gallic cock is present, as are a number of 'ordinary' citizens in the background, waiting to see the king. But although the king is not assertively majestic in this picture, the more radical symbols of revolution are either in-significantly present (the tricolour emblem), or totally banished (the phrygian cap). Gérard's official portrait, completed for display in the Hôtel de Ville in 1831, a copy of which was included in the Versailles collection, adopts a similarly coy approach to the idea of monarchy. Bourbon monarchs were usually painted firmly seated on the throne; Louis-Philippe stands next to a vacant throne. In Gérard's portrait, a crown and gloved symbol of justice are visible, their majesty muted by the inclusion on the king's other side of a copy of the Charter. In 1833, Vernet included Charter, crown, symbols of royal authority together with flags that are not tricolour but decorated with laurel leaves and the watchword of the new regime, 'Liberty and Order'.

Thus Louis-Philippe presented himself as the king of a very controlled, bowdlerised revolution, not made by the 'people', but by a narrow ed-ucated elite. The official portraits eloquently defined the growing conservatism of Orleanism, interspersed with hints of Bonapartism. Louis-Philippe was responsible for the return of Napoleon's ashes to Les Invalides in 1840 and saw himself as, in part, the spiritual heir of the emperor. Indeed, the numerous equestrian portraits have a somewhat Bonapartist air to them, a point which Daumier delighted in ridiculing. A final Vernet portrait, shown at the Salon of 1847 and then at Versailles, displays the king surrounded by all his sons on horseback (including the duke of Orleans who died in 1842) leaving Versailles. Whereas the Bour-bon line strained for an heir, the painting reminds us that Louis-Philippe had four surviving sons. Above the king's head, the palace gates sport the Bourbon symbol, the fleur de lys, removed from all public buildings in

1830. Contemporary Legitimists scorned this attempt to improve on Orleanism's conservative credentials.

The populist image of the citizen-king had long since worn thin and caricaturists, particularly Daumier, cynically revealed the self-seeking and selfish face of Orleanism. In moving lithographs between 1831 and 1835, Daumier illustrated Cabet's aphorism of the 'smuggled away' popular revolution that Orleanists cared little for the poor, except to shoot them. The most enduring image of the period, after the Delacroix, is surely Daumier's lithograph of the massacre in the rue Transnonain. For all the king's efforts in shaping Orleanism, it is striking that Marrinan, in his revealing exploration of over 200 pictures, recalls that his researches led him into 'storehouses'.

To estimate how convincing was the king's re-painting of history one would need to know how many people visited the new museum and what they made of it. How can one disentangle reality from image? Memoralists, official accounts and contemporary newspapers indicate that Cabet and Blanc's picture of 1830 as a popular revolt are more accurate than the tale told in Louis-Philippe's galleries. The July Days were followed by five years in which efforts to push for radical social and political change were at times pronounced.[14] Popular unrest accelerated after the revolution, small towns such as Besançon falling under the control of rebellious small-scale wine-producers supported by the National Guard. New officials sometimes encouraged the sacking of religious establishments, the planting of liberty-trees, the flying of the red flag and the displaying of the phrygian red bonnet. In these conditions Orleanism was pushed to the right.

On the other hand, the desire for a 'modern' and constitutional monarchy was widely shared, given the perceived absence of alternatives. Louis-Philippe genuinely sought to fit the role. He was approachable, his gardens where he strolled were open to the public, he held public audiences, travelled around the country and sent his children to the local lycée. He waged war on court ceremonial and expense; he had been the victim of petty jostlings for status during the Restoration. He was the first European ruler to abolish the court. Although he moved into the Tuileries there were very few formal receptions, no court uniforms and little etiquette. He reduced his civil list demands from Charles X's 32,000,000 francs to 12,000,000 francs, confined civil list pensions to the destitute and leased out hunting rights in the royal forests.[15] His family travelled the country in simple style, without the costly retinues of their predecessors.

There was a tradition of commercial acumen among his ancestors. His Paris family house, the Palais Royal, was traditionally part palace, part thriving business. Although his father was to dissipate the family fortune, in the 1780s the area around the palace was developed as a large square of small, fashionable commercial galleries, which then, as now, gave onto the inner gardens and covered walk-ways as well as onto the street. As well as coffee-houses to accommodate the rich and the professional ladies who did business with them, there were a wide range of retail shops and entertainments including a circus and Curtius's much-acclaimed novelty, the salon de cire. Louis-Philippe redeveloped the area, maintaining its openness and commercial success, while trying to move away from its links with political radicalism, not an easy matter given the proximity of both the national newspapers and a large artisan community. Such royal commercial preoccupations should have secured Louis-Philippe's 'bourgeois' credentials. He stood condemned, not for ostentation, despite his penchant for restoring palaces and buying paintings by the metre, but for meaness, greed and penny-pinching. Critical contemporaries like Cormenin claimed that the lack of respect and ridicule the king suffered was directly related to the absence of royal dignity and ceremonial.

Louis-Philippe set his century's record as a target for assassination. Was this because he tried to be a 'citizen' as well as a king, or because he failed to live up to the 'republican' royal image? There is no doubt that he was determined to be a constitutional monarch, to work with parliament. His efforts to repaint history in the Versailles exhibitions[16] were designed to show that he fitted into an established tradition of constitutional royalism. His eldest son, the duke of Orleans, was a liberal. His death may have contributed to his father's more right-wing orientation in the 1840s, when he realized that though he had a large family, his actual heir, his grandson, was too young to be a viable successor.

While Louis-Philippe was careful to respect the constitution, his actual powers were not noticeably reduced. The monarchy remained hereditary, the king continued to nominate the government, and indeed the degree of ministerial instability in the 1830s actually increased the king's power to select, not merely to name, his ministers. While this, in some respects, was not his doing, it seems clear that he enjoyed an active role in government and would not have liked to be a figurehead, a role which the circumstances of the July Days seemed to augur.

Having considered the ways in which Orleanism was invented, what did the construct signify? The name is misleading; Orleans was merely a convenience, or as they said at the time, one element in a *juste milieu*. Louis-Philippe was not central to the phenomenon we call Orleanism. Orleanism included him almost by chance. It represented the wealthy elite's compromise with the 1789 Revolution, a revolutionary memory and a conservative present embodying stability and security. However, it proved to be a blueprint for how to build a house on sand. Orleanism became a constantly changing recipe for how wealthy property-owners could retain power, ditch equality and uphold their own 'liberty'. It stood for written constitutions and power-sharing, but resistance to the popularization of politics.

Orleanists had a magpie perspective of the Great Revolution, selecting the parts they preferred, but so did everyone. Since the variants unleashed and invented in a quarter of a century of revolution were manifold, Orleanism represented more an attitude, the desire to find a *juste milieu* than an ideology, a precise common ground. Some form of constitutional government, modern centralized state institutions, codes of law, limits on the influence of the Church, were all issues dear to those who thought of themselves as Orleanists. Lest this should seem impossibly vague, Orleanists shared two very concrete characteristics. They and their families had often acquired property, usually Church lands, during the Revolution and had served Napoleon. In a very tangible sense Orleanists had a commitment to 1789. This was not an intransigent war-cry, but a basis for negotiation. Guizot noted in his memoirs, 'Né bourgeois et protestant, je suis profondément dévoué à la liberté de conscience, à l'égalité devant la loi, à toutes les grandes conquêtes de notre ordre social. Mais ma confiance dans les conquêtes est pleine et tranquille et je ne me crois point obligé, pour servir leur cause, de considérer la maison de Bourbon, la noblesse et le clergé catholique comme les ennemis.'[17] How did he reconcile the two? Like many families, his had experienced the violence of revolution. 'J'ai défendu tour à tour la liberté contre le pouvoir absolu et l'ordre contre l'esprit révolutionnaire.'[18] To describe Orleanists as simply right-wing will not do. They share a fundamental acceptance of 1789.

The relationship between the Orleanist regime and the Catholic Church reveals both the limits of this acceptance and the desire for compromise. The July Days were accompanied by, and even more were followed by, widespread popular anticlericalism which climaxed in the sacking of the church of St Germain l'Auxerrois on 14 February 1831 following a Legitimist ceremony honouring their young pretender. During the Restoration, liberals had criticized revived clerical influence in politics and education. After the July Days some more radical liberals connived at popular anticlerical demonstrations against leading ultra-royalist clerics. However, the tone quickly veered towards conciliation, particularly after March 1831. A church blessing was sought for National Guard standards, for the fallen in the July Days, in honour of Louis-Philippe's birthday, for the 14 July celebrations. Most clergy were willing to comply. Ironically, the curé of St Germain l'Auxerrois was notable in tending the wounded during the July Days. Orleanism never lost its anticlerical aura, solidified by Guizot's Education Act of 1833, but the working relationship between prefects and bishops was generally harmonious.

In principle, the move from a Bourbon monarch to Louis-Philippe left Legitimist adherents of Charles X on the outside. In reality, Orleanist officials like Achille Chaper, prefect in Dijon, worked hard to win the backing of Legitimist notables. The obligation to take an oath of allegiance to the new king forced resignations in 1830, but this *émigration à l'intérieur* was brief. While few Legitimists were prepared to work with the July Monarchy at national level, in the provinces they served on local councils and as mayors.[19] In 1840, when Legitimists began to participate in Orleanist politics, they accounted for 7-8 per cent of members of departmental councils.[20] Their presence was more a matter of cohabitation than fusion, but the eagerness with which officials sought Legitimist participation is indicative of where their preferences lay.

If Orleanism can be equated with power for wealthy notables, they were not, of course, a new elite. Blanc was correct when he said that 1830 was a bourgeois revolution in its consequences because the wealthy stayed in control and refused to share power with the less rich.[21] On the other hand, Marx suggested that a new financial aristocracy emerged after the July Days,[22] noting that two bankers headed the second and third governments of the new regime. More recent research has confirmed Louis Blanc's analysis, that traditional elites, particularly professional men and landowners, dominated, as they had done during the Restoration. The proportion of businessmen actually fell from 17 per cent before the revolution to 14 per cent.[23] Analysis shows continuity between the Restoration and the July Monarchy, a statistic which Charles X had briefly disturbed in his anachronistic dreams of a ruling elite composed entirely of landed aristocrats. The Orleanist regime was not a product of a social crisis within the elite, merely a political protest against Charles and Polignac.

Orleanist notables enjoyed thinking of themselves as a bourgeois group, in the sense that they believed that 1789 gave unparalleled opportunities to the middle class. For Guizot, Tocqueville, Rémusat and others 1830 continued the trend which emphasized power for the wealthy, but, Guizot argued, for a meritocracy, an educated, enlightened elite whose right to influence was unconnected with titles or traditional privilege. The claim that Orleanism actually honoured the career open to talent does not bear close inspection. The abolition of hereditary entry to the Chamber of Peers seemed to fit this mould but, interestingly, prefects had difficulty in finding able and willing life peers, while the continued fondness for titles which could be inherited, even invented ones, illustrated their continuing appeal.

That Orleanism was born partly out of a contest between the ultra-royalist Charles X and a liberal majority in parliament might indicate a left- rather than a right-wing axis. To some degree, the extensive administrative shake-up which followed the 1830 revolution witnessed a return to power of Bonapartists out of office since the Hundred Days.[24] However, those who proved to be markedly anticlerical, such as de Trémont, prefect in Dijon, or inclined to sympathize with the problems of artisans, like Dumoulard in Lyon, were soon sacked by Périer in a second round of dismissals from March 1831. Those who survived were the more conservative, like Chaper and Siméon, prefect in the Vosges, men whose families had a long pedigree of professional and state service and were not mere Bonapartist upstarts. There was considerable continuity with *parlementaire* families and the Orleanist regime also offered renewed opportunities to wealthy Protestant clans.

Orleanism can rightly claim a revolutionary inheritance, not in the *frondeur* tradition of Philippe Egalité, but rooted in a genuine acceptance of constitutionalism. 1789 had been the climax to a century of conflict over the organization of the state, embracing a number of possibilities of change ranging from the ideas of Turgot, the various proposals of *philosophes* and the increasingly 'democratic' demands of the parlements. The 1789 Revolution did not have to end in a republic. The experimentation of the following quarter-century meant that there was no straightforward political revolutionary inheritance; constitutional monarchy, republic, empire were all claimants. The revolutionary tradition only became uniquely republican when nineteenth-century attempts to create successively a monarchy and an empire failed. The constitutional monarchy failed in 1792, but aspirations were reawakened in 1814. There was nothing inevitable about 1830. Restoration royalists and liberals shared much common ground and could work together. Only Charles X's short-sightedness and panic in July 1830 torpedoed the compromise. The Orleanist experiment resumed the search for a middle way, linking revolutionary and monarchist traditions.

The more conservative liberals who held on to power after 1831 increasingly isolated themselves from their revolutionary origins. They sought accommodation with Legitimists and the Church to avoid social unrest and political change. Was Orleanism ever a doctrine, of whatever political hue? Orleanism was a moving image, a flickering magic lantern, its acolytes adapting to circumstances, ever mindful of the need to survive. Conciliation all too easily became corruption. Orleanism gave power to a number of intelligent, professional and humane individuals, particularly prefects, but personal rivalries kept too many good men away from power. In the 1840s the political system became petrified through the complacency and fear of those in power. The failure of Orleanists to build on their original revolutionary inheritance by modifying the compromise of 1830 turned Orleanism from a search for a parliamentary *juste milieu* based on the rule of man-made law into a failed right-wing experiment.

Notes

1. Thibaudet, Albert: *Les idées politiques en France* (Paris, 1932)
2. Rémond, René: *La droite en France de la première restauration à la cinquième république* (Paris, 1963)
3. Mansel, Philip: *The Court of France, 1789-1830* (Cambridge, 1988), p 187
4. Aston, Nigel: 'Orleanism, 1789-1830: The Origins of Liberal Monarchy in France', *History Today* October (1988), pp 41-7
5. Broglie, Alexandre de: *Souvenirs* (Paris, 1886), vol 3, p 393
6. Marrinan, Michael: *Painting Politics for Louis-Philippe. Art and Ideology in Orleanist France, 1830-1848* (New Haven, 1988), p 68
7. Guizot, François: *Mémoires pour servir à l'histoire de mon temps* (8 vols, Paris 1858-67)
8. Blanc, Louis: *La révolution française. Histoire de dix ans* (5 vols, Paris, 1841)
9. Thureau-Dangin, Paul: *Histoire de la monarchie de juillet* (7 vols, Paris, 1884-92) was the magisterial climax to a comprehensive range of studies of the period, starting with *Royalistes et républicains* in 1874.
10. Maurras, Charles: *Mes idées politiques* (Paris, 1937), pp 147-212
11. Henri, comte de Paris: *Faillité d'un régime. Essai sur le gouvernement de demain* (Paris, 1936)
12. Furet, François: *La monarchie républicaine. La constitution de 1791* (Paris, 1996)
13. Louis-Philippe: *Mémoires, 1773-1793* (2 vols, Paris, 1973). Louis-Philippe resumed his memoirs in exile in 1848 but had done no more than revise his recollections of his youth when he died in 1850. Henri, comte de Paris, added a circumspect foreword to the 1973 edition.
14. Pilbeam, Pamela M.: *The 1830 Revolution in France* (London, 1991), pp 150-186
15. Mansel: *The Court of France*, pp 191-4
16. Chu, Petra ten-Doesschate and Weisburg, Gabriel: *The Popularization of Images. Visual Culture under the July Monarchy* (Princeton, 1994)

17. Guizot: *Mémoires*, vol 1, p 27
18. Guizot: *Mémoires*, vol 1, p 3
19. Tudesq, André J.: *Les grands notables en France, 1840-49. Etude historique d'une psychologie sociale* (Paris, 1963), vol 2, pp 270-95
20. Tudesq, André J.: *Les conseillers généraux en France au temps de Guizot* (Paris, 1967), p 230
21. Blanc: *La révolution française,* vol 2, p 33
22. Marx, Karl: *Class Struggles in France, 1848-1850* (London, 1895), p 44
23. Higonnet, Patrice B.: 'La composition de la chambre des députés, 1827 à 1831', *Revue historique* 195 (1968), pp 351-78
24. Pinkney, David H.: *The French Revolution of 1830* (Princeton, 1972), p 293

4. LEGITIMISM AND THE CULT OF BOURBON ROYALTY

Geoffrey Cubitt

For a significant and durable portion of the French right in the nineteenth century, right-wing politics were essentially the politics of legitimacy—a politics based not simply on a preference for one form of government over another, for order over disorder, or for conservatism over change, but on recognition of the right to rule inherent in a particular family and, at any given moment, in a particular individual. The politics of legitimacy were no longer necessarily grounded in a fully-fledged ideology of divine right; they might repose, at a theoretical level, on nothing more than the suggestion that an automatic principle of governmental succession was essential to political peace and social order. But political mentalities are seldom reducible to political theory; their strength comes from the imaginative connections and transfers of emotion that take place around and between the symbols that give them focus. In the case of royalism, the symbolic system revolves most obviously around the embodiments of royalty themselves—the royal line and its individual representatives. The purpose of this essay is to explore some of the imaginative connotations that Bourbon royalty possessed in the minds of its supporters—those who would have been called royalists before 1830 and Legitimists after—during the nineteenth century. It is appropriate here to speak of a 'cult' of Bourbon royalty, for, as Stéphane Rials has argued, Legitimism in its more devoted forms is best understood not (in Péguy's terms) as 'une mystique dégradée en politique', but as 'une politique sublimée en mystique'.[1] Its language and conceptual vocabulary were religious—Christian and more or less specifically Catholic—as well as political. The nineteenth-century Legitimist cult of royalty drew not only on long established thinking about the relationship between divine and royal authority and the natural alliance between Throne and Altar, but also on the providentialist turn of mind which saw in the turbulent evolutions of contemporary history the symptoms of divine intervention, and which found in the triumphs and misfortunes of French royalty the best available symbolic evidence of God's intentions for the French nation.

In his ardently royalist biography of the comte de Chambord, published shortly after the latter's death in 1883, Henri de Pène evoked the moment when the king in exile, conscious of his approaching end, received and embraced his Orleanist cousin and rival the comte de Paris. By this gesture of dynastic reconciliation, Chambord seemed to his biographer to have secured for the future the kind of royalist unity, based on an uncontested line of succession, that had never been more than fleetingly glimpsed during his own lengthy career as France's absent and neglected monarch. De Pène commented:

> En vérité, si Dieu n'est pas présent à cet embrassement-là, où est-il? Celui qui protège la France, malgré les épreuves qu'il lui envoie pour l'avertir, avait, à ce qu'il paraît, décidé de nous racheter encore une fois par la mort du juste. Ici, M le comte de Chambord est la hostie, Dieu est le sacrificateur et M le comte de Paris est marqué pour être l'instrument de notre salut. Ainsi l'a ordonné l'éternelle sagesse dont les décrets impénétrables frappent pour ressusciter.[2]

Few passages in Legitimist literature so strikingly combine the concerns of dynastic politics with the language of providentialist religion. Chambord's death becomes a sacrifice ordained by God; his own political gesture becomes part of a larger drama of national salvation governed by divine intention. He is presented to the reader not just as monarch, resolving the succession, but as 'le juste', the victim whose virtue is weighed in the scales of divine justice to the nation's benefit. Such religious understandings of the political were common in the literature of 'chambordisme': de Pène's imaginative conceit is of a piece, for example, with that of the royalist newspaper which, in 1871, compared Chambord's 40 years in exile to Christ's forty days in the wilderness,[3] or with the language of Joseph du Bourg, whose despair at the prince's death led him to declare that it marked not just the passing of a great king, but 'l'écroulement de toutes les espérances humaines de salut'.[4] De Pène's application of such language to the Chambord-Paris embrace placed his readers at a point of intersection between two strands of royalist discourse: the one focusing on the human aspects of royalty, on the importance of the royal line of descent; the other on its supernatural functions, on royalty as the object and the vehicle of divine intentions.

Chambord himself was a figure uniquely well-qualified to dominate that point of intersection. Effusions like de Pène's no doubt owed something to the introspection and frustration of a court in exile, and something also to the sickly intensities of later nineteenth-century ultramontane piety; they reflected also the peculiar influence that had been exerted on the minds of the legitimist faithful throughout his lifetime by the dramatic circumstances of Chambord's own birth. The duchesse de Berry's delivery of a male child in September 1820, seven months after the assassination of her husband had appeared to jeopardize the dynastic future, had been hailed at the time as the ultimate evidence of the Almighty's direct concern with the preservation of the Bourbon blood-line. Lamartine, in famously acclaiming 'l'enfant du miracle', had cast him already as the longed-for hero of the future:

> ... son glaive aux champs de victoire
> Nous rappelera la mémoire
> Des destins promis à Clovis ... .[5]

Memories of his providential beginning affected Legitimist perceptions of Chambord's person and prospects throughout his career: 'l'enfant du miracle' became 'le miracle vivant'[6]—a miracle awaiting its consummation. The realization that, given Chambord's own eventual childlessness, the dynastic extinction evaded in 1820 had merely been postponed, simply encouraged the prince's supporters to assign him a broader providential mission, either as the nation's triumphant deliverer from the Revolution or, when such hopes were frustrated, as self-sacrificing witness to the essential principle of legitimacy. Only with his death would some be forced to conclude that, 'Le miracle a pris fin.'[7]

Chambord's own person, then, supplies an important link between the mystical excesses of royalist devotion in his later years and the royalist hopes and mentalities of the Restoration period. His life was overshadowed by his birth, and his birth by his father's death. That death itself, however, had been overshadowed, in many royalist perceptions, by Louis XVI's death on the scaffold 27 years before. The bishop of Troyes, Mgr de Boulogne, ended his funeral oration for the duc de Berry with the abbé Edgeworth's famous words to Louis: 'Fils de saint Louis, montez au ciel.'[8] Ballanche, likewise, stressed the elements of repetition in the prince's death: 'Tous les crimes, toutes les calamités de la révolution, se sont relevés de leur funeste tombeau. Le sang le plus précieux, ce sang si peu épargné, le sang des martyrs a coulé de nouveau parmi nous.'[9]

A regressive chain of symbolic connections between royal persons thus gave a kind of focus to legitimist sensibilities; perceptions forged in one phase of royalist experience shaped and conditioned the impressions and emotions registered in another. Most of the elements that came together in the cult woven around Chambord during his maturity were already present, and interacting, in the royalist thought and rhetoric of the Restoration, as it focused on the persons of Louis XVI (retrospectively), of Louis XVIII (in 1814) and of the duc de Berry (in 1820). This chapter will seek to explore some of these elements and interactions further, by examining three prominent motifs in the nineteenth-century royalist and Legitimist celebration of Bourbon royalty: the notion of the dynastic inheritance, that of sacrificial suffering, and that of fidelity.

'Henri de France est un de ces vivants résumés de toute une histoire. Sa figure rappelle à la fois Henri IV, Louis XIV, Louis XV et Louis XVI', observed the Legitimist journalist Alfred Nettement, who visited Chambord in London in the 1840s.[10] In alluding to this physiognomic effect, he lent an air of empirical observation, and even of scientific rigour, to the more general habit of relating the actions and characters and prospects of nineteenth-century Bourbons to ancestral models. Louis XVIII, in exile, had himself been a notable exponent of this kind of dynastic back-referencing. Assuming the headship of the dynasty upon the death of Louis XVII in 1793, he had written to his cousin the prince de Condé that he looked forward to the day when, 'après avoir, comme Henri IV, reconquis mon royaume, je pourrai comme Louis XII, mériter le titre de père de mon peuple.' In 1803, rejecting Napoleon's offer of an indemnity in exchange for abdication, he had declared: 'fils de saint Louis, je saurai, à son exemple, me respecter jusque dans les fers; successeur de Francois Ier, je veux du moins pouvoir dire comme lui: "Nous avons tout perdu, fors l'honneur".'[11] Serving no doubt to sustain the self-esteem of an exiled monarch, such references became, at the Restoration, part of a broader strategy for presenting Bourbon monarchy as a system based on the efficient recycling of dynastic glory. 'Ludovico reduce, Henricus redivivus', read the legend on the statue of Henri IV that greeted Louis as he crossed the Pont-Neuf on his return to Paris in 1814.[12] Eulogies on the duc de Berry in 1820 displayed similar referential tastes: 'il représente notre Henri IV tout entier, notre grand roi populaire';[13] 's'il est vécu comme Henri IV, il est mort comme saint Louis.'[14]

More was involved in such references than the celebration of virtuous ancestral examples. The legitimizing force of linkages between present Bourbons and their royal predecessors stemmed, in a post-revolutionary world, at least partly from a linkage of a different kind: between the history of the French monarchy and that of the French nation. This, in the absence of a general belief in divine right, was the most obvious ideological foundation of the Bourbon claim to rule: the Bourbons were the natural representatives of the monarchical tradition, and the monarchical tradition was fundamental to the history, and therefore to the glory and the future, of the nation. It was an argument calculated to counteract both the efforts of the Revolution to elevate the nation above and, if necessary, against the monarchy and the Empire's claim to have recast the nation's glory in a Napoleonic image. The tenacity of the historical connection between dynasty and nation was fundamental to Chateaubriand's influential advocacy of the Bourbons in 1814: 'ils tiennent si fort à la racine de nos moeurs, qu'ils semblent faire partie même de la France.'[15] It supplied the essence also of his more cautious assessment of the strength of Restoration monarchy in 1825: the monarchy had re-established itself without difficulty, 'parce qu'elle est forte de toute notre histoire, parce que la couronne est portée par une famille qui a presque vu naître la nation, qui l'a formée, civilisée, qui lui a donné toutes ses libertés, qui l'a rendue immortelle.'[16] The same idea occurred repeatedly in Chambord's pronouncements later in the century, for example in his Frohsdorf manifesto of 1852:

> La monarchie en France, c'est la maison royale de France indissolublement unie à la nation. Mes pères et les vôtres ont traversé les siècles, travaillant de concert au développement de notre belle patrie. Pendant quatorze cents ans, seuls entre tous les peuples de l'Europe, les français ont toujours eu a leur tête des princes de leur nation et de leur sang. L'histoire de mes ancêtres est l'histoire de la grandeur progressive de la France.[17]

Though such arguments might be expressed in purely secular terms, it was common for them also to possess a religious dimension: the national tradition was held to be Christian as well as monarchical, and the monarchical tradition—from the baptism of Clovis to the scaffold of Louis XVI, as Chateaubriand maintained[18]—Christian as well as national. This, in turn, broadened and shifted the terms of the argument, by associating monarchy in the Bourbon line with the larger phenomenon of Christian civilization. The christianization of Europe, Chateaubriand maintained, had created a kind of interdependence between states: religion was 'le lien maternel qui unissoient toutes les monarchies européennes.'[19] The destabilization of one monarchy destabilized others, and undermined the whole fabric of Christian order. The long and (until the Revolution) continuous links between monarchy, nation and Christian (latterly Catholic) religion had made France the eldest daughter of the Church; it was on this alliance, as far as royalists were concerned, that her natural leadership of Europe was based.

The discourse of Bourbon dynasticism was thus a highly developed one. Its limitations, however, were obvious. By relating the cause of Bourbon monarchy only to the long-term continuities of French history, it ignored the experiences of disruption and conflict that filled the foreground of the recent French past. By dwelling on Henri IV or Saint Louis or Clovis, it begged the question of Louis XVI. In practice, of course, neither the Revolution nor the decapitated monarch was absent from royalist thought and rhetoric. Their inclusion in them, however, involved the use of concepts and languages very different from the essentially traditionalist and predominantly triumphalist ones that were involved in the dynasticist narrative of French and Bourbon history. The essential notions brought into play here were those of providential intervention and of royal martyrdom.

Royalist ideology oscillated, in fact, between the effort to suppress the revolutionary rupture in French history, by linking the present and the future to a supposedly stable dynastic past, and the effort to make sense of it, by relating the events of the present and the recent past to a providential design. The Restoration of 1814, for example, was represented in royalist propaganda sometimes as a smooth resumption of a natural association between the Bourbons and the French people, and sometimes, even simultaneously, as a moment of exceptional providential involvement in French history. In its first issue, published at the moment of their return, *L'ami de la religion et du roi* saw in the Bourbons at once the family which had given France Saint Louis and Henri IV and the family, 'que le ciel sembloit tenir en réserve pour l'amener à notre secours quand le temps marqué dans ses décrets seroit enfin arrivé.'[20] Mgr de Boulogne, for his part, compared the miraculous circumstances of the Restoration to those which had placed the crown of Israel on the head of David, or brought down the walls of Jericho.[21]

Even in the immediate royalist elation of 1814, those who advanced such providentialist understandings of France's sudden deliverance seldom did so with the sole intention of adding a supernatural descant to the fanfares of Bourbon triumphalism. For them, the return from exile of Louis XVIII was essentially part of a more complex and traumatic mystery of national redemption. Making sense of it involved making sense of what had gone before. Salvation did not come without expiation: the sins of nations—like those of individuals—had to be paid for, either by the nations themselves or by individuals who suffered on their behalf. The chapter of suffering—under revolutionary Terror and then Napoleonic tyranny—from which France was providentially released by the Bourbons' return in 1814 had itself been the necessary punishment for the crimes of the Revolution and for the longer derelictions of national Christian duty of which the Revolution was the culmination.[22]

In this economy of national redemption, as royalist literature conceived it, the sufferings of royalty had a central place. The killing of Louis XVI was the pinnacle of the revolutionary criminality for which the nation had to atone.[23] Atonement, however, was a complex process, in which the innocence of victims was weighed on both sides of the balance. Though the efforts made to get the cause of Louis's canonization officially entertained at Rome met with eventual failure, his admirers—encouraged by the initial reactions of Pius VI in 1793—were not slow to accord him a martyr's status.[24] The question—vital in the eyes of Roman officialdom—of whether the king had been killed out of hatred for the Christian faith was of secondary significance to royalist opinion. Attention focused instead on the constancy of his Christian conduct, and on the relationship of his example to a sinful nation's prospects of redemption.

Royalist commentators stressed the tranquillity of conscience and heroic spirit of forgiveness which Louis had displayed in the face of approaching death; these qualities, they argued, amounted to an almost superhumanly efficacious example of the Christian spirit. The abbé Legris-Duval, in a sermon preached before the royal family in 1814, described Louis as, 'ce monarque prédestiné du ciel pour épuiser la coupe entière des humiliations et des douleurs, et triompher de toute la fureur des passions humaines par la magnanimité de sa foi et l'héroïsme de sa clémence.'[25] Preaching in the Vendée the same year, the abbé Jaunet littered his sermon with implicit and explicit comparisons between Louis and the Redeemer of mankind: Christ's words in the garden of Gethsemane were put into Louis's mouth, the king's untroubled sleep on the eve of his execution was compared to Christ's amid the tempest, and the impression his royal demeanour left on the revolutionary Manuel was compared to the conversion of Paul. Louis's last will and testament—a text frequently cited as the finest evidence of his heroic good will towards his people—would serve, according to Jaunet, as, 'le testament de la nouvelle alliance' on which the Restoration would be based. 'Depuis le Sauveur du monde, ce roi des nations, quel autre prince avait laissé aux siens un si bel exemple de douceur et de générosité? Ah! MM, la ressemblance qui se trouve entre la fin de Louis et la mort de JÉSUS-CHRIST, est si frappante, qu'elle doit se présenter d'elle-même aux yeux les moins apercevans.'[26]

For many of its admirers, such a death shone with a splendour of self-sacrifice which transcended the realm of edifying example: it possessed the redemptive significance of martyrdom. Many versions of this theme were developed in the century that followed the Revolution: for Veuillot, Louis's death had expiated his own sins as monarch; for Proyart, the sins of his dynastic predecessors; for Ballanche, it was part of the gigantic drama of progress through trial and expiation by which a fallen mankind struggled towards perfection.[27] For the most part, however, these different versions agreed on an essential point: Louis's suffering was to France's benefit.[28] From the hagiographical and memorial literature on Louis XVI there thus emerged a concept of the relationship between royalty and nation that was strikingly different from the one transmitted by the discourse of dynasticism, though not necessarily incompatible with it. The grandeur of Bourbon royalty was seen to lie, not so much in the long chain of royal achievements through which the nation had taken shape and been endowed with glory, as in royalty's capacity to suffer for the nation, and to do so in a double sense—to suffer for the nation's edification, and to suffer in payment of the nation's sins. The judicial murder of the monarch—the very action which, on a historical plane, revealed the insecurity of the relationship between monarchy and nation, and thus called in question the central premise of the dynastic discourse—became, through a shift in perspective, the moment of the monarchy's greatest service, and its finest title to the gratitude of the nation.

The royalist discourse of sacrificial suffering was not, however, applied to Louis XVI alone; nor did it simply add a new kind of reference to catalogues of dynastic glory. It focused less on dynastic images—ones which prioritized a thin but continuous line of crowned heads—than on images of family. The literature and iconography that commemorated Louis's last days dwelt on his sentiments towards the nation; it dwelt also, in touching and tragic detail, on his ordeal as husband and father, and on the sufferings of the family from which he was torn. The later deaths of other family members—Marie Antoinette, Mme Elisabeth, Louis XVII—were bathed, in royalist literature, with something of the aura of Louis's own martyrdom. The monumental statuary initially proposed in 1814 for the Parisian church of La Madeleine would have included statues of Louis XVI holding his will (the symbol of his heroic good will towards the nation) and of France as a repentant Magdalen; it would have accompanied these figures, however, with images of the other Bourbon victims of the Revolution, including Napoleon's victim, the duc d'Enghien.[29]

Much was also made, under the Restoration (and later, in Legitimist circles) of the symbolic charge attached to the person of the duchesse d'Angoulême, daughter of Louis XVI and sole survivor of the royal family's revolutionary captivity. 'Jamais la terre ne vit une destinée comparable à la vôtre, Madame', the vicar-general of Compiègne told her in 1814, speaking (despite his claim that only angels in the confidence of the Almighty were really qualified to do so) of the 'rigueurs inouïes' and 'éclatantes merveilles' to which God had subjected her.[30] References to the duchesse dwelt on the tragic aura of a woman steeped in the memories of her family's suffering, but also on her charity and Christian virtue. In a circular letter to French bishops, the Ministre des Cultes Beugnot described her attendance at the service held in Notre-Dame to give thanks for the royal family's return:

> Rien ... ne peut rendre le sublime tableau de la fille de Louis XVI, tremblante de ses souvenirs et de ses douleurs, au pied des autels du Dieu qui pardonne, baignant de ses larmes le pavé du temple, invoquant ce Dieu pour les François, pour tous les François qu'elle a retrouvés; ange que le malheur avoit comme élevé au-dessus de la terre, et qui sembloit descendu du ciel pour réconcilier la France avec les manes de son auguste père et avec le vertu.[31]

Chateaubriand, writing his *Mémoires d'outre-tombe* when the duchesse was once again in exile, lavished upon her the full phraseology of noble misfortune—'cette victime immortelle', 'ce modèle parfait des souffrances humaines, cette Antigone de la chrétienté'—and made public the letter he had written her in 1833, in which her suffering and piety were compared to those of the women of the house of David weeping at the foot of the Cross.[32] 'Cette orpheline du Temple, que le roi martyr avait pressée sur son coeur avant d'aller cueillir la palme',[33] acquired the status of a holy relic—at once an embodiment of her family's virtue and a reminder of its sacrifice.

By broadening the theme of royal martyrdom into that of family tragedy, royalist discourse drew not only on the natural poignancy of images of bereavement and of intimate affection but also on resonances derived from the wider uses of familial imagery in discourse on state and society. Restoration propaganda depicted the return of the Bourbons as a reconciliation within the national family. 'Enfans égarés, nous avons revu notre père ...', proclaimed *L'ami de la religion et du roi*. 'Sa joie s'est mêlée à la nôtre. Il a paru oublier notre ingratitude et nos excès. Ses bras se sont ouverts pour nous recevoir, et ses yeux se sont remplis de larmes d'attendrissement. C'est Henri IV qui revient dans sa famille après des jours de dissentions.'[34] The last sentence adroitly incorporates the reference to dynastic glory into the image of family rejoicing; the rest of the passage converts the sufferings of royalty at the hands of the French nation into the torment of family division, now healed by paternal magnanimity.[35] Editorializing on the anniversary of Louis XVI's martyrdom, the same journal compared the discord into which 'la grande famille de l'Etat' had fallen after the king's execution to the celestial malediction visited upon the parricidal Oedipus.[36] Introducing the infant duc de Bordeaux (the future Chambord) to his people in 1820, Louis XVIII again stressed the familial nature of the relationship between royal family and nation: 'il nous est né un enfant à tous. Cet enfant deviendra un jour votre père; il vous aimera comme je vous aime, comme vous aiment tous les miens.'[37] Earlier, in a message to French bishops after the duc de Berry's assassination, he had declared that 'chaque famille a ressenti, comme une blessure faite à elle-même, le coup qui a frappé notre famille royale.'[38] In a whole range of ways, then, the joys and sufferings of the nation were rhetorically interwoven with those of the Bourbon family.

No event did more to fix the minds of royalists on the imagery both of royal martyrdom and of family suffering than the duc de Berry's assassination. As members of the royal family hastened to group themselves around the prince's makeshift deathbed at the opera, the theme of the Bourbons' sacrificial significance was dramatically refocused: what had once seemed an exceptional sacrifice in the context of a unique revolutionary upheaval was now, when repeated in the superficially quieter circumstances of Restoration monarchy, read as a fatal family tradition. Writers and orators renewed the themes of divine justice and human expiation previously woven around the scaffold of Louis XVI. Like that of his uncle, the death of the duc de Berry was understood both as a national calamity that carried warnings of divine vengeance (to be directed, in this case, against the nation's acceptance of liberal and atheistic doctrines)[39] and as a display of Bourbon heroism that offered hope that such vengeance might in the end be averted. The prince's forgiveness of his assassin and his stoically Christian dispositions during his protracted death agony were acclaimed in terms which strongly echoed the hagiographies of Louis—with the difference that, in the duc de Berry's case, the contrast between this final saintliness and the more intemperate character which the royal victim had previously displayed was taken to supply further evidence of God's special designs. 'Fallait-il donc que la mort vint nous apprendre encore une fois ce qu'il y a de magnanime et de généreux dans l'âme de nos rois, dans le sang de nos Bourbons?' asked Ballanche.[40] An anonymous verse compared the duc de Berry's heroic forgiveness to that of Christ:

Ainsi le Sauveur adorable
Du ciel détournant les fléaux
En proie à la rage perfide
D'un peuple aveugle et déicide,
Jésus pria pour ses bourreaux.[41]

By miraculously prolonging the prince's final ordeal to display his heroic magnanimity, Chateaubriand argued, God had allowed the world to benefit from 'une des plus belles leçons qu'il ait jamais reçue.'[42]

Chateaubriand's *Mémoires* on the life and death of the duc de Berry permit us to explore some of the discursive interactions that the prince's assassination could set in motion. The French Revolution, Chateaubriand maintained, had thrown the nation into an abyss from which she had not yet emerged, and in which only the virtue of 'quelques justes issus du sang de nos rois' had saved her from destruction: 'Nous ne doutons point que nous n'ayons été rachetés par le mérite des enfants de saint Louis: quand le sang des Bourbons a cessé de couler pour notre gloire, il a coulé pour notre salut.'[43] One strand in Chateaubriand's rhetorical strategy was thus to establish a continuity and an equivalence between the glories of earlier dynastic history and the spiritual heroism of modern Bourbon martyrs: the duc de Berry's death was presented as the sacrificial culmination of a whole tradition of dynastic service to the French nation. (Indeed, the prince's death was linked to the death of the dynastic hero Henri IV by a host of coincidences which Chateaubriand deemed worthy of record.)[44] By revealing once again 'l'excellence du sang de nos rois', Chateaubriand argued, the tragedy of 1820 made clear the essential bond between the destinies of the nation and of the dynasty: 'Verser le sang d'un Bourbon, c'est ouvrir les veines de la patrie.'[45] The theme of martyrdom here reinforced the message of dynasticism.

This, however, was only half of Chateaubriand's rhetorical strategy of 1820. The other half was to present the duc de Berry's sacrificial death as the culmination of a life governed throughout by an unswerving practice of royalist fidelity. The narrative of the prince's earlier career which follows on from the opening evocation of the dynastic past in Chateaubriand's text is strewn with reminders of his coming death;[46] it is strewn also with the illustrations of his gallant and selfless devotion to royalist duty—his service as a soldier in Condé's royalist army, his admiration for Montrose as an earlier embodiment of the kind of fidelity later practised by those serving the Bourbons in exile.[47] In the duc de Berry's letter to the comte de Ferronays in 1809, declaring his (unrealized) intention of seeking his death in the Vendée, so that 'mon sang versé au champ d'honneur, abreuvant le sol de la patrie, rappellera du moins à la France qu'il existe des Bourbons et qu'ils sont encore dignes d'elle', Chateaubriand located the sense to be assigned to the prince's actual death 11 years later: 'On peut dire que toute la mort de Mgr le duc de Berry est dans cette lettre généreuse et sublime. La fortune refusa à Mgr le duc de Berry la mort de Charette pour lui reserver celle de Henri IV: elle vouloit le traiter en roi.'[48]

The significance of this presentation of the duc de Berry as simultaneously a dynastic hero and a paragon of royalist fidelity emerges more clearly if we consider the discourse of fidelity in rather broader terms. Fidelity was both a central and a problematic value in nineteenth-century royalist discourse. Though decked by royalists with all kinds of medievalizing references to chivalric honour, it was a concept whose meanings and uses had been disturbed by the impact of the French Revolution. Before the Revolution, loyalty to the person of the monarch had been, in theory at least, both routine and obligatory: other political principles or commitments might qualify it, but could not displace it. Thanks to the Revolution's diversification of political creeds and promotion of popular sovereignty, however, fidelity had ceased to be an automatic ingredient in political mentalities; it had become self-conscious and voluntaristic. The cult of fidelity had become central to some political traditions—royalism (or Legitimism) especially—and peripheral to others. This shift in the concept's political significance served also to bring a latent tension within it closer to the surface. Fidelity is always a partially self-referential concept. It is always fidelity over time; it always, therefore, involves a relationship to one's own former self, or to one's tradition, as well as to an external object. By emphasizing the value of fidelity, royalism (or Legitimism) paid tribute not only to continuity in the royal line, but also to the significance of traditions that were not purely dynastic—family traditions among the Legitimist aristocracy, regional traditions in the Vendée, military traditions among (for example) the *zouaves pontificaux* later in the century. The symbolic interweaving of these traditions with those of the royal house was often close, as the draping of the flags of both the Vendée and the *zouaves* over Chambord's coffin in 1883 illustrates.[49] Yet the relationships were complex: reputations for fidelity could sometimes drift apart from external royal referents. Noboby was more active, in the 1830s, in promoting the image of the 'faithful' Vendée than the Vendéan journalist Jacques Crétineau-Joly. Yet the Vendée of Crétineau's imagination was a Vendée faithful above all to its own martyr-traditions, doomed in each generation to re-enact the heroism and to undergo the persecution of the 1790s. Loyalty to the Bourbons was assumed, but it was a loyalty that appeared remote when compared with the tight bonds of a regional identity. Indeed, the ingratitude of the Bourbons (or of their ministers under the Restoration)—their failure to reward services rendered—was increasingly presented by Crétineau as part of what the Vendée had to suffer. Fidelity was all the nobler for being inadequately requited, but it was the Vendée's own spiritual resources, rather than the inspirational nature of Bourbon kingship, that sustained it.[50]

A similar habit of self-reference, focused this time at the level of the individual, informs the most famous of all nineteenth-century French declarations of royalist fidelity—that which is transmitted through the pages of Chateaubriand's *Mémoires d'outre-tombe*. No-one took more pride than Chateaubriand in the grand gesture of fidelity—the sonorous 'Madame! ... Votre fils est mon Roi!', by which he attached himself in romantic gallantry to the duchesse de Berry and in Legitimist loyalty to the cause of her exiled son.[51] Yet no-one, also, was more careful to explain to posterity that his fidelity to the fallen dynasty was part of a strategy of self-consistency: 'Je reconnais au malheur toutes les sortes de puissance, excepté celle de me délier de mes serments de fidélité. Je dois aussi rendre ma vie uniforme: après tout ce que j'ai fait, dit et écrit pour les Bourbons, je serais le dernier des misérables si je les reniais au moment où, pour la troisième et dernière fois, ils s'acheminent vers l'exil.'[52] By dwelling above all on his need to remain faithful to his own oath and former record, and by stressing that (like Crétineau's Vendéans) he did so despite the shabby treatment he had earlier received from those to whom they bound him, Chateaubriand assimilated his post-1830 Legitimism to a broader moral argument (first fashioned for use against the government of the duc de Richelieu in 1818, but now usable against the July Monarchy) about the superiority of societies or régimes based on duty to ones based on material interest.[53] In siding with the exiled Bourbons, he argued, he was not preferring the interests of a family to those of his country; he was preferring 'le monde moral' to 'la société matérielle'.[54] This use of a rather classical language of moral duty served as a counter-weight to Chateaubriand's romantic indulgence in the imagery of royal martyrdom and sacrifice. Where that imagery seemed to focus Legitimist sentiment on the persons of royalty—their suffering bodies and souls, charged with a kind of sacrificial significance—this reading of royalist fidelity as an application of a broader social principle placed the moral qualities of the faithful Legitimist (as exemplified by Chateaubriand himself) at the core of the royalist vision.

If Chateaubriand's celebration of his own Legitimist commitment permits us to glimpse the tensions implicit within the royalist cult of fidelity, his earlier handling of the duc de Berry's life and death had shown how they might, at least momentarily, be surmounted. By casting the ill-fated prince simultaneously as a model of the subject's fidelity and as the bearer of the dynastic heritage of glory and misfortune, Chateaubriand allowed fidelity to be reinterpreted as a specifically Bourbon virtue. The dynastic heritage itself, in Chateaubriand's presentation, was one of service as well as leadership: originating as a cadet branch of the royal line, the Bourbons were 'sujets avant d'être rois' and 'moururent pour les François avant que les François mourussent pour eux.'[55] Sacrifice for the nation and fidelity to the monarch thus ran together in the Bourbon blood-line. The duc de Berry's service in Condé's army—itself, significantly, a royalist army headed by the faithful princes of a cadet branch of the Bourbon line—confirmed the place of fidelity within the dynastic tradition. His readiness to serve under the orders of his elder brother in a regiment which he himself had raised was presented by Chateaubriand not simply as an instance of individual unselfishness, but as a manifestation of the Bourbons' natural instinct for dynastic subordination—a quality through which their conduct became 'une sorte de confession authentique et perpétuelle du principe de la légitimité'.[56] The Bourbons became the exemplary practitioners as well as the objects of legitimist fidelity.

Chateaubriand's text of 1820 focused this complex rhetoric of royal fidelity not on the person of a reigning monarch, but on one who, at the time of his death, was merely third in line to the throne. The equivalences which Chateaubriand and others detected between the duc de Berry's death and those of Louis XVI and Henri IV served, however, to bring the themes of fidelity and of kingly sacrifice into close proximity. The connections thus established were to be part of the comte de Chambord's symbolic inheritance from the deathbed of his father. For it was in Chambord's public image that the conceptual shift whereby the language of fidelity came to be applied not only to the loyal service of the subject but to the king's own devotion to the principle that he himself embodied was most concretely expressed. Encouraged at a general level by the experiences of revolution and of royal exile, both renewed in 1830, this conceptual shift was given a sharpness of definition by the spectacular emergence of Louis-Philippe as an available contrasting symbol. The promotion of Chambord as paragon of legitimist fidelity both accentuated and drew force from the denigration of the July Monarchy as a regime founded on a family and dynastic betrayal.

For his more ardent admirers, Chambord's refusal to compromise the essential principle of legitimacy—or even to compromise its symbols, most notably the white flag—was itself the proof of his kingly dignity and of his value to the nation. This was a perception that Chambord himself insistently encouraged. 'Par mon inébranlable fidélité à ma foi et a mon drapeau', he wrote in 1872, 'c'est l'honneur même de la France et de son glorieux passé que je défends, c'est son avenir que je prépare.'[57] This emphasis on his own fidelity was rooted, not in mere stubbornness of character, but in a specific version of the old belief that royalty confers duties as well as rights. As Chambord put it in 1850: 'La royauté est un attribut qui appartient à la fois au peuple et au prince. Il y a entre eux une union indissoluble.'[58] A king in exile who compromised his own legitimacy—even by appealing to popular sovereignty to restore the monarchy—would thus be guilty of a form of treason. By being unfaithful to his principle, he would be unfaithful both to himself and to his people. He was, as Chambord never tired of repeating, the repository of a sacred trust, which conferred upon him the duty of self-sacrifice. He must be faithful to his people even when his people were not faithful to him. The romance of unrequitedness was as central to the rhetoric of *chambordisme* as it was to Crétineau-Joly's celebration of the faithful Vendée and to Chateaubriand's celebration of his faithful self.

Returning to the duc de Berry's assassination from the far side of 1830 in his *Mémoires d'outre-tombe*, Chateaubriand recalled his own earlier description of the prince's posthumous son as a 'goutte échappée' of the royal blood shed in 1820. 'Hélas!' he now remarked, 'Cette goutte de sang s'écoule sur la terre étrangère.'[59] Chambord's life in exile was imaginatively converted into a continuation of his father's sacrifice. Less resigned and more frustrated, Barbey d'Aurevilly would disparage 'le garçon de là-bas, qui attend béatement, assis sur sa chaise, avec du sang de Henri IV dans ses veines, les volontés de la Providence!'[60] Taken together, the two passages bear witness both to the fluctuating connotations of Bourbon blood in royalist rhetoric, and to the complex patterns of expectation that found a focus in Chambord's exiled figure. The dynastic discourse linked the king in exile to the former glories of a national dynasty. It did so, however, in ways that were inflected by the interacting discourses of fidelity and martyrdom. The activist connotations of fidelity— evident in the duc de Berry's own military career, and in his widow's unsuccessful effort to rake the embers of the faithful Vendée in 1832—were themselves softened through the imaginative impact of more passive kinds of royal heroism. Chambord's lengthening exile was lived in the shadow of the earlier Bourbon exile, so providentially ended in 1814, and of his own providential birth at a special moment of dynastic peril: the belief that it was providence rather than tactics that would determine the fortunes both of the dynasty and of the nation was always prominent in his own thinking. Equally influential, though in more elusive ways, was the association that had been formed between the idea of Bourbon monarchy and the idea of redemptive sacrifice. If Chambord's own sufferings did not attain the dramatic peaks of martyrdom scaled by his father and great-uncle, they were reminiscent in their way of the duchesse d'Angoulême's longer and sadder career as a living reminder of her family's sacrificial ordeal. The bloodstained shirt of Louis XVI lay in its display case in Chambord's residence at Frohsdorf.[61] Firmness in the face of adversity, readiness for self-sacrifice, the capacity to mount an example of saintly forgiveness that would redeem an erring nation—these were now the qualities that the faithful deemed normal in a Bourbon prince. They were the expectations that composed the comte de Chambord's role as a model of Legitimist fidelity.

Notes

1. Rials, Stéphane,'Contribution à l'étude de la sensibilité légitimiste: le "chambordisme"', in his *Révolution et contre-révolution au XIXe siècle* (Paris, 1987), p 221. For a more general exploration of the interactions between Legitimism and Catholicism, see the same author's 'Légitimisme et catholicisme (1830-1883)', in the same volume.

2. Pène, Henri de: *Henri de France* (Paris, 1885, 2nd edn), p 422

3. Quoted (from a Toulouse newspaper) in Jossinet, Alain: *Henri V, duc de Bordeaux, comte de Chambord* (Paris, 1983), p 351. For more on Chambord, see Brown, Marvin: *The Comte de Chambord. The Third Republic's Uncompromising King* (Durham,1967); Bled, Jean-Paul: *Les lys en exil, ou la seconde mort de l'ancien régime* (Paris, 1992). The best analysis of the mystical excesses of 'chambordisme' is Rials: 'Contribution'.

4. Bourg, Joseph du: *Les entrevues des princes à Frohsdorf, 1873 et 1883. La*

vérité et la légende (Paris, 1910), p 41

5. Lamartine, Alphonse de: 'Ode sur la naissance du duc de Bordeaux', in his *Oeuvres poétiques* (Paris, 1963), pp 42-3

6. Quoted in Jossinet, *Henri V*, p 351 (the same newspaper article as in note 3 above). A fairly typical royalist account of the 'suite de merveilleux bienfaits' (p 389) by which providence protected Chambord is contained in Nettement, Alfred: *Henri de France, ou histoire des Bourbons de la branche aînée pendant quinze ans d'exil, 1830-1845* (Paris, 1846).

7. De Pène, *Henri de France*, p 430 (quoting his own article in *Le Gaulois*)

8. Mgr de Boulogne: *Sermons et discours inédits* (Ghent, 1827), p 282

9. Ballanche, Pierre-Simon: *Elégie*, in his *Oeuvres* (Paris, 1833), vol 3, p 326

10. Nettement, Alfred: *Dix jours à Londres pendant le voyage de Henri de France, pour servir d'introduction à la deuxième édition de l'appel aux royalistes contre la division des opinions* (Paris, 1844), p xxxi. In his *Mémoires d'un royaliste* (Paris, 1888), vol 1, p 281, the comte de Falloux recalled the comte de Quatrebarbes's admiring comment on Chambord—'C'est Henri IV, corrigé par saint Louis'—and his own more sceptical but equally dynastically aware rejoinder—'je me contenterais de Charles X, corrigé par Louis XVIII.'

11. These two statements come from documents included in Chateaubriand, François René de: *Mémoires, lettres et pièces authentiques touchant la vie et la mort de S. A. R. Mgr Charles-Ferdinand d'Artois, fils de France, duc de Berry*, in his *Oeuvres complètes* (Paris, 1861), vol 9, pp 588, 594.

12. *L'ami de la religion et du roi* [hereafter *Ami*], vol 1, pp 71-2

13. Ballanche, *Elégie*, p 342

14. Boulogne, *Sermons et discours*, p 282

15. Chateaubriand, François René de: *De Buonaparte, des Bourbons, et de la nécessité de se rallier à nos princes légitimes, pour le bonheur de la France et celui de l'Europe* (Paris, 1814, 2nd edn), p 71. See also his *Réflexions politiques sur quelques écrits du jour et sur les intérêts de tous les français* (London, 1814), p 137.

16. Chateaubriand, *Oeuvres complètes*, vol 8, p 68 (article of 5 July 1825). The caution lay in Chateaubriand's warning that the monarchy, despite these historical foundations, could no longer rely on a kind of religious mystique: 'le temps a réduit cette monarchie à ce qu'elle a de réel.'

17. Manifesto (dated 25 October 1852), included in *Etude politique. M le comte de Chambord. Correspondance, 1841-1859* (Brussels, 1859), p 146

18. Chateaubriand, François René de: *Analyse raisonnée de l'histoire de France depuis la bataille de Poitiers, sous le roi Jean, en 1356, jusqu'à la révolution de 1789*, in his *Oeuvres complètes*, vol 10, p 343

19. Chateaubriand, *Oeuvres complètes*, vol 8, pp 24-5 (article of 15 August 1819)

20. *Ami*, vol 1, p 7

21. Episcopal *mandement* of 10 May 1814, in *Ami*, vol 1, pp 100-101.

Boulogne saw the return of the pope from his Napoleonic captivity as equally miraculous.

22. For further discussion of these interlocking themes of providential deliverance and expiatory suffering, see Cubitt, Geoffrey: 'God, Man and Satan: Strands in Counter-Revolutionary Thought among Nineteenth-Century French Catholics', in F. Tallett and N. Atkin, eds: *Catholicism in Britain and France since 1789* (London, 1996), pp 141-9. On the providentialist strand in Legitimism, see Rials, 'Légitimisme et catholicisme', pp 210-13, and 'Contribution', pp 223-5.

23. See, for example, the editorial on the death of Louis XVI in *Ami*, vol 3, p 407 (January 1815)

24. Boutry, Philippe: '"Le roi martyr". La cause de Louis XVI devant la cour de Rome (1820)', *Revue d'histoire de l'église de France* 76 (1990), pp 57-71. For more general discussion of the theme of Louis XVI as royal martyr, see Dunn, Suzanne: *The Deaths of Louis XVI. Regicide and the French Political Imagination* (Princeton, 1994).

25. *Ami*, vol 1, p 163

26. Abbé Jaunet, 'Oraison funèbre de Louis XVI', in A. de Guerry and T. Heckmann, eds: *Eloge funèbre des Vendéens et autres oeuvres de l'abbé Jaunet* (La Roche-sur-Yon, 1993), pp 120, 122, 127 (quotation), 129. On Louis's last will and testament, see, for example, *Ami*, vol 3, p 403 ('il tiendra sa place parmi les actes des martyrs').

27. Veuillot, Louis:'Vie de Notre Seigneur Jésus-Christ' (1864), in his *Oeuvres*, (Paris, 1924-38), vol 1, p 320; Proyart, abbé L.-B.: *Louis XVI détrôné avant d'être roi, ou tableau des causes necessitantes de la révolution française, et de l'ébranlement de tous les trônes* (London, 1800); Ballanche, Pierre-Simon: 'L'homme sans nom' (1820), in his *Oeuvres*, vol 3, pp 263-5, 276-7. On the latter two writers, see Cubitt, 'God, Man and Satan', pp 147-9.

28. See, for example, Mgr de Boulogne's words at a service of expiation for the death of Louis held at Saint-Denis, reported in *Ami*, vol 4, p 22: 'Oui, Prince magnanime autant qu'infortuné, votre mort le fera ce bonheur de la France, comme la mort de Jésus-Christ a procuré le salut du genre humain. Le sang du juste est monté jusqu'au ciel, non pour crier vengeance, comme celui d'Abel, mais pour crier grâce et miséricorde.'

29. Lemaistre, I. Leroy-Jay: 'L'église de la Madeleine, de la restauration à la monarchie de juillet: un mécénat d'état', in *La sculpture française au XIXᵉ siècle* (Paris, 1986), p 197

30. Quoted in *Ami*, vol 1, p 92

31. Circular of 13 May 1814, in *Ami*, vol 1, p 121

32. Chateaubriand, François René de: *Mémoires d'outre-tombe*, (Paris, 1957, 3rd edn), vol 2, pp 104, 710, 760

33. Chateaubriand: *Mémoires d'outre-tombe*, vol 2, p 753

34. *Ami*, vol 1, p 65

35. For further examples of this insistent presentation of Louis XVIII as the good father, often blending the image of father of the nation with that of father of the royal family, see *Ami*, vol 2, p 223; vol 4, pp 273-4. See more generally Deniel, Raymond: *Une image de la famille et de la société sous la restauration (1815-1830). Etude de la presse catholique* (Paris, 1965).

36. *Ami*, vol 3, p 40

37. *Ami*, vol 25, p 25

38. *Ami*, vol 23, p 166

39. See, for example, the funerary oration pronounced by the future archbishop of Paris, Mgr de Quelen, extensively quoted in Limouzin-Lamothe, Roger: *Monseigneur de Quelen, archevêque de Paris. Son rôle dans l'église de France de 1815 à 1839, d'après ses archives privées*, (Paris, 1955-7), vol 2, pp 111-14.

40. Ballanche: *Elégie*, p 316.

41. Reproduced in *Ami*, vol 23, p 176. See also Mgr de Quelen's acclamation of the prince's virtue: 'vertu d'un Dieu crucifié, vertu d'un roi martyr, vertus des Bourbons persécutés, qui a reparu sur le trône avec eux', (quoted in Limouzin-Lamothe: *Monseigneur de Quelen*, vol 1, p 113).

42. Chateaubriand: *Mémoires, lettres et pièces*, p 571. See also Boulogne: *Sermons et discours*, p 282.

43. Chateaubriand: *Mémoires, lettres et pièces*, p 488

44. Chateaubriand: *Mémoires, lettres et pièces*, pp 552, 556-7, 563

45. Chateaubriand: *Mémoires, lettres et pièces*, pp 580-1

46. Chateaubriand: *Mémoires, lettres et pièces*, for example pp 528, 532, 533, 537, 552, 556-7

47. Chateaubriand: *Mémoires, lettres et pièces*, p. 520

48. Chateaubriand: *Mémoires, lettres et pièces*, pp. 527-8

49. Jossinet: *Henri V*, pp 516-7, 529-31

50. For a fuller development of this reading of Crétineau-Joly's writings of the 1830s, see Cubitt, Geoffrey: 'Memory and Fidelity in Early Nineteenth-Century France: Crétineau-Joly and the Vendée', *Nineteenth-Century Contexts* (forthcoming)

51. Chateaubriand, François René de: *Mémoire sur la captivité de madame la duchesse de Berry* (Paris, 1833), p 120; the passage containing the declaration was reproduced in the *Mémoires d'outre-tombe*, vol 2, p 614

52. The passage comes from Chateaubriand's speech to the chambre des pairs on 7 August 1830, reproduced in his *Oeuvres complètes*, vol 8, p 479, and also incorporated in the *Mémoires d'outre-tombe*, vol 2, p 471

53. The argument was developed in an article in *Le Conservateur*, 5 December 1818, reproduced in Chateaubriand: *Oeuvres complètes*, vol 7, pp 548-56; an abridged version was included in the *Mémoires d'outre-tombe*, vol 2, pp 20-22.

54. Chateaubriand: *Mémoires d'outre-tombe*, vol 2, p 611

55. Chateaubriand: *Mémoires, lettres et pièces*, p. 489

56. Chateaubriand: *Mémoires, lettres et pièces*, p. 514

57. 'Deuxième manifeste de M le comte de Chambord', reproduced in *Du drapeau blanc et de la proclamation de Chambord* (Paris, 1872), p 113. On the white flag affair, see Brown: *The Comte de Chambord*, ch. 6; Rials, Stéphane:'Henri V et l'affaire du drapeau blanc', in his *Révolution et contre-révolution*.

58. Quoted in Jossinet: *Henri V*, p 242

59. Chateaubriand: *Mémoires d'outre-tombe*, vol 2, p 25

60. Quoted in Rials: 'Légitimisme et catholicisme', p 213, n 50. Barbey's frustrations with Chambord ('ce grand Expectant dans l'histoire') reached their culminating expression in the article 'Le comte de Chambord', published after the prince's death and contained in Aurevilly, J. Barbey de: *Les oeuvres et les hommes* (Paris, 1887; repr, Geneva, 1968), vol 8, p 490

61. Jossinet: *Henri V*, p. 283

5. HIPPOLYTE TAINE AND THE MAKING OF HISTORY

Michael Biddiss

Hippolyte Taine was regarded in his own time as one of the undisputed giants of French intellectual life. His work during the second half of the nineteenth century is remarkable both for the scope of its concerns and for the scale of its influence. By the end of the Second Empire in 1870, he was already a figure of considerable renown within a number of scholarly domains. Then—under the impact of national defeat at Sedan and, even more significantly, of the Paris Commune—he further enlarged his range by embarking on a major project of political and social history. The present essay focuses chiefly on the upshot—a multi-volume treatment of *The Origins of Contemporary France.*[1] Its composition consumed the last two decades of Taine's life, from the early 1870s until his death in 1893. Full of conservative warnings about the causes, course, and consequences of the Revolution of 1789, this whole undertaking would serve to reinforce much of the criticism which the right directed against the Third Republic in and beyond the early years of that regime.

A century ago Lord Acton wrote about the *Origins* in these terms: 'Of books that are strong enough to work a change and form an epoch in a reader's life, there are two perhaps on our revolutionary shelf. One is Taine, the other Michelet. No man feels the grandeur of the Revolution till he reads Michelet, or the horror of it without reading Taine.'[2] When considering the latter's achievement it is useful to keep in mind three broad issues, each of which reflects one of the different meanings that we commonly tend to attach to 'history'. First, with reference to its sense as *the past itself,* to what extent does Taine's analysis of modern France sustain his celebrated claim that *race, milieu,* and *moment* are the principal forces that mould historical processes, and how readily do the terms of their alleged operation offer support to a conservative interpretation of events? Second, in the context of history treated as retrospective *writing* about previous epochs, how deeply did his own methodology and polemical motivations unbalance the particular example of its construction which we are considering? Third, in terms of history conceived as a distinctively organized professional *discipline*, what did he contribute to the preservation of a scholarly voice for the right during the Third Republic's opening decades, which themselves proved to be such a crucial period for the intellectual and institutional 'making' of this subject within France?

Let us begin by assessing the nature of the reputation that Taine had already come to enjoy by the time of the Franco-Prussian War.[3] Born in 1828, this lawyer's son from the Ardennes had long been famed for his sheer cleverness. After the death of Hippolyte's father in 1841, an uncle arranged for the boy to come to Paris so that the most might be made of his precocious talents. Having previously collected all the major scholarly prizes at the Collège Bourbon, Taine entered the École Normale Supérieure shortly after the June Days of 1848. By the end of his studies there he had exchanged his initial Catholicism for a loosely Spinozan brand of pantheism. As he wrote to his fellow-student Prévost-Paradol in November 1851, 'Nature is God, the true God, and why so? Because it is perfectly beautiful, eternally living, absolutely one and necessary.'[4] In the increasingly reactionary and clericalist atmosphere of the Second Republic as governed by Louis-Napoleon Bonaparte, this was not the stance most likely to endear Taine, now a young school-teacher in his first post at Nevers, to those who were enlarging their control over the educational system. Professional prospects were further blighted by his refusal, after the coup d'état of December 1851, to pay even lip-service to a regime which was plainly hastening towards the restoration of an authoritarian Empire and the imposition of tighter restrictions upon academic freedom.

Thus Taine soon turned away from teaching, and began to carve out a successful career as Parisian *homme de lettres.* Avoiding any narrow political partisanship, he concentrated his energies on articles and books that spanned the domains of literature, aesthetics, and philosophy. After his thesis on La Fontaine (1853) and a study of Livy (1856), he proceeded to publish an influential series of collected pieces, including *Les philosophes français du XIXe siècle* (1857), *Essais de critique et d'histoire* (1858), and *Nouveaux essais* (1865). Not least, he brought out in 1863-64 his *Histoire de la littérature anglaise,* and in 1870 a work on philosophy and psychology entitled *De l'intelligence.* Meanwhile, he had also succeeded Viollet-le-Duc in the prestigious, albeit part-time, post of professor of aesthetics and art history at the École des Beaux-Arts. On the basis of these achievements, Taine's fame and fortune had been firmly secured by the time that the Second Empire ended. When under circumstances of defeat and civil war he then decided to compile the *Origins,* the range and content of his previous writings had already marked him out as France's leading spokesman for a particular philosophical persuasion—one full of potential implications for the huge project of political and social history upon which he was now embarking.

In brief, Taine had succeeded Auguste Comte as the foremost champion of positivism. This philosophy centred on a belief that the methods of natural science provided the principal, or even the sole, model for the attainment of true knowledge; and, conversely, that any insights claimed by other disciplines were valid only to the extent that they incorporated, or somehow approximated, the procedures of the scientist. Taine's version of the creed was closely related to his pantheistic respect for the necessity of a single logic within nature, such as must cover the workings not only of the physical world but also of the human sphere. He was typical of many contemporaries in seeking what Donald Charlton called 'a knowledge distinguished by both certainty and completeness.'[5] The challenge for such positivists was to attain the second of these two features by constantly extending the domains in which scientific method seemed to be achieving the first. With hindsight we can now readily see that one of their biggest weaknesses was a tendency to repeat the Comtean error of using during the interim some curious form of secular mysticism to fill up whatever short-fall might still remain between the certitude and the plenitude!

Even before he undertook the *Origins,* Taine had already brought secularist positivism to bear upon the task of discovering the 'laws' of history, as manifestations not of some divine will but of the logic of nature operative within the human past itself. His most explicit analyses come in the two prefaces to the *Essais de critique et d'histoire* (one accompanying the original edition of 1858, and the other forming a significant supplement for the reissue of 1866), and at the opening to the *Histoire de la littérature anglaise* of 1863-64. The texts of 1858 and 1866 stress how, at any given epoch, the diverse manifestations of a particular society or civilization—whether shown in family and governmental structures, or in customs of public and private conduct, or in philosophy, religion, and art—are all deeply interconnected. Taine contended that these phenomena were not random but structural, organized according to 'a universal force, every-where present and active, governing all great issues, and directing all major events'.[6] He argued, further, that this *'force maîtresse'* possessed a certain continuity across time in so far as it stemmed from 'the particular character and spirit of the race, transmitted from generation to generation.'[7] Here, so he thought, was the kind of formal patterning which had eluded the romantic-inspirational historiography of Michelet, a writer more skilled at emotionally seducing than at empirically convincing the reader.[8] For Taine a scholarly understanding of the past could not be founded largely upon poetical imagination, any more than it could fulfil itself solely through compilation of detail. Only by progressing from the latter towards the rigorous analysis of systematic regularities would the study of history fulfil its proper destiny of developing into a proper science—even into a form of knowledge containing predictive potential.

The positivistic ambitions were still more famously evident in the introductory section of Taine's attempt at using English literature as a means of recapturing the thoughts and feelings embedded in a particular national past—one all the more easily isolated for observational purposes because of its relative insularity. Through thirty-odd pages he urged upon his audience a welter of scientific analogies, from such domains as algebra, astronomy, zoology, psychology, anatomy, physiology, botany, chemistry, mineralogy, and mechanics. He declared, for example, at one particularly notorious juncture, 'Vice and virtue are products, like vitriol and sugar.'[9] Most significant of all, however, was his refinement of the *force maîtresse*. Here he presented it in terms of three controlling elements. Their triangulation established the framework within whose confines the civilizational development (including the imaginative creativity) of any particular people must occur.[10] Taine restated, first, the significance of race. Though he formally defined this in terms of 'the innate and hereditary dispositions which man brings with him into the world, and which, as a rule, are united with the marked differences in the temperament and structure of the body', he also tended to stretch the concept so as to cover what we might think of more loosely as 'national character'. Second, he cited the surroundings (*milieu*), in the form of those 'physical or social circumstances [that] disturb or confirm the character committed to their charge.' His final conditioning factor emerged as the 'epoch' (*moment*). Here was a device which might capture, at any specific stage in time, whatever alterations had by then occurred to the interactions operative as between the racial element ('the internal mainsprings') and that of the *milieu* ('the external pressure').

To the extent that the 'acquired momentum' represented by this third element offered more flexibility than the other two factors, it allowed Taine in his own historical writing to loosen the trammels which his positivistic determinism otherwise threatened to impose. Even so, the constrictions generally implied by these methodological reflections do suggest one of the most important reasons for his eventual identification with the right. By the 1860s, he had long abandoned any youthful sympathy for certain aspects of revolutionary idealism; rather, he was now stressing that one of the principal criteria for gauging the wisdom of political actors, past or present, must be the degree to which they understood the limits of choice set by the *force maîtresse* and thus accepted the need to work *with*, not *against,* the grain of history. Only on that circumscribed basis could some due measure of individuality and freedom of action be properly asserted. Supremely dangerous were those who instead promised to achieve—seemingly overnight—a remaking of the world, and a radical regeneration of all human kind. Not surprisingly, therefore, the ideological implications of Taine's study of English literature were clearest in the sections devoted to the later eighteenth century. Most notable is the passage where the writings of Edmund Burke (his Irish connections notwithstanding) are praised for conservative prudence and practical moral sense. Taine also explicitly distances these works from the woeful exercises in abstract reasoning and rhetoric displayed across the Channel by so many of the *philosophes.* 'Never', he tells us, 'was the contrast of two spirits and two civilizations shown in clearer characters, and it was Burke who, with the superiority of a thinker and the hostility of an Englishman, took it in hand to demonstrate this to the French.'[11]

The national disaster of 1870 and its sequel of civil conflict simply confirmed Taine in these views, underlining for him just how much of the Burkean wisdom his compatriots still lacked. In May 1871, even while the increasingly eminent anglophile was in Oxford receiving an honorary degree, the Paris Commune entered its final and bloodiest phase.[12] He now put aside plans to produce a sequel to *De l'intelligence,* or to write a book on German literature. If he also moved away from *philosophizing* about history, that was, however, largely in order to concentrate his energies on *writing* it instead. It was necessary, as he wrote to Albert Sorel, 'to show how our faults caused our reverses.'[13] Henceforth, he would devote himself to *The Origins of Contemporary France.* The scale of this enterprise soon exceeded his initial intent, as two volumes eventually grew into six. The first of these, issued in 1875, was a study of the pre-1789 regime. There followed a trilogy covering various phases of the Revolution itself, published in 1878, 1881, and 1884. The fifth and sixth volumes, dated 1890 and 1893, then presented the ailing author's ultimately uncompleted analysis of the nineteenth-century scene. There were numerous and rapid reprintings, to the point where Victor Giraud estimated that by 1900 no fewer than seven million readers had already perused at least part of the

Origins.[14]

Taine composed his sequence with a passion which differed from Michelet's in its political orientation, but scarcely in its ardour. The emotional intensity suffusing the work's condemnatory prejudgment of all that '1789' might be taken to symbolize placed an almost unbearable strain on the author's positivistic principles. As Alfred Cobban once suggested, it could well be the case that, out of all those who have written on the Revolution, 'Taine possessed the greatest genius, and produced the worst history.'[15] Nonetheless, whatever its other weaknesses, the *Origins* did manage a clear and consistent identification of the major targets needing to be attacked. Like Alexis de Tocqueville before him, Taine was arguing that over many centuries France had suffered gravely from a constant enlargement of centralized state power. Yet, so he went on to contend, that malaise, endemic within the absolutist old regime, was itself the product of another disorder operating at the even deeper level of collective psychology. In the opening volume of the *Origins,* which is the one most fundamental to any identification of the principal themes running through the project as a whole, he asserted that, 'The social and political mould into which a nation may enter and *remain* is not subject to its will, but determined by its character and past.'[16] This judgement underpinned his claim that the French tragedy could be explained by a certain orientation of mind, which had been nurtured especially within the ranks of the educated and which had long developed even to the point where its noxious consequences seemed to permeate society as a whole.

The mentality at issue had manifested itself most banefully through the Enlightenment's infatuation with the phenomenon labelled in the *Origins* as *la raison raisonnante.*[17] At first sight, this line of criticism from Taine might appear inconsistent with his own undeniable debt to the whole tradition of secular positivism. Thus we could well wonder whether he was now actually sawing off precisely the same branch of the tree of knowledge as that upon which he himself had chosen to perch. Yet his expressed intent, at any rate, was clearly not to dismiss reason as such. Rather, by condemning *la raison raisonnante,* he was assailing one particular habit of thinking which had proved itself unfitted 'to embrace the fullness and complexity of reality'.[18] Here was the leading theme for Taine's account of French intellectual history during the seventeenth and eighteenth centuries, which concentrated on the way in which the estimable endeavours of scientific empiricism had become increasingly mixed with—but also imperilled by—those of an altogether more abstract *esprit classique.* On the latter he commented as follows:

> To pursue in every research, with the utmost confidence, without either reserve or precaution, the mathematical method; to derive, limit, and isolate a few of the simplest generalized notions; and then, setting experience aside, comparing them, combining them, and, from the artificial compound thus obtained, deducing all the consequences they involve by pure reasoning, is the natural process of the classic spirit.[19]

Taine's critics have rightly observed that some such mind-set already suffused much of his *own* thinking—as, for example, in his efforts to triangulate the *force maîtresse*. However, what he himself clearly intended to argue was that in late-eighteenth-century France this *esprit classique* had become thoroughly parasitic upon science proper, and that an analysis of the resulting debilitation would now give historians the key to explaining the causes and course of the Revolution which in 1789 had replaced one flawed regime with another even worse.

At the core of Taine's argument lies a contrast between *la raison raisonnante* and something which we find encapsulated in the phrase 'une sorte de raison qui s'ignore.'[20] Unselfconscious even about its own operation, the latter is a brand of rationality reminiscent, once again, of that championed by Burke. Its wisdom—to be elicited not through formal logic but through empathetic historical analysis—serves essentially to support some general presumption in favour of the continuity of established tradition. Taine writes about such *préjugé héréditaire* in these terms:

> Careful investigation shows that, like science, it issues from a long accumulation of experiences: men, after a multitude of gropings and efforts, have satisfied themselves that a certain way of living and thinking is the only one adapted to their situation, the most practical and the most salutary, the system or dogma now seeming arbitrary to us being at first a confirmed expedient of public safety. Frequently it is so still; in any event, in its leading features, it is indispensable; it may be stated with certainty that, if the leading prejudices of the community should suddenly disappear, man, deprived of the precious legacy transmitted to him by the wisdom of the ages, would at once fall back into a savage condition and again become what he was at first, namely, a restless, famished, wandering, hunted brute....In general, the older and more universal a custom, the more it is based on profound motives, on physiological motives, on those of hygiene, and on the precautions taken by society.[21]

In effect, the author is urging that the conventions of the *race,* adapted through the ages to the constraints of its particular *milieu,* should not be suddenly disregarded. Least of all should a community abandon them in the vain expectation of finding greater fulfilment through a reckless transformation based on abstract psychological and political principles divorced from concrete historical experience.

Taine believed that this was just the kind of chimera which the French *philosophes* had increasingly offered. While remaining in many ways respectful of Montesquieu and Voltaire, he focused his most impassioned attack on Rousseau—and especially on *Du contrat social* of 1762. This work features in the *Origins* as the most dangerous manifestation of the *esprit classique*. Rousseau's book is roundly condemned for aspiring to construct a new political order on the basis of geometrical axioms which supposedly possess a universal validity quite independent of specific circumstances. Taine claims, by contrast, to be judging from actual historical experience when he argues that an authentic sense of community is something evolved over time, with reason and tradition operating in harmony. He dismisses Rousseau's compact as damagingly fictive—an agreement forged not by living individuals, but simply between 'so many abstract creatures, so many species of mathematical units'.[22] To make matters worse, *Du contrat social* also attributes to these ciphers a fatally exaggerated capacity for reasoning. According to Taine, 'What we call reason in man is not an innate endowment, original and enduring, but a tardy acquisition and a fragile construct.'[23] Its correct application to public affairs is a craft to be mastered only slowly, and, even then, merely by a few. The essence of such an elitist stance is that, contrary to the claims made from the left by Rousseau's legatees, only the right can generate a truly defensible form of political rationalism.

On this view of human nature, prudent governance involves recognizing that the influence of reason upon the mass of mankind is small compared with wilder impulses stemming from 'a steady substratum of brutality and ferocity, and of violence and destructive instincts'.[24] Taine believed that the *philosophes*, instead of helping to control 'the savage, brigand, and madman which each of us harbours',[25] had managed merely to destroy the structures of due restraint. 'Millions of savages', he declared, 'were launched into action by a few thousand babblers.'[26] In one of his letters he explained that the downfall of the Old Regime, though amply deserved, would have been better executed 'in the English and German fashion, upon the principles of Locke and Stein',[27] rather than in the radically destructive mode actually adopted by the French. Taine elaborated these arguments by presenting the opening phase of the Revolution as the epitome of anarchy. Then, paradoxically, he went on to suggest that this condition had soon given way to one involving, instead, 'the unlimited dictatorship of the state'.[28] When the revolutionaries enacted Rousseau's rhetoric about social contract and popular sovereignty, they not only turned living individuals into dehumanized abstractions but also glorified a principle of reason which the government alone could exercise the right to interpret. Here—in this most evil assertion of state monopoly, and especially in its exploitation by the Jacobins—Taine was inviting his own contemporaries to recognize the terroristic fulfilment of the *esprit classique*. As G.P. Gooch once observed, the author in his anger would throw determinism to the winds: 'We are dealing with a pessimist in a passion.'[29]

The trilogy of volumes on the period 1789-99, forming the middle part of Taine's survey, proved thoroughly disappointing to those moderates who were hoping that his hostility to the old regime might yet have led him to be sympathetic towards some aspects of the Revolution itself. Rather, he condemned it all from the outset, and not even merely from the Jacobin Terror. Similar dismay was eventually in store for any readers who expected the logic of the book's treatment of the 1790s to culminate in a defence of Napoleon's attempts to bring order out of the chaos left by Robespierre. The author certainly conveys much of the dynamism of Bonaparte—even to the point of emphasizing the senses in which the new dictator aspired to defy the controlling laws of history, by seeking to transplant a certain *force maîtresse* from one habitat to another. As we read in the *Origins*:

> He is not a Frenchman, nor a man of the eighteenth century; he belongs to another race and another epoch ... We take him for what he is, a posthumous brother of Dante and Michaelangelo ... His genius is of the same stature and of the same structure; he is one of the three sovereign minds of the Italian Renaissance. Only, while the first two operated on paper and on marble, the latter operates on the living being, on the sensitive and suffering flesh of humanity.[30]

It was, however, precisely such Napoleonic misery that Taine chose mainly to highlight in the bleak continuation of his narrative. We learn that, while many of the supposed achievements of the Emperor were too shallow-rooted in French history to be anything other than ephemeral, the wounds which he inflicted proved longer-lasting; that, having made genius the servant of sheer egoism, this *condottiere* further extended the powers of central government, and did so even while turning the state into the tool of his own personal tyranny. The version of Bonapartism which thus emerges from the *Origins*—almost as a supercharged transcendence of Bourbon absolutism on one hand and of Jacobin dicatorship on the other—ensures for the author a prominent place amongst the makers of the black legend of the Corsican ogre.[31] As Taine himself wrote to Friedrich Nietzsche, how better could one describe Napoleon than as the combination of '*Unmensch und Uebermensch*'?[32]

The concluding sections of the *Origins*, dealing with the legacy inflicted upon nineteenth-century France, have more of a thematic than a chronological structure, and focus as much upon sociological as historical issues. Taine's plans to analyse the roles of science, of the family, and of *Association* (involving other groupings from civil society) in the modern *milieu* remained unfulfilled at his death.[33] He did complete, however, his reviews of local society, the Church, and the school system. To the first of these topics he brought his experience as *conseiller municipal* in the Savoyard commune of Boringe. He argued, predictably, against the centralizing state's growing intrusion of its abstract symmetries into the conduct of affairs best reserved for the more nuanced judgements of local notables such as himself. The role of the latter had become similarly diminished through direct universal suffrage. In rural areas, this practice threatened to transfer control to a largely unlettered peasantry, whose 'rude brains rendered torpid by the routine of manual labour' made them even more vulnerable than their betters to manipulation from the centre.[34] Still worse were the effects of popular voting on the urban scene, where a little extra literacy had turned out to be an even more dangerous thing. Taine conjures up the image of *citadins* stirred to callow dogmatism by a popular press, who are then found 'loudly arguing on every subject with confidence, according to Jacobin traditions, being indeed so many fresh Jacobins, the heirs and continuators of the old sectarians ... mainly narrow-minded, excited, and bewildered by the smoke of the glittering generalities they utter'.[35] Rampant corruption everywhere ensues, especially because the prefect—still, in effect, 'the prefect of the year VIII'[36]—is expected by town and country alike to deploy his vast powers of patronage to buy the votes of these mass herds, and because he himself thus becomes the prisoner of electoral opinion at the expense of the real public good.

Since Catholicism harboured many authoritarian pretensions of its own, Taine could hardly look to the Church as providing a consistently reliable check upon the the power of the state. He correctly observed that, under Charles X and during the early Second Empire, the secular and ecclesiastical forces had actually helped each other in their respective quests 'to control the entire man.'[37] But, granted the history of growing state centralization in France, their more customary situation was adversarial. In this rivalry, Catholicism (as distinct from the Protestantism to which Taine himself became increasingly drawn during his final years) had further weakened itself by a reluctance to accommodate many aspects of recent scientific progress. This obscurantism also confirmed that the Church would be just as undeserving as the state to enjoy victory in the ongoing contest for a monopolistic control over schooling. As published in its unfinished form, the *Origins* did indeed culminate with a vigorous attack on French public instruction. At the level of secondary education, this assault was directed against the system of the *internat*, especially as conducted within the barracks of the lycées. There the pupils resembled geese force-fed through a mechanical *gaveuse*, and they now remained, even under the Third Republic, the victims of the Jacobin and Napoleonic idea of 'the teaching state'.[38] How very different, suggested the author, was this caged regimentation of thinking and living—indeed this 'communism'—from the independence of spirit which he so generously associated with the Rugby of Dr Arnold![39] As for primary schooling, Taine concluded with the quintessentially conservative warning that the French state had erred in making excessively elaborate provision for the bulk of pupils, under circumstances where 'nine out of ten are sons or daughters of peasants or workmen and will remain in the condition of their parents.'[40] Was it not damaging, so he insisted, thus to divorce education from *life*?

Viewed as a whole, the *Origins* clearly confirm the need to identify Taine as a man of the right. Yet the issue of where precisely within that part of the French political spectrum we should place him is more problematic. Constantly distancing himself from any specific party, he wrote *à rebours*—against the grain of many conventional configurations. As a positivist he believed in the advance of science, yet, regarding France at least, he also remained deeply doubtful about prospects for political progress. He was a rationalist who also maintained respect for tradition, and an opponent of the clericalist stranglehold upon legitimism who no less roundly protested against Jacobinism too. Having been a prominent critic of the Second Empire, he went on after 1870 to become increasingly hostile to a successor republic which, quickly and (for him) inevitably, abandoned its initial moderation. In 1887, when his personal friendship with the princesse Mathilde was about to collapse, he explained that the wounds which he had inflicted on her fellow-Bonapartists had been matched by those registered against royalists and republicans as well.[41]

Taine's own ideal would certainly have been a regime controlled by the upper orders—men of property, noble and bourgeois together. As he observed to the English-language translator of the *Origins*: 'The essential thing is for the well-informed and wealthy classes to lead the ignorant and those who live merely from day to day.'[42] Yet such conservatism had also to satisfy the criteria of an elitist *liberal*. Taine was, for example, a champion of individual conscience in matters secular and spiritual alike, as well as a defender of the independence of the legislative and judicial functions against encroachments by the executive power. His principal watchword was *limitation* of government: let the state act as a gendarme against robbers within and enemies without, but never permit it then to begin diminishing the right of its subjects 'to seek their happiness or their peace of mind in the style of living, or association, or aspiration which suits them best.'[43] He contrasted the betrayal of this principle by centralized France with the allegedly happier experience of its neighbours. When he looked at Prusso-German dynamism beyond the Rhine and attributed this to the liberal ethos of the controlling aristocracy, Taine was hardly making the soundest of his judgements.[44] But he was arguably on safer ground when, turning westwards, he attributed much of Britain's success to the wisdom of the Whig tradition. As he declared after reading the speeches of Lord Macaulay, 'How happy to be born in a country where one can be liberal!'[45] Among the choices actually available to contemporary Frenchmen, there was only one grouping towards which he expressed some hesitant sympathy. He believed that its particular version of monarchism, though tainted by revolutionary connections, benefited occasionally from a malleability such as Pamela Pilbeam has emphasized elsewhere in the present volume. Put briefly, it was in some vague Orleanism that from time to time he glimpsed a basis for the kind of regime which would have alarmed him least.

Even so, it is Taine's refusal willingly to endorse any partisan engagement which constitutes the most fundamental point. 'The social and political battle,' he declared in 1877, 'has long been lost.'[46] In observing how the great positivist compared his vast historical undertaking to 'a conference of physicians', we approach the heart of the matter.[47] Nothing is more striking about the *Origins* than its reflection of, and further contribution to, the discourse of pathological degeneration which pervaded so much of the social self-analysis conducted within France during the final decades of the nineteenth century. Here we have what Daniel Pick calls 'an attempt to conceptualise the morbid passage of history itself', conducted by 'a kind of doctor of past pathologies—a Lombroso of the archives'.[48] According to Taine's diagnosis, such *dégénérescence* was in the French case nothing less than terminal. In one of his last letters he referred to his 20 year enterprise as a set of investigations which had darkened his old age while also remaining devoid of practical purpose: 'A vast and powerful stream carries us away. What is the use of writing a thesis about the depth and speed of the current?'[49] Much of this sense of futility surely stemmed from his own over-indulgence in the abstractions of the *esprit classique*. He had been led, in Claude Digeon's apt words, 'to fight against French tradition in the name of Tradition, against French history in the name of History, and against French reality in the name of Reality.'[50] Granted Taine's eventual disillusionment with the effectiveness of that struggle, it was not he himself but others on the right (for example, enthusiasts of the Action Française) who would proceed to adapt his arguments so as to serve more truly activist forms of political campaigning. Just as the Germans of the Wagner circle distorted for their racially redemptive purposes the fundamentally pessimistic Aryanism of Arthur de Gobineau,[51] so too did such French propagandists as Edouard Drumont, Léon Daudet, Charles Maurras, and Maurice Barrès need to misrepresent much of the meaning of the *Origins* before they could cite that work in strong support of their own irrationalist cults of violent counter-revolutionary transformation.

As for his fate in a more scholarly context, the influence of Taine on historical writing is greatly entwined with his contribution to the development of sociological discourse as well. The linkage is fundamentally evident in his positivistic habit of searching for general laws applicable to the whole social domain, even if that enterprise was then flawed by his failure to pursue any properly systematic comparisons with the historical configurations of *race* and *milieu* applicable to cases beyond France. Furthermore, the racial rhetoric itself not only underlined the interdisciplinary connection, but also assumed a far greater significance under the circumstances of the Dreyfus case. Commencing in the year after Taine's death, the Affair helped to turn the French versions of anti-Jewish feeling into a set of pressures that became more predominantly rightist than ever before. Stephen Wilson observes that the author of the *Origins* 'never gave the same direct support to antisemitism as did Renan, but his contribution to popularizing the concept of race as a tool in socio-historical explanation was probably greater'.[52] Nor, as another major example of interaction between history and sociology, should we overlook the influence which Taine's outstandingly dramatic presentation of the bestial behaviour of the revolutionary *canaille* would continue to exert on right-wing scholarship.

With reference to this literature on crowd behaviour, Susanna Barrows contends, 'No other nineteenth-century writer created such frightening, yet memorable machines of savagery.'[53] Taine's pathological obsessions were supremely evident in his evocations of the madness and criminality, the drunkenness and regressive animality, of the mob. Contagious disorder dominates the passages that depict the *peuple-roi* coming into its own: the pages where we read, for instance, about the men of Paris—and (in a significant moment of concession to gendered history-writing) the women also—forcing Louis XVI to return with them from Versailles in October 1789, or about the Jacobins of 1793 embarking upon their Terror with the aid of 'those recruited from the human waste which infects all capital cities, the epileptic and scrofulous *canaille.*'[54] Well into the first half of the twentieth century similar descriptions would feature constantly in the popular histories of France purveyed from the right by such authors as Jacques Bainville, Louis Madelin, Frantz Funck-Brentano, and Pierre Gaxotte.[55] The same images would also influence those pioneering classics within the sociological study of collective psychopathology that were produced around 1900 by Gustave Le Bon and Gabriel Tarde.[56] Indeed, when the most seminal of all modern studies of the revolutionary crowd came out in 1959, it was Taine's presentation of the mob—now assessed 'as a frank symbol of prejudice, rather than as a verifiable historical phenomenon'—that George Rudé would still be seeking to dispel, even through to the very last sentence of his own book.[57]

In so far as the author of the *Origins* eventually enjoyed an institutional base for his renown, this was provided not by the centralized system of the state-dominated University but by the French Academy.[58] The conservatives who dominated the latter decided towards the end of 1878 that, despite their discomfiture at his attacks on clericalism, they should elect Taine to join them by virtue of his even more strident assaults against the political left. Conversely, his work came increasingly under challenge at the Sorbonne. That was particularly the case once Alphonse Aulard had become enthroned in the new chair of the history of the French Revolution, which he occupied there from 1886 to 1922. Between 1905 and 1907 this radical republican, who took Danton as his hero, delivered a series of lectures on the *Origins* which remorselessly exposed the many technical deficiencies apparent in the book's handling of historical evidence. Aulard even prefaced his analysis with the celebrated warning that, at the Sorbonne, failure must befall those diploma or doctoral candidates who lapsed into citing Taine as an authority for anything at all![59] Might not we, however, regard such a threat as forming also an unintended compliment to the scale of the latter's posthumous significance? As Rudé was still effectively acknowledging 50 years after Aulard's own attack, the *Origins* would long continue to influence the making of French history from the conservative flank. In essence, Taine's final and monumental venture had offered a powerful blending of positivism and passion which those opposed to the right could persistently disparage but never afford to ignore.

Notes

1.   *Les origines de la France contemporaine* appeared originally in six volumes (Paris, 1875-93). For printings from 1899 onwards the publishers, Hachette, reset the work in the format of 11 volumes, plus a separate general index. It is to this latter 'standard' edition, cited hereafter as *OFC*, that the present notes refer. A selection of chapters from the English translation swiftly produced by John Durand (6 vols, London 1876-94) have been reprinted in a single-volume format, edited by Edward T. Gargan for the 'Classic European Historians' series (Chicago, 1974).
2.   Quoted in Gooch, George P.: *History and Historians in the Nineteenth Century* (London, 1952, revised edn), p 225
3.   A recent study of the life is Leger, Francçois: *Monsieur Taine* (Paris, 1993), and this also includes a useful summary guide to further reading. Also notable within the secondary literature is Evans, Colin: *Taine. Essai de biographie intérieurei* (Paris, 1975). An indispensable general source is the compilation of documents made by the author's widow: *Hippolyte Taine. Sa vie et sa correspondance* (4 vols, Paris, 1902-7), cited hereafter as *VC*.
4.   16 November 1851, *VC*, vol 1, p 150.
5.   Charlton, Donald: *Positivist Thought in France during the Second Empire, 1852-1870* (Oxford, 1959), p 131
6.   *Essais de critique et d'histoire* (Paris, 1904, 10th edn), preface to the first edition of 1858, pp x-xi
7.   *Essais de critique*, preface to the second edition of 1866, pp xviii-xix
8.   See the analysis of Michelet in *Essais de critique*, pp 84-129
9.   *History of English Literature* (tr. H. Van Laun, Edinburgh, 1873-4), vol 1, p 11
10. *English Literature*, vol 1, pp 17-25
11. *English Literature*, vol 3, p 89
12. For Taine's views on England, see generally his *Notes sur l'Angleterre* (Paris, 1872); and, for a warning prediction about something like the Commune, see the letter to his mother of 12 February 1871, *VC*, vol 3, p 51.
13. 16 December 1870, *VC*, vol 3, p 35
14. Giraud's *Essai sur Taine. Son Oeuvre et son influence* (Paris, 1901), as cited by Barrows, Susanna: *Distorting Mirrors. Visions of the Crowd in Late Nineteenth-Century France* (New Haven, 1981), p 91 n
15. Cobban, Alfred: *Aspects of the French Revolution* (London, 1971), p 43. Note also the same author's, 'Hyppolyte Taine: Historian of the French Revolution', *History* 53 (1968), pp 331-41
16. *OFC*, vol 1, p iv

17. *OFC*, vol 1, p 300
18. *OFC*, vol 1, p 300
19. *OFC*, vol 1, p 315
20. *OFC*, vol 2, p 6
21. *OFC*, vol 2, p 7
22. *OFC*, vol 2, p 66
23. *OFC*, vol 2, p 56
24. *OFC*, vol 2, p 61
25. *OFC*, vol 2, p 62
26. *OFC*, vol 2, p 311
27. To Georges Saint-René Taillandier, 20 July 1881, *VC*, vol 4, p 126
28. *OFC*, vol 2, p 65
29. Gooch: *History and Historians*, p 232
30. *OFC*, vol 9, pp 5, 61
31. The context is well summarized in Geyl, Pieter: *Napoleon. For and Against* (Harmondsworth, 1965), pp 127-39. See, also, Gildea, Robert: *The Past in French History* (London, 1994), chap 2.
32. 12 July 1887, *VC*, vol 4, pp 241-2
33. For some of his relevant notes, see the appendix to the *VC*, vol 4, pp 351-63
34. *OFC*, vol 10, pp 276-7
35. *OFC*, vol 10, p 286
36. *OFC*, vol 10, p 289
37. *OFC*, vol 11, p 170
38. *OFC*, vol 11, pp 347-55
39. *OFC*, vol 11, p 322
40. *OFC*, vol 11, p 361
41. To princesse Mathilde Bonaparte, 19 February 1887, *VC*, vol 4, pp 227-30
42. To John Durand, 29 November 1871, *VC*, vol 3, p 173
43. To Joseph Hornung, 19 November 1875, *VC*, vol 3, p 288
44. See generally Digeon, Claude: *La crise allemande de la pensée française, 1870-1914* (Paris, 1959), pp 215-35
45. To Émile Boutmy, 1 June 1877, *VC*, vol 4, p 28. The accompanying stress on wise evolutionary development is seen, for example, in E. Hyams, ed: *Taine's Notes on England* (London, 1957), p 126.
46. To Alexandre Denuelle, 21 May 1877, *VC*, vol 4, p 22
47. To Ernest Havet, 24 March 1878, *VC*, IV, p 45
48. Pick, Daniel: *Faces of Degeneration. A European Disorder, c.1848-c.1918* (Cambridge, 1989), pp 67-8. See also, generally, Nye, Robert A.: *Crime, Madnes, and Politics in Modern France. The Medical Concept of National Decline* (Princeton, NJ, 1984); and Harris, Ruth: *Murders and Madness. Medicine, Law and Society in the Fin de Siècle* (Oxford, 1989).
49. To Gaston Paris, 23 July 1892, *VC*, vol 4, p 338
50. Digeon: *Crise allemande*, p 228
51. See Biddiss, Michael: *Father of Racist Ideology. The Social and Political*

Thought of Count Gobineau (London, 1970), pp 244-61: and the same author's chapter on 'Arthur de Gobineau (1816-1882) and the Illusions of Progress', in J. Hall, ed: *Rediscoveries. Some Neglected Modern European Political Thinkers* (Oxford, 1986), pp 27-45.

52.   Wilson, Stephen: *Ideology and Experience. Antisemitism in France at the Time of the Dreyfus Affair* (London, 1982), p 472

53.   Barrows: *Distorting Mirrors*, pp 85-6. See also, generally, McClelland, John: *The Crowd and the Mob. From Plato to Canetti* (London, 1989), pp 127-54.

54.   See *OFC*, vol 3, pp 127-67; and vol 6, pp 255-67

55.   See, with particular reference to the treatments of the Revolution undertaken by these authors, the summary offered in Cobban: *Aspects*, pp 46-56

56.   See Le Bon, Gustav: *La psychologie des foules* (Paris, 1895); and Tarde, Gabriel: *L'opinion et la foule* (Paris, 1901).

57.   Rudé, George: *The Crowd in the French Revolution* (Oxford, 1959), p 239

58.   The overall context for the institutionalization of French historical scholarship at this epoch is discussed in Carbonell, Charles-Olivier: *Histoire et historiens. Une mutation idéologique des historiens français, 1865-1885* (Toulouse, 1976).

59.   See Aulard, Alphonse: *Taine, historien de la révolution française* (Paris, 1907), especially p viii; and, for a prompt effort of rebuttal, Cochin, Augustin: *La crise de l'histoire révolutionnaire, Taine et M Aulard* (Paris, 1909).

6. THE FRENCH RIGHT AND THE OVERSEAS EMPIRE

Michael Heffernan

The idea of empire and a belief in the legitimacy of European imperial expansion are generally seen as right-wing concerns. Imperialism, it would appear, has 'natural' ideological affinities with militarism, authoritarianism, racialism and uncompromising nationalism, the other forces which have shaped the development of the modern European right.

There is much to be said for this interpretation. The conviction that Europeans are biologically, culturally, morally and intellectually superior to Africans or Asians and therefore have a right, indeed a duty, to expand their civilization, laws and institutions around the world is virtually axiomatic for many right-wing thinkers. The fact that the most powerful critiques of European imperialism have come from those on the left has served further to underline the assumption that the cause of empire is somehow intrinsically a right-wing project.[1]

An ideological consensus seems to exist on this matter, even in the polarized political culture of modern France. The French left regularly uses terms such as 'neo-colonialist' or 'neo-imperialist' to describe the racism and xenophobia of the extreme right which seems positively to revel in such accusations, unashamedly representing itself as the modern custodian of the old imperial spirit in whose name France's huge colonial empire was originally established.[2] The Front National (FN), claim its leaders, is the natural home for all those who believed in the justness of French imperialism and who remain convinced that the idea of *la plus grande France* was an honourable and righteous geopolitical ambition. It is for this reason that the FN has focused so much attention on the *pied-noir* community, the 'European' Algerians who settled mainly in the south of France in the early 1960s after the bitter struggle for independence in Algeria. The powerful *pied-noir* collective memory of betrayal, humiliation and sell-out, passed on from generation to generation, has been carefully cultivated by the FN over the last two decades. During the last-but-one presidential election campaign, I vividly recall well dressed FN supporters on the eve of a major rally in Marseilles, men and women in their early 20s, sons and daughters perhaps of the bewildered immigrants from Algiers or Oran who stepped blinking onto the quayside of the Vieux Port in the summer of 1962, their pathetic belongings squeezed in battered, bulging suitcases. These young enthusiasts were busying themselves posting colourful stickers onto lamp-posts and boardings across the city. 'Pied-noir!' screamed the red, white and blue lettering, 'Remember your heritage. Support the National Front.' The swaggering rhetoric of Jean-Marie Le Pen, whose smiling face beamed down from these same posters and whose disturbing speech at the following day's rally was broadcast around the country, provided a clear echo of the rabid anti-Muslim prejudice which emerged so violently during the Algerian war. Here is a man openly proud of his role as a veteran of France's doomed military struggle to retain its status as a global imperial power, contemptuous of anyone who would challenge the justice of France's role in North Africa and Indochina.[3]

Nostalgia for the days when school atlas maps carried 'a deuce of a lot of blue' is a significant component in the political programme of the extreme right in France; a corrosive version of the more general yearning for the age of empire which Paul Azoulay calls 'la nostalgérie française'.[4]

There is, of course, a tension here between the FN's misty-eyed longing for the old days of empire when the *tricoleur* fluttered proudly over unmistakeably French buildings from Dakar to Hanoi, and the party's unapologetically racist contempt for the non-white immigrants from these same former colonies. This is by no means the only intellectual and ideological confusion of the extreme right; nor is it recognized as such by FN supporters who tend, on the whole, to devote little time to pondering 'subtle' questions of this kind. The nearest we get to a coherent argument here is the assertion (or at least the implication) that the old empire functioned as a kind of geopolitical fix, maintaining a balance between white, European France and the different peoples, races, cultures and religions of the sprawling overseas empire. Imperial France was thus more than the sum of its constituent parts. Each imperial region benefited from its position within the whole. This symbiosis was only successful, however, when the peoples of each region played their distinctive role within their appropriate place. The end of empire, it is suggested, brought this happy imperial order to an end. Deprived of the civilization, dynamism and economic prosperity which France brought to the colonies, the impoverished and ever-increasing populations of the empire sought out these same qualities by flocking in vast numbers to France itself which naively opened its doors to them in a period of economic boom and labour shortage. According to many on the extreme right, modern, ethnically diverse France is now living with the racial consequences, not of an imperial past, but of a misplaced, post-colonial guilt which has failed to recognize that the overseas empire brought not only power and prestige to France but also political stability and relative economic prosperity to the colonies.[5]

In this essay, I want to explore the connections between French imperialism and the French right in greater detail. The argument can be summarized fairly easily. The apparently close association between the French right and the cause of the French overseas empire is, I suggest, an historical myth.[6] It is, however, a politically significant myth which raises important questions for all shades of opinion in today's multicultural, post-colonial France. The familiar division between a right-wing pro-colonialism and a left-wing anti-colonialism is, I shall claim, a hugely simplistic duality which, in so far as it has ever really existed, emerged only very slowly and uncertainly. This categorization seems to have been valid only during the trauma of decolonization, a tragic breeding ground for the kind of virulently racist, extreme right-wing colonialism represented by the Organisation de l'Armée Secrète (OAS) and the other paramilitary groups which emerged during the last days of French Algeria.[7] In so far as one can detect any clear ideological impulse behind the actual process of French colonisation during the nineteenth and early twentieth centuries (and this is extremely difficult because French imperial expansion was frequently motivated by a mixture of idiosyncratic military adventurism and cynical political expediency), this came not from the right but from liberal or even left-wing perspectives. Many of the individuals and constituencies which we would now characterize as belonging to a right-wing tradition within French political culture were unconvinced by the need for imperial expansion and often resolutely opposed to the idea of an overseas empire.[8]

Let me attempt to elaborate this argument by examining some of the ideological foundations upon which French imperialism was constructed, particularly during the Third Republic. There is a vast literature on this, in both English and French.[9] Most commentators seem to agree on an essential paradox at the heart of the French imperial project.[10] While France acquired a huge overseas empire, beginning with the seizure of Algiers in 1830 and ending with the establishment of the French mandates in the Middle East after the Great War, for most of this period, French public opinion was indifferent to the colonies. This paradox arose from the limitations and instabilities of French political institutions. During the middle decades of the nineteenth century—from Bugeaud's bloody campaigns in North Africa in the 1840s through Faidherbe's conquest of West Africa in the 1850s and 1860s— the drive to expand the empire came from within the ranks of the French army operating effectively beyond the restraining control of their political 'masters' in Paris. Imperial objectives and colonial policies were fashioned 'on the hoof', so to speak, and in response to immediate local strategic considerations. The progressive expansion of the French empire in Africa up to 1870 thus assumed an inexorable dynamic of its own, fuelled partly by military adventurism and partly by the desire of senior army officers to protect their new-found positions of colonial authority. The unimaginative solution to any threat to existing colonial possessions, real or imagined, was yet more colonial conquest in the areas from which that threat was deemed to originate. Once conquered, colonial territory proved extremely difficult to surrender without great loss of face and honour. Worried ministers in Paris were thus reduced to the status of impotent onlookers whose post-hoc justifications for each round of conquest rang increasingly hollow.[11] The situation was summed up with his usual insight by Alexis de Tocqueville in 1846 in respect of French economic policy towards Algeria. 'Cette grande affaire d'Afrique a été dirigée jusqu'à présent par qui? Par le hasard.'[12]

It was only after 1870 that the centre of gravity of the French imperial impulse began to shift from the colonial periphery to the metropolitan core and from the army to various sections of the middle-class intelligentsia in France. The civilian advocates of imperialism, organized into a plethora of colonialist clubs and societies, comprised a small group of provincial businessmen, academics (especially geographers), assorted civil servants, lawyers and medics. This so-called *parti colonial* was small in number (probably fewer than 10,000 adherents at the peak of the movement in the 1890s) but wielded an influence that belied its size and strictly limited public support. Ably led by Eugene Etienne, the charismatic *député* for Oran, and with the active support of prominent liberal republican converts to the cause such as Léon Gambetta and Jules Ferry, the colonial lobby was able to exploit the chronic instability of the Third Republic and the constant to-ing and fro-ing of ministers to keep colonial questions high on the political agenda. Operating in the interstices of political power, French colonialists directly influenced the decision-making process, despite continuing opposition. According to Christopher Andrew and Alexander S. Kanya-Forstner, it was largely through the activities of this amorphous pressure group, rather than the efforts of elected governments with a pro-colonial agenda, that the second largest empire of the imperial age was carved out in the name of France.[13]

The colonial lobby was partially successful in swaying public opinion behind the imperial cause by the turn of the century but it was never a united force ideologically or strategically. The most obvious disputes were simple geographical ones between those who championed Africa, the Middle East or Indochina, as the most desirable arenas for French imperial action.[14] Some of the broader arguments in favour of French expansion were also contradictory, if not mutually exclusive, and certainly a source of debate.[15] There was, for example, a powerful constituency, particularly among the business elites of provincial port cities with trading links to the empire, which saw overseas expansion as a means of enhancing their commercial success.[16] According to these 'municipal imperialists', as John Laffey has dubbed them, the raw materials and resources of a large empire would be critical for France's industrial and commercial future, particularly after the loss of Alsace-Lorraine to Germany.[17]

Other colonialists had a very different vision of empire which was less narrowly focused on trade and commerce. It is possible to detect, even into the 1880s, a lingering utopian and quasi-socialist vision of France's imperial destiny, the offspring of early nineteenth-century, Saint-Simonian arguments in favour of the European colonization of North Africa and the Middle East.[18] This is most obvious in the work and writings of the campaigning journalist and North African entrepreneur, Jules Duval; the geographer and Saharan explorer, Henri Duveyrier; and, of course, in the ceaselessly energetic activities of Ferdinand de Lesseps, the architect of the Suez Canal.[19] Duveyrier's father, the playwright Charles, was a leading member of the Saint-Simonian sect during the 1820s and early 1830s. Along with Prosper Enfantin and others, he fashioned this most unusual social, economic and political philosophy which, as Eric Hobsbawm has noted, 'can be assigned neither to capitalism nor to socialism, because it can be claimed by both.'[20] The distinctly spiritual Saint-Simonian faith in the power of science and technology to overcome the natural barriers which held different cultures and civilizations apart is immediately evident in many of the grand canal and railway schemes which the colonial lobby supported across the empire in the wake of de Lesseps' success with the Suez Canal during the 1860s, perhaps the ultimate Saint-Simonian dream which Enfantin had speculated upon at length 30 years earlier.[21] This vision of empire was often expressed, in characteristically florid prose, as a fruitful union between two distinctive realms, an essentially masculine, dynamic and expansive European power such as France and the more feminine, passive and receptive world of Africa and Asia, a union facilitated by modern communications. The objective for Duval, Duveyrier and their like was the emergence of a new, 'hybrid' imperial civilization but one in which French culture, language and values would always have the dominant role.[22]

The wilder flights of French utopian imperialism are easily mocked, now as then, but it is surprising how frequently such views recur. Overlapping with this perspective, however, and of far greater significance, was a less mystical and more overtly nationalist strand of cultural imperialism. Many of the early prophets of the imperial cause developed this line of argument, including Anatole-Prévost Paradol whose *La France nouvelle* (1868) was a deeply troubled assessment of French cultural dynamism. Despite its superficial transformations and glitz, Prévost-Paradol saw Second Empire France as a nation facing stagnation and decline. The failure of the French population to increase as quickly as that of other European nations was only one manifestation of this deeper malaise. The only cure for this decadence, he insisted, was aggressive colonial expansion. 'If our population, obstinately attached to our native soil, continues to grow so slowly, or even (as has happened over the last ten years) to remain static or to decline, we will be overrun in an Anglo-Saxon world, just as Athens was overwhelmed in past times by the new Roman order ... we shall become as Greece is now— an ancient though dead civilization.'[23] Reversing what might seem the logical argument— that if there were too few people in France itself there was little point in encouraging them to colonize the far-flung regions of the globe— Prévost-Paradol insisted that it was only through colonization that cultural and national vigour would return. The example of Britain was revealing. Britain had not become a great imperial power because of its rapid population growth, as was often argued. Rather, Britain's demographic strength— so endlessly embarrassing to virile Frenchmen— was the result of the psychological and cultural prestige brought by empire.[24] If France could colonize more enthusiastically, it would regain its dented *amour propre* and create a new, imperial France of '100 hundred million Frenchmen'.[25]

France's *annus horribilis* of 1870-71 seemed to confirm Prévost-Paradol's gloomy prognosis. The idea that a well cultivated and populous overseas empire could help France to overcome its demographic weakness, compensate for its loss of territory in Europe and thus facilitate a national re-birth began to gain many converts. The idea that waves of French migrants would be able to settle around the world was clearly unrealistic but France still possessed a uniquely expansive language and culture, the building blocks of a universal civilization, or so it was often claimed by good republicans reared on a potent mythology derived from the Enlightenment, the Revolution and the early phases of the Napoleonic First Empire. 'England has set foot in no country without setting up her counting houses', wrote Louis Blanc, 'France has nowhere passed without leaving the perfume of her spirituality.'[26]

French imperialism could develop in an entirely new, distinctive and uplifting direction. It would be inspired not by greed or grubby commercial motives, nor would it be facilitated by a large-scale population exodus. Rather, the French empire would be suffused forever by the light of French civilization. Native peoples lucky enough to live beneath the *tricoleur* would have bestowed upon them the precious gift of French language, education, law and institutions. They would become, in short, Frenchmen and women—or near enough to be of use to the mother country when they were needed. Thus would the overseas empire solve the demographic problems of European France.

It was this long-held conviction in the expansive power of French civilization which spawned the strongly educational and cultural dimension of French imperialism and its characteristic preoccupation with language, an idea subsequently summed up in the idea of *la mission civilisatrice* and most perfectly reflected in the work of institutions such as the Alliance Française, established by Pierre Foncin and others in 1883.[27] One can readily trace a lineage from this early emphasis on the cultural basis of French imperial authority through to the theories of assimilation (and even association) which were so prevalent in twentieth-century colonial rhetoric.[28]

Clearly, those who advocated the cultural argument could easily end up on a collision course with those saw in the empire an opportunity to make serious financial profit; the former emphasized the costs of empire for the greater glory of France, the latter stressed the need to minimize expenditure and maximize profits. Fortunately for the imperialist lobby, there were plenty of skilful colonial commentators able to steer a judicious path between these two extremes. The influential economist Paul Leroy Beaulieu, for example, drew a clear distinction in his widely read *De la colonisation chez les peuples modernes* (1874) between colonies of settlement, which he saw as having limited use, and colonies of commercial exploitation, which he insisted would be of crucial importance for the European powers in the future. France, with insufficient people within Europe, would never be able to compete with other colonizing European powers in respect of colonies of settlement. However, the inclusive internationalism at the heart of French culture would make it comparatively easy to establish a network of French trading outposts and commercial colonies, if only this opportunity were seized.[29]

Notwithstanding a continuing economic argument in favour of empire, it is fair to say that the cultural and nationalist rhetoric was to remain, as the British imperial historian Ronald E. Robinson remarks, the dominant theme in French imperialist writing. While 'the liberal Anglo-Saxon painted the map red in pursuit of trade and philanthrop', Robinson notes, 'the nationalistic French painted it blue not for good economic reasons, but to pump up their prestige as a great nation.'[30] As Andrew and Kanya-Forstner put it, French imperialism was 'the highest stage not of French capitalism but of French nationalism'.[31]

My point is not merely to demonstrate the complex and disputatious nature of French imperial reasoning. Rather, it is to claim that the principal arguments in favour of French imperial expansion during the early decades of the Third Republic, and to some extent through the early twentieth century, were inspired by a broadly liberal, even a left-of-centre, republican political philosophy, although, as I shall argue later, the spiritual and nationalist register of French imperialism was to become the main route way through which a more overtly right-wing imperialism was eventually to emerge. Thus we find a young François Mitterrand rehearsing familiar arguments about the cultural and political necessity of France overseas in the midst of the Algerian war. 'Sans Afrique', he wrote in 1957, 'il n'y aura pas l'histoire de France au XXIᵉ siècle.'[32]

One must not overstate this, for much liberal economic opinion, following the early anti-colonial lead given by Jean-Baptiste Say, remained scornful of imperial expansion and ever willing to condemn the colonial drain on the domestic economy.[33] 'Le fardeau des colonies' became a veritable incantation for later generations of liberal free-trade economists, notably Charles Gide.[34] It is also true that while many on the left were content to support the idea of empire as a peaceful and mutually beneficial means to facilitate economic and cultural exchange during the early decades of the Republic, this view began to change once the rapacious and exploitative nature of European imperialism was fully revealed after the 'Scramble for Africa' in the wake of the Berlin Conference of 1884-85 and the undignified race to grab colonial possessions elswhere. The great 'steeple-chase into the unknown', as Jules Ferry memorably called this frenetic period, unleashed all the old destructive adventurism and colonial militarizm, anathema to an increasingly humanitarian and internationalist left. Jean Jaurès captured the unease of his socialist followers following the

French conquest of Morocco in 1912:

> I have never painted an idyllic picture of the Muslim populations and I am well aware of the disorder and oligarchic exploitation by mighty chiefs which takes place. But if you look deeply into the matter, there existed a Moroccan civilization, capable of the necessary transformation, capable of evolution and progress, a civilization both ancient and modern. There was a seed for the future, a hope. And let me say that I cannot pardon those who have crushed this hope for pacific and human progress—African civilization—by all sorts of ruses and by the brutalities of conquest.[35]

However, while many on the left were instinctively and often passionately anti-colonial, left-wing politicians were often willing to suppress their beliefs when colonial interests seemed to coincide with national interests, as often they did. Georges Clemenceau provides a classic illustration. Vigorously and noisily anti-imperialist for much of his career, particularly during the disastrous Tonkin affair of the mid 1880s which ended with the collapse of Jules Ferry's administration, Clemenceau was nevertheless prepared to play the imperial game and to assert France's colonial interests when confronted with British claims to former German and Turkish lands in Africa and the Middle East in the aftermath of the First World War.[36]

Once the Parti Communiste Français (PCF) emerged as a separate political force after 1921, it seemed likely that a familiar, Marxist anti-colonialism would become a feature of French political life, though French socialists were fully reconciled to the idea of a greater, colonial France.[37] The PCF certainly took an uncompromising anti-imperial stand during the Rif War in Morocco in the mid 1920s, in the face of much rancour and controversy.[38] Yet the party's anti-imperial stance was rarely unqualified, as Danièle Joly's excellent survey of the organization's internal conflicts and ruptures during the Algerian War makes abundantly clear.[39]

For most of the early Third Republic, it was the French right rather than the left which provided the main opposition to the idea of imperial expansion. Most of the criticism levelled at Ferry in 1883 over the Tonkin affair came from his more familiar political opponents on the right; monarchists like Paul de Cassagnac who detected a sinister, republican plot to conquer Tonkin solely in order to offer mining concessions to republican sympathizers in the business community. For the Orleanist camp, the ageing duc de Broglie railed against the Republic's imperial projects as 'contrary to the lessons of history and of reason'. Paul Déroulède was, for his part, equally forthright. 'Before planting the French flag where its has never flown before', he famously observed in a speech at the Trocadéro on 26 October 1885, 'we should re-plant it first where once it flew, where (in Alsace-Lorraine) we have all seen it with our own eyes.'[40] Here, of course, was the most familiar conservative anti-colonial lament. Overseas colonies were costly and extravagant distractions. France needed to a keep firm eye on 'the blue line of the Vosges' rather than the far horizons of empire. One must accept, however, that to some extent the conservative opposition to colonial expansion in the 1880s was based not on an ideological argument but on the fact that this policy was being pursued by a liberal, republican regime.

The first stirrings of a distinctive right-wing imperialism began in the 1890s, part of a wider increase in enthusiasm for empire which affected all shades of political opinion.[41] The emergence of a popular imperialism was the hard-won result of the colonial lobby's tireless proselytizing and was reinforced by educational reforms at secondary and tertiary level which stressed the civic virtues of patriotism and devotion to both nation and empire. The rapid expansion of subjects such as geography, 'unquestionably the queen of all imperial sciences', was especially important in promoting popular understanding of, and commitment to, the empire.[42] The increasing popularity of 'colonialist' novels by Pierre Loti and Ernest Psichari was also both cause and symptom of changing popular attitudes towards the empire.[43]

The emergence of right-wing imperialism was a more hesitant and partial process than the general conversion of public opinion, and was far from complete even by the end of the interwar period. Several factors influenced the gradual reconfiguration of the right behind the empire, one of the most important being the role of the army, especially the colonial forces. The Dreyfus Affair destroyed, probably forever, any lingering notion that the army might rally to the cause of liberal bourgeois republicanism; henceforth, the army seemed to represent the forces of reaction, conservatism and intransigent nationalism in their purest incarnation, an image widely accepted by both left-wing opponents and right-wing admirers. The utterances of senior army figures thus automatically became part of the right's agenda, even though identical views might previously have been expressed by liberal or left-wing commentators. As so many of the more charismatic and articulate figures in the army were strongly pro-colonial (having earnt their reputations on colonial service), the empire started to become, almost by definition, a right-wing cause. The traditional conservative fear that the empire was a drain on France's over-stretched European army was gradually replaced by two, quintessentially right-wing imperial beliefs about the benefits which the empire brought to the mother country. First, a large overseas empire was presented as a virtually unlimited source of colonial 'manpower'. If wisely cultivated and trained, Africans and Asians could be used to swell the ranks of the French army wherever it needed to operate, including the all-important European theatre. Charles Mangin's *La force noire* (1911) was but one example of this military reasoning, an obvious extension of broader pro-natalist arguments previously developed by nationalist and liberal republicans but now associated firmly with a right-of-centre ideology.[44] The fact that France's major international crises before August 1914 all took place in the non-European, colonial arena (from Fashoda in 1898 to Morocco in 1911) simply reinforced the significance of the empire. France's national interest could thus be readily equated with her colonial interests.[45]

Second, the writings of soldiers and men of action such as Joseph Gallieni and Louis-Hubert Lyautey (whose *Du rôle social de l'officier dans le service militaire universel* was a roaring success in 1891) generated a vision of the empire as a testing ground for the flower of the nation's youth, a challenging and character-building environment through which national vitality, virility and military prowess would return.[46] The role of an increasingly sympathic popular press which eagerly reported the colourful 'heroics' of French colonial soldiers in Indochina, Madagascar or Morocco was important in this respect.[47] Within French right-wing circles, a rather British imperial idea gradually began to emerge which saw the empire as the natural playground of the masculine hero, whether soldier, explorer, or even priest. The heroic, and usually fatal, exploits of the great soldier-explorers of the Sahara touched a powerful nerve with a sedentary French bourgeoisie, starved of tales of derring-do in a deeply unheroic age.[48]

The idea of the dedicated and exemplary individual pitting his selfless courage against the forces of nature in the far-off parts of the empire corresponded with an emerging right-wing preoccupation with death, sacrifice and the power of the individual. This is best exemplified, of course, in the writings of Maurice Barrès who was slowly converted to the imperial cause through his interest in the exemplary individual, the embodiment of the national psyche. Initially cool, if not actively hostile, to the imperial project, Barrès began to lavish extravagent praise on leading colonial soldiers, notably Gallieni whose administration of Madagascar Barrès saw as approaching perfection. '(Gallieni's) importance', Barrès wrote in 1902, 'is that he belongs to a species we most lack today: he is an authoritarian in government.'[49] For Barrès, the empire could become an important breeding ground for the great men who were destined to carry forth the national spirit.

An important theme here is the diffusion into France of the idea of the colonial frontier as a spiritually, morally and physically redemptive environment, a notion developed with respect to the westward expansion of the USA by Frederick Jackson Turner and then popularized in relation to the British Empire by Lord Curzon and others.[50] The overseas empire, especially for Barrès, provided an important arena in which the flower of France's youth could extend themselves physically and morally, an area where they could escape, temporarily or permanently if necessary, from a Europe which was possibly in decline. Thus could national degeneration be reversed by the rigours of imperial life.

The idea of heroic sacrifice and the selfless pursuit of spirituality in a contemplative colonial life, particularly in the Sahara, was also deeply attractive to many French Catholics and this may partially explain the cult status enjoyed by the hermit priest Charles de Foucauld whose exploits in the desert wastes were well known to every Catholic schoolchild.[51]

Right-wing converts to the imperial cause such as Barrès were eventually to appropriate the cultural and educational arguments in favour of empire, traditionally the preserve of liberal republicans. In his two-volume account of his journey through the Middle East on the eve of the First World War, Barrès described the role of French schools in the region in the most rhapsodic terms 'It is ravishing', he noted, 'to see those little Oriental girls welcoming and so wonderfully reproducing the *fantaisie* and the melody of the Ile-de-France. There is, there in the Orient, a feeling about France which is so religious and strong that it is capable of absorbing and reconciling all our diverse aspirations. In the Orient, we represent spirituality, justice, and the category of the ideal. England is powerful there; Germany is all-powerful; but we possess Oriental souls.'[52] Other advocates of the extreme right, such as Pierre Taittinger, also rallied to the imperial cause, though his arguments in favour of empire groaned under his conflicting desire to maximize colonial profits to the mother country while also advocating investment in the costly business of spreading French language and culture amongst the native peoples.[53]

Other figures on the extreme right, such as Paul Déroulède and Charles Maurras, resisted the lure of empire for much longer, the latter insisting in 1920 that the advocates of France's imperial destiny sought 'la gloire facile' rather than 'le courage véritable'. But even Maurras relented and began to write fleetingly in favour of empire which he conceived as a kind of grand global experiment in which the supposedly positive role of intellectual and racial inequalities could be examined.[54]

As Ageron and others have shown, imperial questions rarely, if ever, dominated political or intellectual debate in the interwar period. The Colonial Ministry on the Rue Oudinot was the least coveted assignment for an aspiring civil servant or politician.[55] A broad consensus existed on the need for an empire and most Frenchmen and women seemed happy to accept the myth that the colonies offered commercial, political and cultural security.[56] This sense of well-being was reinforced by the great Colonial Exhibition in Paris in 1931.[57] Colonial questions were, on the whole, uncontroversial and hence of little interest either to right or left in the interwar years.[58] On the extreme right, the Action Française had remarkably little of interest or originality to say on the colonial question though in 1935 it did inaugurate a column in its newspaper entitled 'Lettre aux amis d'outre-mer'.[59] It is, therefore, difficult to classify pro- and anti-imperial voices between the wars according to any simple political division. Imperial topics were generally seen as national issues, transcending factional political debates. French imperialism, perhaps rather more so than French fascism, can thus legitimately be claimed to have been 'ni droite, ni gauche'.[60]

That said, although right and left could readily agree on several imperial questions during the 1920s and 1930s, their rationales tended to diverge. The right-wing advocacy of empire was generally based on the idea of 'empire man', of regeneration of national spirit, military prowess and collective energy through the experience of empire. Liberal and left-wing imperialism was, for the most part, still expressed in terms of *la mission civilisatrice*, of the spread of enlightenment and reason coupled with a more politically agnostic, developmentalism—the so-called *mise-en-valeur* school of economic imperialism associated with Albert Sarraut, Camille Fidel, Henri Simon and Edmond Vivier de Streel.[61] Marc Michel is, therefore, surely correct when he observes that the imperialist right in interwar France was like the great pavilions which were erected in the Bois de Vincennes for the Colonial Exposition of 1931: 'belle façade [mais] sans véritable réalité constructive'.[62]

The frequently invoked association of the right with the cause of France's overseas empire is, therefore, an historical myth. For much of the period since 1830, the cause of empire was championed most enthusiastically by liberal or even left-wing voices. In the early decades of empire building, from the 1830s to the 1870s, it was the colonial army which promoted the cause of empire in ways which are difficult to categorize according to any simple right-left division. After 1870, a liberal and republican colonialism began to gather momentum based on a nationalist and cultural rationale, although there was no consensus on this across the range of liberal-left republican views. The left's enthusiasm for the empire was shaken, but far from eradicated, by the imperial scrambles of the 1880s and 1890s whereas this same period witnessed the first stirrings of a right-wing imperialism. Between the wars, the empire was not a major source of division between left and right. After 1945, however, and particularly after the violent trauma of decolonization, the French left definitively re-positioned itself as an anti-imperial force whereas elements on the right became firmly associated with the cause of empire.

These complex shifts are, I suggest, of more than merely historical significance. In the current climate of *fin-de-siècle* nostalgia, the age of empire has become terribly fashionable throughout Europe and North America, a fact revealed by the enormous popularity of Merchant Ivory films and their French equivalents about the Raj, Indochina or Senegal. Those contemporary politicians who lay claim, however fraudulently, to be the custodians of Europe's imperial legacy are able to exploit a rich vein of popular longing for the perceived certainties, elegance and style of that by-gone age. In France, and to a lesser extent in Britain, this is ultimately a problem for the left which, understandably, is somewhat reluctant to accept that so many in its pantheon of heroes had colonialist convictions and that the French empire was, to a considerable extent, a project associated with the liberal-left rather than the right. Such an acceptance would undermine the moral high ground which the left adopts in its legitimate assault on the neo-colonialism of the right while also tarnishing its own image as the intellectual source of modern notions of anti-racism, cosmopolitanism and multiculturalism. Viewing the French right through the optic of the empire, from the vantage point of Casablanca or Djibouti so to speak, shows once again the immense historical complexity of ideological forces which have shaped the emergence both of France itself and of its former colonial arena.

Notes

1. Amongst the earliest detailed anti-imperialist statements are those written at the beginning of this century by Hobson and Lenin. See Hobson, John A.: *Imperialism. A Study* (London, 1902) and Lenin, Vladimir I.: *Imperialism. The Highest Stage of Capitalism* (Moscow, 1966 edn). For examples of more recent Marxist-influenced analysis, see Brewer, Anthony: *Marxist Theories of Imperialism. A Critical Survey* (London, 1980); Cohen,

Benjamin J.: *The Question of Imperialism. The Political Economy of Dominance and Dependence* (London, 1973); Etherington, Norman: *Theories of Imperialism. War, Conquest and Capital* (London, 1984); Kiernan, Victor: *Marxism and Imperialism* (London, 1974); Kiernan, Victor: *Imperialism and its Contradictions* (1995); R. Owen and B. Sutcliffe, eds: *Studies in the Theory of Imperialism* (London, 1972); Warren, Bill: *Imperialism. Pioneer of Capitalism* (London, 1984).

2.   The left has also levelled these same accusations against the current conservative regime, particularly in respect of its intransigence regarding France's right to continue nuclear testing in the Pacific. Widely condemned around the world, French nuclear policy has been interpreted on the left as an illustration of the latent, vainglorious neo-colonialism of the French right. Chirac's aggressive stance is represented as the predictable response of an incoming conservative president desperate to reassert France's global military prowess in the wake of a long socialist interlude. Such a reading of the current regime's nuclear policy is, of course, less than fair, for in most aspects of foreign and defence policy, the attitude of previous socialist regimes was virtually indistinguishable from that of the existing government. The most notorious example is the continuing support which France has given to the genocidal Habyarimana regime in Rwanda. It has been suggested that French calls for a European military intervention in Rwanda were motivated not by a humanitarian concern to keep the warring Hutu and Tutsi factions apart but by an ongoing desire to protect and enhance French cultural and political interests in the region by offering preferential treatment to the largely Francophone Hutu leadership. See Krop, Pascal: *Le génocide Franco-Africain* (Paris, 1994); Vershave, François-Xavier: *Complicité de génocide?* (Paris, 1994); Prumier, Gérard: *The Rwanda Crisis, 1959-94. History of a Genocide* (London, 1995); Lang, Kirsty: 'France Plays African Power Game', *The Sunday Times*, 10 November 1996, p 19 of main section. For a general survey, see Chipman, John: *French Power in Africa* (Oxford, 1989).

3.   See Pervillé, Guy: 'L'Algérie dans la mémoire des droites', in J.-F. Sirinelli, ed: *Histoire des droites en France* (Paris, 1992), vol 2, pp 621-56. For more general accounts of the political culture of the FN, see Birenbaum, Guy: *Le Front National en politique* (Paris, 1992); Mayer, Nonna and Perrineau, Pascal: *Le Front National à découvert* (Paris, 1989); and Perrineau, Pascal: 'Le Front National: 1972-1992', in M. Winock, ed: *Histoire de l'extreme droite en France* (Paris, 1993), pp 243-98.

4.   Azoulay, Paul: *La nostalgérie française* (Paris, 1980). The quotation 'a deuce of a lot of blue' is taken from Conrad, Joseph: *Heart of Darkness* (Harmondsworth, 1985 [1902]), p 36.

5.   The relationship between France's colonial legacy and its immigration policy are discussed in different ways in George, Pierre: *L'immigration en France* (Paris, 1986); Noiriel, Gérard: *Le creuset français. Histoire de*

l'immigration, XIXe - XXe siècle (Paris, 1988); several of the essays in R. Aldrich and J. Connell, eds: *France in World Politics* (London, 1989); and Stora, Benjamin: *Ils venaient d'Algérie. L'immigration algérienne en France, 1912-1992* (Paris, 1992).

6. This is not, let it be said, a startlingly original insight, for similar arguments are made in Marseilles, Jacques: 'La gauche, la droite et le fait colonial en France des années 1880 aux années 1960', *Vingtième siècle* 24 (1989), pp 17-28; and Michel, Marc: 'La colonisation', in Sirinelli: *Histoire des droites*, pp 125-63.

7. The literature on decolonization and its impact on French political culture is vast. For general accounts, see C.-R. Ageron, ed: *Chemins de la décolonisation de l'empire colonial français* (Paris, 1986); Ageron, Charles-Robert: *La décolonisation française* (Paris, 1991); Betts, Raymond F.: *France and Decolonization, 1900-1960* (London, 1991); Clayton, Anthony: *The Wars of French Decolonization* (London, 1994); Kahler, Miles: *Decolonization in Britain and France. The Domestic Consequences of International Relations* (Princeton, 1984); Sorum, Paul Clay: *Intellectuals and Decolonization in France* (Chapel Hill, 1977). On specific decolonization conflicts and their legacy, see H. Alleg, ed: *La guerre d'Algérie* (3 vols, Paris, 1981); Dalloz, Jacques: *La guerre d'Indochine, 1945-1954* (Paris, 1987); Droz, Bernard and Lever, Evelyne: *Histoire de la guerre d'Algérie, 1954-1962* (Paris, 1982); L. Gervereau, J.-P. Rioux and B. Stora, eds: *La France en guerre d'Algérie* (Paris, 1992); Horne, Alistair: *A Savage War of Peace. Algeria, 1954-1962* (London, 1987 edn); J-P. Rioux, ed: *La guerre d'Algérie et les français* (Paris, 1990); Ruscio, Alain: *La guerre française d'Indochine* (Paris, 1992); Stora, Benjamin: *La gangrène et l'oubli. La mémoire de las guerre d'Algérie* (Paris, 1991); Stora, Benjamin: *Histoire de la guerre d'Algérie, 1954-1962* (Paris, 1993); Talbott, John: *The War Without a Name. France in Algeria, 1954-1962* (London, 1981); White, Dorothy S.: *Black Africa and de Gaulle. From the French Empire to Independence* (Maryland, 1979).

8. For more detailed studies of French anti-colonialism, see Ageron, Charles-Robert: *L'anticolonialisme en France de 1871 à 1914* (Paris, 1973); Ageron, Charles-Robert: *France coloniale ou parti coloniale?* (Paris, 1978); Biondi, Jean-Pierre and Morin, Gilles: *Les anticolonialistes, 1881-1962* (Paris, 1992); Lacouture, Jean and Chagnollaud, Dominique: *Le désempire* (Paris, 1993).

9. See, for example, Aldrich, Robert: *Greater France. A History of French Overseas Expansion* (London, 1996), pp 89-121; Betts, Raymond F.: *Assimilation and Association in French Colonial Theory 1890-1914* (New York, 1961); Betts, Raymond F.: *Tricoleur. The French Overseas Empire* (London, 1978); J. Bouvier and R. Girault eds: *L'impérialisme francais d'avant 1914* (Paris, 1976); Thobie, Jacques, Bouvier, Jean and Girault, René: *L'impérialisme à la française, 1914-1960* (Paris, 1986);

Brunschwig, Henri: *French Colonialism, 1871-1914. Myths and Realities* (London, 1966); Cook, James J.: *New French Imperialism, 1880-1910. The Third Republic and Colonial Expansion* (Newton Abbot, 1973); Ganiage, Jean, *L'expansion coloniale de la France sous la troisième république, 1871-1914* (Paris, 1968); Girardet, Raoul: *L'idée coloniale de la France de 1871 à 1962* (Paris, 1962); Marseille, Jacques: *Empire coloniale et capitalisme français: histoire d'un divorce* (Paris, 1984); Murphy, Agnes: *The Ideology of French Imperialism, 1871-1881* (Washington, 1948).

10.   The argument developed here is a bald synopsis of Andrew, Christopher M. and Kanya-Forstner, Alexander S.: 'Centre and Periphery in the Making of the Second French Empire, 1815-1930', *Journal of Imperial and Commonwealth History* 16 (1988), pp 9-34, itself a summary of their extensive earlier research.

11.   For an excellent study of French overseas imperialism and the French army, see Kanya-Forstner, Alexander S.: *The Conquest of the Western Sudan. A Study in French Military Imperialism* (Cambridge, 1969). The Algerian experience after the seizure of Algiers in 1830 set the tone for French imperial expansion during the remainder of the nineteenth century and is expertly covered in Schefer, Christian: *La politique coloniale de la monarchie de juillet. L'Algérie et l'évolution de la colonisation française* (Paris, 1947); Julien, Charles-André: *Histoire de l'Algérie contemporaine* (Paris, 1979, 2nd edn), vol 1; Danziger, R.: *Abd-al-Qadir and the Algerians. Resistance to the French and Internal Consolidation* (New York, 1979); Sullivan, Antony T.: *Thomas-Robert Bugeaud, France and Algeria, 1784-1849. Politics, Power and the Good Society* (Hamden, Connecticut, 1983); and Hamdani, Amar: *La vérité sur l'expédition d'Alger* (Paris, 1985).

12.   Quoted in Michel: 'La colonisation', p 129. See also Tocqueville, Alexis de: 'Notes du voyage en Algérie de 1841', in *Oeuvres complètes* (Paris, 1958), vol 5, p 190; Richter, Melvin: 'Tocqueville on Algeria', *Review of Politics* 25 (1963), pp 369-98; Heffernan, Michael:"The Parisian Poor and the Colonization of Algeria during the Second Empire', *French History* 3, 4 (1989), pp 377-403.

13.   See Andrew, Christopher M. and Kanya-Forstner, Alexander S.: 'The French "Colonial Party": Its Composition, Aims and Influence, 1885-1914', *The Historical Journal* 14/1 (1971), pp 90-128; Andrew, Christopher M. and Kanya-Forstner, Alexander J.: 'The Groupe Colonial in the French Chamber of Deputies 1892-1932', *The Historical Journal* 17/4 (1974), pp 837-66; Andrew, Christopher M. and Kanya-Forstner, Alexander S.: 'Gabriel Hanotaux, the Colonial Party and the Fashoda Strategy', *Journal of Imperial and Commonwealth History* 3 (1974), pp 55-104; Andrew, Christoper M., Grupp, P. and Kanya-Forstner, Alexander S.: 'Le mouvement colonial français et ses principales personnalités (1890-1914)', *Revue française d'histoire d'outre mer* 62 (1975), pp 640-73;

Andrew, Christopher M. and Kanya-Forstner, Alexander S.: 'French Business and the French Colonialists', *The Historical Journal* 19/4 (1976), pp 981-1000; Andrew, Christopher M. and Kanya-Forstner, Alexander S.: 'The French Colonialist Movement during the Third Republic: The Unofficial Mind of Imperialism', *Transactions of the Royal Historical Society* 26 (1976), pp 143-66 ; Abrams, L. and Miller, D.J.: 'Who were the French Colonialists? A Reassessment of the Parti Colonial, 1890-1914', *The Historical Journal* 19/3 (1976), pp 685-725; Persell, Stuart M.: *The French Colonial Lobby, 1889-1938* (Stanford, 1983). On Etienne, see Sieberg, Herward: *Eugène Etienne und die Französische Kolonialpolitik* (Cologne, 1968). The colonial enthusiasms of Gambetta and Ferry are discussed in Ageron, Charles-Robert: 'Gambetta et la reprise de l'expansion coloniale', *Revue française d'histoire d'outre mer* 59/215 (1972), pp 165-204; and Ageron, Charles-Robert: 'Jules Ferry et la colonisation', in F. Furet, ed: *Jules Ferry. Fondateur de la république* (Paris, 1986), pp 191-206. On the final phase of French imperial expansion, after World War One, see Andrew, Christopher M. and Kanya-Forstner, Alexander S.: *France Overseas. The Great War and the Climax of French Imperial Expansion* (London, 1981). The role of academics and scientists has been much discussed of late. See, for example, Bonneuil, Christophe: *Des savants pour l'empire. La structuration des recherches scientifiques coloniales au temps de ' la mise en valeur des colonies françaises ', 1917-1945*, (Paris, 1991); Lejeune, Dominique: *Les sociétés de géographie en France et l'expansion coloniale au XIXe siècle* (Paris, 1993); and Pyenson, Lewis: *Civilizing Mission. Exact Sciences and French Overseas Expansion, 1830-1940* (Baltimore, 1993); Osborne, Michael A.: *Nature, the Exotic and the Science of French Colonialism* (Bloomington, 1994); Heffernan , Michael: 'The Science of Empire: The French Geographical Movement and the Forms of French Imperialism, 1870-1920', in A.Godlewska and N.Smith, eds: *Geography and Empire* (Oxford, 1994), pp 92-114; Heffernan, Michael: 'A State Scholarship: The Political Geography of French Science during the Nineteenth Century', *Transactions of the Institute of British Geographers* NS 19/1 (1994), pp 21-45; Heffernan, Michael: 'The Spoils of War: the Société de Géographie de Paris and the French Empire, 1914-1919', in M. Bell, R. Butlin and M. Heffernan, eds, *Geography and Imperialism. 1820-1940* (Manchester, 1995), pp 221-64; Lorcin, Patricia M.E.: *Imperial Identities. Stereotyping, Prejudice and Race in Colonial Algeria* (London, 1995).

14.   Some of the 60-odd clubs and societies which made up the colonial lobby championed the cause of empire on general moral, religious or commercial grounds (for example, the *Comité Républicain aux Colonies, La France Colonisatrice*, the *Société Antiesclavage de France*) but the more powerful colonialist organizations had clear regional identities (for example, the *Comité de l'Afrique Française*, the *Comité de l'Asie Française*, the *Comité*

de l'Océanie Française, the *Comité de l'Orient*). For an instance of the conflict between different elements within the French colonial lobby, see Reclus, Onésime: *Lâchons l'Asie, prenons l'Afrique. Où renaître? Et comment durer?* (Paris, 1904).

15. Some of the different forms of French imperialism under the Third Republic are summarized in Bouvier, Jean: 'Les traits majeurs de l'impérialisme français avant 1914', *Le mouvement social* 86 (1974), pp 99-128; and Heffernan: 'The Science of Empire'.

16. There was certainly plenty of scope for this as French colonial trade remained notoriously underdeveloped. As late as 1914, just 10 per cent of France's external trade and an even smaller percentage of the nation's overseas investment were directed towards the empire. Hampered by the smallness of its merchant navy (only one-tenth the size of the British fleet), France was rarely able to capture even one half of the trade from its own empire. Some 25 per cent of French overseas investment went to Russia, however, and France was easily the dominant source of external capital for the Ottoman Empire. See Andrew and Kanya-Forstner: 'French Business'; Andrew and Kanya-Forstner: *France Overseas*, pp 14-17, 40-54; Marseille: *Empire coloniale et capitalisme français*; Pamuk, Sevket: *The Ottoman Empire and European Capitalism, 1820-1913. Trade, Investment and Production* (Cambridge, 1987); Thobie, Jacques: *Intérêts et impérialisme français dans l'empire ottoman* (Paris, 1978); and Shorrocks, W.I.: *French Imperialism in the Middle East* (London, 1976).

17. Laffey, John F.: 'Roots of French Imperialism in the Nineteenth Century: The Case of Lyon', *French Historical Studies* 6/1 (1969), pp. 78-92; Laffey, John F.: 'Municipal Imperialism in Nineteenth-Century France', *Historical Reflections/Réflexions historiques* 1/1 (1974), pp 81-114; Laffey, John F.: 'The Lyon Chamber of Commerce and Indochina during the Third Republic', *Canadian Journal of History* 10 (1975), 325-48; Laffey, John F.: 'Municipal Imperialism in Decline: The Lyon Chamber of Commerce, 1925-1938', *French Historical Studies* 9/2 (1975), pp 329-53; Schneider, William H.: 'Geographical reform and municipal imperialism in France, 1870-80', in J.M. MacKenzie, ed.: *Imperialism and the Natural World* (Manchester, 1990), pp 90-117. For an excellent study of 'municipal imperialism' in the earliest phase of the nineteenth-century French overseas empire, see Guiral, Pierre: *Marseille et l'Algérie, 1830-1841* (Aix-en-Provence, 1956).

18. Other pioneers of the European left were also enthusiastic about the idea of European expansion into the non-European world. Writing in the Chartist paper, the *Northern Star*, on 22 January 1848, Friedrich Engels memorably welcomed the French conquest of Algeria as 'an important and fortunate fact for the progress of civilization'. Quoted in Marx, Karl: *Surveys from Exile* (Harmondsworth, 1981 edn), p 24.

19. Duval's writings were particularly important, especially *Les colonies et la*

politique coloniale de la France (Paris, 1864) and *L'Algérie et les colonies françaises* (Paris, 1877). See Girardet: *L'idée coloniale*, pp 43-5; and Vallette, J.: 'Socialisme Utopique et Idée Coloniale: Jules Duval (1813-1870)' (Unpublished Doctoral Thesis, Université de Lyon II, 1976). On Duveyrier, see Heffernan, Michael: 'The Limits of Utopia: Henri Duveyrier and the Exploration of the Sahara in the Nineteenth Century', *Geographical Journal* 155 (1989), pp 342-52. For studies of de Lesseps, see Beatty, Charles: *Ferdinand de Lesseps. A Biographical Study* (London, 1956); and Edgar-Bonnet, Georges: *Ferdinand de Lesseps* (Paris, 1959).

20.   Hobsbawm, Eric J.: *The Age of Empire 1875-1914* (London, 1987), p 339. There is a huge literature on Saint-Simon and Saint-Simonianism. See, for divergent interpretations, J.-R.Derré, ed.: *Regards sur le saint-simonisme et les saint-simoniens* (Lyons, 1986); Iggers, Georg G.: *The Cult of Authority. The Political Philosophy of the Saint-Simonian. A Chapter in the Intellectual History of Totalitarianism* (The Hague, 1958); Manuel, Frank E.: *The New World of Henri Saint-Simon* (New Orleans, 1963); Manuel, Frank E.: *The Prophets of Paris* (New York, 1965).

21.   See, for example, Porch, Douglas: *The Conquest of the Sahara* (Oxford, 1983), pp. 83-125; Heffernan, Michael: 'A French Colonial Controversy: Captain Roudaire and the Saharan Sea, 1872-83', *The Maghreb Review* 13 (1988), pp 145-59; Heffernan, Michael: 'Bringing the Desert to Bloom: French Ambitions in the Sahara Desert during the Nineteenth Century', in Cosgrove, D.E. and Petts, G.E. eds.: *Water, Engineering and Landscape. Water Control and Landscape Formation in the Modern Period* (London, 1990), pp 94-114.

22.   Enfantin's sexualised reading of French imperial expansion is developed at length in Enfantin, Barthélemy P.: *Colonisation de l'Algérie* (Paris, 1843) and is discussed in Sagnes, O.: *Enfantion et la colonisation de l'Algérie* (Poitiers, 1904) and in Heffernan, Michael: 'An Imperial Utopia: French Surveys of North Africa in the Early Colonial Period', in J.Stone ed: *Maps and Africa* (Aberdeen, 1993), pp 81-107. On Saint-Simonian imperialism, see Emerit, Marcel: *Les saint-simoniens en Algérie* (Paris, 1941); Emerit, Marcel: 'Les explorateurs saint-simoniens en Afrique orientale et sur les routes des Indes', *Revue africaine* 87 (1943), pp 92-116; Emerit, Marcel: 'L'idée de colonisation dans les socialismes françaises', *L'âge nouveau* 24 (1967), pp 103-15; Emerit, Marcel: 'Diplomates et explorateurs saint-simoniens', *Revue d'histoire moderne et contemporaine* 22 (1975), pp 397-415; Fakkar, Raoul: *Reflets de la sociologie pre-marxiste dans le monde arabe. Idées progressistes et pratiques industrielles des saint-simoniens en Algérie et en Egypte au XIXe siècle* (Paris, 1974); M.Morsy, ed: *Les saint-simoniens et l'orient. Vers la modernité* (Paris, 1989).

23.   Prévost-Paradol, Lucien-Anatole: *La France Nouvelle et pages choisis* (Paris, 1981), pp 286-7

24. A similar despairing attempt to reconcile France's weak population growth with a perceived need to colonize overseas was developed by Jules Duval; see Charbit, Yves: *Du malthusianisme au populationisme. Les économistes français et la population, 1840-1970* (Paris, 1981), pp 185-92. The literature on the fear of population decline in France is vast. Spengler, Joseph J.: *France Faces Depopulation* (Westport, 1938); McLaren, Angus: *Sexuality and the Social Order. The Debate over the Fertility of Women and Workers in France, 1770-1920* (New York, 1983); Nye, Robert A.: *Crime, Madness and Politics in Modern France. The Medical Concept of National Decline* (Princeton, 1984); Nye, Robert A.: 'Honor, Impotence and Male Sexuality in Nineteenth-Century French Medicine', *French Historical Studies* 16 (1989), pp 48-71; Offen, Karen: 'Depopulation, Nationalism and Feminism in fin-de-siècle France', *American Historical Review* 89 (1984), pp 648-75; Ogden, Philip E. and Huss, Marie-Monique: 'Demography and Pronatalism in France in the Nineteenth and Twentieth Centuries', *Journal of Historical Geography* 8 (1982), pp 283-98 are especially entertaining accounts.

25. This became a rallying cry of the assimilationist strand of France cultural colonialism which emphasized the possibility of creating Frenchmen (and presumably women) from the disparate peoples of the empire through the aggressive promotion of French language and civilization around the world. See Lewis, Martin D.: '"One Hundred Million Frenchmen": The Assimilation Theory in French Colonial Policy', *Comparative Studies in Society and History* 4 (1961-62), pp 129-53.

26. Quoted in Andrew and Kanya-Forstner: *France Overseas*, p 26.

27. The expansive potential of French *civilization* was frequently invoked as the key feature distinguishing it from the German notion of *Kultur*, an altogether more earthy, rooted and immobile concept. See Elias, Norbert: *The Civilizing Process. The History of Manners. State Formation and Civilization* (Oxford, 1994); Febvre, Lucien: 'Civilization: Evolution of a Word and a Group of Ideas', in P.Burke, ed: *A New Kind of History from the Writings of Febvre* (New York), pp 219-57; Vogt, E.A.: '*Civilization and Kultur*: Keywords in the History of French and German Citizenship', *Ecumene* 3/2 (1996), pp 125-45. On the Alliance Française, see Bruézière, Maurice: *L'Alliance Française, 1883-1983. Histoire d'un institution* (Paris, 1983). See also Calvet, L.-J.: 'Le colonialisme linquistique de la France', *Les temps modernes* 324-6 (1973), pp 72-89; and Burrows, Mathew: '"Mission Civilisatrice": French Cultural Policy in the Middle East, 1860-1914', *The Historical Journal* 29/1 (1986), pp 109-35.

28. Betts, *Assimilation and Association*; Lewis, 'One Hundred Million Frenchmen'

29. Leroy Beaulieu, Paul: *De la colonisation chez les peuples modernes* (Paris, 1874). On Leroy Beaulieu and his *côterie*, see Murphy: *The Ideology of French Imperialism*, pp 103-222.

30. Robinson, Ronald E.: 'Introduction', in Brunschwig: *French Colonialism*, p vii
31. Andrew and Kanya-Forstner: *France Overseas*, p 26
32. Mitterrand, François: *Présence française et abandon* (Paris, 1957), p 237
33. On early liberal economic opposition to imperial expansion, Buheiry, M.R.: 'Anti-Colonial Sentiment in France during the July Monarchy: The Algerian case' (Unpublished PhD thesis, Princeton University, 1974).
34. Michel: 'La colonisation', pp 127, 132. Gide is probably best known for his *Principes d'économie politique* (Paris, 1884).
35. Quoted in Aldrich: *Greater France*, p. 112; and in Biondi and Morin: *Les anticolonialistes*, p 99
36. Andrew and Kanya-Forstner, *France Overseas*
37. The SFIO (Section Française de l'Internationale Ouvrière), particularly under Léon Blum, sought out a modern, progressive form of colonialism. Blum once remarked that socialists were 'too imbued with the love of our country to disavow the expansion of French thought and civilization. We recognise the right and even the duty of superior races to draw unto them those which have not arrived at the same level of culture'. Quoted in Aldrich: *Greater France*, p 115.
38. Aldrich: *Greater France*, p. 117; Biondi and Morin: *Les anticolonialistes*, pp 135-42; Slavin, David H.: 'The French Left and the Rif War, 1924-5: Racism and the Limits of Internationalism', *Journal of Contemporary History* 26 (1991), pp 5-32.
39. Joly, Danièle: *The French Communist Party and the Algerian War* (London, 1991). See, also, Ageron, Charles-Robert: 'L'opinion française devant la guerre d'Algérie', *Revue française d'histoire d'outre-mer* 63 (1976), pp 256-85.
40. Quoted in Michel: 'La colonisation', pp 133-5
41. Michel: 'La colonisation'
42. The quotation is from Richards, Thomas: *The Imperial Archive. Knowledge and the Fantasy of Empire* (London, 1993), p 13. On geography, education and colonialism, see Heffernan: 'The Science of Empire'; Semidei, Manuela: 'De l'empire à la décolonisation à travers les manuels scolaires français', *Revue française de science politique* 16/1 (1966), pp 56-86.
43. Hargreaves, Alec: *The Colonial Experience in French Fiction. A Study of Pierre Loti, Ernest Psichari and Pierre Mille* (London, 1981)
44. Mangin, Charles: *La force noir* (Paris, 1911). It is intriguing to note Mangin's role in the diffusion into the French language of the English imperial word 'man-power', a term first coined in 1905 by Sir Halford Mackinder, the MP and geopolitical theorist. See Mackinder, Halford J.: 'Man-Power as a Measure of National and Imperial Strength', *The National and English Review* 45 (1905), pp 136-43.
45. Michel: 'La colonisation', p 139
46. The careers of these two men were closely interwoven, though the enduring

fascination with Lyautey has generated a much larger literature. See Scham, Alan: *Lyautey in Morocco. Protectorate Administration, 1912-1925* (Berkeley and Los Angeles, 1970); Porch, Douglas: *The Conquest of Morocco* (London, 1982); Révérend, André: *Lyautey* (Paris, 1983); Singer, Barnett: 'Lyautey: An Interpretation of the Man and French Imperialism', *Journal of Contemporary History* 26 (1991), pp 131-57; Aldrich: *Greater France*, pp 134-8. More complex readings of both men's work in Morocco and Madagascar is provided in Rabinow, Paul: *French Modern. Norms and Forms of the Social Environment* (Cambridge, Mass., 1989), pp 277-318; and Wright, Gwendolyn: *The Politics of Design in French Colonial Urbanism* (Chicago, 1991), pp 85-160, 235-300.

47.   The conversion of the popular press to the imperial cause was of critical importance. See Schneider, William H.: *An Empire for the Masses. The French Popular Image of Africa, 1870-1900* (Westport, 1982); August, Thomas G.: *The Selling of Empire. British and French Imperialist Propaganda, 1890-1940* (Westport, nd).

48.   See, for a lively recent account, Porch, Douglas: *The Conquest of the Sahara* (Oxford, 1986) and also Broc, Numa: 'Les explorateurs français du XIXe siècle reconsidérés', *Revue française d'histoire d'outre-mer* 69/256 (1982), pp 237-73 and 69, 257 (1982), pp 323-59; Broc, Numa: 'Les français face à l'inconnue saharienne: géographes, explorateurs, ingénieurs, 1880-1881', *Annales de géographie* 535 (1987), pp 302-38; Broc, Numa: *Dictionnaire illustré des explorateurs et grand voyageurs français du XIXe siècle* (Paris, 1988), vol 1; Brunschwig, Henri: 'French Exploration and Conquest in Tropical Africa from 1865 to 1898', in L.H.Gann and P.Duignan, eds: *Colonialism in Africa, 1870-1960* (Cambridge, 1969), vol 1, pp 132-64; Tuck, Patrick J.N.: 'Auguste Pavie and the Exploration of the Mekong Valley, 1886-95', *Terrae Incognitae* 14 (1982), pp 41-60.

49.   Soucy, Robert: *Fascism in France. The Case of Maurice Barrès* (Berkeley and Los Angeles, 1972), p 219

50.   On the influence of American frontier thinking in British imperialism, see Kearns, Gerry: 'Closed Space and Poitical Pactice: Frederick Jackson Turner and Halford Mackinder', *Environment and Planning. Society and Space* 2 (1984), pp 23-34. Curzon's views on this matter are expressed in *Frontiers* (Oxford, 1907), pp 56-7, delivered as the Romanes Lecture at Oxford University, where he was Chancellor. 'Outside of the English universities,' he claimed, 'no school of character exists to compare with the Frontier; and character is there moulded, not by attrition with fellow men in the arts or studies of peace, but in the furnace of responsibility and on the anvil of self-reliance. On the outskirts of empire, where the machine is relatively impotent and the individual is strong, is to be found an ennobling and invigorating stimulus for our youth, saving them alike from the corroding ease and the morbid excitements of western civilization.'

51.   There is a huge literature on de Foucauld, most of it Catholic hagiography

of limited value. See, however, Bazin, René: *Charles de Foucauld. Explorateur du Maroc, ermite au Sahara* (Paris, 1921); Lepetit, Charles: *Two Dancers in the Desert. The Life of Charles de Foucauld* (London, 1981). On the broader religious and cultural significance of the Sahara, see Etienne, Bruno: 'Ecritures saintes, désert, monothéisme et imaginaire', in J.-R.Henry, ed: *Le Maghreb dans l'imaginaire français: la colonie, le désert, l'exil* (Aix-en-Provence, 1985), pp 133-149; Heffernan, Michael: 'The Desert in French Orientalist Painting', *Landscape Research* 16/2 (1991), pp 37-42.

52.   Barrès, Maurice: *Une enquête aux pays du Levant* (Paris, 1923), vol 1, p 20; vol. 2, p 181. Translated and quoted in Said, Edward W.: *Orientalism* (London, 1978), pp 244-5. See Soucy: *Fascism in France*, pp 37-8. It is important to note that, despite the perennial conflict between rival religious and secular educational systems in France itself, the anticlerical left was usually happy to accept Catholic French educationalists as a useful ally within the colonial arena. 'Anticlericalism', claimed the resoundingly secular Léon Gambetta, 'is not an article for export.' This imperial alliance was powerful—there were over 500 French Catholic secondary schools in the Levant with over 100,000 pupils, 10 per cent of all those educated to that level in the entire Ottoman Empire. See Andrew and Kanya-Forstner: *France Overseas*, p 41.

53.   Soucy, Robert: *French Fascism. The First Wave 1924-1933* (New Haven, 1986), pp 84-6

54.   See Maurras, Charles: *Pages africaines* (Paris, 1940); Maurras, Charles: 'La plus grande France', *L'Action Française* 12 June, 1939, p 2

55.   Ageron, Charles-Robert: 'Les colonies devant l'opinion publique française, 1919-1939', *Revue française d'histoire d'outre-mer* 77/286 (1990), pp 31-73; Cohen, William B.: *Rulers of Empire. The French Colonial Service in Africa* (Stanford, 1971).

56.   Ageron, Charles-Robert: 'La perception de la puissance française en 1938-1939: le mythe impérial', *Revue française d'histoire d'outre-mer* 69, 254 (1982), pp 7-22; Ageron, Charles-Robert: 'La survivance d'un mythe: la puissance par l'empire coloniale, 1944-47', *Revue française d'histoire d'outre-mer* 72/269 (1985), pp 387-403

57.   Ageron, Charles-Robert: 'L'exposition coloniale de 1931: mythe républicain ou mythe impérial', in P.Nora, ed: *Les lieux de mémoire* (Paris, 1984), vol 1, pp 561-91; Marseille, Jacques: *L'âge d'or de la France coloniale* (Paris, 1986), pp 117-36; Hodeir, Catherine and Pierre, Michel: *L'exposition coloniale* (Paris, 1991); Lebovics, Herman: *True France. The Wars over Cultural Identity, 1900-1945* (Ithaca, 1992), pp 51-97

58.   Laguna, Marc: 'L'échec de la commission d'enquête coloniale du Front Populaire', *Historical Reflections/Réflexions historiques* 16/1 (1989), pp 79-97

59.   Michel: 'La colonisation', p. 146. See also Blanchard, Pascal: 'Idéologie

coloniale et regard sur l'Afrique à travers la presse de "droite-extrême" au temps du mythe impérial' (Unpublished doctoral thesis, Université de Paris I, 1989)

60. Sternhell, Zeev: *Neither Right Nor Left. Fascist Ideology in France* (Berkeley and Los Angeles, 1986)

61. See, for example, Fidel, Camille: *La paix coloniale française* (Paris, 1918) and, for a detailed analysis, Heisser, David D.R.: 'The Impact of the Great War on French Imperialism, 1914-24', (Unpublished Ph.D thesis, University of North Carolina, 1972)

62. Michel: 'La colonisation', p 148

7. FROM NOSTALGIA TO PRAGMATISM: FRENCH ROYALISM AND THE DREYFUS WATERSHED

Richard Griffiths

There is no denying that French royalism underwent a profound change at the turn of the century. The accepted picture runs as follows: royalism, though it had a lot of support in certain areas of society in the last decades of the nineteenth century, was a declining political force, with less and less chance of a breakthrough; from the turn of the century onwards, with Maurras and Action Française, one had a far more vital and effective movement which gained a great deal of new popular support, in those classes which had found a new home on the right after Boulangism, and which completely revitalized support for the monarchy. In large part, so this explanation runs, this was based on new policies stemming from a coherent political doctrine, as opposed to the reliance on nostalgia and on simple dislike for the Republic, which had marked royalism up to this time.

This is the usual picture; and, though there are strong elements of truth within it, it is also a very misleading one, as we shall see.

Let us take the elements of truth first. There is little doubt that monarchism, by the 1890s, was something of a spent force. Charles Maurras himself, arriving in Paris as a young man in the 1880s, already had a strong tendency to the right, which was translated into a Boulangist vote in 1889; but he had no faith whatsoever in monarchism, which he believed to be dead, without any hope of a restoration:

Le premier Boulangisme m'avait répugné par son aspect de démagogie. Je me rendis peu à peu à ses allures de réveil national, et l'évolution conservatrice du Général me décida même à avaler, pour l'amour de lui, un assez dur crapaud: majeur en 1889, et vivant rue Cujas, au cinquième arrondissement, je donnais mon premier bulletin de vote au juif Naquet, bien que je fusse antisémite de coeur! La vérité profonde est que l'indiscipline des partis de droite avait été si souvent blâmée devant moi que j'avais voulu débuter par la plus méritoire des obéissances. Il ne me déplaisait pas non plus de voir un prince comme le comte de Paris, qui passait pour 'parlementaire', s'allier à la sorte au peuple et à l'armée. Néanmoins, j'étais sans foi dans sa Restauration, je croyais la monarchie morte, en me demandant néanmoins si, tout au contraire, l'avenir n'était pas à quelque cinquième dynastie![1]

This is not to say that the monarchists themselves did not continue to believe in their future. There is nothing more sad than to read the police records of this period, in which the royalists' aspirations are so little matched by events. The coded telegrams to the Pretender, perpetually calling on him to come near the frontier to await the call, related to internal events within France which never matched the hopes that had been placed in them. I propose to take two examples: the resignation of the War Minister, General Chanoine, in October 1898, and Déroulède's attempted coup d'état in February 1899.

General Chanoine's *démission*, though its causes were originally mysterious, has correctly been surmised, after certain newspaper revelations some years later, to have been inspired by the royalists. Police documents I have recently unearthed in the Fonds Waldeck-Rousseau bear this out, but their detail is particularly fascinating as an insight into royalist hopes.

On 26 September 1898, the head of the royalist movement, Buffet, had received a letter from one of his leading members, which ran as follows:

Monsieur, quelqu'un qui connaît bien le Ministre actuel de la Guerre, me dit qu'on lui ferait faire facilement un coup d'état au profit de Monseigneur. N'ayant aucun avenir au point de vue militaire, ne pouvant être placé à la place de FF, il aimerait jouer un second rôle éminent: un titre de duc, une dotation sourirait énormément à sa fille.[2]

This letter, in the police file, has been crossed out, and replaced with the words: 'indiquant l'espoir de s'assurer le concours d'une haute personnalité.'[3]

Were it not for later events, this letter would seem to have been little more than a fantasy; but the fact that Chanoine's eventual action was linked to this letter is made clear by Buffet's actions thereafter. Chanoine's public resignation took place on *25 October*. On the *22nd* Buffet sent a coded telegram to the duc d'Orléans, the Pretender (who was at Königswinter in

Bohemia), calling him urgently to Brussels *by the 24th*. (The telegrams were easily decoded by the police): 'Buffet-duc d'Orléans (Königswinter, Bohème): Bruxelles 24 indispensable'.[4]

The Pretender's telegram in reply merely asked how urgent this was, as he had urgent affairs where he was.

On 25 October Chanoine resigned unexpectedly in the Chamber of Deputies, with tumultuous results on the Place de la Concorde and the surrounding streets. The police reports show that the demonstrations *must* have been set up beforehand:

> Graves événements ... La démission imprévue du général Chanoine à la suite d'une mise en cause préméditée, donnée, fait sans précédent, à la tribune, déchaînait un véritable tumulte: On l'attendait au dehors.
> Sur la place de la Concorde, toutes les ligues sont présentes: patriotes, nationalistes, royalistes, antisémites, rivalisent dans l'agitation.[5]

The duc d'Orléans had meanwhile sent a further telegram, asking whether he *really* needed to come to Brussels: duc d'Orléans-Comte Chevilly (Château d'Eu): *'Prière télégraphier de suite ici réponse dépêche hier. Dois-je revenir de suite ou puis-je attendre encore. Crois dernière solution meilleure et la préfère amities.'*

On the 26th Buffet, however, sent another urgent telegram to the Pretender: *'Rapprocher frontière nécessaire'*.[6] But the Pretender never came. And he was probably right, in that the 'émeute' was in no way the kind of coup d'état which had been envisaged in the original letter. Indeed, though the Dreyfus Affair may have seemed the great opportunity for which the royalists had been waiting, with all the forces of the right being able to work together in a common cause from which the royalists could derive profit, this particular opportunity in fact showed just how unreal the royalists' hopes for a coup d'état were (and the Pretender seems to have realized it!).

This is even more clear in the case of Déroulède's attempted coup d'état in February 1899, to which the royalists had latched on in the hope of Déroulède, a republican, becoming their catspaw. The attempt was staged, it will be remembered, amid the confusion following the death of Félix Faure, President of the Republic, and was due to take place on the day of his state funeral.

On 17 February 1899, immediately following Faure's death, a telegram was sent to the duc d'Orléans, who was in Turin: 'Chevilly-Duc d'Orléans (Turin): *Présence prince Bruxelles désirée par amis afin prouver son intérêt situation.*'

Further, more urgent telegrams were sent on the 18th and 19th, as demonstrations mounted in the capital. The second of these ran: 'Buffet-duc d'Orléans (Turin): *Nombreuses et imposantes manifestations de protestation hier soir. Conseil partir avec Luxembourg.*'

This time the Pretender *did* come to Brussels, where, on the 22nd, the eve of Faure's funeral, he received the following news from Buffet, which confirmed preparations for the projected coup d'état on the 23rd: 'Buffet-duc d'Orléans (Bruxelles): Tous seront demain à leur poste.'

There is no need to go into the details of Déroulède's grotesque and bungled attempt. The effect of its failure upon the royalists is, however, significant. On the day itself, the 23rd, Buffet telegraphed to Brussels: 'Buffet-duc d'Orléans (Bruxelles): Inutile venir. Enverrons demain nouvelles.'

A day later, he seemed more hopeful, and called on the prince to remain in Brussels awaiting events: 'Buffet-duc d'Orléans (Bruxelles): *Gouvernement affolé. Supplie Mgr rester.*'

The next day, 25 February, he wrote: 'Buffet-duc d'Orléans (Bruxelles): *Rien nouveau. Gouvernement ne sait que faire Déroulède.*'

But the Pretender was by now fed up. His telegram, in reply on the same day, ran: 'Duc d'Orléans-Buffet: *Maintiens dépêche hier. Partons ce soir.*'

The unreality of the beliefs and hopes of Buffet and his men is shown by the initial reactions of both police and newspapers to Déroulède's plot. As Stephen Wilson has pointed out, they did not take it seriously at all: '*Le Matin* referred on 29 February to "a poet's coup d'état"; *Le Journal du peuple*, on the same day, to "the grotesque attempt".'[7]

This was, however, to take it too lightly. If the army *had*, as planned, supported Déroulède, it would have been a serious matter indeed. But this pinpoints the essential weakness of the right in general, and the royalists in particular, at this time. In the absence of extensive popular support, they had to rely on the power which could be conferred by the army, which was seen as a royalist bastion.

A royalist bastion it certainly was, but it was in no way a counter-revolutionary force. As Stephen Wilson writes, 'The police reported in December 1898 that the duc d'Orléans could "not find a single high-ranking officer who was willing to foreswear his duty in order to promote a Restoration".'[8]

While the army had strong feelings about the Affair, it did not extend those feelings to support for a coup d'état, whether royalist or otherwise. Fear of the army, in the 1890s, was on the whole unjustified; as Martin

Alexander demonstrates elsewhere in this volume, it was not until the twentieth century that the army, for various reasons, was to become a potent political force in its own right.

The Affair had appeared to help the royalist cause, by adding strings to its bow, and by facilitating possible alliances with other right-wing groups. Among the new strings added to its bow was political antisemitism. But these were illusory advantages. As we have seen, royalism remained politically impotent.

Yet within six or seven years, when the Action Française movement came fully to fruition, the future of royalism looked completely different. This, too, as part of the traditional interpretation of events, holds water. But *what was it* that had changed?

Yes, there was the appearance of a new philosophy; but that was likely to appeal only to a small minority. Maurras's invocation of Comtian logic, his insistence on the intellect, did not inspire much trust in the intelligent public, either. As his friend Barrès was to put it, this was merely a smoke-screen with which to hide presumptions which had already been arrived at:

> Les procédés d'argumentation régulière donnent l'illusion de la méthode scientifique. C'est un magnifique symptôme d'activité intellectuelle, mais il ne mène nulle part. Maurras a résolu d'avance par une adhésion inébranlable à la monarchie le problème politique; avec sa ferme et douce insistance, il a l'air de raisonner librement; mais il n'a pas le droit de se laisser convaincre.[9]

What, then, did Action Française bring that was new, which can explain its success where others had failed? Its policies, after all, were not exactly new. Among the negative ones, anti-democracy had been a mainstay of 'old' royalism, and xenophobia and antisemitism had become so by the time of the Affair. Among the positive ones, too, nationalism had been central to royalist rhetoric in the 1890s, and the appeal for social justice for the workers had a long royalist pedigree.

The difference is not one of policies, but one of activity, and of attitude; above all, the conscious cultivation of a wider appeal for these traditional doctrines. Nowhere can this be seen more clearly than in the 'social question', which was one of the areas on which the Action Française built most strongly in its early days. I would like to take this as my main example of what happened over a whole range of other policies which Action Française took over from old-style royalism.

The 'appeal to the workers' was not an invention of Action Française.

It had played a strong part in the propaganda of the Pretenders from the 1860s onwards, as they called for 'liberté d'association', which was being denied by both the Second Empire and the Third Republic. In this way, the royalists associated themselves with the workers against the restrictive practices of the dominant capitalist regimes of post-revolutionary France.

As early as 1865, we find the comte de Chambord writing, in his *Lettre sur les ouvriers*, in a way that is remarkably akin to the later reasonings of Maurras:

> La royauté a toujours été la patronne des classes ouvrières. Les *établissements* de Saint-Louis, les *règlements* des métiers, le système des *corporations* en sont les preuves manifestes.
>
> Lorsque les jurandes et les maîtrises disparurent, la liberté du travail fut proclamée. Mais la liberté d'association fut détruite du même coup. De là cet individualisme dont l'ouvrier est encore aujourd'hui la victime. L'individu demeuré sans bouclier pour ses intérêts, a été de plus livré en proie à une concurrence sans limites, contre laquelle il n'a eu d'autre ressource que la *coalition* et les *grèves*. En même temps se constituait par le développement de la prospérité publique une espèce de privilège industriel qui, tenant dans ses mains l'existence des ouvriers, se trouvait investi d'une sorte de domination qui pouvait devenir oppressive, et amener par contrecoup des crises funestes. En un mot, ce qui est démontré c'est la nécessité d'associations volontaires et libres des ouvriers pour la défense de leurs intérêts communs.[10]

Over 20 years later, in the climate of Boulangism, the comte de Paris, in a reply to an address from the workers of Paris, stressed the same themes: the self-seeking of the capitalist classes, the slavery brought by apparent freedoms, and the importance for the workers of grouping their forces to defend their interests. He continued:

> Vous avez longtemps fait crédit à ceux qui vous abusant par de vaines promesses, n'ont songé qu'à satisfaire leur ambition personnelle.
>
> Que vous ont-ils donné? Le suffrage universel. Mais il ne peut seul assurer votre indépendance et votre bonheur. Il a besoin de la liberté d'association, et comme vous me le rappelez, cette liberté vous a été impitoyablement refusée. Lorsque d'anciennes institutions ont disparu devant l'aurore d'une société nouvelle, on vous a dévié les moyens de grouper vos forces pour la défense de vos intérêts.[11]

Similarly the duc d'Orléans, Pretender at the time of the Dreyfus Affair, produced the same arguments for the need for 'liberté d'association' to protect the workers against an omnipotent state:

> Le droit d'association doit fournir aux classes ouvrières le moyen de défendre elles-mêmes leurs intérêts .... en les empêchant d'abdiquer leurs plus précieuses libertés entre les mains d'un Etat omnipotent.[12]

The cry was, of course, taken up by other sections of the right in the 1890s, and in particular by the antisemitic leader, the marquis de Morès, whose movement 'Morès et ses amis' based those parts of its doctrine which were not specifically aimed at the Jews, on the necessity to authorize the creation of *syndicats d'ouvriers*. Indeed, this issue took up so much prominence in the movements' tracts that, in many of them, it is impossible to find references to the Jews. In, for example, a one-page tract entitled 'La Fête du Travail, le 1er mai 1890', Morès calls on the electors to the Conseil Municipal to 'faire avancer la question sociale sur des points déterminés' and 'démontrer, une fois pour toutes aux fonctionnaires, la souveraineté du peuple'. He proposes practical measures including:

> 1) Constitution d'un crédit ouvrier, alimenté avec les fonds des assurances contre les accidents et prêtant aux associations ouvrières libres, sur la signature solidaire de leurs membres.
> 2) La convocation d'une Haute Cour de justice populaire destinée à faire rendre gorge aux voleurs de la fortune publique.
> 3) Révision démocratique et sociale, par le peuple, du Code et de la Constitution.[13]

But all this rhetoric did not lead to a movement based on the workers. Instead, small sections of the working class who were particularly suited to street-fighting were recruited for antisemitic action. Above all, the workers in the abattoirs of La Villette, who predominated in 'Morès et ses amis' around 1890, were later recruited by the royalists. In a police report in 1899, the activities of the royalist candidate for La Villette, the comte de Sabran-Pontevès, are described thus:

> M de Sabran recrute de nombreux partisans parmi les garçons bouchers de la Villette, et lors des derniers événements ... il en a embauché par l'entremise de Gaston Dumay, marchand boucher, ancien ami de Morès, un certain nombre pour manifester sur la voie publique.

That this support was in large part based on antisemitism is shown by the role played by Jules Guérin, the leader of the Ligue Antisémitique

Française, in these activities. The police reported that 'Sous le couvert de l'antisémitisme, Jules Guérin travaille en réalité pour le parti orléaniste (et en reçoit des subventions).'

Guérin had been giving money to his lieutenants, to distribute to those taking part in *manifestations*:

> Ces Messieurs recrutent leurs hommes dans les quartiers de Belleville, La Villette, du Pont de Flandre et principalement parmi le personnel des Abattoirs. En général tous ces gens là lui sont très dévoués. Tous appartiennent au Comité Royaliste de la Villette et ont fait campagne pour M le comte de Sabran.[14]

The use of such thugs was not merely confined to the street. They were also accorded a meeting with the Pretender himself, on a visit to Brussels in January 1899. A Belgian police spy, 'l'indicateur à l'hôtel de Flandre', where the duc and duchesse d'Orléans were staying, reported to his superiors at the Belgian Sûreté Générale that 'Aujourd'hui cinquante ouvriers royalistes de Paris (Quartier de la Villette) arrivés à Bruxelles dans la matinée, ont été reçus par le duc et la duchesse d'Orléans.'[15]

The royalist appeal to the workers, up to the turn of the century, remained however on this level. High-minded statements by the Pretenders about workers' rights contrasted with the actual practical approach made to workers on the ground. Here the royalists conscripted small groups of racialist thugs in the same areas as Morès had been recruiting around 1890; and their use of Guérin and his henchmen underlines this approach.

It is true to say that, in July 1898, the duc d'Orléans dictated to Buffet a note in which he suggested that a trade union leader had agreed to bring to the royalist cause the supporter of a large number of unions throughout France.[16] But nothing appears to have come of this, and it seems to be yet another example of the royalist wishful thinking of those years.

So the appeal to the workers, in those years, turned out to be rather small beer. It was at most an appendage, and was not seen as central by the royalists themselves. It was the Action Française which was to build up, on the basis of this same doctrine, widespread support in classes which until then had had no interest in royalism. With Action Française, one had direct action in favour of workers, rather than speeches. Also, by the time of the daily *Action Française*, from 1908 onwards, one had violent press campaigns offering direct support to the workers, rather than pious generalizations.

The social unrest of the years 1907-8 was the great opportunity for this.

The republican government was seen as being impotent in the face of a militant working class; and, in its contempt for parliamentarism and its love of direct action, Action Française found itself in alliance with the forces of the extra-parliamentary left.

All this did not spring from nothing, however. Action Française had been building up support in working-class and lower-middle-class areas for a number of years before this, in a way that old-style royalism had never done. It is interesting to read, for example, the reports of the Action Française Conference in December 1907, which show just how far the party had come.

The *séance* on 12 December 1907 was described, in the reports, as follows:

> Cette séance a été consacrée à la propagande dans les milieux ouvriers, agricoles et commerçants, et d'une façon générale, dans les classes moyennes. Elle a eu d'autant plus de vivacité et d'éclat que la plupart des sections ont onbtenu, dans cet ordre, des résultats absolument surprenants et qui renferment les plus riches promesses pour un avenir très prochain.

At this *séance*, the workers from Roubaix spoke, identifying themselves as coming from a milieu that was 'ni universitaire, ni aristocratique, mais exclusivement travailleur de l'Usine'. The commentary on the *séance* noted that, 'Nous devons une mention spéciale à ce groupe ouvrier de Roubaix, qui a su discerner les nécessités primordiales.'

Later in the same session, the following points were made in relation to the representation from Rouen:

> Le milieu bourgeois, conservateurs par tradition et par égoïsme, mais timorés, prudents, craignant de se compromettre et de compromettre des intérêts, n'est pas favorable à notre mouvement d'idées, dont il ne veut pas discuter le fond. Il le trouve dangereux et inopportun, ne pouvant élever ses conceptions au-dessus des intérêts électoraux immédiats. Le milieu des petits commerçants, employés et ouvriers est plus favorable.[17]

So, while apparently using the same tactics of appealing to the workers that the old royalists had done, Action Française, while maintaining a strong theoretical base through Maurras himself, and through above all Jean Rivain and Georges Valois, had translated this into positive action. The workers were no longer a ploy or an accessory, but had been imported centrally into the movement. This was not an ideological shift, but a practical one; the policies were not changed, but their application was.

The industrial unrest of 1907-8 appeared to provide, as we have already stated, an outlet for such practical action. The emergence of a powerful extra-parliamentary left in the shape of the anarcho-syndicalists of the Confédération Générale du Travail (CGT) seemed to offer the possibility of an anti-republican alliance. Much play was made of the inability of republican governments to cope with this crisis. The Pretender himself, under the influence of Action Française, began adding to his social message allusions to the contemporary situation:

> S'agit-il du plus important (des problèmes sociaux), de l'organisation du travail, l'impuissance de la république à le résoudre apparaît à tous les yeux. Le mouvement syndical actuel, avec ses alternatives d'agitations sourdes et d'explosions violentes, traduit en réalité l'impérieux besoin d'organisation qui tourmente la classe ouvrière. Le gouvernement républicain s'en alarme: devant cette force naissante qui, dédaigneuse de la politique, ne paraît plus disposée à servir ses desseins, il demeure déconcerté, et d'ailleurs incapable de la faire concourir au bien général. La royauté nationale peut seule remplir cette tâche.[18]

Action Française itself, however, went beyond this. The birth of the daily *L'Action Française*, in 1908, coincided with the worst of the strikes, which Clemenceau, 'briseur de grèves', was to put down so bloodily. Tactically, Action Française placed itself in alliance with the CGT on the side of the striking miners, against 'politicians' of all hues. Léon Daudet's editorials were, from the start, violent denunciations of his old Dreyfusard enemies (above all Clemenceau), the so-called 'liberals', who were now in power, grinding the workers down. One such editorial of 5 April 1908 declared:

> Enfin un bruit a couru, un bruit d'essai, d'après lequel le vieux Clemenceau songerait à dissoudre la Confédération du Travail, sous prétexte de complicité avec le parti royaliste. Car plus les choses vont, plus l'ouvrier français se dégoûte de cette République qui a répandu la plus grande quantité de sang ouvrier en Europe au cours des douze dernières années. La sentimentalité romantique, habilement exploitée par la maçonnerie—institution éminemment bourgeoise—avait autrefois persuadé au quatrième Etat que son bonheur et ses droits étaient liés au régime républicain et parlementaire. Cette blague a eu cours pendant une trentaine d'années. Il a fallu maintes fusillades inutiles et féroces—depuis Fourmies jusqu'à Châlons et à Narbonne—pour réveiller le quatrième Etat de son erreur et lui montrer ses pires ennemis dans les politiciens identiques qui vont de Ferry à Millerand et à Briand. En réalité, la République, selon que son

existence est en danger ou non, fait de l'ouvrier tantôt son mercenaire et tantôt son paria.[19]

Maurras, too, stressed the same points in his articles for the new daily. On 20 June 1908, in an article entitled 'Les morts', he commemorated the anniversary of the 'fusillades' in the Languedoc in 1907, which he blamed squarely on Clemenceau and Picquart.

As the troops were being sent from Paris to Villeneuve-St Georges and to Draveil on 30 July 1908, at the height of the coal strike, Maurras produced a powerful article, in general terms, on 'La question ouvrière'. This turned into violent and specific polemic the following day, when the troops had fired on the striking miners. Maurras attacked, above all, Clemenceau—even hinting, in his headline, by the use of an English word, at the old libel about Clemenceau the English spy, which had had such currency in the 1890s. The article declared:

LE SANG OUVRIER

NOMBREUSES VICTIMES

DES MORTS ET DES BLESSÉS

BLOODY!

Tous les journaux français devraient paraître aujourd'hui dans un cadre de deuil (...) Nous ne dirons pas à ce vieillard sanglant qu'il se trompe. Nous lui dirons qu'il ment. Car il a voulu ce carnage. Cette tuerie n'est pas le résultat de la méprise ou de l'erreur. On ne peut l'imputer à une faute de calcul. Il l'a voulue. Il l'a visée.[20]

A few days later, Maurras showed his solidarity with the leaders of the CGT, who had been arrested by Clemenceau, and castigated the conservatives who did not realize the importance of the syndicalist movement:

A la suite de la journée sanglante du jeudi, par la conséquence directe du massacre qui a déterminé l'arrestation des chefs du mouvement syndical, la Confédération Générale du Travail va tomber aux mains de M Clemenceau. Celui-ci l'espère du moins, et, jusqu'ici, tout semble autoriser son espérance. Les premiers dans la presse, nous avons signalé le manoeuvre; il nous faut maintenant signaler le danger de cette manoeuvre, car les conservateurs applaudissent à tour de bras. Les conservateurs ne comprennent rien.[21]

Throughout the month, Maurras was stressing that all the press was united against the workers, except *L'Action Française*:

> Qu'on soit opportuniste ou radical, nationaliste ou conservateur, c'est le travailleur organisé, c'est l'organisation ouvrière que l'on rabroue! Dans cette unanimité touchante, il n'y a guère qu'une exception. Elle est royaliste. Nous en sommes fiers.[22]

Alongside Maurras, there was of course the more knock-about approach of Léon Daudet, mocking the 'lefties' who were now terrified of the proletariat. In a hilariously funny article entitled 'Un homme embêté', Daudet graphically described Jaurès's embarrassment, as a parliamentary 'Socialist' who felt he had to support government action to the extent of calling the soldiers who had fired on the miners 'les ouvriers de la caserne!'[23]

So it was that, at this stage of its career, the Action Française movement tapped pragmatically and practically into areas of support with which the old royalists had just played. The difference was not so much one of doctrine, but one of tactics. And the appeal to the workers is merely one example. The same tactics are to be perceived in relation to all the other groups which Action Française brought to the support of royalism: Catholics, antisemites, patriots, nationalists, conservatives, workers. Often the commitments in all these different directions clashed, as they were bound to; but that did not deter Maurras and his followers. In the *Revue de l'Action Française* in February 1908 Maurras himself cynically revealed his tactics:

> Ainsi, pour les conduire au roi, avons-nous dit aux patriotes: 'Si vous voulez vraiment le salut de votre Patrie ... '; aux nationalistes: 'Si vous tenez à secouer le joug de l'étranger de l'intérieur ... '; aux antisémites: 'Si vous désirez terminer le règne des Juifs ... '; aux conservateurs: 'Si la préservation de l'ordre public est plus forte chez vous que vos divisions, vos préjugés, vos prudences ... '; au prolétariat de la grande industrie: 'Si l'organisation sociale vous paraît vraiment plus nécessaire que tout ... '; aux catholiques enfin: 'Si votre volonté tend bien à triompher des persécuteurs de l'Église ... '. Selon nous, chacun de ces postulats contient et appelle la monarchie. Rien de plus facile que de montrer, par notre examen de la situation—si complet et si rigoureux qu'on ne l'a jamais discuté—comment le roi seul pourra rendre au catholicisme sa liberté, à l'ouvrier nomade un statut vraiment social, à la fortune acquise l'influence publique, la protection et le contrôle que leur doit l'Etat, à l'antisémitisme la victoire

prompte et paisible, aux nationalistes français leur délivrance des métèques, à la Patrie entière la sécurité et l'honneur.[24]

It was when Action Française abandoned this pragmatic universality after the First World War, and became the party of a class and of capitalism, that it lost much of its vigour and appeal. Its doctrines, logical and coherent, became more important that its tactics; pragmatism disappeared, and Action Française locked itself into an intellectual prison.

The revitalization of royalism by the Action Française movement in the first years of this century was not therefore a change of doctrine, or even of discourse, but a change of tactics. Old royalism had adopted, by the 1890s, the same doctrines as Action Française was to espouse: nationalism, antisemitism, the appeal to the workers, Catholicism. Action Française aggressively marketed these doctrines on a wide scale, both through its party organization and through its violent journalism, and created a vast and receptive audience, which remained unaware of the contradictions inherent in the indiscriminate adoption of this wide range of policies.

Notes

1. Maurras, Charles: *Au signe de flore* (Paris, 1933), p 37
2. FF= Félix Faure, Président de la République
3. Fonds Waldeck-Rousseau (Bibliothèque de l'Institut): MS 4577
4. Fonds Waldeck-Rousseau: MS 4578
5. Fonds Waldeck-Rousseau: MS 4577
6. Fonds Waldeck-Rousseau: MS 4578
7. Wilson, Stephen: *Ideology and Experience. Antisemitism in France at the time of the Dreyfus Affair* (London andToronto, 1982), p 25
8. Wilson: *Ideology and Experience*, p 79
9. Barrès, Maurice: *Mes cahiers* (Paris,1900)
10. Henri, comte de Chambord: *Lettre sur les ouvriers*, 20 April 1865
11. Philippe, comte de Paris: *Réponse à l'adresse des ouvriers parisiens*, 17 July 1888, quoted in Valois, Georges: *La révolution sociale ou le roi* (Paris, 1908), p 4
12. Philippe, duc d'Orléans: Préface à une nouvelle édition de l'étude *Une liberté nécessaire*, October 1901, quoted in Valois: *La révolution sociale ou le roi*, pp 4-5
13. Morès, marquis de: *La fête du travail, le 1er mai 1890*, pamphlet published in 1890
14. Fonds Waldeck-Rousseau: MS 4578
15. 'Sûreté Générale, Bruxelles, 29 janvier 1899.' In Fonds Waldeck-Rousseau: MS 4579
16. Report of July 1898. Fonds Waldeck-Rousseau: MS 4577

17. *L'Action Française. Revue bi-mensuelle,* 1 January 1908, pp 36-43
18. Philippe, duc d'Orléans: Préface de *La monarchie française*, June 1907. Quoted in Valois: *La révolution sociale ou le roi*, p 5
19. Daudet, Léon : 'La république et l'ouvrier', *L'Action Française*, 5 April 1908
20. *L'Action Française*, 31 July 1908.
21. Maurras, Charles: 'Le quatre août des conservateurs', *L'Action Française*, 3 August 1908
22. Maurras, Charles: 'Liberté d'esprit', *L'Action Française*, 4 August 1908
23. Daudet, Léon: 'Un homme embêté', *L'Action Française*, 5 August 1908
24. *L'Action Française. Revue bi-mensuelle*, 1 February 1908

8. DUTY, DISCIPLINE AND AUTHORITY: THE FRENCH OFFICER ELITES BETWEEN PROFESSIONALISM AND POLITICS, 1900-1962

Martin Alexander

'Although it was not apparent at the time', wrote Paul-Marie de La Gorce in 1963, 'the political involvement of the officers' corps was for France militarily the most significant fact of the 1930s.' But, he added:

> At the time the reliability of the army, its strength, its technical capacity seemed beyond question. The readjustment in thinking required by 1940 was to be therefore all the more painful. Only in the distressing circumstances of that year would it become plain that a segment of the military had definitely gone political. It was only then that the immediate consequences of defeat [would] bring up for examination the total relationship between Army and country.[1]

Since La Gorce's book was published the French army (and to a lesser extent naval) corps, has received extensive scholarly attention. Some treatments have adopted a historico-sociological ap-proach.[2] Many writers, on the other hand, have endorsed and expanded upon La Gorce's theme that members of the military High Command took leading parts in key moments of French national destiny and regime transitions in the decades between the crushing defeat of Napoleon III's Second Empire by Prussia and its allies in 1870-71 and de Gaulle's consolidation of the Fifth Republic in the early 1960s. But research on the French military's periodic interventions in national politics has generally taken the form of case studies. Most works have focused on just one civil-military convulsion, on a single change of political direction.[3]

This essay seeks to elucidate the trends of French military participation in politics by adopting an approach based on a 'long-view' institutional analysis. The methodology follows that applied by Klaus-Jürgen Müller and Michael Geyer to Germany's military in the Wilhelmine, Weimar and Nazi eras.[4] This essay enquires into the overall traits in the French army officers, and explores continuities and discontinuities in the behavioural responses of French officers to politico-military crisis in the age of total war.

Geyer has suggested that professionally defensive characteristics define and unite the interwar French and German officer castes. He has argued that the concerns of German Reichswehr generals such as Hans von Seeckt and Ludwig Beck were similar to those that preoccupied their French contemporaries such as General Maxime Weygand (Commander-in-Chief-Designate and Inspector-General of the Army, 1931-35) and General Maurice Gamelin (who held the same posts between 1935 and 1940). French and German officers fashioned around their vocation a cocoon of supposedly professional mystique or specialist/technical know-how. By doing so, Geyer argues, senior commanders and staff sought to release the two armies from political interference and from political, and particularly from democratic, accountability.

This was a reaction, Geyer suggests, of nineteenth-century military notables. It represented a response by men whose formative youth experiences, lifestyles, thought-processes, prejudices, self-image, were pre-twentieth century. It was behaviour indicative of the generals' lack of self-confidence, as they sought to erect an impenetrable wall of technical specialization around their business of arms. Career officers asserted that they alone possessed a special body of knowledge or skills unique to the military High Command and incomprehensible to literally incompetent, professionally-untrained civilian politicians.[5]

Does this model work for the twentieth-century French army officers? Can it be extended to explain those officers' politicized behaviour in the decades before and after the crisis of 1940? Or was there something seminal about the army officers' entrance onto the political centre-stage during the Fall of France? Were the actions of French generals in 1940, as Philip Bankwitz has argued, qualitatively different, of such significance that they legitimized the subsequent excursions of French officers into politics in 1958 and 1961, in the name of those old nineteenth-century shibboleths of the French nationalist right, *la patrie* and *la vraie France*?[6]

It may be instructive to reverse Geyer's assertions about 'military professionalism', or at any rate to modify them. For the French military elite's singular shortcoming in the age of mass politics and total war was arguably that it was *insufficiently* professional. Senior French officers repeatedly hid behind *political* explanations at times of military defeat, when these demanded honest self-criticism within a *military* phenomenology of failure. How, except as part of an extended indulgence in a form of denial therapy, can one explain the French High Command's recurrent response to close brushes with military disaster (1914, 1958), or the reality of defeat, surrender and withdrawal (1940, 1954, 1961-62), by a repudiation of governments and regimes (and sometimes, most disreputably, of the entire French people)?[7]

The phenomenon of a search by senior officers for non-military scapegoats to blame for strictly military shortcomings was in fact discernible before 1914. As the military competition between the European great powers intensified and the rival alliance systems took shape from *circa* 1905, French military writers presented a professionally complacent and bland perspective on the prospects for war against Germany. Reflections on French defeat in 1870-71 were increasingly informed not by strategic-military explanations, but by socio-political ones. 'In the great literary organs, as well as in the professional journals, elaborate strategic analyses appeared, pointing out the errors of 1870-71 and suggesting how they could be avoided next time.'[8] French 'decadence and bad luck' loomed larger and larger in pre-1914 commentaries on the causes of the débâcles that had overtaken the armies of Napoleon III. By 1912, the German military attaché in Paris was reporting a growing tendency of military writers to underrate the strength of the German army.[9]

Alongside the comparative absence of a critical assessment of the technical capabilities of the French army was a sharpening focus on perceived weaknesses in the French civilian spirit and psyche. Between the war scare provoked by the Agadir crisis in 1911 and the coming of war in 1914, France witnessed a 'systematic attempt to arouse the nation', a conscious effort to generate a spirit of national revival, accompanied by tirades 'against the enervating forces of "humanitarianism"'.[10] Together with the teaching of the 'spirit of the offensive' by Colonels Charles de Grandmaison and Ferdinand Foch to officers at the Ecole de Guerre, the priority of military publicists who engaged in public debate lay with what might be termed 'psychological' or 'moral' rearmament. The French officers strove to remilitarize public consciousness. Some, such as Hubert-Louis Lyautey (later Marshal of France, pro-consul in French Morocco, and Minister of War in 1915-16), went as far as to assign themselves a mission. This amounted to nothing less than the rebirth of a sense of civic duty, the elevation of military ideals, and the defeat of the pernicious influence on French youth of schoolteachers who promoted pacifism and internationalism.

But the French military 'wished to do more than thrust their ideas upon the school system.' They wished to reorient the habits, the ethics, the value-systems, of the political regime itself. 'What must be indicted', wrote an officer during the Agadir crisis, 'is our entire, lamentable internal politics, the criminal unconsciousness of our parliamentary set, juggling portfolios like those of foreign affairs and war and giving our country an appearance of weakness and disorder.'[11]

France's military performance from 1914 to 1918 was sufficiently alarming that many professional officers remained doubtful that the Third Republic could be trusted with the nation's security. Even loyal generals were inclined to blame strategic and operational failures on the traits of the regime, rather than on technically deficient military planning, training or doctrine. Thus Marshal Joseph Joffre, Chief of the General Staff from 1911 and Commander-in-Chief in 1914-16, retrospectively laid partial responsibility for deficient war preparation on parliamentary pressures to reduce military programmes and on the ministerial instability which had seen eight prime ministers come to office between January 1911 and August 1914.[12] This readiness by one of the Third Republic's most trusted military sons to censure the regime indicated the 'general military thought on the role and competence of the legislature'.[13]

Equally, Pétain (a regimental infantry colonel only two years from retirement in 1914), persistently attributed France's near-fatal reverses in the Battle of the Frontiers in August 1914 to the rank-and-file's 'poor fighting spirit'. He especially excoriated the reservist divisions whose men, he alleged, lacked aggressiveness ('aucune flamme'). Deficient patriotism, inadequate élan, insidious anti-militarist instruction peddled by socialist-leaning teachers in the primary schools: these factors, for Pétain, underlay the disasters which the French armies suffered in the war's opening clashes.[14] Socio-ideological undercurrents were eagerly tapped as alibis for a lamentable military performance. For, if analysed with integrity, that performance would have uncovered grotesque incompetence, inefficiency and inhumanity among the higher officer corps itself.

Blaming anti-militarists in the educational system, syndicalist-internationalists and unpatriotic *agents-provocateurs* was more convenient and congenial. In the volatile atmosphere of the war's early months it was neither difficult nor unwelcome to identify scapegoats, thus obviating a potentially embarrassing admission that battlefield failure might be a High Command responsibility. Scapegoats in the form of unfit and insufficiently bellicose reservists spared the generals and staff college instructors the need to enquire into their own disastrous decisions and teachings. As John Cairns has observed, quoting Joffre: 'Those who wore uniform were, after all, "an intellectual and moral—even physical—elite".'[15] The retention of almost Napoleonic infantry uniforms of blue greatcoats and vivid red pantaloons, the persistent use of obsolete infantry tactics (which eschewed fire-and-movement and dispersal in favour of dense linear advances with fixed bayonets), the paucity of artillery of heavier calibre than the *soixante-quinze*, the 75 mm field gun: these were decisions of the senior officers. Yet any admission of such errors would have fatally broken the spell of High Command infallibility, of professional 'guild' skills and a monopolistic military competence. Instead Joffre, publishing his memoirs in 1932, blamed the French military performance in 1914 on parliamentary vacillation over the military budget in 1913-14, and on tangled lines of authority in the war ministry's bureaucracy.[16]

Placing responsibility onto civilians (or, in the case of reservists, civilians in uniform) emerges as a recurrent device. It was repeatedly used by French officers to exculpate themselves from military disasters which had political ramifications. The process of creating scapegoats became refined, almost rehearsed. It also became essential. For whether or not resulting from military débâcles, national crises enabled the army High Command to present itself in a political role of national leadership which it found highly agreeable.

To do this with conviction, and to persuade the wider nation of their legitimacy, senior officers had to ensure two things. First,they had to focus the natural national concern to find *responsables* onto individuals, or preferably institutions belonging to the current regime. Second, the military command itself had to remain untouched by all criticism. With these two ground rules in place, the High Command was able to idealize the army as embodiment of the 'nation', and to insist on the contingent character, and hence the disposability, of the regime.

This connection has been defined by Bankwitz, in his analysis of Weygand's behaviour in the crisis of May-June 1940, as the 'Army-Nation tradition' in the modern French army.[17] He traced its origins to the conflicts between the generals and republicanism of the later nineteenth century: Marshal MacMahon's confrontation with the parliamentary republicans in the Seize Mai crisis of 1877; General Georges Boulanger's tilt for power in the 1880s, and the implicit threat of an army flexing its political muscles personified by Generals Mercier and Gallifet during the Dreyfus Affair of the 1890s.[18]

After the First World War, however, it was noticeable that this phenomenon became more generalized. Pétain himself served as army Commander-in-Chief-Designate and vice-president of the Conseil Supérieur de la Guerre (CSG) from 1921 until February 1931. As head of the High Command and France's most distinguished serving soldier, Pétain was actually ineffectual as a guardian of the directly professional concerns of the army's cadres. During the 1920s, he failed to arrest either a precipitous decline in the value of officers' salaries, or a morale-sapping loss of public esteem for military officers. One of the pervasive themes of military discontent in twentieth-century France has been this sense of being under-valued. From 1904 to about 1911, the officers suffered a backlash because of the widely-publicized indiscretions of those who had fabricated evidence for the prosecution during the Dreyfus Affair.

At a technical level, the 'incontestable' superiority enjoyed by French artillery over that of possible enemies at the start of the century was eroded by technological complacency and doctrinal dogmatism among artillery officers. 'A lengthy period when we were half-asleep took the place of the intensive activity which had brought the artillery to the pitch [of excellence] it enjoyed in 1905,' wrote Joffre.[19] Morale suffered: pay and conditions were poor. In these years, 'the army was unpopular not because war was horrid, not because officers were reactionary, but simply because existence in it was brutish and unprofitable.'[20] These factors contributed to disillusionment, manifested in a sharp decline in enrolments at Saint Cyr, which fell by half between 1897 and 1910. Another consequence was a steep rise in mid-career resignations. Nor did these trends appear only in the wake of the Dreyfus Affair. The army sank to a low ebb again during the 1920s. Paul Painlevé, War Minister at the end of 1926, admitted that the army 'is at present the prey of a deep uneasiness. Its cadres are dispirited and look for an opportunity to leave the service. The youthful elite turns away from our military schools.'[21] An officer's prospects, pay and prestige became so poor in this era that observers described the army as sickly and cadaverous. One commentator, Lucien Suchon, published a polemical lament in 1929 within this metaphor of disease and mortality, under the provocative title: *Feu l'armée française*.[22]

Nor did matters improve, from an officer's perspective, for much of the 1930s. For the first half of that decade Pétain remained a dominant but largely ineffective figure. He was Commander-in-Chief-Designate in 1930-31, then Inspector-General of Territorial Air Defence (1931-34), and finally War Minister in Gaston Doumergue's putative Government of National Union of 1934. But he was more concerned with the politics of school education and pre-military youth training than with the military issues that increasingly worried Gamelin, the Chief of the General Staff from 1931-40.[23] For Gamelin, the army needed France's political leaders to tackle the shortcomings of the procurement budget, shortages of modern plant and productive capacity in the armaments industries, relations with defence contractors. He also needed support to bring about the modernization of operational and tactical doctrine in the face of fierce inter-arm rivalries and bureaucratic turf wars.[24] In the wake of the Stavisky scandal and rioting in Paris in February 1934, Pétain was invited to serve as Minister of War. He accepted the post reluctantly, for he wished above all to be Minister for National Education.[25] Indeed, though nominally responsible for the army, Pétain 'devoted himself during these months in office to making public speeches that amounted to moral admonishments which offered, even at this stage, a sketch of his future doctrine [at Vichy].' Paying homage at Lyautey's funeral in 1934, Pétain ventured that France needed 'work, conscience and self-restraint' more than she needed ideas which were, he said, 'divisive'. Faced by the unfamiliar practices of parliament, Pétain was, in the words of Jacques Nobécourt, 'like all soldiers, rather disarmed'.[26]

Though treated with immense respect by the deputies, Pétain behaved with curious detachment during his tenure of the war ministry. He made little attempt to reduce the daunting pile of problems facing the High Command as Nazi Germany rapidly rearmed.[27] Indeed, he appears to have tamely accepted his own lack of power. Cabinet meetings of the Third Republic were not minuted. It is difficult, therefore, to reconstruct Pétain's role in governmental discussions. But the record lists no significant achievement, and no obvious alarm on his part at this. Meanwhile, Doumergue tabled proposals for constitutional reform over which his government eventually fell.[28] More generally, the period between the 6 February 1934 riots and the coming to office of Léon Blum's Popular Front government in June 1936 saw a vigorous public debate about the need to overhaul republican institutions such as the Chamber of Deputies, the presidency and the Senate.[29] Pétain's experience of office left him sceptical of the feasibility of an internally inspired renovation of political morality and national cohesion. Speaking of the Doumergue ministry's meetings, Pétain remarked that, 'Nothing comes of them, nothing can come of them.'[30]

Plainly, in terms of military policy and the tackling of the most glaring deficiencies in training, equipment and combat-readiness, the High Command itself was bitterly disappointed by Pétain's tenure of the war ministry.[31] After years of budgetary retrenchment and hostility under centre-left governments dominated by supporters of international disarmament, senior officers had expected Pétain's arrival at the rue Saint-Dominique to mark the end of their beleagured position, yet they were soon disappointed.[32] As Nobécourt has concluded:

> Far from reclaiming a privileged position for national defence in the name of the security of France, Pétain behaved every bit as scrupulously as any civilian minister and never tried to set his own imperatives at odds with the concern for governmental solidarity. Recruitment to Saint-Cyr remained feeble. The number of cadet-candidates declined, as did the average academic quality of those admitted. At the rue Saint-Dominique Pétain did neither better nor worse than his predecessors and successors.[33]

In large part, Pétain's Olympian detachment and low expectations of the job that could be done by any minister of war already reflected his loss of faith in the regime itself. He would probably have experienced equal frustration had he become education minister. By 1935, Pétain's conviction was growing that it would require an ideological and institutional overhaul of the nation to purify a public and political culture that was irredeemably materialistic, decadent and individualistic. The severity of the 'French malaise' was too great to be overcome by cosmetic reform of the Third Republic. Right-wing newspaper straw polls in 1935-36 asked their readers which public figure would make the best strong-man to assume special powers and lift France from the 'political riff-raff' of the fractious, stalemated parliamentary republic. 'It's Pétain we need!'was a headline and rallying call increasingly in evidence by 1936. The trend was not one that the marshal discouraged.[34]

Likewise, other senior generals of ultra-conservative disposition committed themselves in this period to a brazen political guerrilla war against the regime. General de Castelnau, an army commander in the First World War, was a Catholic reactionary who had acquired the sobriquet 'Le capucin botté'. His acerbic style was exemplified by his vilification of the Spanish Popular Front as '*le Frente crapular*', and by his dubbing of Blum's centre-left coalition as the 'Chambre rouge horizon' (a sardonic al-lusion to the 'Horizon Blue Chamber', packed with disabled and decorated veterans such as Sergeant André Maginot and Colonel Jean Fabry, elected in 1919).[35]

Weygand was another ultra-conservative for whom Blum's arrival in office came to mark a crossing of the political Rubicon. During the First World War and the peace-making in 1919, Weygand had been Chief of Staff to Foch, succeeding Pétain as Inspector-General of the Army from 1931 to 1935.[36] Weygand's experience of battling against centre-left ministries headed by Edouard Herriot, Camille Chautemps, Edouard Daladier and Joseph Paul-Boncour from 1932 to 1934 had permanently alienated him from the Third Republic. Squeezed between the moral force of the 'spirit of Geneva' and the inescapable pressures of a trade collapse and shrinking tax-base, these governments had sought to curb military appropriations, offer up French forces for negotiated disarmament and reduce the length of conscription.[37] In December 1934, a month before stepping down from active service, Weygand wrote that, 'With practices as they currently are, the intrusion of parliamentary commissions, the megalomania and intrigues, conditions are impossible for the exercise of army high command.And I've had enough of seeing my name serve as storm-proofing for ministers who never listen to a word I say.'[38]

Gamelin, Weygand's successor, had a different style when dealing with politicians. He thought sulking was counter-productive, and he never raised his voice. A republican by conviction, he was more politically supple and accomplished than his irascible predecessor. Genuinely friendly with parliamentarians of conservative stamp such as André Tardieu as much as with Radical Party grandees such as Maurice and Albert Sarraut and the dissident socialist Paul-Boncour, Gamelin also got on with newspaper editors. André Pironneau of L'Echo de Paris and Etienne Gaboriau of L'Ere Nouvelle were among those he knew well. A man of learning, with a taste for foreign travel, Gamelin was as comfortable reading Bergsonian philosophy or entertaining a novelist such as Jules Romains as he was bantering with a foreign journalist such as The New Yorker magazine's Paris correspondent, A. J. Liebling.[39] A consummate committee man, Gamelin believed in the outstretched hand of cooperation with ministers, not the table-thumping confrontations practised by Weygand.

Yet Gamelin, too, had an agenda. He wished, as had Weygand, to lengthen the term of compulsory military service to meet the rising numbers in Hitler's armed forces. He also sought to mechanize at least three cavalry divisions, creating manoeuvrable and hard-hitting form-ations, thus providing a means of assisting a threatened neighbour such as

Belgium. They also provided a capacity to counter attack any assault by Germany's rapidly expanding armoured forces, whose establishment was monitored closely in the later 1930s by France's Deuxième Bureau (military intelligence).[40]

Gamelin's relations with his political masters, while pursuing this modernization and strengthening of French forces, remained harmonious. Unlike Weygand, he worked well with Daladier, the Minister for National Defence and War between June 1936 and May 1940. Daladier, in Gamelin's estimation, was a Jacobin patriot who had proved his worth in the 1914-18 war on the Western Front, winning a commission from the ranks. Gamelin readily acknowledged Daladier's success in obtaining generous financial allocations for the army's modernization and rearmament in 1938 and 1939.[41]

Nevetheless, even Gamelin experienced anguish over the conduct of the civilian political authorities in making national security policy. An insight into the general's disquiet is evidenced by his reaction in the summer of 1938 to disputes with Daladier over a belated fortifications programme along France's frontier with Belgium. There were disagreements, too, over budgets, delays in delivery of munitions from industry and the rejection of calls to create a ministry of armaments.[42] Gamelin wrote to Daladier: 'If my overriding duty is to remain [publicly] silent, it requires me once again, personally and respectfully, to lay out for you the significance of the decisions you have believed you should take.'[43] He was deeply disturbed by his need to preserve a façade of French military omnipotence, for fear of demoralizing watching foreign powers. Allies and wavering neutrals, especially, looked to the French army to give them courage to withstand Hitler's sabre-rattling diplomacy.[44] Even when uncomfortable with government policy, Gamelin lived by a strict code of subordination and loyalty to France's duly constituted political authority. This makes comprehensible his response to those who later wondered why he had not resigned before 1940. As General Pierre Héring, also a member of the CSG and Military Governor of Paris in 1940, explained for the wartime Vichyite show trial at Riom, it was 'no longer admissible' by 1938 for France's highest commander to quit his post. Gamelin's resignation would have been 'an abdication' of responsibility in the eyes of his officer corps.[45] It would have prompted unedifying post-mortems in the press and parliament. No officer could see France or her allies benefiting from publicly laundering the dirty linen of French defence deficiencies, a point Gamelin acknowledged in his memoirs.[46]

Gamelin's failure was not insufficient personal loyalty to the Third Republic but a wider inability to infuse an unquestioning allegiance to the Republic throughout the officer corps. Gamelin had not eradicated an often concealed but visceral contempt for the Republic shared by many officers. Indeed, it seems unlikely that he realized how commonplace this contempt still was. These officers therefore easily embraced the politics of the authoritarian right after the mental shocks administered by military failure in 1940.

Swept away on 18-19 May 1940, in the first of several fateful reshuffles of the High Command and government, Gamelin was replaced by his own disaffected and defeatist predecessor, Weygand (who had been commanding French Middle East forces at Beirut since August 1939). Weygand was one of the most senior and prominent of those who had lost faith in the Republic. A page had been turned.

With the Fall of France, many senior generals instinctively rounded on the rank-and-file of the army and the parties and politicians of the left. There had to be scapegoats, for the generals were unable to ascribe such a dreadful débâcle to the defects of the institution in which they had spent their lives.[47] In a terse exchange upon the transfer of supreme command on 20 May 1940, Gamelin caught an early and unnerving glimpse of the agenda that would soon result from this alliance of the political right and the military. 'All this politics', exclaimed Weygand, 'that's what's got to change. We've got to be done with these politicians. There's not one of them worth any more than the others.'[48]

As Reynaud's government retreated first to Tours and then Bordeaux to escape the German advance on Paris, Weygand indulged in a stunning political forcing play. He challenged the Prime Minister with a threefold refusal: he refused to assume responsibility for a purely military capitulation; he refused to retreat to French North Africa; and he refused to resign. Now backed by scarcely half his ministers, Reynaud faced checkmate. He ceded power to his deputy, Pétain, the 84 year-old erstwhile 'Hero of Verdun', whom he had recalled from his post as ambassador in Madrid a month before, when he had also replaced Gamelin by Weygand. Reynaud had hoped that Pétain's unrivalled prestige would infuse a spirit of resistance into a wobbly government and a nervous public. Instead, *le maréchal's* prestige merely trumped the authority of Reynaud himself.[49]

Pétain eagerly seized his 'providential' moment. The military débâcle enabled him to impose on France the radical, reactionary change of ideological, educational and political direction he had dreamt of since 1934. He could now ignore republican constitutional norms and no longer pay lip-service to the republican trinity of liberty, equality and fraternity, for these had been discredited by defeat. On 10 July 1940, in the incongruous setting of the Second Empire's gambling casino at Vichy, Pétain received unfettered powers from a majority of browbeaten and bamboozled parliamentarians.

Scholars continue to dispute whether the Third Republic was murdered or committed suicide. To pursue the medical metaphor, we have a contemporary note by Anatole de Monzie, Minister of Public Works in Reynaud's government and a consistent advocate both of prewar appeasement and, after September 1939, of a negotiated compromise peace with Germany. Monzie scathingly censured Reynaud's conduct in May 1940 as an attempt to meet a real strategic crisis, a technical military crisis, with a symbolic gesture aimed not at regaining any military initiative but only at reviving popular morale. 'The search after psychological shocks', mused Monzie, 'occupies Reynaud. He mistakes himself for a psychiatrist.'[50] France's tragedy was that Reynaud's therapy, so inappropriate to the malady of military crisis, soon killed off the patient. But whether the Third Republic's death was a case of murder, suicide or botched treatment, its funeral director and the chief executor of the estate was Pétain, France's most illustrious army officer.[51]

By the Armistice, the Germans permitted Vichy a military force of just 100,000 men. It was not allowed tanks or conscription. This scarcely mattered to Pétain who was not interested in fighting. He set out to employ the officer corps, and especially his generals, in the 'parades and politics' of what swiftly became, with the October 1940 Pétain-Hitler meeting at Montoire, a collaborationist regime of a viciously anti-democratic, antisemitic and anti-modernist character. Just as Vichy turned back the clock to restore the teaching prerogatives and civic status of the Catholic Church, so it restored the privileges and prestige of the army officer. Indeed, for those officers able to put the pain of the 1940 defeat from their minds, the next few years saw the army revered by the regime in a way not seen since the General Staff's bungled cover-ups had destroyed the military's special mystique during the Dreyfus Affair.[52]

Simultaneously, in an equally crucial act of political disobedience, General de Gaulle raised the standard of Fighting France. From London, and then from the French colonies, de Gaulle proclaimed that France had not lost the war. He condemned Pétain's collaboration as politically illegitimate and morally dishonourable. On the latter count, he was on firmer ground than on the former. Indeed, his own claim to personify the authority of France, however morally magnificent, was more constitutionally dubious than anything perpetrated by Pétain.[53] Self-styled saviour or 'constable' of France, de Gaulle, too, was beset by a problem of legitimacy. Moreover, from 1943, an internal resistance emerged within occupied France, with its own armed wing, the Forces Françaises de l'Intérieur (FFI). These forces had a loosely coordinated but competitive relationship with de Gaulle's France Combattante. The FFI came under the political control of the French Communist Party, de Gaulle's sworn adversaries. Thus in 1944-46 the general's goal in the military sphere was to restructure the army into a single, unitary and obedient force. De Gaulle's method of achieving this was to merge the former FFI units into the brigades and divisions that had landed in France in 1944-45 under the command of Free French generals such as Koenig, Leclerc, de Lattre de Tassigny and Legentilhomme. This military reorganization by de Gaulle's Provisional Government saw the absorption of some 2,000 FFI officers into the French Army. Incorporated, too, was a substantial part of Vichy's officer corps, mostly the junior and field-rank officers who had kept their heads below the political parapet during the Occupation.[54]

Inconvenient as it was, the traditions of the old regiments were incontestably sustained after 1945, mostly by the retention of former Vichy officers. De Gaulle tacitly acknowledged this reality. Immediately after the Second World War, therefore, the Army-Nation tradition survived within a confection of an officer corps. This corps owed more to its antirepublican antecedents, its mythic self-image as guardian of 'the nation', than de Gaulle could publicly acknowledge. The old had not been replaced by the new—at best, it had been subsumed within it.[55] More persuasively, one might argue that it had been grafted like the surviving stem of a disfigured and sundered shrub. The resulting hybrid officer corps contained a strong strain grown from the old political residues of the rightwing and Vichyite sympathizers. This freely circulated after 1946 within the branches of the Fourth Republic's army. In particular, it affected the outlook of officers of the Foreign Legion, the *infanterie de marine* and the colonial forces, men whose attitudes were seldom watered by the more republican currents of metropolitan public opinion.[56]

The schisms of 1940 had opened a Pandora's Box, although this was not widely appreciated in 1945. Officers and politicians supposed for a time that they could revert smoothly to older patterns of authority. They preferred to regard the Fall of France as an aberration, its political consequences a divisive nightmare from which society had woken up and moved on. 'When the war in Indochina broke out', wrote Mitterrand in

1957, 'France was able to believe that the 1940 defeat was nothing more than a lost battle, and that the armistice of 1945 was going to restore its power at the same time as its glory.'[57] In fact, it was a trauma of transforming significance. The unity between the army and the political regime from 1945 to the early 1950s was more apparent than real. In the shrewd words of Guy Chapman, 'none perceived that with the abdication of the Republic [in 1940], the question of loyalty was thrown open.'[58]

However, this could not long be disguised as stresses were created by new wars against indigenous independence movements; and, as many French officers persuaded themselves, against the global march of communism. It was disastrous that the French army was assigned missions of colonial pacification and counter-insurgency— an inevitably politicized kind of warfare—within the broader context of the ideological Cold War between east and west.[59] This occurred not once but twice: in Indochina (1946-54) and Algeria (1954-62).[60] In both instances, as in 1914, as in the diplomatic defeats of 1936-38, and as in 1940, senior French officers sought to account for military failure through explanations that were extraneous to the military issues at hand.

The generals were temperamentally, educationally and psychologically unable to conduct a professional analysis of their own military performance. They were also incapable of the fundamental self-evaluation which might have revealed the irrelevance of military 'solutions' to conflicts that were rooted in political struggle.[61] In Indochina, a generation of incredibly courageous French field officers were powerless to prevent their inept and arrogant higher commanders losing the battle for Dien-Bien-Phu. These field officers then had to watch peace talks unfold at Geneva, in which the government of Pierre Mendès-France conceded the loss of the war for Indochina.[62]

Conflict in the Far East cost the French expeditionary corps 75,200 killed and missing, 20,700 of them metropolitan French.[63] Among those who returned to France were some profoundly radicalized and deep-thinking majors and colonels. They included Hélie Denoix de Saint-Marc, Antoine Argoud, Charles Lacheroy, Jean Gardès, Yves Godard, Roger Trinquier and Marcel 'Bruno' Bigeard.[64] Some had been among the 10,754 non-Indochinese prisoners of the Vietminh released after the signature on 21 July 1954 of the Geneva accords (6,132 of them being admitted immediately to hospitals because 'their physical state recalled that of the survivors of the Nazi camps').[65] All had been dealt haunting first-hand lessons in counter-insurgency, revolutionary war and indoctrination.[66]

In the mid 1950s, often as disillusioned with their own generals as with the politicians in Paris, few officers asked, self-critically, whether a war against the Maoist guerrilla tactics of General Vo Nguyen Giap could have been 'won' by a military corps trained in western traditions of strategy.[67] Much of the French professional army instead responded to defeat in Indochina by articulating an even more hostile view of their governments and of the despised Fourth Republic. General Paris de Bollardière criticized it because, 'instead of coldly analysing with courageous lucidity its strategic and tactical errors, it gave itself up to a too-human inclination and tried—not without reason, however—to excuse its mistakes by the faults of civil authority and public opinion.'[68] Many believed that sacrifices in Asia had been sabotaged by those ruling in France. In the summation of General Boyer de Latour, Commissaire de la République for North and South Vietnam: 'the loss of Indochina was due to the incoherence of our politics under the Fourth Republic, to military errors resulting in part from the regime.'[69]

A particularly potent accusation from some senior officers in 1954-55 was that defeat had been accepted without any government initiative to allow the deployment of conscripts outside metropolitan territory. Many officers on active service believed that, because the Indochina War was only ever the concern of a small number of professional and colonial troops, it had lacked the support of the metropolitan population. Denied sufficient troop strength and a connection to French public opinion (which field commanders unthinkingly assumed would be supportive), Indochina veterans formed the view that the army had been obliged to fight with one hand tied behind its back.[70]

These cadres did not have time to analyse the lessons of defeat and withdrawal in Indochina before a new nationalist insurgency plunged them into Algeria.[71] There, on 1 November 1954, the Armée de Libération Nationale (ALN) commenced an armed struggle for independence.[72] Within 18 months, French commanders secured the use of the reservists and conscripts denied them in Indochina. Algeria was legally a part of France and thus there was no constitutional barrier this time to deployment of the metropolitan army. From May 1956, in a dramatic widening of the war's ferocity and its social impact in France, conscript draftees were shipped south to Algeria.[73] Paradoxically and controversially, the decision was that of a 'Government of Republican concentration' formed four months earlier, under the Socialist Party's leader Guy Mollet, precisely to negotiate an *end* to the war. Political authority had again bent the knee, Mollet cravenly permitting his policy to be reversed by pressure from the settlers, backed by 'ultras' in the army.[74]

The situation in Algeria differed fundamentally from the limited war France had waged in Indochina. In south-east Asia, a small professional army had been decoupled from metropolitan public opinion and politics, and French soldiers had always been thin on the ground. But in Algeria there was no shortage of troops. And in Algeria the nation-in-arms was once again engaged.[75] This was a war that directly affected millions of metropolitan French families: wives of reservists, mothers and sisters of conscripts, electors and taxpayers.[76]

Partly because the war had such a high profile, prominent officers continued to challenge politicians over the direction of national policy. Others continued to intrigue against the regime. The mid 1950s witnessed many high-ranking resignations or early retirements, usually orchestrated to attract maximum coverage from sympathetic newspapers. Among those to depart were Marshal Juin, and General Zeller, the Inspector General of the Army, later a participant in the attempted April 1961 Algiers putsch against de Gaulle. Another was Boyer de Latour, the Resident-General in Tunisia and Morocco while the Protectorates prepared for the independence to which Mendès-France's ministry had agreed in 1954. For publishing *Vérités sur l'Afrique du Nord* in 1956, condemning the regime's entire Maghreb policy, Boyer de Latour found himself summarily retired by a government which, only months before, had promoted him to *général d'armée*. Further embittered, he inveighed in a second book published just as de Gaulle extricated France from Algeria against 'the traitors at home' who, 'with the tacit complicity of the civil power, supported the enemy.'[77]

How could this disaffection and anger among the generals come about in spite of the employment of the reserves and conscripts? Perhaps the answer is that it occurred precisely because of it. For the war's escalation in 1956 crucially raised the stakes for the military. Jean-Jacques Servan-Schreiber, publisher of the news-magazine *L'Express*, called up as a reservist lieutenant for service in Algeria, was warned in the autumn of that year by one hard-bitten officer, Major Marcus:

> It just is not possible—mark my words, *not possible*—for an army of five hundred thousand Frenchmen, the biggest that's ever gone overseas, backed by the efforts of the entire country, with all France's resources at its disposal, to stand by indefinitely with folded hands, watching itself being defeated or dishonoured. No, this time it's not just the Indochina expeditionary corps that's involved—-this time it's the whole country. Remember this: what with the reservists, the conscripts and regular

armymen, it's an entire generation that's passing through our hands. We're turning them into moral failures, sometimes into monsters.[78]

By the time Servan-Schreiber's six-month tour of duty was over, in January 1957, ruthless counter-insurgency tactics had been extended to the cities of Oran, Constantine and Bône. These reached a climax from April to December 1957 in General Massu's 10th Parachute Division's urban 'cleansing operations' known as the Battle of Algiers.[79] House-arrests and sweeps of the souks and casbahs were backed by threats to FLN/ALN detainees' families, to turn nationalists into agents of French counter-intelligence, and by the torture of detainees.[80] The 'dirty war' of the paras and police was condemned within France by academics, writers and reservists such as André Mandouze, Pierre Vidal-Naquet, Georges Mattéi and Robert Bonnaud. Both inside and outside formal politics, passions ran high. Families were divided. French methods attracted opprobrium from liberal newspapers around the world, and were censured in the General Assembly of the United Nations.[81] The episode damaged France's good name as the 'Land of the Rights of Man'. In narrowly military terms, admittedly, FLN urban terrorist cells and intelligence networks were all but eliminated.[82] But as Paul Teitgen, secretary-general at the Algiers prefecture remarked: 'All right, Massu won the Battle of Algiers; but that meant losing the war.'[83]

Furthermore, Mollet's defeat in the National Assembly in May 1957 plunged France into renewed governmental turmoil. In the next eleven months three more prime ministers, Maurice Bourgès-Maunoury, Félix Gaillard and Pierre Pflimlin, came and went with bewildering speed. The changes re-emphasized the fragility of civilian authority in the Fourth Republic, and they prompted senior officers in Algeria, notably a former Indochina Commander-in-Chief, General Raoul Salan, to flex their political muscles again. Colluding with Gaullist agents, in May 1958 the army in Algeria imposed the restoration of de Gaulle to power.[84] It acted in this way because the very conduct of the war against the Front de Libération Nationale (FLN), the political wing of Algerian nationalism, had gradually intoxicated many professional officers with what has been termed the 'narcotic of revolutionary war'.[85]

During his first 18 months back in power, de Gaulle appeared to encourage the quest for military victory. The army 'had settled itself somewhat bureaucratically into the war' during Salan's command.[86] To inject a new impetus into operations, de Gaulle appointed General Challe as Commander-in-Chief. Bluff and plain talking, Challe scored a series of notable military successes between April 1959 and April 1960.

The FLN political cadres had to flee to Morocco, Tunisia and Egypt. Their armed wing, the ALN, suffered unprecedented casualties in battles in the desert *bled* as well as in the Atlas and Aurès mountains. In the 'Challe Plan', which the general directed in person, aggressive divisional-scale operations were mounted, codenamed *Courroie*, *Etincelles* and *Jumelles*, supported by helicopters and tactical air power.[87] At the same time the Morice Line, a trip-wire barrier separating Algeria from Tunisia, was electrified and protected by searchlights and mines. Patrolled by heavily armed French motor columns, it almost choked off the supplies from outside Algeria which were essential to the ALN.[88] French field officers were swept by a new sense that military victory lay in their grasp. 'The military phase of the rebellion is terminated', claimed Challe.[89]

Yet, during 1960, it also emerged that de Gaulle's representatives were secretly negotiating at Evian-les-Bains with the FLN for Algerian independence. By March 1962, a ceasefire was in place and by July that year an independent Algeria had been born.[90] Bewildered, many French military commanders complained of a sell-out.[91] As in previous crises, some generals, led this time by Salan, Challe and Edmond Jouhaud (a *pied-noir*), thought what had occurred was a political betrayal. The settlers certainly did not hesitate to label de Gaulle's abandonment of French Algeria as 'treason'.[92] For many officers serving in Algeria at the time of Evian, France stood humiliated for the third time in 20 years because of lassitude, decadence and failure of political will.

Proponents of 'revolutionary war' had been given their head in the field. In tactical, military terms, they claimed great success.[93] But this was a counter-insurgency war.[94] And the use of torture, psychological warfare, 'brain washing', double-agents and the resettlement of the indigenous Moslems made it impossible to win hearts and minds. This, in turn, made the war itself unwinnable.[95] Field commanders, in John S. Ambler's judgment, should have 'viewed revolutionary-guerrilla war in less manipulative terms' and 'given more attention to grievances actually felt.' For even 'when acting as agents of reform French officers were inescapably aliens working with an unassimilated native population.'[96] Few could face such an unpalatable truth.[97]

Almost reflexively, therefore, they denounced de Gaulle, the public face of the regime. In so doing, many officers displayed another recurrent trait of the modern French military elite's politicization. De Gaulle was censured and despised for assuming formal political office, as Boulanger had been in 1886-87. It did not matter that, a mere three years earlier, many of these same officers had pressed him to do so. De Gaulle's conduct was regarded as underhand, if not downright treacherous.[98] Believing that they had recalled him expressly to help clinch victory in Algeria, the officers were aghast at his abandonment of the struggle, especially coming after unparalleled military success.[99]

De Gaulle, however, interpreted his mandate in an infinitely more flexible manner. His ambition was to liberate France, a second time, on this occasion from the shackles of the 'war without a name', to permit the national recovery of 'grandeur'. As he stated when nominating a new, impeccably Gaullist, Commander-in-Chief for Algeria, General Fernand Gambiez, to prepare the January 1961 referendum on Algerian self-determination: 'The war was all but over. Military success was achieved. Operations had been reduced to next to nothing. Instead, politics dominated the scene.'[100] This was for de Gaulle so natural, normal and essential, as to be almost unremarkable.

In June 1940, Weygand had insisted, as a matter of personal honour, that the sordid game of politics was not something he played—even as he was refusing to seek terms from the Germans or resign his post. He refused to see just how singular a political role he had appropriated to the High Command, in burying the Third Republic's last democratic government.[101] And similarly, 20 years later, the officers who participated in the April 1961 Algiers Putsch, or who joined the illegal Organisation Armée Secrète (OAS) to employ terror in the effort to halt de Gaulle's abandonment of French Algeria, were also those who most trenchantly denied that their conduct was in any way 'political'.[102] Discussing his choice in favour of insurrection in 1961-62, a company commander of the 1st Foreign Legion Parachute Regiment (a unit deeply embroiled in the Algiers putsch and, on this account, disbanded afterwards by de Gaulle), Captain Pierre Sergent, argued that it had been worse than 'when our elders had torn themselves between de Gaulle and Pétain', because '*many of us* believed that it was a matter quite simply of choosing between de Gaulle *and France*.'[103] It therefore demanded the ultimate and self-consciously political general, de Gaulle, to drive out the political inclinations of the officer corps.

The flirtations between French career officers and explicitly political forces and movements, usually of the right, in the first six decades of the twentieth century had a recurrent feature. This was the inclination of officers to stray from a 'professional' approach, whenever they faced crises of national security. Time and again, French officers set aside short-comings in their systems of selection, education, training, doctrinal development and operational planning. Those who did identify these problems within a military analytical framework dared not, or could not, speak out.

Gamelin, as noted earlier, kept quiet in the late 1930s about the shortcomings riddling the French army for fear of losing the country's few remaining allies. Marc Bloch, while serving as a reservist officer in 1939-40, saw much to cause him alarm. But he could record his 'statement of evidence' only after the Fall of France.[104] And in Algeria in late 1956, Servan-Schreiber recorded the same syndrome. He recounted how Major Marcus told him that the army was 'behaving like idiots almost everywhere', and implored Servan-Schreiber, the journalist to, 'see that all this is made known. We are a silent service, we haven't the means to communicate.' Servan-Schreiber promised that after his discharge he would do what he could, but warned the regular officer:

> You must know that the army in Algeria has been turned into a national taboo to which you can only pay compliments. Anyone who criticized its methods would immediately be suspected. We're in a vicious circle; soldiers, whose opinion on the way the army's being used would carry great weight, can't make their opinion known; civilians, when they talk, are discredited.[105]

After an earlier conversation with Captain Julienne, another officer, Servan-Schreiber noted that, 'No one knows better than the army itself the harm that is being done to the army of Algeria by some of its generals.'[106] Julienne lamented that, 'behind the communiqués, with their daily dozens of "*fellagha* killed and arms captured" the entire Arab population is joining the resistance against us. Aren't there any high-ups, civilians or soldiers, who can see that day by day we are building up the classic conditions for a disaster?' Marcus replied that many higher ranks knew these truths. But people were, 'lying from the top to the bottom of the ladder. Lying has become second-nature here. You lie from a sense of duty, you see. Once you've got that far, there's no way out.'[107] Unable to analyse their own problems with candour, unfettered by the lack of integrity within the military institution, many officers again reverted to political rather than 'technical' explanations of France's predicament. 'It is a matter of record', remarks Ambler, 'that the colonels who were instrumental in military revolt were almost without exception enthusiasts and theorists of *la guerre révolutionnaire*.'[108]

Perhaps if the Weimar and Nazi German military was too insular and isolated, too blinkered, too narrowly and amorally 'professional', the failing of the modern French officer corps was the opposite one. It lacked a clear and professional self-definition. Normatively conditioned to expect only shiftiness, drift and default from civilian governments, French officers came to assume that it was their right, almost their sacred duty, to take a lead in policy making. They had a coherence, a common culture of the uniform, that successfully excluded independent, external, inquiries into their shortcomings and military blunders. The same bonding and background laid them open to the siren advances of right-wing politicians. For these figures represented, in the eyes of the military, the only reliable and disciplined force capable of implementing policies congenial to the upper officer corps.

The opportunities for the French political right from the Dreyfus Affair to the Algerian denouement existed because, until de Gaulle depoliticized them, French officers were never truly 'just military professionals'.[109] For decades, right-wingers supposed that they would find supporters among senior military officers if they staged a bid for power. To depoliticize all the officers required action by a general who had been schooled in both war and politics.

This took two stages. First, in 1960-61, the insubordinate officers in Algeria had to be disciplined. Significant progress had been made by March 1962. 'At the time of the cease-fire in Algeria', observed La Gorce, 'the military apparatus was gradually settling down to a definitive obedience to the state.'[110] The second stage required overwhelming and explicit popular authority. This was a power that de Gaulle possessed only once he secured a majority in the constitutional referendum of 1962 for the direct election of the president by universal suffrage.[111] The troubled spiritual wanderings of French career officers would end only when a politician who had himself begun as a career officer obtained 'sovereignty' through a constitutionally legitimized mechanism of mass politics.[112]

Genuinely empowered, de Gaulle refocused French popular and professional military thought about defence around an ancient, unchanging, uncontested national necessity. This was the protection of the 'Hexagon', the defence of metropolitan France and the adjacent French-garrisoned zone of Germany. 'With the end of the empire, the army lost its privileged terrain of manoeuvre. What de Gaulle did was replace it with the image of a modern army based on the possession of its own nuclear deterrent.'[113] The military focused on this metropolitan, European and nuclear role from the middle and later 1960s. The modern, nuclear armed forces renewed the faith of French officers in the worth of a military career, and renewed their belief that France was a great power.[114] This hugely facilitated de Gaulle's other objective of re-embedding them into 'the Nation', so that 'opportunity was provided for French officers to find a place once more in French society, from which they had too long remained separated.'[115]

By the time de Gaulle left the Elysée in 1969, he had conclusively exorcized the spectre of a rightist-military coalition assuming power in the manner of 1852, 1940 or 1958. The Fifth Republic instead constructed a new civil-military equilibrium, renewing the reciprocal understanding of the respective boundaries of civil and military authority. It did so, both in de Gaulle's era and between 1981 and 1995, under the general's adversary, Mitterrand, by embracing a modernized version of Jacobin patriotic nationalism. De Gaulle and Mitterrand both passionately loved to study France's past, especially its politics, its statecraft and its wars.[116] Each was keenly aware of the historic tensions between periods of authoritarianism and periods of republicanism in the post-1789 heritage, and of the army officers' importance in so many of the convulsive transitions between the two types of regime. So it can hardly be surprising that the Fifth Republic, under Mitterrand as well as under de Gaulle, should solve the question of the future of civil-military relations by recourse to the current in the past that had, since 1789, stood as the principal alternative to the narrow, socially and politically reactionary professional 'army apart from the nation'. The Fifth Republic depoliticized its officer corps by making it a part of the nation once more. From the 1960s to the 1990s career army officers, as much as the rank-and-file, again became, first and foremost, soldier-citizens.[117]

Notes

An earlier form of this essay was published as 'Loyalität, Autorität und Disziplin: Die französische Militärelite seit 1914 zwischen Professionalismus und Politik', in E.-W.Hansen, G.Schreiber and B.Wegner eds: *Politischer Wandel, organisierte Gewalt und nationale Sicherheit. Beiträge zur neueren Geschichte Deutschlands und Frankreichs. Festschrift für Klaus-Jürgen Müller* (Munich, 1995), pp 111-29. I am grateful to Professor J. F. V. Keiger of the University of Salford for help in identifying further references for this revised version.

1.   La Gorce, Paul-Marie de: *The French Army. A Military-Political History* (New York, 1963), p 252

2.   See Serman, William: *Les officiers français dans la nation, 1848-1914*
      (Paris, 1982); Bodinier, Gilbert et al.: *L'histoire de l'officier français des*
      origines à nos jours (St.-Jean-d'Angély, 1987); Martin, Michel: *Warriors*
      into Managers. The French Military Establishment since 1945 (Chapel Hill,
      1981).
3.   See, for example, Ralston, David B.: *The Army of the Republic. The Place*
      of the Military in the Political Evolution of France, 1871-1914 (Cambridge,
      Mass., 1967); his 'From Boulanger to Pétain: The Third Republic and the
      Republican Generals', in B. Bond and I. Roy, eds: *War and Society. A*
      Yearbook of Military History (London, 1976), pp 178-201; Horne, Alistair:
      The French Army and Politics, 1870-1970 (London, 1984).
4.   See Müller, Klaus-Jürgen: *Armee, Politik und Gesellschaft in Deutschland,*
      1933-1945 (Paderborn, 1979)]; his 'The Army in the Third Reich: An
      Historical Interpretation', *Journal of Strategic Studies* 2/2 (1979), pp 123-
      52; Geyer, Michael: 'The Crisis of Military Leadership in the 1930s',
      Journal of Strategic Studies 14/4 (1991), pp 449-62; his 'German Strategy
      in the Age of Machine Warfare, 1914-1945', in P. Paret, ed: *Makers of*
      Modern Strategy. From Machiavelli to the Nuclear Age (Princeton, 1986),
      pp 527-97 and his 'Professionals and Junkers: German Rearmament and
      Politics in the Weimar Republic', in R. Bessel and E. Feuchtwanger, eds:
      Social Change and Political Development in Weimar Germany (London,
      1981), pp 77-133.
5.   Geyer: 'The Crisis of Military Leadership', pp 452-6
6.   See Bankwitz, Philip C. F.: *Maxime Weygand and Civil-Military Relations*
      in Modern France (Cambridge, Mass., 1967); his 'Maxime Weygand and
      the Fall of France: A Study in Civil-Military Relations', *Journal of Modern*
      History 31/3 (1959), pp 225-42; Jauffret, Jean-Charles: 'The Army and the
      Appel au Soldat, 1874-1889', in R. P. Tombs, ed: *Nationhood and*
      Nationalism in France. From Boulangism to the Great War, 1889-1918
      (London, 1991), pp 238-47.
7.   Pétain's radio broadcast to the French nation on 22 June 1940, for example,
      announced that France had been defeated and forced to seek an Armistice
      because it had been fighting Germany with 'too few arms, too few allies, too
      few children'. See, too, Gamelin's infamous attempt to shift blame for High
      Command failures onto the rank-and-file soldiery in his report of 18 May
      1940. Gamelin, General Maurice: *Servir* (Paris, 1946-47), vol 3, pp 421-26.
8.   Cairns, John C.: 'International Politics and the Military Mind: the Case of
      the French Republic, 1911-1914', *Journal of Modern History* 25/3 (1953),
      p 282
9.   Cairns: 'International Politics', p 282
10.   Cairns: 'International Politics', p 282
11.   Cairns: 'International Politics', pp 283-4
12.   Joffre, Joseph-J.-C.: *Mémoires du maréchal Joffre, 1910-1917* (Paris, 1932),
      vol 1, pp 58-9

13. Cairns: 'International Politics', p 284
14. Pétain's allegations about low quality and poor fighting spirit in French reservist units in 1914 occur in: Conseil Supérieur de la Guerre (CSG), Séance du 18 décembre 1933: procès verbal', Service Historique de l'Armée de Terre (SHAT), carton 1N 22, vol 17, p 42. The matter is well dealt with in Kiesling, Eugenia C.: *Arming Against Hitler. France and the Limits of Military Planning* (Lawrence, 1996), pp 99-104.
15. Cairns: 'International Politics', p 284
16. Joffre: *Mémoires,* vol 1, p 58
17. Bankwitz, Philip C. F.: 'Maxime Weygand and the Army-Nation Concept in the Modern French Army', *French Historical Studies* 2/2 (1961), pp 157-88
18. See Garrigues, Jean: *Le général Boulanger* (Paris, 1991).
19. Joffre: *Mémoires*, vol 1, p 61
20. Chapman, Guy: 'The French Army and Politics', in M. Howard, ed: *Soldiers and Governments. Nine Studies in Civil-Military Relations* (London, 1957), p 65
21. Quoted in La Gorce: *The French Army*, pp 191-2
22. La Gorce: *The French Army*, pp 180-96
23. See Griffiths, Richard: *Pétain* (London, 1970), pp 127-70.
24. See Alexander, Martin S.: *The Republic in Danger. General Maurice Gamelin and the Politics of French Defence, 1933-1940* (Cambridge, 1993), pp 27-30, 34-76.
25. Griffiths: *Pétain*, pp 160-4, 169-72, 189-95
26. Nobécourt, Jacques: *Une histoire politique de l'armée* (Paris, 1967), vol 1, p 206
27. Griffiths: *Pétain*, p 152
28. See Simard, Marc: 'Doumergue et la réforme de l'état en 1934: la dernière chance de la troisièmer république', *French Historical Studies* 16/3 (1990), pp 576-96.
29. See such contemporary contributions as Bardoux, Jacques: 'La réforme de l'état', *Revue des deux mondes* 26 (March, 1935), pp 268-86; Blum, Léon: *La réforme gouvernementale* (Paris, 1936)..
30. Cited in Nobécourt: *Une histoire politique de l'armée,* vol 1, p 206. See, too, Griffiths: *Pétain*, pp 189-95.
31. See Bankwitz: *Maxime Weygand and Civil-Military Relations*, pp 108-9; Cornet, Jean-Perrier: 'Le maréchal Pétain et le problème du commandement unique, 1931-1936', *Guerres mondiales et conflits contemporains* 168 (1992), pp 51-7.
32. Requin, General Edouard: *D'une guerre à l'autre, 1919-1939* (Paris, 1949), p 182
33. Nobécourt: *Une histoire politique de l'armée,* vol 1, pp 206-7
34. See Griffiths: *Pétain*, pp 171-86; Nobécourt: *Une histoire politique de*

l'armée, vol 1, pp 238-9, 247-8; Warner, Geoffrey: *Pierre Laval and the Eclipse of France* (London, 1968), pp 135-9. See, too, Gamelin's reflection, near the end of his life, that 'It's undeniable that Marshal Pétain rendered great service to France. But when one was alongside Joffre, Foch and Lyautey one had the impression they were supermen. It was not the same with Pétain: it was desperately sad that he ended up as an ambitious old dodderer.' (Gamelin, 'Les causes de nos revers en 1940', pp 9-10, undated, signed typescript from 1956 or 1957, in Fonds Gamelin, 1K 224, Carton 7, SHAT).

35. Nobécourt: *Une histoire politique de l'armée*, vol 1, pp 153-9, 166-7

36. Bankwitz: *Maxime Weygand and Civil-Military Relations*, pp 49-289

37. Bankwitz: *Maxime Weygand and Civil-Military Relations*, pp 36-115; Destremau, Bernard: *Weygand* (Paris, 1989)

38. Cited in Nobécourt: *Une histoire politique de l'armée*, vol 1, p 208. See CSG, 'Séance tenue le 15 janvier 1935 au Ministère de la Guerre, sous la présidence de M le Ministre de la Guerre: procès-verbal. Exposé par M le Général Weygand, Vice-Président du Conseil Supérieur de la Guerre, Inspecteur Général de l'Armée, de certaines considérations relatives à l'état présent et futur de l'Armée française', Carton 1N 22, vol 17, pp 60-7, SHAT.

39. See Romains, Jules: *Sept mystères du destin de l'Europe* (New York, 1940), pp 68-9, 80-99; Liebling, Abbot Joseph: *The Road Back to Paris* (New York, 1988), pp 25-33.

40. Gunsburg, Jeffery A.: 'General Maurice-Gustave Gamelin, 1872-1958', in P.H.Hutton, ed: *Historical Dictionary of the Third Republic* (Westport, 1986), vol 1, pp 412-13. For Weygand's dissemination of his political and military ideas during the years of his retirement from 1935 to 1939, see his articles: 'L'état militaire de la France', *Revue des deux mondes* 35 (15 Oct. 1936), pp 721-36; 'L'armée d'aujourd'hui', *Revue des deux mondes* 45 (15 May 1938), pp 325-36. See, also, Bankwitz: *Maxime Weygand and Civil-Military Relations*, pp 208-89.

41. See Nobécourt: *Une histoire politique de l'armée*, vol 1, p 202 and Alexander: *The Republic in Danger*, pp 88-91.

42. See Alexander: *The Republic in Danger*, pp 132-4.

43. Le général Gamelin, lettre à M le ministre de la Défense Nationale et de la Guerre, le 8 juin 1938, no. 2633/S, in Fonds Gamelin, 1K 224 Carton 8, dossier labelled 'Organisation du Haut Commandement (Notes de principe, 1935-1938)', SHAT

44. See Kiesling: *Arming against Hitler*, p 104; Alexander: *The Republic in Danger*, pp 103, 381-2.

45. Héring deposition for the Supreme Court of Justice (19 March 1942) reproduced in Soupiron, Paul: *Bazaine contre Gambetta, ou le procès de Rion*(Lyons, 1944), p 189; Bourret, General Victor: *La tragédie de l'armée française* (Paris, 1947), pp 129-31

46. Gamelin: *Servir*, vol 2, pp 280-1
47. Villatte, Colonel Robert: 'Le changement de commandement de mai 1940', *Revue d'histoire de la deuxième guerre mondiale (RHDGM)* 2/5 (Jan 1952), pp 27-36; Reussner, André: 'La réorganisation du haut commandement au mois de mai 1940', *RHDGM*, 3/10-11 (June 1953), pp 49-59
48. Gamelin: *Servir*, vol 3, p 486
49. Warner: *Pierre Laval*, pp 158-77
50. Monzie, Anatole de: *Ci-devant* (Paris, 1941), p 230; Beaufre, General André: *Le drame de 1940* (Paris, 1965), pp 240-1
51. See Pertinax: *Les fossoyeurs. Défaite militaire de la France. Armistice. Contre-révolution* (New York,1943) vol 2; Challener, Richard D.: 'The Third Republic and the Generals: The Gravediggers Revisited', in H.C.Coles, ed: *Total War and Cold War. Problems in Civilian Control of the Military* (Columbus, 1962), pp 91-107.
52. See Paxton, Robert O.: *Parades and Politics at Vichy. The French Officer Corps under Marshal Pétain* (Princeton, 1966), pp 3-94, 183-213, 253-81.
53. Chapman: 'The French Army and Politics', p 69
54. *De Gaulle et la nation face aux problèmes de défense, 1945-1946. Colloque organisé par l'Institut d'Histoire du Temps Présent et l'Institut Charles-de-Gaulle, les 21 et 22 octobre 1982* (Paris, 1983)
55. Paxton: *Parades and Politics*, pp 410-32
56. Ambler, John S.: *Soldiers against the State: the French Army in Politics, 1945-1962* (New York, 1966); Kelly, George Armstrong: *Lost Soldiers. The French Army and Empire in Crisis, 1947-1962* (Cambridge, Mass, 1965), pp 13-30, 54-75
57. Quoted in Horne, Alistair: *A Savage War of Peace. Algeria, 1954-1962* (London, 1977), p 175
58. Chapman: 'The French Army and Politics', p 69
59. Typical of contemporary soldierly analyses of the defeat of 1940 contextualized within the renewed civil-military crisis brought on by the war in Algeria and the crumbling authority of another political regime, the Fourth Republic, is Boucherie, General Marcel: 'Les causes politiques et morales d'un désastre: 1940', *Revue de défense nationale* 14 (March 1958), pp 409-16. On the post-1945 reflections of the commander of the French 5th Army in 1939-40, see Bourret: *La tragédie*, pp 125-34, 209-17.
60. An excellent overview is Clayton, Anthony: *The Wars of French Decolonization* (Harlow, 1994); see also Betts, Raymond F.: *France and Decolonisation, 1900-1960* (London, 1991), pp 63-113; Ruscio, Alain: *1945- 1954. La guerre française d'Indochine* (Brussels, 1992).
61. Kelly: *Lost Soldiers*, pp 31-90
62. Folin, Jacques de: *Indochine, 1940-1955. La fin d'un rêve* (Paris, 1993), pp 233-91; Randle, Robert F.: *Geneva 1954: The Settlement of the Indochinese War* (Princeton, 1969)

63. Folin: *Indochine*, p 290
64. See Horne: *Savage War of Peace*, pp 165-78; Beccaria, Laurent: *Hélie de Saint-Marc* (Paris, 1988); Argoud, Colonel Antoine: *La décadence, l'imposture et la tragédie* (Paris, 1974); Godard, Colonel Yves: *Les trois batailles d'Alger* (Paris, 1972), vol 1; Trinquier, Colonel Roger: *La guerre moderne* (Paris, 1961); Bigeard, General Marcel: *Contre-guérilla* (Paris, 1957); his *Pour une parcelle de gloire* (Paris, 1975); and his *De la brousse à la jungle* (Paris, 1994).
65. Folin: *Indochine*, pp 290-1
66. See the classic account of the experiences of a prisoner of the Vietminh after Dien-Bien-Phu in Pouget, Jean: *Le manifeste du camp no. 1* (Paris, 1991).
67. Kelly: *Lost Soldiers*, pp 91-106; Pimlott, John: 'The French Army: From Indochina to Chad, 1946-1984', in I.F.W. Beckett and J. Pimlott, eds: *Armed Forces and Modern Counter-Insurgency* (London and Sydney, 1985), pp 46-76.
68. Quoted in Horne: *Savage War of Peace*, p 176. For an example of the jaundiced analysis emanating from French commanders implicated in the Dien-Bien-Phu catastrophe see Navarre, General Henri: *L'agonie de l'Indochine* (Paris, 1956).
69. Boyer de Latour: *Le martyre de l'armée*, p 275
70. See Ruscio, Alain: 'French Public Opinion and the War in Indochina, 1945-1954', in M. Scriven and P. Wagstaff, eds: *War and Society in Twentieth-Century France* (New York, 1991), pp 117-29; Horne: *The French Army and Politics*, pp 73-7.
71. Marill, Jean-Marc: 'L'héritage indochinois: adaptation de l'armée française en Algérie (1954-1956)', *Revue historique des armées* 187/2 (June 1992), pp 26-32; Pellissier, Pierre: *Saint-Cyr, génération Indochine-Algérie* (Paris, 1992)
72. See Jauffret, Jean-Charles: 'L'armée et l'Algérie en 1954', *Revue historique des armées* 187/2 (June 1992), pp 15-25; 'The Origins of the Algerian War: The Reaction of France and its Army to the Emergencies of 8 May 1945 and 1 November 1954', in R.F. Holland, ed: *Emergencies and Disorder in the European Empires after 1945* (London, 1994), pp 17-29
73. After decades of neglect, much is now being written about the experiences of the reservists and draftees. See Bergot, Erwan: *La guerre des appelés en Algérie, 1956-1962* (Paris, 1980); Sigg, Bernard W.: *Le silence et la honte. Névroses de la guerre d'Algérie* (Paris, 1989); Stora, Benjamin: *La gangrène et l'oubli. La mémoire de la guerre d'Algérie* (Paris, 1991): Lemalet, Martine: *Lettres d'Algérie, 1954-1962. La guerre des appelés, la mémoire d'une génération* (Paris, 1992); Rotman, Patrick and Tavernier, Bertrand: *La guerre sans nom. Les appelés d'Algérie, 1954-1962* (Paris, 1992); Fleury, Georges: *Appelés en Algérie* (Paris, 1992).
74. See Horne: *Savage War of Peace*, pp 147-52; Clark, Michael K.: *Algeria in Turmoil. A History of the Rebellion* (New York 1959), pp 259-88.

75. For the functions that French republicanism imputed to obligatory military service as the organizing basis for the national army, see Challener, Richard D.: *The French Theory of the Nation-in-Arms, 1866-1939* (New York, 1955).

76. Talbott, John: 'French Public Opinion and the Algerian War: A Research Note', *French Historical Studies* 9/2 (1975), pp 354-61; Smith, Tony: 'The French Colonial Consensus and People's War, 1946-58', *Journal of Contemporary History* 9/4 (1974), pp 217-47.

77. Boyer de Latour: *Le martyre de l'armée*, p 11

78. Servan-Schreiber, Jean-Jacques: *Lieutenant in Algeria* (London, 1958), pp 58-9. A perceptive discussion of fault-lines opened within the French military because of the deployment of the reservists and conscripts is in Evans, Martin: 'The French Army and the Algerian War: Crisis of Identity', in Scriven and Wagstaff, eds: *War and Society*, pp 147-61.

79. Massu, General Jacques: *La vraie bataille d'Alger* (Paris, 1971); Horne: *Savage War of Peace*, pp 183-219

80. Horne: *Savage War of Peace*, pp 258-61

81. First-hand statements include Rey, Benoîst: *The Throatcutters* (London, 1961); Alleg, Henri: *The Question* (London, 1961); Vidal-Naquet, Pierre: *Torture: Cancer of Democracy. France and Algeria, 1954-62* (Harmondsworth, 1963); Behr, Edward: *The Algerian Problem* (Harmondsworth, 1961). An autobiographical novel of the experiences of a reservist who spent six months in Algeria in 1956 is Mattéi, Georges M.: *La Guerre des gusses* (La Tour d'Aigues, 1994). See his: 'Jours Kabyles (Notes d'un rappelé)', *Les temps modernes* (July 1957), pp 138-59. For historians' analyses, Horne: *Savage War of Peace*, pp 195-202, 231-5, 243-7, 415-17; Wall, Irwin M.: 'The French Communists and the Algerian War', *Journal of Contemporary History* 12/3 (1977), pp 521-43; and Joly, Danièle: *The French Communist party and the Algerian War* (London, 1991), pp 42-67, 100-44.

82. Valuable overviews of the war include O'Ballance, Edgar: *The Algerian Insurrection, 1954-1962* (London, 1967); Talbott, John: *The War Without a Name. France in Algeria, 1954-1962* (London, 1981); Droz, Bernard and Lever, Evelyne: *Histoire de la guerre d'Algérie* (Paris, 1982); Le Mire, Henri: *Histoire militaire de la guerre d'Algérie* (Paris, 1982). A rich first-hand account is Kettle, Michael: *De Gaulle and Algeria, 1940-1960. From Mers el-Kébir to the Algiers Barricades* (London, 1993). Essential for the war's international ramifications and impact on French society is Rioux, Jean-Pierre ed: *La guerre d'Algérie et les français* (Paris, 1990).

83. Quoted in Horne: *Savage War of Peace*, p 207

84. See Rémond, René: *1958, le retour de De Gaulle* (Brussels, 1983); Rudelle, Odile: *Mai 58. De Gaulle et la république* (Paris, 1988)

85. Alexander, Martin S. and Bankwitz, Philip C. F.: 'From *Politiques en Képi*

to Military Technocrats: De Gaulle and the Recovery of the French Army after Indochina and Algeria', in G.J. Andreopoulos and H.E. Selesky, eds: *The Aftermath of Defeat. Societies, Armed Forces and the Challenge of Recovery* (New Haven, 1994), p 96. See, also, Girardet, Raoul: 'Civil and Military Power in the Fourth Republic', and Trinquier, Colonel Roger: 'Modern Warfare', both in C.S. Maier and D.S. White, eds: *The Thirteenth of May. The Advent of de Gaulle's Republic* (London, 1968), pp 108-47; Vidal-Naquet, Pierre: *Face à la raison d'état. Un historien dans la guerre d'Algérie* (Paris, 1989), pp 214-17; Bankwitz: *Maxime Weygand and Civil-Military Relations*, pp 363-4; Lemalet: *Lettres d'Algérie*, pp 283-94; Kelly: *Lost Soldiers*, pp 107-25, 126-42, 235-52.

86. Cointet, Michèle: *De Gaulle et l'Algérie française, 1958-1962* (Paris, 1995), p 65

87. Cointet: *De Gaulle*, pp 64-6.See Challe, General Maurice: *Notre révolte* (Paris, 1968), pp 91-128; Horne: *Savage War of Peace*, pp 330-40

88. Horne: *Savage War of Peace*, pp 263-5

89. Quoted in Horne: *Savage War of Peace*, p 339; and Clayton: *Wars of French Decolonization*, pp 159-61

90. Carréras, Fernand: *L'accord FLN-OAS. Des négociations secrètes au cessez-le-feu* (Paris, 1967); Buron, Robert: *Carnets politiques de la guerre d'Algérie* (Paris, 1965)

91. See Meisel, James H.: *The Fall of the Republic. Military Revolt in France* (Ann Arbor, 1962); Menard, Orville D.: *The Army and the Fifth Republic* (Lincoln, 1967); Vaïsse, Maurice: *Alger, le putsch* (Brussels, 1983).

92. See Perez, Jean-Claude: *Le sang d'Algérie* (Paris, 1992)

93. Ambler: *The French Army in Politics*, pp 308-36

94. See Kelly: *Lost Soldiers*, pp 143-95. One senior officer, General de Bollardière, was placed under arrest for 60 days after publishing an unauthorized protest in Servan-Schreiber's *L'Express* in March 1957 at the army's use of torture (the resulting publicity seriously embarrassing Mollet's government). From 1957, doubt and demoralization affected junior officers and other ranks as evidenced in Horne: *Savage War of Peace*, pp 203-4; Lemalet: *Lettres d'Algérie*, pp 267-301.

95. Ambler: *The French Army in Politics*, p 316

96. Ambler: *The French Army in Politics*, p 318

97. But see the words of Company Sergeant-Major Gambert, to Servan-Schreiber: 'What we're doing doesn't make any sense. We might be living in a Communist caricature, we're turning all the inhabitants into *fellagha*. For one rebel we kill, we're making 20 ready to replace him.' And those of Julienne: 'I've seen enough here to be convinced that what they're making us do here is leading straight to the loss of Algeria.' (*Lieutenant in Algeria*, pp 50-1, 54)

98. See Garrigues: *Boulanger*, pp 34-116, 356-60; Porch, Douglas: *The March to the Marne. The French Army, 1871-1914* (Cambridge, 1981), pp 50-3;

Ralston: *Army of the Republic*, pp 167-73, 178-80, 187-94; Planchais, Jean: *Le malaise de l'armée* (Paris, 1958); Fauvet, Jacques and Planchais, Jean: *La fronde des généraux* (Paris, 1961).

99.   See Furniss, Edgar S., Jr.: *De Gaulle and the French Army. A Crisis in Civil-Military Relations* (New York, 1964); Maier and White, eds: *The Thirteenth of May*, pp 213-390.

100. Quoted in Horne: *Savage War of Peace*, pp 424-5. See Debré, Michel: *Entretiens avec le général de Gaulle, 1961-1969* (Paris, 1993), pp. 17-55; Peyrefitte, Alain: *C'était de Gaulle* (Paris, 1994), pp. 48-91

101. See Nobécourt: *Une histoire politique de l'armée*, vol 1, pp 217-18, 221-4, 226-30; Bankwitz: *Maxime Weygand and Civil-Military Relations*, pp 362-79; Beaufre: *Le drame*, pp 258-66.

102. See Challe: *Notre révolte*; Zeller, General André: *Dialogues avec un général* (Paris, 1974); Gandy, Alain: *Salan* (Paris, 1990); *Le procès du Général Raoul Salan. Sténographie complète des audiences. Réquisitoire. Plaidoiries. Verdict* (Paris, 1962); Minella, Alain-Gilles: *Le soldat méconnu. Entretiens avec le général Massu* (Paris, 1993). On the OAS, there are now many memoirs and histories, the best of the latter being Delarue, Jacques: *L'OAS contre de Gaulle* (Paris, 1981); Kauffer, Rémi: *L'OAS. Histoire d'une organisation secrète* (Paris, 1986); Harrison, Alexander: *Challenging de Gaulle. The OAS and the Counterrevolution in Algeria, 1954-1962* (New York, 1989); Duranton-Crabol, Anne-Marie: *Le temps de L'OAS* (Brussels, 1995).

103. Sergent, Pierre: *Lettre aux officiers* (Paris, 1975), p 57

104. Bloch, Marc: *Strange Defeat. A statement of evidence written in 1940* (New York, 1968)

105. Servan-Schreiber: *Lieutenant in Algeria*, pp 54-5

106. Servan-Schreiber: *Lieutenant in Algeria*, p 48

107. Servan-Schreiber: *Lieutenant in Algeria*, p 55

108. Ambler: *The French Army in Politics*, pp 325-6. For key examples of thinking among the 'activist' officers of 1960-2, see Beccaria: *Hélie de Saint Marc*; Sergent, Pierre: *Je ne regrette rien* (Paris, 1972), pp 228-403; his *Lettre aux officiers*, pp 55-64; Kuntz, François: *L'officier français dans la nation* (Paris, 1960); Bastien-Thiry, Geneviève, ed: *Jean Bastien-Thiry. Sa vie. Ses écrits. Témoignages* (Paris, 1973); Labadie, Gilbert: *Bastien-Thiry, mon camarade* (Paris, 1989); Müller-Blessing, Inge and Müller, Klaus-Jürgen: 'Ehre und Gewissen. Zur Motivation eines katholischen Attentäters', in A.E.Hierold and E.J.Nagel, E. Josef, eds: *Kirchlicher Auftrag und politische Friedensgestaltung* (Stuttgart, 1995), pp 165-77.

109. General Victor Bourret, military Chief of Staff to War Minister Daladier in 1936-37 and 5th Army commander in 1939-40, reflected after the Second World War that, 'The two powers, civil and military, lived in parallel universes, without either one infusing the other, some of the time in a state

of semi-incomprehension and mistrust. The soldier had the last word, when all was said and done. The Third Republic had allowed the supremacy of the civil power to fall to the distaff side.' (Bourret: *La Tragédie*, pp 130-2)

110. La Gorce: *The French Army*, p 547. Yet the hatred felt for de Gaulle by senior officers who regarded retreat from Algeria as a military and national catastrophe cannot be over-emphasized. In a book published in October 1962, seven months after the cease-fire, Boyer de Latour made an astonishing and deeply ironical comparison to show that, for him, de Gaulle has plumbed new depths of national disgrace: 'General Gamelin has tried in his memoirs to justify himself in terms of the defeat. He will remain, however, the man who was vanquished in 1940! From the events of this present time, General de Gaulle will remain the man who brought the Empire crashing down and caused the decadence of France, perhaps of the entire West.' (*Le martyre de l'Armée*, p 14)

111. See Kelly: *Lost Soldiers*, pp 373-81; Furniss: *De Gaulle and the French Army*, pp 147-79. See Martin: *Warriors into Managers*.

112. *Le Souverain* was the sub-title given by Jean Lacouture to the last volume of the French version of his biography of de Gaulle, published in the 1980s.

113. Evans: 'The French Army and the Algerian War', p 161

114. In February 1960, France's first atomic weapon test at Reggane in the Sahara was greeted by de Gaulle 'with joy, proclaiming that henceforth France was stronger and prouder.' Evans: 'The French Army and the Algerian War', p. 161

115. La Gorce: *The French Army*, p 551

116. For the broader impact of historic policy reflexes in French security thinking during the 1980s and 1990s see Keiger, John F. V.: 'France and International Relations in the Post-Cold War Era: Some Lessons of the Past', *Modern and Contemporary France* 3/3 (1995), pp 263-74.

117. See Furniss: *De Gaulle and the French Army*, pp 221-91; and Hernu, Charles: *Citoyen-Soldat* (Paris, 1977), an argument in this sense by the Socialist Party politician who was President Mitterrand's Minister for National Defence from 1981 to 1985. However, see the warning in 1975 by a bitterly anti-Gaullist former Foreign Legion paratroop captain (Sergent: *Lettre aux officiers*, p 169), that conscription had become 'useless, even harmful, and better to do away with it immediately than have it continue to mass produce anti-militarists', foreshadowing a fresh chapter in the relationship between the French and their military, opened with President Jacques Chirac's announcement in 1996 of an end to compulsory service in favour of professional forces by 2002.

9. COUNTER REVOLUTION BY CONSPIRACY, 1935-37

D.L.L. Parry

In 1935-37, a number of clandestine organizations were formed by right-wing civilians and soldiers, either to oppose a communist revolution or to stage an insurrection of their own. The main military network called itself the 'Corvignolles' while the most important civilian body, the Organisation Secrète d'Action Révolutionnaire Nationale (OSARN), was nicknamed the 'Cagoule', in mockery of the hoods its members were supposed to wear at their secret meetings.[1] But the Cagoule's actions and intentions were far from laughable, for it carried out a number of terrorist attacks and murders and took its plans for a coup d'état to the brink of execution, thus leading France to the edge of civil war.

The Cagoule's importance has been consistently underestimated by historians for several reasons. To begin with, too much was made of it in the post-war trials; Pétain's relations with members of the Cagoule before the war featured in the *acte d'accusation* against him in order to imply complicity in a plot to overthrow the Third Republic dating from the 1930s.[2] Historians subsequently, and correctly, dismissed this interpretation as a conspiracy theory but overcompensated for it, so that by 1965 Georges Lefranc's standard history of the Popular Front came close to doubting its very existence, allowing only that the Cagoule had tried to seize power in November 1937 'd'après certains témoignages'.[3] The unreliability of evidence discouraged historians from taking stories about the Cagoule and Corvignolles too seriously, especially since there were relatively few political repercussions when the leading Cagoulards were arrested in November 1937. In any case, the Cagoulards' fantasies about coups d'état appeared to lead to a dead-end: either their plans were purely defensive, to oppose a communist rising, or they planned to mount their own coup with military support, but could only secure this by convincing the High Command that a communist rising was imminent. Since there was no such communist threat and since the High Command knew that full well, the Cagoule's manoeuvres were doomed. If the Cagoule had taken to the streets without the pretext of a communist insurrection, it would have had no supporters and would have been broken by military opposition or a general strike.

However, the evidence available has improved in the past few years, and has made the extent of the Cagoule's operations clearer. The 'hardest' evidence comes from the weapons seized by police searches at a dozen addresses in and around Paris: nearly 250 machine-guns and automatic weapons; 300-400 army and hunting rifles; about 300,000 cartridges; and over 7,000 grenades.[4] Other evidence reliably mentions 300 Schmeisser submachine-guns seized by Belgian police from arms-traffickers,[5] and less reliably talks of 650 submachine-guns which were still in Spain in November 1937.[6] One must assume that there were other weapons held in the provinces too. Few underground or terrorist organizations would not envy these arsenals, the financial resources they imply, the number of men mobilized by the Cagoule, the links to senior army officers and the aid the Cagoule received from sympathetic foreign governments. Moreover, the Cagoulards were not entirely defensively minded, and could conceivably have attempted a putsch. While this would certainly have failed militarily, the subsequent train of events is harder to predict. The Easter Rising of 1916 in Dublin was launched by about 1,600 men answering the call of an organization which was, at that point, in decline; in military terms it was doomed—but its impact went way beyond the street-fighting of April 1916. What other events would have been set in motion by an attempted coup in France in November 1937?

Evidence about the Corvignolles and other military groups remains much less satisfactory, and will not improve for a long time—police investigators were under instructions not to question active officers, while the relevant army personal service records remain closed for several decades. The military groups were not planning to stage any revolutions of their own, only to act defensively against rebels from left or right; these officers did not consider the Third Republic, and especially the Popular Front government, capable of defending France, in which case they saw it as their duty to intervene covertly. Contacts between civilian and military conspirators were frequent and even intimate, but they were ultimately split by a question which ran through these years: was France's worst enemy Germany or communism? For the most part, the soldiers were primarily opposed to Germany, and the civilians were primarily opposed to communism.

Cagoulards and Corvignolles

The first sources of information about these clandestine bodies came from the post-Liberation trials, especially the 1948 trial of the Cagoule. Much of this information is available from the 'Cabinet René Bluet' papers; dossiers of the original investigations are held in the Archives de Paris.[7] A number of memoirs were published between 1946 and 1967, of varying credibility. Police memoirs include Jean Belin's personal account of life at the Sûreté Nationale, but his remarkable inaccuracy about 6 February 1934 does not inspire confidence; the memoirs of Louis Ducloux presented a standard account from a policeman's perspective. For the army, Loustaunau-Lacau and Groussard published their versions of events shortly after the war. Cagoulard memoirs are rarer; Henry Charbonneau provided some information, but not always as an eye-witness: he was a rank-and-file Cagoulard until he became Deloncle's secretary in 1938.[8] Tournoux's 1962 book was the first detailed study of the Cagoule, followed by Philippe Bourdrel in 1970. Further information came from Pierre de Villemarest (using the papers of his father-in-law, the insatiable conspirator and conspiracy theorist Dr Henri Martin) and Pierre Ordioni (with access to the private papers of some officers, notably Jean Chrétien).[9] De Villemarest and Ordioni both sympathized with the right (de Villemarest was in the Organisation de l'Armée Secrète [OAS]), and, alarmingly, both believed that the Synarchy plot was genuine.[10] An additional source was provided by the diary of Aristide Corre, published in 1971.[11]

The historiography of the subject was much improved by Bourdrel's 1992 edition (revised with access to police records and now naming its informants, notably Gabriel Jeantet and Jacques Corrèze), and by Pierre Péan's *Le mystérieux Docteur Martin*, written with the papers of Dr Martin and André Brouillard, an army intelligence officer.[12] There is now a substantial body of information on the Cagoule, but the Corvignolles remain much more shadowy.

The OSARN was founded by dissidents from the Action Française (AF). Attracted by the AF's verbal violence, they were repelled by its lack of serious revolutionary intentions, especially on 6 February 1934. At the end of 1935, 97 members were expelled for signing the 'Mémoire sur l'immobilisme', drawn up by Eugène Deloncle and Corre; these dissidents were mostly from the 17e section of AF, Deloncle's group, and the Camelots du Roi of the XVIe arrondissement of Paris, led by Jean Filliol. The dissidents formed the legal Parti National Révolutionnaire et Social in

February 1936, but the ban on leagues and a police search of its offices on 10 June ended its activity. Instead, the clandestine OSARN was formed in June 1936 (after the election victory of the Popular Front and at the height of the strikes), by Eugène and Henri Deloncle, Filliol, Corrèze and Jeantet. The OSARN was organized on military lines with four bureaux. The 1er Bureau (recruitment and discipline) was run by Eugène Deloncle and Corrèze; the 2e Bureau (information) was kept by Corre, though Dr Martin did much of the information gathering; the 3e Bureau (operations) was under Colonel Georges Cachier; the 4e Bureau (logistics) was briefly run by Henri Benoît, replaced by Jean Moreau de la Meuse. An 'Action' branch existed too, comprising Jeantet, Henri Deloncle, François Méténier, Corre and Maurice Duclos.[13]

A legal cover for the OSARN was provided by the Union des Comités d'Action Défensive (UCAD), an independent creation which was then incorporated into the OSARN's structure.[14] In addition, the leaders of a number of other nationalist groups affiliated to the OSARN without their members' knowledge. Police sources name the Cercle d'Etudes National-istes and the Office de Documentation Nationale et Social of Armand Crespin; the Centre d'Information et de Coopération of Lainey; the Comité de Rassemblement Antisoviétique of Jurquet de la Salle; the Front Lorrain; the Union Nationale des Combattants de la Seine; the Association des Milices Secrètes d'Action Révolutionnaire (alias the Milices Nationales) run by Corrèze; the Union des Enfants d'Auvergne and the Patriotes d'Auvergne of Clermont-Ferrand; Algérie Française; the Groupement Militaire Patriotique Français in Toulouse; and the Cercle Bleu-Blanc-Rouge of Hanus in Nancy.[15] Deloncle described his organization as being 'surtout un Etat-Major et un encadrement pour les troupes d'autres groupements qui lui étaient subordonnés.'[16]

Nine-tenths of those in the affiliated bodies detailed above had never heard of Deloncle, so the important question about the size of the OSARN was not how many self-confessed Cagoulards there were, but how many would have followed his orders into action. During the war, Deloncle boasted that he had 40,000 men in France, of whom 12,000 were in Paris, and 5,000 were ready for combat—but these figures were meaningless. More accurate numbers suggest around 2,000 men: the UCAD had 2,800 members according to the police; Corre's coded list of names, when seized by the police, contained about 1,260 entries; and, on 28 June 1937, he spoke in his diary of 'la grande faiblesse de nos effectifs dont les troupes de choc n'atteignent pas deux milles hommes.'[17]

The material resources of the Cagoule extended beyond their dozen or more arms caches and mundane items like clothing and laboratory equipment for germ warfare. Fortunately, their expert Rodiot failed in his attempts to get botulism samples from the Institut Pasteur.[18] Arms supplies came from diverse sources. Some were bought or stolen in France, or dug up from First World War battlefields; others came from Germany, Italy and Spain, via arms dealers or the Italian secret services, often diverted from the massive traffic in arms which supplied the Spanish Civil War. Deloncle was interested in a Rome-Paris-Madrid axis, and the OSARN worked closely with Italian and Spanish secret services: the Rosselli brothers were killed in return for 100 Beretta rifles. The post-war trial of the Italian counter-espionage chief Colonel Emanuele Santo revealed the extent of these connections, as did the refuges provided in Italy and Spain for fleeing Cagoulards in late 1937 (Filliol, Corre, Martin and Corrèze among others).[19]

The OSARN's terrorist activities form a familiar story, both because they were sensational events and because they formed the heart of the 1948 trial. Two of the Cagoule's arms-smugglers, Paul Jean-Baptiste and Maurice Juif, were murdered in October 1936 and February 1937 for defrauding the OSARN, and their deaths provided leads for the police. The other well documented events of 1937 were the murders of a Soviet banker, Dimitri Navachine, in the Bois de Boulogne on 25 January 1937; the murders of the Italian anti-fascist Rosselli brothers at Bagnoles-de-l'Orne on 9 June; the bombing of aeroplanes destined for the Spanish Republic at Toussous-le-Noble on 29 August; and the 'Etoile bombs' of 11 September, which destroyed the offices of the Confédération Générale du Patronat Français at 4, rue de Presbourg and of the Union des Industries Métallurgiques at 45, rue Boissière. These bombs, which killed two policemen, were meant to be blamed on the Parti Communiste Français (PCF).[20]

The worst event associated with the OSARN was an explosion at the Villejuif police laboratory on 26 January 1938, when 6,400 grenades and 150 kg of explosives seized from Cagoulard depots exploded accidentally, killing 14 people. The Cagoule has been accused of two additional 'provocations': the attack on Blum during the funeral of the royalist historian Jacques Bainville on 13 February 1936, and the Clichy riot of 16 March 1937. The attack on Blum occurred soon after the expulsion of Filliol's 17ᵉ équipe from the AF, and was intended to produce outrage against the AF. It succeeded, and several AF organizations were banned immediately afterwards. No conclusive evidence has been produced for this commonly repeated story. The men arrested for the attack said that they had followed a *chef d'équipe* and men wearing AF armbands, who formed part of the AF's *service d'ordre*. Paul Guichard, head of the Police Municipale, said that the AF was never allowed to provide its own *service d'ordre*; if this were true, it supports the provocation hypothesis.[21]

The Clichy riot occurred when communist-led Popular Front demonstrators attacked policemen who were protecting a legal meeting of the Parti Social Français (PSF). It left five civilians dead and 107 injured, 48 by gunshot; 257 policemen were hurt, 5 by gunshot. It was alleged that Corrèze boasted of having provoked this riot. According to the police investigation, the first shots were probably fired from the rear of the crowd when the bulk of the demonstrators were on a march away from the scene of the violence. The police also commented on the presence of many unknown faces in the crowd; these facts certainly allow for provocation by the Cagoule. However, the 'fusillade de Clichy' itself came from police reinforcements who had been stoned in their vans as they arrived from the other 19 arrondissements. This implies a much wider geographical scope than the Cagoule could have covered;[22] violence between demonstrators and police was common enough at that time, and a riot was possible without any extra provocation.

The culmination of the adventure of the Cagoule came on the night of 15-16 November 1937, when the OSARN mobilized its forces in Paris, either to prevent a communist coup or to mount a putsch of its own. That this mobilization took place is not in question. It led to the opening of a judicial investigation on 16 November and to a press communiqué from the Minister of the Interior, Marx Dormoy, on the 23rd, which declared that, 'C'est un véritable complot contre les institutions républicaines qui a été découvert les coupables s'étaient assigné pour but de substituer à la forme républicaine que notre pays s'est librement donnée, un régime de dictature précédant la restauration de la monarchie.'[23] Ironically, virtually identical words had been used by *Le Populaire* in February 1934 to describe the 6 February riot, which had not been an organized conspiracy but had in large part inspired Deloncle to form a real plot.[24] Deloncle attempted to convince the General Staff and ministry of war that a communist rising was under way through such well known and respected figures as General Dufieux (Inspector-General of the Infantry), Duseigneur, Lebecq (a Paris municipal councillor and president of the Union Nationale des Combattants) and Ernest Mercier. They, in turn, alerted Daladier (as Minister of War), Generals Gamelin, Georges, Jeannel and Prételat (military commander of the Paris region), and Colonel de Bellefond (of the Elysée palace military staff). However, neither these men, nor the Corvignolles, nor any other army contact, were persuaded, and the mobilized Cagoulards returned home in the early hours of 16 November.[25] Arrests followed in the following weeks, but the police investigation was so complicated that no trials had occurred by the time war began in 1939, and all the remaining prisoners were released, including Deloncle.

Some of the Cagoule felt betrayed by the refusal of their army contacts to support them—but what was the relationship between civilians and soldiers? The military organizations shared some of the same 'patrons', in the English rather than French sense: Marshals Pétain and Franchet d'Esperey, and General Lavigne-Delville. Pétain knew what was underway, but did and said nothing, while the other two actively encouraged the civilian and military plotters. A number of other senior officers may have approved of their actions, notably General Dufieux, who was a member of the Conseil Supérieur de la Guerre (CSG) along with Pétain and Franchet d'Esperey. Many of the officers involved in the military conspiracy were from Pétain's staff, including the leading army conspirator, Commandant Loustaunau-Lacau, and Captain Bonhomme, or were from the army's intelligence services, such as General Gérodias, Colonel Rivet and Captain Beaune (of the 2ᵉ Bureau), Captain Brouillard (head of the Paris military region's 2ᵉ Bureau), Chef de bataillon Schlesser (director of the Service Central de Renseignement [SR] of the 2ᵉ Bureau) and Charles de Cossé-Brissac (also of the SR). According to Pierre Péan, Loustaunau-Lacau drew many of these men together in a military 'société de pensée', known as 'les Sioux' from the pin they wore, which depicted a Sioux warrior.[26]

Loustaunau-Lacau and the other main figure in the military organization, Colonel Groussard, were concerned by the external threat of Germany and the internal threat of communist subversion. They gathered information about German rearmament from their contacts in military intelligence, and established a network of officers across France to supply them with information about communist cells in the army, which was then passed to their superiors in a bulletin. This activity began in 1935, when Groussard formed a secret network with Jean Chrétien (then a captain on the General Staff) which was approved by Franchet d'Esperey around September 1935. According to Chrétien, this network merged with the parallel organization of Loustaunau-Lacau—the Corvignolles—at the end of August 1936, though this conflicts with Loustaunau-Lacau's memoirs, which stated that he formed the Corvignolles in December 1936. Whatever the case, these three officers ran the network until Groussard was sent to Morocco and Chrétien to Dakar early in 1937. No figures have been given for its total membership.[27] Loustaunau-Lacau claimed that it broke up 150-200 communist cells before he was expelled from the army in 1938. It should be remembered that the PCF was never very active in the army, but Loustaunau-Lacau's definition of a communist cell was probably rather broad.

The Corvignolles had another purpose: to form the active arm of the Sioux in their plans to oppose a coup d'état. They believed that both the PCF and extreme-right militants were preparing a coup, which would have devastating consequences for French security against Nazi aggression. Their solution was to prepare a counter-coup to turn this to their advantage, and to establish a government of public safety under Pétain.[28]

Contacts between civilians and soldiers became frequent during 1937, but it was the nature of these contacts that mattered most. Here, the Cagoulards appear to have been over optimistic. For example, in his summary of 1937, Corre wrote that relations with the army had been good from June, when General Prételat had asked Deloncle for his support,[29] but according to Prételat, it was Deloncle who had asked for help which he, Prételat, had refused. On 29 September 1937, three OSARN-style explosives were placed outside Prételat's home, either to threaten him or to convince him of the communist menace; neither option suggests good relations.[30] Corre's diary entry for 8 July recorded that 'l'accord entre l'armée et nous est complet', and credited this agreement to technical discussions. Their contacts included the 2e Bureau, the 72 e artillery at Vincennes, the 30 e artillerie, the 182e régiment, the Orléans garrison, the 8 e chasseur à cheval and some members of the airforce.[31] Relations between the Cagoule and these units probably existed; that there was complete agreement between them is highly unlikely.

If there was an alliance between civilian and military conspirators, it was to be found in the 'Conseil Supérieur', described by de Villemarest, Ordioni and Péan from information left by Dr Martin, which brought together the Corvignolles, UCAD and OSARN.[32] The Conseil Supérieur originated from an encounter between Deloncle, Groussard and Martin, arranged by Lavigne-Delville. Lavigne-Delville had retired from the army in 1928, was a member of the directing committee of the veterans' association Décorés au Péril de leur Vie, and gathered information on the Comintern and PCF. According to Martin, this first meeting was at the end of February or the start of March 1936. Another encounter followed in June 1936, when each brought along their closest contacts to what became the first meeting of the Conseil Supérieur. It contained eight men: Eugène Deloncle, Filliol, Duseigneur, Groussard, Martin and two friends of his,

Professeur Vaudremer and Raphaël Alibert, then *maître des requêtes* on the Conseil d'Etat. The presence of the eighth member is disputable. Péan placed Colonel Heurteaux (an air-ace of the Great War) on the Conseil Supérieur, while de Villemarest and Ordioni claimed that he joined later, perhaps replacing Groussard at the turn of 1936-37; it was also claimed that the eighth member was the still-anonymous secretary-general of the Comité (or Syndicat) des Armateurs de France, another late addition according to de Villemarest.[33] However, the Corvignolles were directed by Loustaunau-Lacau after the departure of Groussard and Chrétien, and no account of the Conseil Supérieur placed Loustaunau-Lacau on it. The first attempts to bring Loustaunau-Lacau and the civilians together seem to have failed, before an understanding of sorts was reached at a meeting arranged by Franchet d'Esperey between Deloncle and Loustaunau-Lacau on 3 March 1937, which committed the Cagoule and Corvignolles to an exchange of information and men. Thus serving officers left the Cagoule for the Corvignolles, and vice versa for civilians. According to Chrétien, Loustaunau-Lacau had recruited from the Parti Populaire Français (PPF) while Groussard had links to the AF.[34] However, Ordioni mentions another argument between Loustaunau-Lacau and Deloncle on 8 May 1937, at a meeting of about 30 members of the Corvignolles, UCAD and OSARN, once again over the military's opposition to a coup which would endanger French security.[35] This fatal rift meant that there was no effective unified command between the conspiracies, whether a formal Conseil Supérieur existed or not. Meetings between the two sides became focal points for disagreement, not for joint command.

The restraint of the military conspirators persuaded the government not to enquire too closely into their activities. Gamelin suspected that Pétain, Franchet d'Esperey and Dufieux were aware of the clandestine organizations, but took no action against them; Daladier disciplined only Loustaunau-Lacau and Gérodias.[36] Loustaunau-Lacau claimed that he had had the approval of his superiors, but as long as his activity was limited to discussions of German military capacity, technical reforms and opposing communist subversion within army barracks, there was nothing of which they could disapprove. The officer corps in general would also have approved of these measures, given that many of them did not think that the Popular Front government or the parliamentary Third Republic were competent to defend France. While La Gorce felt that complicity between officers and the OSARN marked 'the moral rupture between an important segment of the army and the republican state', Alexander, Dutailly and

Attignies held that the officer corps remained loyal to the state because the state was France first and the Republic second.[37] This loyalty was increasingly conditional, as shown by the numerous relations between soldiers and the Cagoule, but these links were ultimately more conflictual than collaborative.

Counter revolution and Conspiracy

Counter revolution was synonymous with the right in the sense that the original 'right wing' of the French Revolution had opposed the revolutionaries of the 'left wing'. However, the nature of this counter revolution changed with the national and international context. By the 1930s, a republic was accepted by most of the right, the AF excepted. Although most of the OSARN's leaders began their political life in the AF, they seem to have abandoned royalism when they left. Corre alone records a meeting between Deloncle, Duseigneur and a representative of the Anjou branch of the royal family in Brussels on 27 March 1937, although this is not corroborated by any other source. It can, in any case, be assumed to have had no significant consequences.[38] However, the *parliamentary* regime of the Third Republic was detested by the far right. While calls for a more effective executive were common in the 1930s across the political spectrum, the Cagoule's preference was for an authoritarian government in the French tradition of *césarisme* and in the European context of fascism. The *césarisme* of Napoleon III, Boulanger or Déroulède veered between electoral politics and coups d'état; the Cagoulards had rejected electoral means entirely and were unequivocally bent on a coup. Their intended leader was Deloncle himself, while the Corvignolles would have made Pétain head of state.

The Cagoule opposed the revolution of 1917 far more than that of 1789. The Popular Front's electoral victory of 1936, with 72 communist deputies returned and over 12,000 strikes in the weeks following, convinced many nationalists that a communist revolution was imminent.[39] The Cagoule was formed in June 1936 to block such an insurrection. Deloncle knew that the Cagoule had to be, or appear to be, counter revolutionary in its tactics too, remembering that 6 February 1934 had been followed by a massive general strike and vast demonstrations by the left. When Filliol reproached Deloncle for his caution, saying that 'tu attendras qu'on vienne t'égorger chez toi. Il faut agir et agir rapidement', Deloncle replied that, 'Si nous descendons les premiers dans la rue, *personne ne nous suivra*: tandis que si c'est pour se défendre, tout le monde marchera.'[40] Many nationalists made what they called 'defensive' preparations in 1935-37,[41] but only the Cagoule sought to 'get retaliation in first'. By planning a paramilitary coup, it not only rejected electoral politics but also the tradition of the *journée*. Although the first *journées* of the French Revolution came from the left, Boulanger, Déroulède and the demonstrators of 6 February had appropriated this action, aspiring to a spontaneous, combined rising of 'the people' and the army; such an action was seen as legitimate because the people of Paris and the army were moral embodiments of the nation superior to the discredited representatives of the people sitting in the Palais-Bourbon. The failure of 6 February—and the success of October 1917—convinced Deloncle that spontaneous indignation was no match for well planned violence.

To mount a successful putsch one needed a conspiracy, and while other groups on the far right were secretive to a degree, none were as covert as the OSARN and Corvignolles. For example, the Croix de Feu prepared their motor-rallies using passwords and cryptic messages, but the rallies themselves were very public. The conspiratorial element was pyschological as well as tactical. The leaders of the Cagoulards and Corvignolles were obsessive conspiracy theorists, who believed that the world was run by a series of conspiracies, and that the best way to counter them was through one's own plot. In his royalist days, Dr Martin was asked by the duchesse de Guise how he should be rewarded in the event of a royalist restoration. He replied, 'En m'expédiant comme gouverneur à Tombouctou; c'est votre seule chance que je vous laisse tranquilles.' When Corre heard that the Soviet ambassador in Paris had been changed, he could not decide if this was a device of British freemasonry to have their man, Potemkin, working for them in Moscow, or if it was a Soviet ploy because the new ambassador, Suritz, was Jewish and therefore had access to Blum's government. After his election as deputy for the Basses-Pyrénées in 1951, Loustaunau-Lacau's first words were said be be, 'Enfin, je pourrai comploter à l'abri de l'immunité parlementaire.'[42]

Where should the OSARN be situated within the far right? Can it be dismissed as a small group of isolated extremists? The general political beliefs of the Cagoulards were little different from the rest of the far right of the 1930s. They were nationalists, nominally Catholic without being deeply religious, who desired a strong, authoritarian government. Their enemies were entirely predictable—communists, socialists, Jews, freemasons and deputies. They recruited from the AF, the Croix de Feu, PSF, PPF, Jeunesses Patriotes, Solidarité Français and a swarm of smaller extremist groups.[43] The OSARN's paramilitarism was equally unremarkable.

Some of the other groups favoured uniforms, like Marcel Bucard's Francistes; and, although the Croix de Feu eschewed uniforms, 'paramilitarism was an intrinsic part of the self-definition of the league's militants', who also practised 'mobilizations'.[44]

Where de la Rocque and Deloncle differed was the lesson they drew from the failure of paramilitary parades to stop the Popular Front's electoral victory. De la Rocque turned from parades to electioneering, and Deloncle turned to paramilitary action and terrorism. The success of the PSF after June 1936 showed that the far right as a whole preferred de la Rocque's solution, but many others were enticed into Deloncle's web, including Gaudiot, a former Volontaire National and PPF member, who joined some 'groupes d'auto-défense' around 1937, thinking that they belonged to the PPF, and was surprised to be arrested for membership of the Cagoule. He met Deloncle for the first time inside La Santé prison.[45] Verbal and physical violence were staples of the far right, and had a communist coup been attempted, it would undoubtedly have been opposed forcefully by many nationalists. As long as Deloncle insisted that he was only preparing 'auto-défense', he was in line with the leagues, PSF and PPF. De la Rocque and the AF warned their members against involvement with clandestine organizations. This was partly to defend their own interests as they competed for the same nationalist constituency as the OSARN and also because the AF never forgave renegades, fearing that the movement might be compromised by conspirators. But even if one accepts that de la Rocque and the AF were genuinely hostile to a putsch, it was clear that they did not trust all their supporters to be so scrupulous.

Given the scale of their arsenals and the lavish lifestyles of some Cagoulards, the OSARN must have received substantial backing from business leaders. The police could only guess at a total expenditure of 40-80,000,000 francs, but could not find the source of the funding, despite inspecting the bank accounts of a number of companies, including Michelin and Citröen. Deloncle and his aides had access to a number of companies as directors or shareholders, and through Jacques Lemaigre-Dubreuil (head of Huiles Lesieur and of a taxpayers' league) and Colonel Heurteaux (Franchet d'Esperey's representative), they gathered funds even more widely. Martin recalled collecting 3,500,000 francs from Michelin, while Corre credited a 'grand industriel de l'automobile' (Renault, this time) with a donation of 2,000,000 francs. The police also suspected Chantiers de St Nazaire, the Syndicat de l'Industrie Lyonnaise and Pont-à-Mousson.[46] A host of other companies have been named, though it is impossible to gauge the truth of these allegations. According to

Charbonneau, Heurteaux introduced Deloncle to de Peyrecare, director of Renault. Other alleged donors included Gibbs, Bernard of Revel, Pavin of Lafarge, Violet of Byrrh (Jeantet's brother-in-law), the bankers Mirabaud, Hottinguer and de Neuflize. Franchet d'Esperey personally gave 1-1,500,000 francs; Lemaigre-Dubreuil donated 1,000,000 francs himself while also gathering funds for Deloncle from companies in a multitude of industries: oil, coal, metallurgy, shipping, cosmetics, finance, aviation, commerce, textiles and electricity.[47]

What was the significance of this funding? Duseigneur and Deloncle presented themselves, with Franchet d'Esperey's blessing, as patriots with purely defensive aims, invoking the communist peril to encourage donations. Some businessmen may have paid them because they too were anti-communist, and others as a form of insurance; probably none would have approved of an armed coup. The Etoile bombs suggest that business leaders had ceased to be so generous by September 1937, when the menace of June 1936 had long since gone; the bombs were meant both to discredit the PCF and to frighten the *patronat*. If the OSARN's fund-raising had become nothing more than a protection racket, one can assume that businesses were not enthusiastic supporters.

Yet even if the Cagoule was more extreme than AF, the PSF and business leaders, did it mark the very limit of the political spectrum? In ideological terms, no, because it was neither fascist nor radical. The Cagoule was by definition not populist, and it had no interest in the aesthetics of the mass rally. Its ideal government was authoritarian, but with no cult of a charismatic leader; the regeneration it desired was technocratic not spiritual, rooted in the Ecole Polytechnique not the *Volk;* there were no left-wing antecedents to it; the Cagoulard seizure of power did not model itself on the Beer Hall putsch or the March on Rome, which were closer to the *journée* than to Trotsky's coup. The social background of many Cagoulards was outlined in the prosecution documents.[48] They came from the *classes moyennes* and the bourgeoisie; they were frequently highly educated; they included several highly decorated veterans of the First World War, and a number of officers in the Légion d'honneur. Deloncle was educated at the Ecole Polytechnique while Corre attended the Collège de France. Deloncle then became a naval engineer and was a director of the Chantiers de Penhoët (among other posts); Moreau de la Meuse was also a wealthy engineer, while Cachier left the ministry of finance to become a company director. Jeantet had been the president of the Etudiants d'Action Française, and later became a company secretary. Only a couple of the leaders had been badly affected by business failures, notably Henri Benoît and Moreau de la Meuse. In short, they were not the *déclassés* so prominent in many fascist movements, nor did they have the criminal records of many leading Nazis.

The absence of *déclassés* was perhaps not surprising since the OSARN was primarily an ideological movement, not a social one; but even in this respect their ideology was not so extreme. Many far-right movements attacked the decadence of bourgeois and capitalist society; the Cagoulards were bourgeois capitalists who wanted a political revolution in order to prevent a social revolution, to preserve their own social and economic interests. In their ideology and their social origins, the Cagoulards were placed well inside the right wing.[49] It was their methods—murder, terrorism and insurrection—which placed them at an extreme.

Better Hitler than Blum?

The French far right of the 1930s was torn between two hatreds: of Germany and of communism. Though army officers and civilians could be found on either side of this divide, soldiers tended to regard Germany as the main threat while civilians were more opposed to communism. This division split the military and civilian conspirators irrevocably. For example, the Cagoulards were unanimous in their support for the nationalist rebellion in Spain and in their hostility to the Soviet Union, while many of the 'Sioux' favoured the Spanish Republicans and approved of the 1935 Franco-Soviet pact as the best ways to counter Nazi Germany. The Spanish Civil War produced another clandestine operation, to smuggle arms to the Spanish Republic. It was run by the customs official Gaston Cusin working with the PCF's shipping company France-Navigation, and was approved by Pierre Cot, Vincent Auriol and Blum himself. While some members of the Deuxième Bureau helped Cusin to supply the republicans, others helped the Cagoule to disrupt his operations.[50] According to Grisoni and Hertzog, Blum's policy of non-intervention in Spain disguised arms-running on a vast scale, as Soviet weapons were shipped from the Arctic ports to Spain via France.[51] The novelistic style of Grisoni and Hertzog's book does not inspire confidence, but Burnett Bolloten commended it in his exhaustive study of the Spanish Civil War. Bolloten quoted two Soviet sources from 1974 which gave the following figures for arms shipped to Spain: half a million rifles, 362 or 347 tanks, 15,113 or 20,486 machine guns, 1,555 or 1,186 artillery pieces, 806 or 648 military aircraft. However, while he accepted that a sizeable amount of this material was shipped by France-Navigation, he continued to treat the policy of the French government as that of non-intervention, for it did not send substantial quantities of arms itself.[52]

The defeat of 1940 also forced the conspirators to choose between fighting France's internal or external enemies. It has been said that the Cagoule and Corvignolles were 'couillonnés par l'Histoire',[53] for they had hoped to begin the *révolution nationale* in order to save France from defeat by Germany, not to enact the revolution via this defeat. Only a few joined the resistance immediately, notably Maurice Duclos. Alibert, Charbonneau, Corrèze, Darnand, Deloncle, Filliol, Groussard, Heurteaux, Jeantet, Loustaunau-Lacau, Martin, Méténier and Vaudremer were all to be found in *vichyste* circles in 1940, hoping both to purge France from its enemies and to combat the German occupiers. As they realised that there was no Vichy 'double game', Groussard and Loustaunau-Lacau moved towards resistance (the former escaped to Britain in 1941, and the latter was deported to Germany in 1942) while many of the civilians went deeper into collaboration. Deloncle was shot on 7 January 1944 by Gestapo agents sent to arrest him for intrigues with Admirals Darlan and Canaris; Darnand, Filliol and Charbonneau finished the war in the Milice. On 11 October 1948, the prosecution of nearly 50 Cagoulards began. Corrèze, Jeantet, Méténier and Maurice Duclos were present (as a resistance hero Duclos had not been summoned, but he turned up voluntarily and unrepentant); 13 of those charged were absent, including Henri Deloncle, Filliol and Martin, while Eugène Deloncle, Franchet d'Esperey, Darnand, Duseigneur, Moreau de la Meuse and Corre were all dead. The jury acquitted Duclos and 11 others, while the harshest sentence was forced labour for life for the murder of the Rossellis, passed against Fernand Jakubiez. Several of those missing, including Filliol, were sentenced to death *in absentia*.[54] Undeterred by this, some of them, notably Martin, were still active against the Fourth and Fifth Republics on 13 May 1958 and in the Organisation de l'Armée Secrète (OAS).

The army's refusal to support Deloncle on 15-16 November 1937 also lay in its view that civil conflict was worse than a Popular Front government because it would expose France to aggression by Germany. This was one of several reasons given to minimize the importance of the Cagoule's mobilization. The others are that the PCF and Comintern had no intention of mounting an insurrection; that the Cagoule had no hope of fooling army intelligence that such an insurrection was imminent; and that, had the Cagoule begun a rising, it would have been crushed either by the army or by a general strike. However, it was far from certain that the Cagoule were doomed never to attempt a coup. There were several complications. First, the police were closing in. In September and October, they had arrested minor figures such as Michel Harispe and Henri Place; Corre's apartment was searched; and Deloncle himself was questioned. So one possibility was that Deloncle might have decided to act before it was too late. A second possibility was that Deloncle might have been convinced by Filliol's view: if the Cagoule did begin a civil war it would provoke the PCF into action; the army would be forced to intervene, and would surely side with the nationalists.[55] Yet further possibilities are raised by Péan. On the one hand, the Sioux deceived the Cagoule into exposing itself to the eyes of the Sûreté Nationale, because they deemed it to be dangerously turbulent; Loustaunau-Lacau was personally blamed for betraying the Cagoule, a charge he denied.[56] On the other hand, Péan has suggested that the OSARN was simply blinded by its own conspiracy theories. Charbonneau, who was 'mobilized' on the 15th but was not at the meetings of the leading Cagoulards, claimed that by November Deloncle was desperate for an opportunity to strike when Martin brought him news of a communist insurrection. He, and others, have described Martin as lacking one crucial quality necessary for intelligence-gathering, 'l'esprit critique', and that he believed the rumour of a rising, albeit without evidence.[57] Considering these possibilities, the Cagoule's failure to launch its putsch did not depend on racing certainties such as the lack of a communist threat or the army's distaste for insurrection, but on the better judgement of Deloncle, Filliol and Martin—which was far from certain.

Marx Dormoy's statement to the press, the arrest of many Cagoulards and the police investigation had little political impact, which has been taken to mean that they had no political significance. However, this depended on the circumstances of the time, not on any law of proportionality between cause and effect. The right wished to distance itself from the Cagoule as much as possible, and the government decided to leave the army outside the inquiry. While the Popular Front coalition would have made much of this conspiracy in 1935 or 1936, by late 1937 the Blum experiment had lost its momentum and was disintegrating from within. After the communiqué of 23 November, only one deputy spoke about the plot in the Chamber in 1937. René Dommange asked if it was not a diversion, and lamented the ill-treatment of imprisoned Cagoulards. As evidence for their terrorism grew, and especially after the Villejuif explosion, sympathy for them lessened.[58] Left-wing politicians barely mentioned the affair in the Chamber, although the left-wing press gave it much attention. It did not believe that Deloncle and Duseigneur were the real chiefs, and detected the hands of Tardieu, Laval, Doriot, royalists and/or the 'trusts', abetted by Germany and Italy.[59] This staleness of this list illustrated how the left was trapped in a rigid interpretation of politics, and was unable to appreciate the novelty of the Cagoule. 6 February 1934 had produced political repercussions far beyond the original significance of the event; paradoxically, the repercussions of 15-16 November 1937 fell far short of its real importance.

The adventure of the Corvignolles and the Cagoule showed just how little confidence military and civilian elites had in the parliamentary Third Republic, and the lengths some of the far right had gone to in preparing armed insurrection. These rebels were not a handful of *exaltés*, but were numerous, well armed and well connected, and they took France to the brink of a bloody civil conflict. In the end, they were disarmed by their own loss of nerve, by the Sûreté Nationale and by an often underestimated political weapon. An example of this came in a cartoon which depicted one woman saying to another that, 'On dit même qu'ils avaient construit un grand âne de bois, dans lequel les conjurés devaient entrer au Palais-Bourbon sans attirer l'attention.'[60] In France, ridicule has long been the best way to vanquish an opponent with minimum effort and maximum effect.

Notes

1. It was referred to as the Comité Secret d'Action Révolutionnaire when exposed in 1937 and during the 1948 trials. Maurice Pujo of the Action Française gave it the 'Cagoule' nickname.

2. *Le procès du Maréchal Pétain* (Paris, 1945), pp 25-6

3. Lefranc, Georges: *Histoire du front populaire, 1934-1938* (Paris, 1974 edn), p 263

4. Archives de Paris: 1434 W.219, reg. no. 37(A), letter from Etat-Major de l'Armée, 1ᵉʳ Bureau, no. 11999, 14 May 1940, to the Greffier of the Cour d'Assise de la Seine, records 242 automatic weapons, 333 rifles, 297,249 cartridges, 36 hand-guns. Archives Nationales (AN) 334 AP 74: 'Réquisitoire définitif' of 1939, p 221, records 324 automatic weapons, 304 rifles, 300,938 cartridges and 7740 grenades.

5. Ibid, p 111

6. According to Corrèze in exile. C. Bernadac, ed.: *Les carnets secrets de la Cagoule, par 'Dagore'* (Aristide Corre) (Paris, 1977), pp 242-3.

7. See AN: 334 AP 29 and 334 AP 74 for papers from the Cour de Justice and the Cour d'Assises de la Seine, especially the 1102 page 'Réquisitoire définitif'; Bibliothèque de Documentation Internationale Contemporaine (BDIC), Nanterre: F. Rés. 339/8/1-3 (Cour d'assises de la Seine, 'Affaire de "la Cagoule"', sessions of 12-24 November 1948), includes some

defence speeches; Archives de Paris dossiers are 212/79/3, articles 11-53, while 1434 W.291 Rég. no. 37(A) lists police seizures. Archive de Paris dossiers remain closed unless permission is granted by *dérogation*.

8. Belin, Jean: *My Work at the Sûreté* (London, 1950), esp pp 189-221; Ducloux, Louis: *From Blackmail to Treason* (London, 1958), pp 159-92; Loustaunau-Lacau, Georges: *Mémoires d'un français rebelle* (Paris, 1948), esp pp 87-128; Groussard, Georges A.: *Chemins secrets* (Paris, 1948), vol 1, esp pp 92-119, and his *Service secret, 1940-1945* (Paris, 1964), pp 77-100 for a slightly different version; Charbonneau, Henry: *Les mémoires de Porthos* (Paris, 1967), vol 1, esp pp 175-230.

9. Tournoux, Jean-Raymond: *L'histoire secrète* (Paris, 1973); Bourdrel, Philippe: *La Cagoule. 30 ans de complots* (Paris, 1973); Villemarest, Pierre de: 'La Cagoule dans légende', *Le charivari*, 7 (July-September 1969), pp 41-5; Ordioni, Pierre: *Le pouvoir militaire en France* (Paris, 1981), vol 2, pp 348-92.

10. Ordioni: *Le pouvoir militaire*, pp 375-82; Péan, Pierre: *Le mystérieux Docteur Martin, 1895-1969* (Paris, 1993), p 294, note 18, for de Villemarest's claim that Synarchy was part of an international technocratic conspiracy centred on the Fabian Society in London.

11. Bernadac: *Carnets secrets*

12. Bourdrel, Philippe: *La Cagoule. Histoire d'une société secrète du front populaire à la Ve république* (Paris, 1992); see, also, Freigneaux, Frédéric: 'La Cagoule: enquête sur une conspiration d'extrême droite', *L'histoire*, 159 (October 1992), pp 6-17.

13. This structure is generally agreed, except that Tournoux and Bourdel have Mertin as head of the 2e Bureau. Péan and Bernadac give it to Corre, on the evidence left by both Martin and Corre.

14. So much so that de Villemarest claimed that the OSARN's 2e and 3 Bureaux doubled for the UCAD as well; 'Cagoule', p 44

15. AN: 334 AP 74, 'Réquisitoire définitif', pp 233-63

16. Ibid, p 232

17. Ibid, p 235; Bernadac: *Carnets secrets*, p 97

18. Clothing supplies included 1,700 haversacks, over 1,000 mock-leather jackets and several hundred pairs of breeches. AN: 334 AP 74, 'Réquisitoire définitif', pp 230-2; for Rodiot, ibid, pp 313-14.

19. Tournoux: *Histoire secrète*, published a selection of documents from this and related trials, pp 324-61.

20. Though *L'Insurgé*, a publication close to the OSARN, reported the Etoile bombs as 'Bombes de police'—a sign of the hostility between the OSARN and the policemen hunting them. See Bernadac: *Carnets secrets*, diary entry for 14 September 1937, p 139.

21. Archives de la Préfecture de Police (APP): Ba 1648, dossiers '13 février 1936—obsèques de Jacques Bainville' and 'Agression sur Léon Blum'. According to Bernadac, Filliol once proposed to murder AF's leaders to get

the PCF banned. See Bernadac: *Carnets secrets*, pp 41-2.

22. Police report in AN: F⁷ 13985, 'Rapport Imbert', 23 March 1937. Fontenay, Fernand: *La Cagoule contre la France* (Paris, 1938), pp 105-6 on Corrèze. Bourdrel: *Cagoule* (1992 edn), pp 112-17 concludes that Corrèze did play a role in the events.

23. Reprinted variously, for example in Tournoux: *Histoire secrète*, pp 99-100. See Tournoux, Jean-Raymond: *Secrets d'état* (Paris, 1964), vol 2, *Pétain et de Gaulle*, pp 392-402 for documents on the mobilization, including Deloncle's statement to *juge d'instruction* Béteille on 31 December 1937.

24. 'C'était une véritable émeute, préparée, organisée avec soin, avec méthode, par les formations fascistes. C'était un complot armé contre le régime républicain', *Le Populaire*, 7 February 1934.

25. Fontenay: *Cagoule*, pp 162-4; Tournoux: *Histoire secrète*, pp 92-100; Bernadac: *Carnets secrets*, pp 252-3, 265, 269; Bourdrel: *Cagoule* (1992 edn): pp 210-13, 222-4; Péan: *Docteur Martin*, pp 161-5

26. For the Sioux, see Péan: *Docteur Martin*, esp. p 100; his information is from Brouillard's memoirs. As Ruth Harris notes, this name contrasted the noble Sioux warrior with *les apaches*, a colloquialism for ruffians.

27. Ordioni: *Pouvoir militaire*, vol 2, pp 348-58 on Groussard, Chrétien and the merger; pp 386-8 on the bulletin, which went to Dufieux, the Minister of War, the General Staff and CSG. It has been given various names, 'La Spirale', 'Le Barrage', 'Notre prestige français' and 'Baltimore'; some of these were presumably titles of particular numbers. See also Loustaunau-Lacau: *Mémoires*, pp 110-14, 124-5; Péan: *Docteur Martin*, pp 93-5.

28. Ibid., pp 99-101

29. According to Corre, they had met on 10 March without result, then Prételat asked for aid in June. See Bernadac: *Carnet secrets*, p 303. Cachier provided the link to Prételat according to BDIC: F.Rés.339/8/2, defence of Corrèze, p 34.

30. AN: 334 AP 74, 'Réquisitoire définitif', pp 271-2

31. Bernadac: *Carnets secrets*, pp 103, 112 (26 July) and 121-2 (11 August)

32. The archives of this body escaped the police searches of 1937 and, according to de Villemarest, are housed outside of France, while Ordioni suggests Switzerland; 'Cagoule', p 44, *Pouvoir militaire*, vol 2, pp 373, 536 (where Ordioni calls this body first 'Comité' then 'Conseil').

33. Péan: *Docteur Martin*, pp 96-8, 103-4; de Villemarest: 'Cagoule', pp 43-4; Ordioni: *Pouvoir militaire*, vol 2, pp 372-4

34. Loustaunau-Lacau: *Mémoires*, pp 114-16; Péan: *Docteur Martin*, p. 95

35. Ordioni: *Pouvoir militaire*, pp 389-90

36. Gérodias was dismissed to the provinces in January 1937 for circulating alarmist information about communist insurgency, provided by Loustaunau-Lacau. Gamelin, Maurice: *Servir* (Paris, 1946), vol 2, pp 259-66, 303-4; *Le procès du Maréchal Pétain*, pp 117-18.

37. La Gorce, Paul-Marie de: *The French Army. A military-political history*

(London, 1963), p 250; M.W. Attignies (a pseudonym): 'Complot franquiste: la Cagoule', *Cahiers Léon Trotsky*, 31 (1987), pp 79-102; Dutailly, Henry: 'Une puissance militaire illusoire, 1930-1939', in P. Contamine, ed: *Histoire militaire de la France* (Paris, 1992-4), vol 3, pp 347-62, esp 348, 361; Alexander, Martin S: 'Soldiers and Socialists: The French Officer Corps and Leftist Government, 1935-37', in M.S.Alexander and H. Graham, eds: *The French and Spanish Popular Fronts* (Cambridge, 1989), pp 62-78, and Alexander, Martin S: *The Republic in Danger. General Maurice Gamelin and the Politics of French Defence, 1933-40* (Cambridge, 1992), pp 80-109.

38. Bernadac: *Carnets secrets*, p 303 (in Corre's summary of 1937)
39. For example Bardoux, Jacques: *Les soviets contre la France* (Paris, 1936)
40. AN: 334 AP 74, 'Réquisitoire définitif', p 273. Evidence of Wiart to police; original emphasis.
41. Witness the exchanges between Jacques Duclos and Jacques Doriot after the Clichy riot (*Journal Officiel*, Chambre des Députés, Débats parlementaires, [*JO*] 23 March 1937, pp 1208-17), or a questionnaire sent to members of the Croix de Feu about their military experience, whether they owned any arms or a car (APP: Ba 1901, dossier 'Croix de Feu et Briscards', letter from Director of the Sûreté Nationale to the Prefect of Police, 15 June 1937, no. 7770).
42. Bourdrel: *La Cagoule* (1970 edn), p 334; Bernadac: *Carnets secrets*, pp 52-4; Tournoux: *Histoire secrète*, p 27 n
43. The police thought that they recruited more from AF than the PSF: AN 334 AP 74, 'Réquisitoire définitif', pp 68-70
44. Passmore, Kevin: 'Boy-Scouting for Grown-Ups? Paramilitarism in the Croix de Feu and the Parti Social Français', *French Historical Studies*, 19/2 (1995), p 542
45. AN: 334 AP 29, Cour de Justice, dossier 'Harispe, Delioux, Locquet, Gaudiot, Macon, Corrèze', 1st set of papers pp 18-20, 2nd set p 116. Delioux also unknowingly joined an association under OSARN control; 2nd set pp 3-5.
46. Péan: *Docteur Martin*, p 99; Bernadac, *Carnets secrets*, pp 102-3, 107, entries of 8 and 15 July 1937; Bourdrel: *La Cagoule* (1992 edn), pp 107-8, citing evidence of Méténier and Harispe, and police enquiries.
47. Loustaunau-Lacau: *Mémoires*, pp 114-16, specifies that d'Esperey gave to the Corvignolles and was less keen on the Cagoule; Charbonneau: *Mémoires*, vol 1, p 192; Ordioni: *Pouvoir militaire*, vol 2, pp 384-6
48. AN: 334 AP 74, 'Réquisitoire définitif', vol 2 (in alphabetical order)
49. Milza, Pierre: 'L'ultra-droite des années trente', in M. Winock, ed: *Histoire de l'extrême droite en France. XXᵉ siècle* (Paris, 1993), pp 157-89, thinks that the Cagoule was not fascist because of its respectable bourgeois origins and clientele, its counter-revolutionary ideology, and its plan for a militarist-paternalist regime under Pétain.

50. Péan: *Docteur Martin*, pp 129-34, 147-8
51. Grisoni, Dominique and Hertzog, Gilles: *Les brigades de la mer* (Paris, 1979)
52. Bolloten, Burnett: *The Spanish Civil War. Revolution and Counter Revolution* (Chapel Hill, 1991), pp 107-9, 155, 157, 798n; see 89-91, 176-7, 184, 803-4n on the non-intervention policy.
53. Ascribed to André Brouillard. Péan: *Docteur Martin*, p 101.
54. For the trial and reproductions of some of the evidence, see Bourdrel: *Cagoule* (1992 edn); Tournoux: *Histoire secrète* and *Secrets d'état*, vol 2
55. Bourdrel: *Cagoule* (1992 edn), pp 217-225, including the views of Corrèze.
56. Bernadac: *Carnets secrets*, p 202: Corre's diary entry for 15 November 1937 (after he had fled to Spain) quoted Jeantet on 'le trahison de Loustaunau'. See Loustaunau-Lacau: *Mémoires*, p 127.
57. Charbonneau: *Mémoires*, vol 1, p 194, 202-5; confirmed by Péan: *Docteur Martin*, p 113; de Villemarest defended Martin against this charge: 'Cagoule', p 41.
58. *JO*, Dommange on 4 December 1937, pp 2685-6, 2691-3; interpellation on Villejuif by Raymond Guyot, 4 February 1938, pp 230-2. Dommange was allied to the Fédération Républicaine; Guyot was a communist. Chautemps also referred to the plot in declarations made as premier, and other interpellations on the subject were placed but not debated.
59. For example, *La Lumière*, 26 November and 3 December 1937; *L'Humanité*, 19-22 and 25 November 1937; *Le Populaire*, 19-26 November 1937
60. Varé: *Gringoire*, 26 November 1937, p 5

10. CLASS, GENDER, AND POPULISM: THE PARTI POPULAIRE FRANÇAIS IN LYON, 1936-1940

Kevin Passmore

The Parti Populaire Français (PPF) was launched on 27-28 June 1936 in the Parisian suburb of Saint-Denis by Jacques Doriot, deputy of the constituency and one-time communist. The ambition of the PPF's founders was to build a mass movement that would transcend the division between left and right. In terms of national membership— possibly some 75,000 in the winter of 1936-37—the PPF experienced a certain success. But the party never rivalled its chief competitor on the far right, the Parti Social Français (PSF), which may have had as many as 600,000 members. Thanks to the collapse of the Third Republic in 1940, the PPF would not test its strength in a general election. Doubtless it would not have fared well, for it had not won any by-elections, and in 1939 membership had fallen to perhaps 50,000.[1] The level of support for the PPF in Lyon—the location of one of the party's more important sections—suggests that even these relatively conservative estimates of party membership were optimistic. The party only recruited a few hundred activists in the region and never matched the local PSF's membership of 20,000.[2]

The PPF has had a greater impact upon historians than it ever had upon the political scene of the Third Republic. One reason for historiographical interest is that some, notably René Rémond, have seen the party as the only mass fascist movement in interwar France.[3] Philippe Burrin suggests, on the other hand, that before 1940 the PPF contained a fascist potential that remained, for the time being, not fully realized. In his view, the PPF was a 'national-populist' movement. National-populism shares many of the features of fascism but, argues Burrin, it is ultimately demarcated by its 'reference to popular sovereignty'.[4] This distinction between a fascist and

183

a non-fascist radical right is potentially useful, for it might reveal something about the extent to which the PPF accepted the framework of the Third Republic's democracy and pluralism. However, a degree of conceptual refinement is needed, given Burrin's blindness to the centrality of the notion of the people in German, Italian and French fascism.[5] Greater emphasis should be made of the fact that fascists differed from other strands of the radical right in that they conceived the people in unitary, even totalitarian, terms, and coupled this to mass mobilization in a paramilitary formation.[6] In this essay, we shall see that the PPF imagined the people in reactionary and anti-pluralist terms, but did not fully realize its conceptions in the practical form of paramilitarism. It therefore hesitated between the fascist and non-fascist radical right.

A related reason for historical preoccupation with the PPF is that it had originated in a schism of the Parti Communiste Français (PCF). In Saint-Denis, many PCF activists, and at first many voters, were to follow Doriot on a political odyssey that was to end with exile among the ultras of collaboration in Bavaria in 1944-45. This highlights the issue of whether fascism, or the radical right in a more general sense, is essentially revolutionary or reactionary. Rémond and Brunet both see Doriot's communist past as *sustaining* the radicalism on which, in their view, the PPF's fascism depended. Conversely, Robert Soucy argues that Doriot *rejected* communism and developed a consuming hatred of it. For Soucy, the PPF's fascism lay in its authoritarianism, social conservatism, and dependence on big business money and middle-class votes.[7] The roots of the debate about whether fascism is revolutionary or reactionary lie in differing assumptions about the nature of social conflict. Soucy assumes that the principal axis of struggle is between capital and labour. He demonstrates convincingly that the PPF desired the destruction of the PCF and labour movement, and so in his terms the PPF must have been reactionary. Those, on the other hand, who see the PPF as radical, implicitly regard the mobilization of the 'people' or 'masses' against the state as the more fundamental source of tension. Both alternatives ignore the possibility that social conflict is organized simultaneously around several oppositions. The purpose of this essay is therefore to explore the PPF in the context of inter-related struggles concerning capital and labour, people and state, and gender.[8]

Antagonism between government and the governed need particular emphasis.[9] In one way or another, this antithesis shapes all modern societies. Yet only in certain historical circumstances, such as 1930s France, does the opposition of the people to the state, government, or 'establishment', become an explicit organizing principle of political struggle.

The concept of 'populism' encapsulates the resultant hostility to the established order of movements like the PPF, which aspired to the construction of a mass movement and a new kind of state—the *état populaire français*. It is, however, essential to stress that to describe the PPF as 'radical' does not mean that it was in any sense left wing. Populist opposition to the 'establishment' (in any case, a pliable concept) was cross-cut by class, gender and religious antipathies. Close inspection reveals that the PPF's idea of the people was inseparable from conservative views of gender and property relations. Yet, at the same time, its search for mass mobilization imparted a radical quality to its attitudes to labour relations and women that differentiated it from conventional parties of the right. Thus the PPF represented a synthesis of conservatism and radicalism: it was located on the far right of the political spectrum by its commitment to destruction of the left; it was also radical and populist because it sought to achieve its goals through mass mobilization against the 'establishment'.

The Political Origins of the PPF in Lyon

In the late 1930s, the city of Lyon and its satellite communes was home to some 750,000 people, only a handful of whom ever joined, or sympathized with, the PPF. Attraction to the party was not typical of any social group in the way that loyalty to the PSF was in some parts of the city. The task of situating the party in its local environment therefore poses delicate problems. The historian must take account of the more 'personal' circumstances which encouraged individuals to make the untypical choice of joining the PPF. But this does not absolve the historian from relating 'individual' motives to broader social pressures. This is all the more important because the PPF's programme did not, as William Irvine argues, differ radically from that of the PSF.[10] It is therefore possible to see both parties as products of the same general conditions. Both must be understood in the context of long-term changes in the social structure of Lyon, a related crisis of the right, and the social and political polarization of the mid 1930s. The PPF differed from the PSF in that it profited from the dissolution of the leagues and in its ability to attract a minority of supporters from the parties of the extreme left.

Until 1936, Lyonnais politics had been dominated by Radicalism, represented above all by Édouard Herriot, mayor of Lyon from 1905 until 1956, apart from the Occupation interlude. In the mid 1930s, the middle ground of politics in the city melted away. The Radical vote in Lyon and its communes fell from 28 per cent of the registered electorate in 1932 to

16 cent in 1936, with the loss of four of the party's seven seats. The chief beneficiary was the PCF, hitherto of marginal importance in the city. The communists gained votes in all working-class districts, and won seats in the 7th arrondissent of Lyon and the canton of Villeurbanne. [11] The advance of the extreme left was parallelled by reinforcement of the right, which increased its seats from one to three. Polarization was underlined by the victory of Pierre Burgeot in the 6th arrondissement. He was elected under the banner of the nationalist wing of the Fédération Républicaine, and had received support from the Croix de Feu. Although the Lyonnais right had, contrary to the pattern in the rest of France, gained both seats and votes, there was no mistaking its disarray. There had been a record number of dissident conservative candidates in the Rhône, while the Croix de Feu already attracted a considerable proportion of the conservative electorate. The weakness of the right was dramatically exposed when, on 18 June 1936, the new Popular Front government dissolved the leagues.

Bourgeois fears of revolution were reinforced by the strikes and factory occupations that spread across France in June 1936. In Lyon, the first major industrial action began on 8-9 June, when workers in large metallurgical firms such as Berliet downed tools. Strikes soon affected most sectors of the local economy. The peak of the movement was on 25 June, when there were perhaps 35,000 on strike. By 13 July, some 71,000 workers had been involved in strikes in Lyon and its suburbs—about half of the workers and employees in the conurbation. [12] In the wake of the strikes, there was an expansion in the membership of the CGT, which rose from 30,000 in 1935 to 200,000 in 1938. [13] Industrial strife continued until the defeat of the general strike of 30 November 1938. Particularly affected were the Gillet dyeing factories in Villeurbanne where there was a bitter conflict in the summer of 1937, and the building industry,which experienced a violent strike in August-October 1938.

The PPF, like the PSF, successfully emerged from this climate of an anti-communist panic and a disintegrating right. In terms of political origins, its membership can be divided into three unequal parts, all of which contributed to its blend of anti-communism and radical populism. [14] First, the great majority of PPF activists had not hitherto been politically active. It is likely that most had previously been right-wing voters, for in both of the two constituencies where the PPF stood under its own colours in the 1937 local elections, it gained almost exclusively conservative votes. [15] The leader of the Rhône PPF, Albert Beugras, must be included in this category. As the son of an army officer turned businessman, as a Catholic, and because of his 'belief in France' he had been 'inexorably destined for the right'. He had been a reader of *Gringoire* and especially *Je Suis Partout*, from which he had learned of the PPF.[16] Thus, like the Croix de Feu and PSF, the PPF was part of the mobilization of rank-and-file conservatives, frightened by the progress of communism, yet also doubtful of the ability of the right to deal with the Popular Front.

Second, the PPF recruited from the cadres of the recently dissolved leagues. Adrien Anscheling, former president of the Solidarité Française, joined the PPF. There were five former activists in Action Française. One ex-royalist told police in 1945 that he had been recruited by Paul Chartron, former leader of the Camelots du Roi, who had persuaded him that the PPF now represented the only means of continuing the anti-communist struggle.[17] Another four had belonged to the Jeunesses Patriotes, one of whom, Joanny Berlioz, had been the local president. The other three came to the PPF via the Francistes. The most notorious of these was Fernand Sape, who had put his journalistic talents at the service of the Jeunesses Patriotes, an obscure Maurrassian journal, *La Patrie Lyonnaise*, the Fédération Républicaine and the Francistes. Because of the dearth of sources, only two recruits from the Croix de Feu/PSF can be identified. There may well have been more for police reports suggested that in late 1936 several younger members of the PSF moved to the supposedly more dynamic PPF.[18] The moderate right, by contrast, was represented by only two individuals, both from the Christian democratic Parti Démocrate Populaire (PDP). One of them, Émile Roux, was a councillor in Lyon and a leading figure in the local veterans movement.

Beugras journeyed to Paris to meet Doriot shortly after the 'Rendez-vous de Saint-Denis', joining the PPF five days after its formation. Because Doriot knew nobody else in Lyon, Beugras was immediately named *délégué* for the south-east. He held his first meeting in Lyon on 7 July. Among the founder members were a number of former leaguers. In the summer of 1936, some of the latter had joined the obscure Comités de Rassemblement Anti-Soviétique (CRAS). CRAS had been intended as a front for the dissolved Francistes, but served as means of linking former members of all the outlawed leagues, and even included members of the Fédération Républicaine.[19] In the following months, CRAS members, such as Anscheling of Solidarité Française and Sape, the Franciste leader, joined the PPF.[20] The son of a sexton in the parish of St Pothin, Sape had worked his way up from a printer's job at the *Nouveau Journal* to become a journalist on the *Nouvelliste* in Lyon, subsequently working for news-papers in Brittany and St Etienne. In 1934, Marcel Bucard charged him with setting up a Franciste section in St Etienne. The next year, he returned to Lyon to found a Franciste journal, published as *L'Attaque* in April 1936. After dissolution of the Francistes, Sape became sympathetic to the PPF and, in June 1937, he joined Doriot's party, taking *L'Attaque* with him.[21]

We shall see that some of those who gravitated to the PPF from dissolved leagues were, like Sape, subsequently expelled from the party.[22] Nevertheless, ex-leaguers provided many of the cadres of the PPF, as well as the party journal. They also brought with them a long-standing anticommunism, together with a love-hate relationship with the parliamentary right. Like the dissolved leagues, the PPF attempted to balance denunciations of big capital and the right-wing establishment with a willingness to take money from the former and to collaborate politically with the latter. Distrust of the parliamentary right was reinforced by outright hostility to the PSF. The latter's predecessor, the Croix de Feu, had been the target of abuse from rival leagues for its supposed pusillanimity in the winter of 1935-36. The PSF was seen as even more moderate than its predecessor. In 1937-38, PSF/PPF relations declined to the point of violence.

It is possible to identify only three recruits from the left, two of whom had been PCF members. One was Francis André, known as 'guele tordue' because of his disfigurement. André took his talents as a sports journalist from the communist *Voix du Peuple* to *L'Attaque* where he wrote under the pseudonym 'Andrex'. Like Doriot, André was to fight with the Légion des Volontaires Français contre le Bolchevisme (LVF). In Lyon, he became notorious as an organizer of the armed wing of the PPF in 1942-45.[23] A second communist, Ennemond Chambon, secretary of the regional CGT metallurgy union, joined in 1939 in protest against the Nazi-Soviet Pact. Joseph Desgeorges had been a member of Gaston Bergery's Front Social and secretary of the building section of the anarcho-syndicalist Confédération Générale du Travail Syndicaliste et Révolutionnaire (CGTSR).[24] The example of Lyon thus suggests that the proportion of ex-communists in the PPF has been exaggerated.[25] For the level of attraction to the PPF claimed by some historians to have been real, there would have had to have been far more dissidence in the PCF across France—in Lyon there is no evidence of any significant support for Doriot. In effect, the PCF quarantined Doriot in Saint-Denis.[26] Studies of the PPF in Marseilles and the Alpes-Maritimes confirm the failure of the party to bite into PCF support. Even in Saint-Denis, Doriot gradually lost the backing of left-wing voters as he moved to the right.[27] All the same, there is reason to suppose that the number of ex-communists in the Lyon PPF is understated by the sources: the database on which this study draws, contains only militants of conservative parties, making it easier to trace right-wing itineraries. Even though they were a minority, the presence of former communists in the PPF must be taken seriously, for there was no equivalent in any other party of the right. Ex-communists brought with them the anti-communist fury of recent converts, while retaining an hostility to elites.

The PPF clearly originated largely on the right and extreme right—even the previously non-active had probably been right-wing voters. Like the PSF, the PPF sprang from the hostility of rank-and-file conservatives to the left and to their own leaders, who were perceived as incapable of combating the left. Their antipathies were reinforced by the presence of former leaguers. Nevertheless, these were not the only routes to the radical right and fascism. The shift of the Saint-Denis communists to the far right, parallelled by a minority in Lyon, shows that the radical right could also originate in a crisis of the left. In this case, the contradictory nature of the right-wing populist movement derived from the desire to destroy the PCF while retaining an oppositional stance.

Social Origins

The complex mixture of radical-populism and reactionary anti-communism that inspired the PPF can also be seen in the occupational backgrounds of PPF members. Since the mission of the PPF was to mobilize the masses in a new formation that would transcend differences of class, status and wealth, it claimed that its members were representative of the population in general.[28] The reality was different. The sociology of PPF sympathizers must be explained in terms of the crisis of the right and extreme right referred to above, and of the changing socio-economic structures of Lyon.

During the Third Republic, the economy and society of Lyon was transformed. In the 1870s, the economy had been based on the manu-facture and trading of silk textiles. The organization of the silk industry remained pre-industrial, reliant on merchant capital and artisan producers. By the 1930s, the city had felt the full weight of the Second Industrial Revolution. The silk industry had turned to the production of artificial fibres in huge factories located in satellite communes such as Vaulx en Velin. New sectors also appeared. Large chemical works such as Rhône-Poulenc were located to the south of Lyon, especially in St Fons. The engineering and electrical industries also expanded rapidly, rising from 25,000 employees in 1914 to 44,000 in 1930. The Berliet lorry plant in Vénissieux alone employed 11,000 workers. Growth of modern industry was accompanied by changes in occupational breakdown. Lyon itself became increasingly bourgeois. The older ruling class—merchant manufacturers, lawyers, doctors and nobles—remained numerous in the *presqu'île*, while employers in the new industries, together with the increasingly numerous engineers and experts associated with them, preferred the more recently developed Brotteaux on the left bank of the Rhône. Thanks to the growth of service industries, state employment and the bureaucratization of the private firm, the number of white-collar workers living in the centre of the city expanded. In the Croix Rousse, once the home of the silk weaver, clerks and shopkeepers became the dominant social group. White-collar workers, professionals and employers also created commuter suburbs, such as Tassin la Demi-Lune, to the west of Lyon. Large-scale modern industry was located to the west and south, in the 7th arrondissement of Lyon, Villeurbanne, Vaulx en Velin, Vénissieux, Bron, St Fons, Oullins and Pierre-Bénite. In these communes lived concentrations of semi-skilled workers, many of them immigrants. The PPF must be related to the emergence of large-scale industry, the growth of salaried managerial and technical employment and of a semi-skilled working class, for those most discontented with the conservative establishment in 1936 were often drawn from occupational groups that did not feel themselves to be well represented within existing right-wing parties.

The relative youth of PPF militants doubtless reinforced a sense of exclusion and radical dynamism. The graph below shows that the PPF's age structure was a reverse image of that of the Fédération Républicaine, and that its members were younger than those of the PSF.[29]

Age of Right Wing Activists in the Rhône, 1936-39

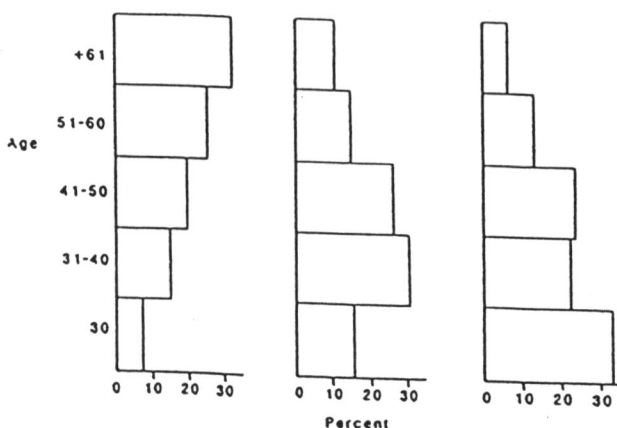

As for geographical distribution, shown in *map 1* (page 192), the PPF resembled the Fédération Républicaine and the PSF in that it was well implanted in the bourgeois centre of the city and suburban Tassin. This reflected recruitment from the dissolved leagues, which had been strong in those areas. The PPF differed from PSF and Fédération in that it had a following in working-class districts, especially Villeurbanne and Bron, where its most important section was located.[30] While not all these members were working class, they were all conscious of their status as an embattled minority in a communist stronghold.

The graph below compares the occupational breakdown of PPF members in the Lyonnais conurbation with that of the PSF and Fédération Républicaine.

Occupation of Right Wing Activists in the Rhone, 1936-39

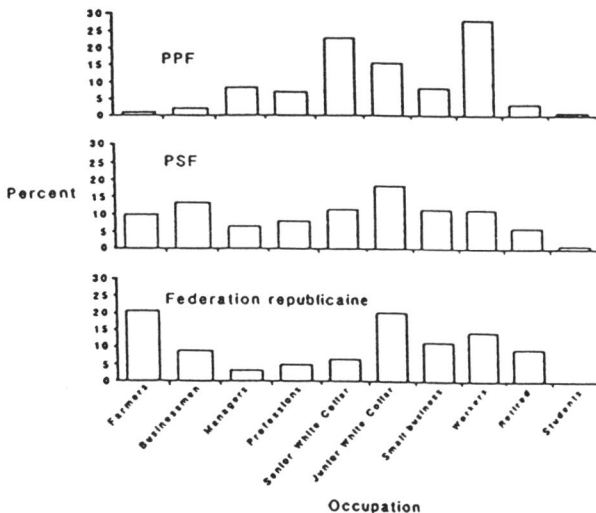

On the one hand, the PPF was well represented among the bourgeoisie, and included representatives of some of the best known families in Lyon.[31] Unlike the PSF and Fédération, the PPF did not have a high business membership, but it gained support from the ranks of senior management and higher grade white collar workers. On the other hand, the PPF had a higher proportion of workers (28 per cent) than both the PSF and the Fédération. These figures reveal that there is *some* truth in the PPF claim

Map 1: Residence of PPF activists in the Lyon conurbation 1936-39

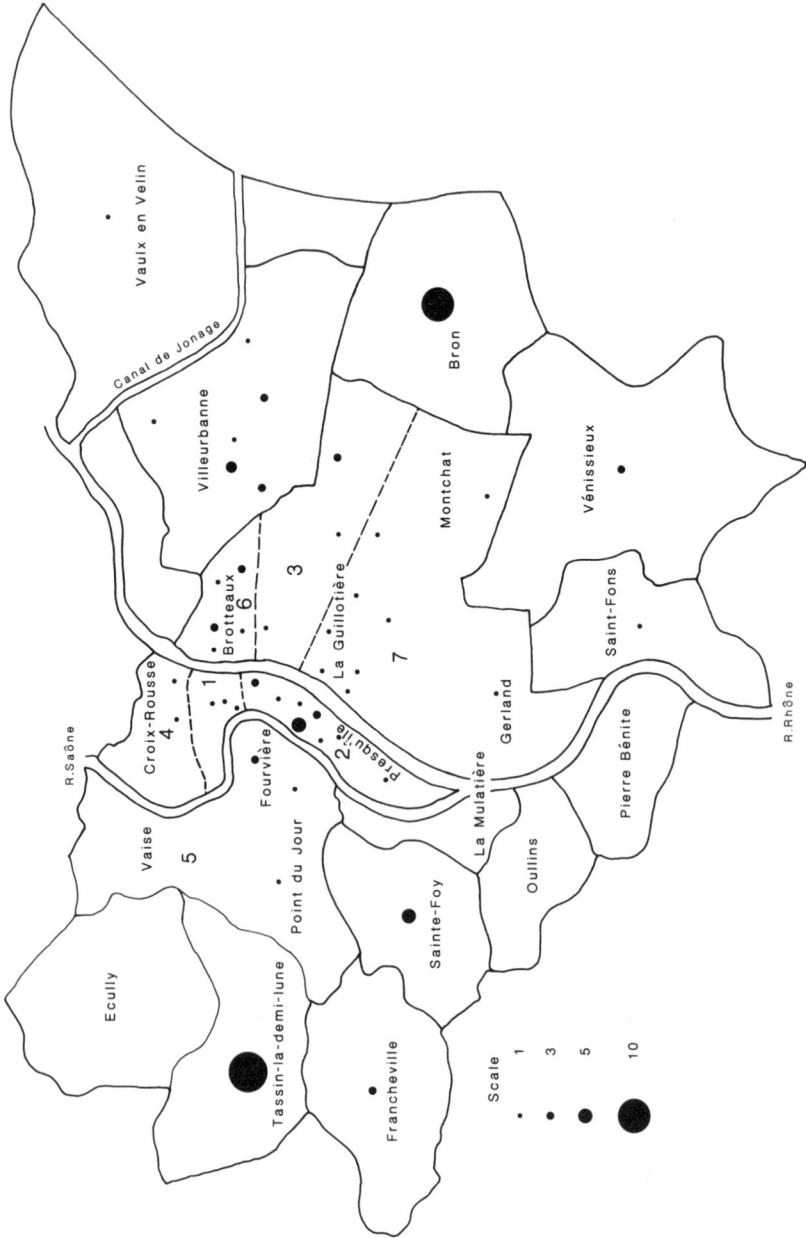

to recruit from both bourgeoisie and working class. The party was more proletarian than the Fédération or PSF, although workers were still under represented in relation to the population as a whole, and were absent from the party leadership. It is not possible to read off political attitudes from social composition, however, for the most radical elements of the league were not workers, but the young bourgeoisie in the bourgeois centre of the city. A closer look at PPF militants in the context of a changing city will do more to illuminate their motives and preoccupations. This essay is unable to examine all the groups attracted to the PPF, and will instead focus upon two of the more important: the 'cadres' and industrial workers. Both reveal the amalgam of anti-communism and populism that nourished the movement.

The 'Cadres' and the PPF

Senior managers and engineers—'cadres' in the terminology of the 1930s—were over-represented in both the PSF and PPF.[32] The support of engineers for both movements resulted from the impact of the labour unrest of 1936-38 on groups influenced by the dream of a middle way between capital and labour.[33] For many engineers, the PCF represented both a personal and a professional danger. Some were targeted by the CGT, often because of their role in enforcing unpopular work practices. For example, in June 1937 an engineer at the Rhodiaceta artificial fibre factory in Vaise had his car overturned by demonstrators.[34] Albert Beugras was a senior manager at the Rhône-Poulenc factory at Péage-de-Roussillon (to the south of Lyon in the Isère). In June 1936, strikers scattered offensive tracts in front of his house, and may have threatened to kidnap his family.[35] To personal grievances like these, must be added resentments resulting from a crisis of the profession. Luc Boltanski has argued that engineers in the 1930s experienced a profound threat to their identity. An excess of engineers devalued their 'cultural capital' and ensured that many failed to realize the hopes raised by a lengthy education.[36] In such circumstances, engineers resented the pretensions of the CGT. The trades unions often claimed to control hiring and firing and, in September 1936, strikers at Rhodiaceta boasted of their ability to run the machines without the help of engineers.[37]

Although engineers abhorred the CGT, they were nevertheless suspicious of their employers. A majority who joined the PPF described themselves in the electoral lists as 'engineers' rather than 'senior managers', suggesting that they were not at the summit of responsibility within the enterprise. Only those who had attended the Parisian *grandes écoles* could aspire to the most elevated positions. If PPF managers possessed any qualifications at all, they were more likely to be from establishments such as the École de Chimie de Mulhous, attended by Beugras, than the École Polytechnique. PPF engineers were, then, at one remove from their employers. Indeed, in the PPF engineers were not clearly differentiated from technicians, senior white-collar workers or foremen, also relatively numerous in the party. The PPF press used the terms 'engineer', 'technician' and 'foreman' interchangeably, while the engineers and technicians sections of the party often held joint meetings.[38]

Representative of those on the margin of the profession of engineer was Louis Chazal, a member of the regional leadership. Born in Geneva, Chazal arrived in Lyon at the age of 11, and during the war worked as a telephonist at the Hospices Civils. After training in his spare time as a refrigeration engineer, in 1935 he set up a firm making refrigeration equipment. When that business failed in 1937, he became manager of the Lyon branch of Markt et Cie.[39] The PPF also appealed to supervisory personnel. Armond Mamanti, for example, was a foreman at the Cazes biscuit factory in Villeurbanne, and joined the PPF in protest against the strikes of June 1936.[40]

This confluence of all those who exercised authority within the enterprise reflected the influence the PCF model, with its assumption that all managers were ultimately wage earners. In this respect, the PPF differed from the PSF. In the latter, engineers were more sensitive to professional distinctions and took care, implicitly, to assert the leadership within the 'cadres' movement of the best qualified.[41] Whatever their grade, engineers and technicians in the PPF would have agreed with Beugras that the cowardice and selfishness of the bosses had been responsible for the victory of the CGT. Beugras claimed that enlightened management in his own workshop had ensured that workers did not strike. Ultimately, the bosses of Rhône-Poulenc had given in, and Beugras was sent on extended leave. Thus, like many engineers, he combined hostility to the CGT with a conviction that backward management and the feebleness of big business were responsible for labour troubles. Like the engineers' unions of the 1930s, the PPF took from social Catholic thought a tripartite model of society which permitted the 'cadres' to regard themselves as uniquely placed to reconcile bosses and workers. Louis Roger, for example, argued that engineers and technicians were the precious and immediate collaborators of their employers. They were anti-communist, 'knew' the firm and identified with it. Yet the bosses had treated them worse than the workers.

The only solution was for engineers and technicians to organize autonomously within the PPF.[42] Thus, in the PPF, the 'cadres' were motivated simultaneously by anti-communism and a desire to organize collectively to defend their own interests, even against the patronat.

Workers and the PPF

The same mixed motives explained the backing of a minority of the working class for the PPF. Most workers who joined the party had undoubtedly been long-standing sympathisers of the right, for in the local elections of 1937 support for the two candidates presented by the PPF and PSF in working-class Villeurbanne was almost identical to that for the right in the general election of the previous year. Even in the most communist of suburbs there had always been a substantial minority of conservative workers. In the 1936 elections, 16 per cent of the Villeurbanne electorate had voted for the right, while 14 per cent had done so in Vénissieux. The main party of the parliamentary right, the Fédération Républicaine, possessed some of its most active sections in these districts. In the mid 1930s, there is reason to believe that some conservative workers felt that they had been forsaken by the traditional right. With the onset of the economic crisis the parliamentary right had abandoned the social reformism that had characterized it in the late 1920s. In 1928-32, many conservatives in Lyon had embraced the moderate reformism represented on the national level by the ministries of Tardieu and Laval, which had produced the Social Insurance Acts of 1928 and 1930, and the Family Allowances Act of 1932. In Lyon, the moderate Alliance Démocratique, and to a lesser extent the PDP, had profited from the reformist mood. Yet, in autumn 1931, sympathy for reform evaporated as the world economic crisis took its toll on local industries, silk in particular. The right's only remedy for the crisis was wage and price deflation, a programme which offered little to the working class. Catholic trades unions expressed in vain the opposition of conservative workers to deflation.[43]

Discontent with the parliamentary right coincided with the PCF's capture of the town halls of working-class communes such as Villeurbanne, Vénissieux and Bron in 1935, communist gains in the general elections of 1936, and the massive expansion of the CGT that followed. The status of conservative workers as an embattled minority was especially evident in the factories, where there was pressure to conform. Collections for strikers and the strikes themselves occasioned collective solidarity and suspicion of those who failed to participate in the popular movement. Some of the latter were subjected to community sanctions such as the notorious 'conduite de Grenoble'. In November 1937, this was the fate of a worker at the Société Electro-Chimie at Pierre-Bénite. The victim was surrounded by a crowd of women, who forced him off his bicycle and made him walk three kilometres to the Maison du Peuple, accompanied by a jeering crowd of 400. The ordeal ended at the Town Hall, where a trades union leader harangued the crowd.[44] In this climate of fear, activity by the Fédération Républicaine in working-class districts declined. Whereas the Croix de Feu had held a series of motorized rallies in working-class districts in 1934-35, its successor, the PSF, rarely ventured there. On the rare occasions when the PSF did show itself publicly, violence often resulted, as in October 1937 when a local election rally in Saint-Fons led to clashes with communists.[45] Isolated activists of right-wing parties, including the PPF, were also the subject of attacks from communist counter-demonstrations. In August 1937, the PPF press reported that the communists had attacked three of their activists and driven their lorry into the Jonage canal.[46]

It is possible that the backgrounds of PPF workers reinforced a sense of exclusion. Working-class militants in the PPF were younger than those in the PSF or Fédération Républicaine: 66 per cent of PPF workers were aged 40 or less. Most were recent arrivals in the city, only two out of 14 having been born there. Typical was Henri Carton. In 1938, aged 28, he left his birthplace at Miribel (Ain). He worked for a number of firms in Villeurbanne. After a stay in Marseille, followed by his military service, he returned there in 1933 to work for the dyeing firm, Nombret-Gaillard. Carton joined the PPF on its foundation, becoming secretary of the Villeurbanne section.[47]

Thus, right-wing workers combined an enhanced resentment of the PCF with a feeling of abandonment by the traditional right. For its working-class members, the PPF represented a means to fight the PCF, while protecting social reforms, and to defend their persons from physical attack. Through the PPF workers could integrate themselves into the popular community and reassert their identity as workers and men. In this sense, involvement in the PPF was the opposite of the symbolic emasculation by trades union leaders and women in the 'conduite de Grenoble'.

'Nous sommes le peuple'

The PPF's desire to mobilize the people, to assert 'popular sovereignty', and to construct the *état populaire français* was central to its identity. This supposedly distinguished it from parties of the left (allegedly based on the sectional interests of the working class) and the right (said to reflect the selfishness of the wealthy) something that Sape was keen to emphasize. He did not, of course, regard the governing class of the Republic as the legitimate expression of popular sovereignty. The ruling elite had betrayed the people by its desire for war, by alliance with the USSR, and by devaluing the franc. The current regime had not been chosen by the people; it was a self-appointed clique. Drawing on the language of 1789, Sape claimed that under the 'reign' of the 'seigneurs of the regime', the people had never been free, and that those who exploited the masses were 'criminals'. It followed that the people possessed the right of insurrection. Whereas populist discourses of the left, particularly of the Radical Party, were inseparable from representative democracy, the PPF appealed to a notion of direct democracy drawn from the Jacobin tradition. The PPF did not merely represent the people—it was, literally, synonymous with it. In Sape's words, 'Nous sommes le peuple'. He ironically warned the governing class, which he held to be isolated from the real world, that it would soon 'get to know the people', and learn that it was a 'tidal wave', rather than a 'phantom'. 'It is rising up', he said, 'you cannot continue to ignore it.' He stressed, too, that the revolution desired by the PPF would be a 'TOTAL national revolution, that is to say a revolution that would not stop at the extermination of communism.' The guarantee of this, said Sape, was that Doriot had emerged neither from the army nor the aristocracy, but from the people. Given that Sape's popular uprising never materialized, it is possible only to make an informed guess as to what all of this would have amounted to in practice. It would doubtless have involved the kind of irruption of party into the state apparatus that had occurred in Fascist Italy and in Nazi Germany.[48] This does not, however, mean that the PPF was in any sense left wing. Indeed, populism derived partly from the conviction that the ruling elites had failed to prevent, and had perhaps even secretly encouraged, the advance of communism.

It is not surprising that Sape's conception of the people was inseparable from conservative views of class, gender and citizenship. He distinguished the 'true people' from the 'howling multitude', the latter identified with 'bistros, smoky meetings, raised fists and recent naturalizations'. The 'true people' were defined firstly by work—rather than the leisure represented by the bistro. Sape likened the PPF itself to the 'workers who produce all the better when they are crushed by toil', thereby rejoining traditional right-wing thought in raising self-sacrifice above materialism and pleasure-seeking. So the ideal worker valued profession and nation more than class interest and, would not resort to industrial action. Second, the people eschewed politics and, in particular, the PCF. For Sape, communism was symbolized by the egocentric hatred expressed in the clenched-fist salute, the reverse of the class collaboration desired by the PPF. Third, communism was excluded from the people by its foreignness, for it was an 'Asiatic' doctrine that appealed largely, in Sape's eyes, to immigrants. This stereotype was extended to include non-communists like the CGT leader Léon Jouhaux, whose mass of oily flesh, multiple chins with isolated hairs sprouting from them was said to explain his flirtation with 'asiatics'.[49] Fourth, women were implicitly excluded because of their non-productive status. Sape accepted that some women might reach the heights of the professions, yet most would never be more than pseudo-intellectuals who had forgotten that woman's true vocation was to forgo material success in order to raise children.[50] Thus Sape's idea of the people excluded trades unionists, communists, immigrants, and women. Nevertheless, these reactionary assumptions were combined with populism to produce a distinctive type of conservatism.

The nature of PPF discourse and political practice can be further elucidated by examining the relationship of the PPF to gender and class issues. These are particularly important because PPF writers did not see popular sovereignty as the sum of individual wills expressed through parliament. Rather the Jacobin idea of the people was combined with the traditional conservative assumption that family and profession were the building blocks of society.

Populism and gender

Identification of the people with the family points to the gendering of the PPF's populism. We have already seen that women were, in principle at least, excluded from the people as non-producers. Furthermore, female 'frivolity'did not suit them to participation in the PPF. Pierre Buffière assumed that women were more sensitive to social rank and that it was therefore harder for them to participate in a popular party. Men, on the other hand, were able to communicate across class boundaries because of their natural 'simplicity'.[51] The recurrence in PPF discourse of adjectives such as 'franchise' and 'loyauté' betrays the same assumption that the ideal PPF militant was male: these characteristics were implicitly contrasted with the egocentric materialism that characterized both women and communists. Hence the gendered connotations of the PPF's insistence that, 'Only frank and loyal collaboration between bosses and workers will permit peace and social justice.' Only men could overcome social conflict, which was regarded as feminine in origin.[52]

The masculinity of PPF populism was reinforced by its view of the nation. As Dr Léonet explained in *L'Attaque*, the nation was based on the recognition by the individuals within it of common characteristics. This restrained the natural combativity of individual men. Struggle was instead directed towards the achievement of national unity and to competition between nations, for love of the similar was necessarily accompanied by rejection of the dissimilar.[53] PPF activists were therefore identified with 'natural' male virility and competitiveness. Similarly, Sape preached love of the 'heroic life' to the elite who had gathered in the PPF.[54] In this register, the male values of the PPF were implicitly an antidote to the corruption of contemporary France.

The masculinity of PPF activists contrasted with the femininity of the nation as an ideal. The nation performed the socially useful function of disciplining the selfish aggressiveness of the malel. This subordination of individual concerns allowed PPF writers to portray the regenerated nation as a 'serious woman', deserving of sacrifice.[55] More generally, women represented a living reminder of the higher purpose of political activity. As one writer put it, whenever men experienced depression, whenever life seemed pointless and insipid, the ideal, the eternal utopia within him, could always be revived by a sign of support from the mother, sister or wife. This apparently contradicted the assumption that women were more likely than men to descend to petty intrigue. The truth was that PPF writers shared a paradoxical, and age-old, view of femininity in which women represented both the transcendent goals of political action, and the temptations of the flesh which threatened to divert men from the true path. Hence the identification of a corrupt contemporary France with a 'tart' given over to luxury, impulsive behaviour and fantasy.[56] Whereas men could save the nation actively, women could do so only as a passive representation of the ideal. Women were, then, excluded from the people by their non-productive status, their lack of virile and heroic aggressiveness, and their predilection for social distinctions. The PPF's masculinization of the people, the agent of national regeneration, contrasted with the conviction of nineteenth-century conservatives that the people, an object of fear, were marked by feminine irrationality.

It is not surprising that the PPF shared the view of the conservative natalist movement that women could best serve the nation by producing children. The spread of materialist values by Marxists and freemasons had diverted women from this duty.[57] From their position within the family women were expected to support the male PPF activist. Alberte denounced those wives who paralyzed the work of the husband by difficult scenes, bad tempers or sulks. Some, she wrote, welcomed the husband home from meetings, where he had often risked his life, with as much irritation as if he had spent the evening playing cards. She concluded, 'The PPF will triumph! Thanks to Doriot and thanks to the valiant fighters, our husbands, we will soon live in a peaceful France.'[58] Thus men risked their lives for the nation, while the task of women was to overcome their inclination towards selfishness in order to ensure that their husbands encountered no domestic obstacle to their political activities. This pattern prevailed in the Beugras household. Albert told his wife little of his activities even neglecting to inform her that he had left his job with Rhône-Poulenc to work for the PPF.[59]

Reactionary though the PPF's view of women was, it nevertheless possessed distinctive traits. These derived from the PPF's commitment to mass mobilization. The ideal wife would support her husband by internalizing party doctrine, reading the party's arid newspaper and learning its anthem, 'France! libère-toi'.[60] Additionally, the PPF placed the needs of the family below the cause of the nation, and therefore of the PPF. Men and women must sacrifice some aspects of family life in order to consecrate themselves to the rescue of France.[61] The ambiguity of the family's place in PPF discourse was reinforced by its portrayal of those males who did not participate in the party. Wives of activists should be grateful that their husbands struggled for a beautiful cause, and did not wear out their slippers in front of the fire from six o'clock each evening.[62] If the family was the basis of society, it was also the site of easy satisfactions which destroyed active love of the nation.

The tension between opposition to female emancipation and the desire for political mobilization of all citizens, emerges particularly clearly from the creation of women's sections, announced by the regional bureau of the party in December 1937.[63] In some respects, these sections were conventionally conservative in outlook. Madeleine Bry rejected the model of the female activist and soldier promoted by the Spanish communist Dalores Ibàrruri, 'la Pasionaria'.[64] Instead, women's sections were to help restore women to their proper place in society. The 'fallacious pretext' of emancipation should not divert women from domestic duties. Yet the contradiction is already apparent in that the PPF aimed to take women out of home and family, to mobilize them 'within the framework of the PPF, in order to restore the "traditional" equilibrium between the sexes.'[65]

Furthermore, the commitment to mass mobilization enabled women to make their voices heard within the party. Indeed, there are some hints that there had been pressure from female activists for the creation of women's sections. The initial announcement stated that such sections would make the PPF 'complete', and added that many would say 'At last! The country and Doriot need us'.[66] Female writers in *L'Attaque* shared the traditional assumptions about women, but with the important difference that they were not regarded as natural. Women's lives, wrote Alberte, were full of 'pointless futilities, pointless tasks, and pointless prejudices, which have always had an unfortunate influence on our manner of thinking and of judging our neighbour.'Yet such failings could be overcome. Women could learn to love others, and might, through fraternal simplicity and intelligent friendship, cross social barriers.[67] Similarly, Madeleine Bry accepted that the true place of women was in the home, not the factory, office, civil service, or even the fields. Yet the war had shown that women were able to take the place of men. This was partly because they were cheaper and easier to exploit, but they had nevertheless shown that they 'were able to deal intelligently with all tasks.' Women, Bry implied, were not necessarily unproductive. She explained that women had a triple burden, as factory workers, mothers, and as the bearers of a grave moral burden.[68] Women were not therefore defined by an unchanging essence, but could choose their role. Another writer argued that women could use their powers of persuasion to spread the message of the party. The main disadvantage of women was that they would have to struggle against the scepticism of men.[69]

The account of femininity that emerges from these writers was not based on the assumption of gender equality. Rather, some female activists turned conventional ideas about women to their advantage. This permitted incorporation of women into the oppressed people as producers, carriers and also disseminators of the national ideal. It followed that women could participate in the PPF, if not on the same terms as men, especially since they could make a particular contribution to the party's mission. As one writer explained, the task of uprooting communism should be left to 'our husbands'. But women could play a central role in overcoming the social deprivation which had permitted communism to flourish in the first place. Women, in this case assumed to be the repository of the ideal of self-sacrifice and mutual understanding, would make a vital contribution to overcoming the selfishness which underlay class struggle.[70] The belief that feminine values were the solution to class conflict provided another justification for removal of women from the home. In this case, women were admitted to the party on condition that they confined themselves to traditionally female activities. The issue of peace potentially brought women more centrally into the party. As mothers and wives they had a special reason for opposing communist attempts to drag France into war against fascism. According to Bry, neutrality and inaction were impossible and all women who wanted order, peace and work should rally to the PPF.[71]

Thus the PPF, particularly its female activists, adopted a flexible approach to gender roles which permitted female agency. Alberte divided female activists into two categories: those who supported the male activist domestically , and the 'vibrant and enthusiastic phalanx' of women who worked within the PPF. Even some male writers accepted a blurring of gender identities. This emerges from an article on the pro-PPF aviator Madeleine Charnaux. The author stated that, 'The PPF is a virile party. It is a party of combat. Those women who are found among its troops accept the harsh necessities of its activity, and above all they accept those virtues which our masculine fatuity normally causes us to attribute to ourself.'[72] Gender identities could not necessarily be read off from biological sex. Yet the female activist was regarded as an exception, like the popular heroine Charnaux.

Thus, although the PPF drew upon traditional views of gender, its desire to mobilize women within a new national community called these values into question. The arguments advanced here do not imply that the PPF had 'progressive' views on gender issues. On the contrary, one suspects that the very existence of 'feminism' within the PPF reinforced the misogyny of male activists such as Sape. Rather, the populism of the PPF made it possible for some, mainly middle-class, women to endeavour to advance their interests through a movement of the far right and to demand their incorporation into the people. They, too, drew upon traditional gender discourse, yet articulated views which differed subtly from those of male activists. This was possible for two reasons. First, although all right-wing movements are hostile to feminism as an idea,they respond to this in different ways. Second, women brought their own agendas and cultures to the PPF.[73] However much dominant ideologies shaped the opportunities open to women, they were not merely 'constructed' by such systems.[74] Similar points can be made about the relationship of the PPF to the working class.

Populism and Class

PPF writers were profoundly uncomfortable with the notion of class. Sape, as we have seen, rejected Marxist notions of class struggle in favour of Proudhon's division of society into parasites and producers.[75] The people were defined by work rather than by ownership of the means of production. The people therefore embraced those with 'white hands', such as intellectuals, and those with 'greasy overalls and worn hands,' in a cross-class 'fraternity'.[76] It was difficult, however, to define class out of existence. One reason was that the PPF opposed egalitarianism as understood by the left. Pierre Buffière argued that progress depended on the efforts of a few disinterested men [sic]. Because such individuals were found in all classes, Buffière preferred equality of opportunity to an 'imbecilic egalitarianism' that would promote mediocrity. He was also careful to preserve the advantages of the wealthy. He followed conventional right-wing thought in insisting that the success of a family was more important than that of the individual. Inherited wealth was therefore legitimate.[77]

Buffière's desire to preserve bourgeois culture within a populist movement is also evident in his account of a dance held after the 1938 regional party conference which had confirmed that the PPF was synonymous with the people, understood in the true sense of the term. It had not been used by the wealthy as an excuse for vulgar carousing and the casting off of social constraints. On the contrary, bourgeois members of the PPF had effortlessly established a rapport with the most simple proletarian while remaining true to themselves. They had not disguised the superiorities acquired thanks to fortunate birth and upbringing. PPF members behaved in this way because they were aware of the dignity of all human beings, irrespective of their upbringing or class.[78] Just as the people were made in the image of the bourgeoisie, so the working class was to be incorporated on bourgeois terms. Sape explained that the worker would count for nothing in society until he possessed property. When he had something to defend he would be an active member of the community.[79]

The PPF devoted much of its energy to fighting, in print and in the factories, the Popular Front and the organized labour movement. The PPF's attitude towards the reforms of the Popular Front often paralleled that of conventional conservatives. Like employers and the parliamentary right, the PPF accepted reform in principle, yet insisted that measures such as the 40 hour week must be introduced only when conditions were favourable.[80] The PPF was also involved in the struggle against the CGT. The police reported that the party's relations with employers' organizations were well known.[81] Links with bosses in the building industry, in the forefront of the employers' counter-offensive, were especially close.[82] During the violent general building strike, the PPF called for the arrest of flying pickets and of CGT leaders and claimed to have 'led the anti-CGT struggle'. Workers at Etablissements Borie complained in June 1938 that the manager had sacked 30 workers and attempted to force others to join the PPF. Doriot's party had indeed been behind the creation of an 'independent committee' and of a section of the Confédération Français des Travailleurs Unique.[83] At Berliet, during a strike in April 1938, the PPF set up an 'independent committee' to agitate for a return to work.[84] The PPF also received money from employers. Beugras continued to receive his salary from Rhône-Poulenc, even though he had become a full time worker for the PPF.[85] Fernand Sape's interrogation in 1945 revealed that in 1936-37 L'Attaque had received subsidies of 5-10,000 francs from a number of well known Lyonnais business leaders. These included Georges Villiers, president of the engineering employers federation and leader of the national employers movement after 1945; Aimé Bernard, president of the Lyon branch of the Confédération Générale de la Production Française; Henri Lumière, the inventor of cinematography and Paul Lombard, manager of the Rhodiaceta artificial fibre firm. This support probably continued after Sape left the PPF in October 1937. Sape also told his interrogators that his financial backers left him total liberty in matters of foreign policy, while imposing restrictions on what he could write on domestic issues.[86]

The PPF was not merely a puppet of the ruling class. The traditional right, like the employers' movement, sought to weaken and destroy the CGT. They saw 'independent' trades unions as a means to this end and displayed no long-term commitment to them. The PPF's goal, was to mobilize the working class within a new national trades unionism. In L'Attaque Sape preached the doctrine of 'national-syndicalism', which he later described as a 'sort of synthesis of Italian corporatism and Spanish syndicalism'.[87] This meant that a single union would replace the CGT, Catholic and independent unions. Employers, 'cadres', and raw material suppliers would also join such 'syndicats'. They would be brought together in the corporation, which would represent the general interest. The edifice would be regulated and arbitrated by the state.[88] Existing trades unions, as Beugras explained, had to be purged of communist influence, and the PCF dissolved, before they could be truly representative. The party also set up its own 'Sections d'entreprise' as the nucleus of a corporatist system. Yet Beugras also warned the workers against 'house unions', for domination by the employer was as harmful as political interference.[89] Another writer insisted that autonomous unions must fight the CGT while simultaneously defending workers' demands.[90]

Some historians have dismissed PPF syndicalist schemes as window dressing designed to deceive the workers,[91] yet these plans should be taken seriously. First, PPF corporatism derived from a real hostility not just to communism, but to the supposed liberalism of the elites. After evoking the necessity of the anti-communist struggle, Beugras urged his readers not to forget that 'the real cause of the proletarian and middle-class rebellion, exploited by Stalin's lackeys, was misery and injustice'. The PPF would therefore oppose social conservatism along with Marxism.[92] In other words, social conservatism and capitalism (albeit defined in a manner that prevented an all-out attack on private ownership of the means of production) were to blame for the rise of communism. More practically, we have seen that the PPF appealed to groups, such as workers and managers, that were certainly anti-communist, but which believed themselves to have genuine grievances against the elites. Corporatism offered the 'cadres' a means to restore their power within the enterprise, by eliminating the communists, but also by giving managers and engineers the right of consultation in certain decisions.[93] Similarly, the 'syndicat' as understood by the PPF offered conservative workers the chance to eliminate communism and to defend social reforms. These reforms would not be accorded universally, but limited to the 'loyal' worker, in effect male heads of families, French citizens and the politically reliable. The PPF, as we have seen, defined the people in exclusive terms, but this still left a considerable number of individuals who might potentially benefit from social reform. The PPF also included within its programme the proposal that surplus profits be paid into a social fund for redistribution to the workers. While the PPF was imprecise on the mechanics of this reform, the principle of collective appropriation of profit was a departure from conventional right-wing thinking.

The meaning of PPF attitudes to the 'social question' is also ambiguous when looked at from the point of view of the employers. On the one hand, they attempted, with some success, to use the party for their own ends, and were able to do so because the PPF had originated partly from a conviction that the PCF could not be defeated by traditional methods. On the other hand, employers distrusted the radical potential of PPF discourse. Sape reported that his financial backers had attempted to moderate the social programme of L'Attaque. His business sponsors had been particularly upset by an article in June 1937 calling for simultaneous closure of parliament and the stock exchange, and had used this as a pretext to oblige him to put his journal at the service of the PPF.[94] Under the wing of the PPF, L'Attaque became more moderate. Yet business support always remained conditional upon fear of the Popular Front. Shortly after the defeat of the CGT on 30 November 1938, Buffière complained that the

PPF had disappointed those who had looked upon it as a servile gendarme useful for the ignoble task of dividing the working class. The departure of reactionaries had purified the party, but at the cost of financial difficulties.[95] In 1938-39, L'Attaque appeared intermittently as its funds dried up. For its part, the PPF was aware that if it was to prevent itself from falling into the hands of the patronat then it must create its own autonomous labour movement. This was particularly true once the communist threat had receded after 30 November 1938. Subsequently, the PPF reaffirmed the necessity of a unified national trades union movement, though one independent of politics.[96] In practice, the PPF never created such a role for itself.

The PPF and the Right

As the PPF slipped into the wake of the employers' counter-offensive, it struggled to remain independent from the parliamentary right. During 1937 the party's failure to make the desired political breakthrough became evident. On the national level, Doriot's revocation as mayor of Saint-Denis and his subsequent defeat at the hands of the municipal and legislative electorates were crushing blows to the movement. In Lyon, the PPF's plight was hardly better. Despite issuing 60-80,000 invitations to a showpiece regional conference in July 1937, only 1,200 people turned up. Beugras described the conference as the 'point of departure' for a movement which so far had failed to reach the masses. In fact, summer 1937 was the PPF's high-point in the region. In the two Rhône constituencies where it stood under its own colours in the October 1937 local elections, it won less than 5 per cent of the vote.[97] The PPF also failed to assert its presence on the streets. This was demonstrated by the fiasco of a visit by Doriot to the city on 17-18 December 1936. Rallies planned for the Salle Donjon were banned by the Prefect. Instead, 150 PPF members attended a private meeting in a restaurant, while 4-5,000 communist supporters demonstrated outside. As PPF members left the hall under police protection, one of Doriot's bodyguards accidentally shot an inspector in the foot.[98] This was the last occasion on which the party attempted a high profile public meeting in Lyon.[99]

It was against this depressing background that, on 27 March 1937, Doriot appealed for all those parties opposed to the Popular Front to join an anti-communist alliance. The Front de la Liberté was launched on 8 May. It had a minimum programme, but constituent parties were, beyond that, free to develop their own agendas. In the event, only the Fédération

Républicaine agreed to join the Front, seeing it as a means to prevent the PSF from putting up candidates against it in the forthcoming general elections. The PSF refused to join, rightly detecting an attempt to steal its troops.[100]

More important were the effects of the Front de la Liberté on the PPF in Lyon, for Philippe Burrin has argued that in 1937-38 the party underwent a process of 'fascistization'.[101] In Lyon, participation in the Front de la Liberté led to a marked softening of the PPF's line. Beugras hammered home the message that no single party could hope to defeat the communists, and that the only meaningful opposition was between Marxists and anti-Marxists, Frenchmen and disciples of the foreigner, cowards and brave men, the free and the enslaved.[102] Buffière provided theoretical justification for prioritization of the anti-PCF struggle: whereas conservatives created misery only for some, communism would create famine for all.[103] The local Fédération, Parti Républicain National et Social (PRNS, the former Jeunesses Patriotes), and even royalists enthusiastically welcomed the call for unity. From May 1937, the activists of the constituent organizations dined together at the Café Morel on Place Bellecour, and the PPF concluded an alliance with the Fédération, to which the PSF was loosely attached, for the local elections of October 1937.[104] The PPF also provided security for Fédération meetings. This help was not always effective, for in February 1938 a PPF squad failed to prevent a group of PSF militants from breaking up a Fédération assembly at which Philippe Henriot was to have spoken.[105] This incident reflects the extent to which the PPF had become an adjunct of the old right, and also points to why this had happened. Both the PSF and the PPF were populist parties, which had originated out of real hostility to the elites. But thanks to its possession of a mass membership the PSF was able to achieve greater freedom of action.

The increasing moderation of the PPF in Lyon also caused internal dissidence. Some of the party's recruits from Action Française had lasted only a few months in the party. Paul Chartron, for example, was expelled in early 1937. We know only that his royalist opinions had brought him into conflict with Beugras.[106] We are better informed about the reasons for Sape's departure. A notoriously difficult individual, he found it hard to work as part of a team. He had additionally embezzled 5,600 francs from *L'Attaque*'s accounts. While Sape's relations with the German and Italian embassies may also have caused unease, the most important reason for his expulsion was his view of the Front de la Liberté. Sape, who had joined the PPF shortly after the creation of the Front, claimed that he had long detested the term 'Union Nationale', but had been convinced of the need for unity by a visit to nationalist troops in Spain. He refused, however, to define it merely as a defensive anti-communist alliance. Within the Front, the PPF would turn defence into attack, and would refuse to sacrifice the social to the national revolution. In the same issue of *L'Attaque* in which Beugras attributed a supposed communist defeat in the local elections to the unity of the right, Sape warned that electoral victories would be worthless, and that France would expire, unless 'leaders, real leaders, taught the love of the heroic life to the elite around us [the PPF].' Sape concluded by asserting his preparedness to confront an attempt by the communists to win power by violent means. His denunciation of non-productive, speculative and dishonest capitalism in the following week proved to be his last contribution to the journal he had founded. On 6 November 1937, *L'Attaque* announced the expulsion of Sape and nine of his allies. In 1938 Sape funded a new journal, *L'Union Française*, through which he was to preach the cause of collaboration throughout the war. He was executed in 1945 at the age of 34.[107]

Conclusion

The expulsion of Sape and his friends from the PPF meant that Beugras's authority was now unquestioned. It also showed the distance the party had moved from its original intention to break the mould of French politics. It might also suggest that the party's claim to represent a populist revolt against the political establishment and selfish capitalism had never possessed real substance. This article has attempted to demonstrate that the populism of the PPF was sustained by its origins in a rebellion of rank-and-file right wingers and ex-leaguers, reinforced by a minority of former communists, against the social and political establishment. The aim of the party was both to destroy the communist party and to create a new elite, drawn from the people, to replace the failed political class. However, the balance between radical and reactionary impulses within the populist party depends on favourable conditions, and is always difficult to maintain. Parties of the radical right, by their very nature, tend to oscillate between sectarianism and compromise with conventional conservatives. Because of its failure to recruit more than a handful of activists, the PPF ended up playing a secondary role in the employers' counter-offensive and defending the meetings of the Fédération Républicaine from a more successful movement of the far right. The departure of the most extreme exponents of 'national revolution' accentuated the party's drift towards the old right.

None of this, however, means that the PPF ceased to be a populist party. Rather, it was a failed populist party.

Whether the PPF before 1940 can be characterized as 'fascist' is more difficult to say. The definition of fascism used here relies on three components, two of which were undoubtedly present in the party. First, it displayed a reactionary hostility to communism, feminism and liberal democracy. The party had no sympathy for the pluralism of the Republic. It called for dissolution of the PCF, purges or suppression of the CGT, and conceived the 'people' in exclusive, even totalitarian, terms. Second, the PPF displayed a radical populism expressed in hostility to the social elites and in the desire to mobilize the people against politicians of left and right. On these criteria the PPF certainly contained a fascist potential. But the third component of fascism—a mass activism expressed in paramilitarism and real or symbolic political violence—is less easy to detect. Admittedly, Sape envisaged violence, justifying this as a means of defence against communisn, and some PPF members were armed. But before 1940 the PPF did not develop a paramilitary wing, and in 1936-39 it resorted less readily to violence than did the PSF. One reason is that PPF activists, in Lyon and in France as a whole, were not numerous enough to confront the PCF on the streets. More importantly, it is likely that in creating the PPF, Doriot wanted to avoid the charge that he was duplicating the methods of the paramilitary Croix de Feu. Whatever the reason, before 1940 the PPF's fascist potential was not fully realized.

Notes

The author thanks Garthine Walker for her comments on this essay.

1.   Burrin, Philippe: *La dérive fasciste. Doriot, Déat, Bergery* (Paris, 1987), pp 285-6; Brunet, Jean-Paul: *Jacques Doriot. Du communisme au fascisme* (Paris, 1986), pp 228-9

2.   Archives Départementales du Rhône (ADR): 4m 263, 23 December, 1936, 29 July, 1937; *L'Attaque*, 21 August, 1937; Wolf, Dieter: *Doriot. Du communisme au collaboration* (Paris, 1971), p 220, quotes a figure of 6,000 in the region. Since Beugras claimed only 3,000 in 1938 this is an overestimate. (*L'Attaque*, 19 February, 1938).

3.   Rémond, René: *Les droites en France* (Paris, 1981), pp 216-7. Brunet: *Jacques Doriot*, pp 245-67 also emphasizes the connection between the PPF's revolutionary spirit and its fascism.

4.   Burrin, *La dérive fasciste*, pp 278-312; Burrin, Philippe: 'Fascisme', in J.-F. Sirinelli, ed: *Histoire des droites en France* (Paris, 1992), pp 631-2

5.   See the 'Postulates of the Fascist Programme' of 1920 cited in C. Delzell,

ed: *Mediterranean Fascism 1919-1945* (London, 1970), pp 14-15 and Göring's remarks on the Nazi seizure of power cited in J. Noakes and G. Pridham, eds: *Nazism 1919-1945* (Exeter, 1988), vol 1, pp 150-1.

6. Passmore, Kevin: *From Liberalism to Fascism. The Right in a French Province* (Cambridge, 1997); Passmore, Kevin: 'The Croix de Feu. Bonapartism, National-Populism or Fascism?', *French History*, 9 (1995), pp 93-123; Passmore, Kevin: '"Boy-Scouting for Ggrown-Ups?" Paramilitarism in the Croix de Feu and PSF', *French Historical Studies*, 19 (1995), pp 527-57

7. Soucy, Robert: *French Fascism. The Second Wave* (Yale, 1995), pp 204-279

8. For a pioneering analysis of fascism and gender see Koos, Cheryl: 'Engendering Reaction: The Politics of Pronatalism and the Family in France, 1919-1944' (unpublished Ph.D thesis, University of Southern California, 1996).

9. This does not mean that the people/state conflict is to be regarded as more important than gender, class or other forms of conflict in a theoretical sense, only that it has been privileged for the purposes of this essay. On 'populism' see Laclau, Ernesto: *Politics and Ideology in Marxist Theory* (London, 1977).

10. Irvine, William D: 'Fascism in France: The Strange Case of the Croix de Feu', *Journal of Modern History* 63 (1991), pp 271-95

11. Pinol, Jean-Luc: *Espace social et espace politique. Lyon époque du Front Populaire* (Lyon, 1980). The canton of Villeurbanne comprised the communes of Vénissieux, Bron, Saint-Fons, Bron, Villeurbanne and Vaulex en Venin (See *map 1*)

12. For the strikes of June 1936 in the Rhône, see Archives Nationales (AN): BB[18] especially 3010, and *Procès verbeaux de la Chambre de Commerce de Lyon.*

13. Prost: Antoine: *La CGT à l'époque du front populaire* (Paris, 1963). pp 212, 219

14. The analysis that follows is based on a sample of 159 members of the PPF in Lyon and the Rhône, part of a larger database of several thousand sympathisers of right wing parties. See Passmore, Kevin: 'The Right and the Extreme Right in the Rhône, 1928-1940' (unpublished Ph.D. thesis, University of Warwick, 1992)

15. Villeurbanne and the southern canton of the 7th arrondissement of Lyon

16. AN: CJS, 514 4073[1]; Chaix, Marie: *Les lauriers du lac de Constance* (Paris, 1974); Chaix, Marie, *Juliette Chemin des Cerisiers* (Paris, 1985). These two novels were written by the daughter of Albert Beugras, and inspired by an autobiography written by him while awaiting trial for his wartime activities.

17. AN: Cour de Justice de la Seine (CJS), 514 4703[1]

18. ADR: 4m 236, 5 November, 1936

19. *L'Attaque*, June/July, October, 1936. Guy Jarrosson, one-time president of

the Jeunesses Patriotes, told me in 1987 that the PSF in this period were engaged in clandestine contacts with other leagues.

20. AN: F[7] 14 818, 17 September, 1936. Sape wrote under the pen-name of Philippe Dreux.

21. ADR: Cour de Justice du Rhône (CJR), 1294. The headline appeared in *L'Attaque*, 22 May, 1937

22. CJR: 1294 and 635

23. CJR: 794(2) 794(3); Chauvy, Gérard: *Lyon, 1940-1944* (Paris, 1985), pp 324-5. On Chambon see CJR: 1420 (1).

24. CJR: 1420[1]

25. Brunet: *Doriot*, pp. 230-231 accepts the PPF's claim that 33 per cent of PPF conference delegates came from the left, 27 per cent from the right, while 39 per cent had no prior political affiliation.

26. Brunet: *Doriot*, pp 174-5

27. Jankowski, Paul: *Communism and Collaboration. Simon Sabiani and Politics in Marseille, 1919-1944* (New Haven, 1989); Schor, Ralph: 'Le Parti Populaire Français dans les Alpes-Maritimes,1936-1939', *Cahiers de la Méditerranée*, 33/34 (1986-9), pp 99-125

28. For example, Beugras in *L'Attaque*, 24 July 1937 claimed that those who attended the party's first meeting were from all classes and all parties.

29. For comparison with rival movements of the right and far right, see Passmore: 'The Right and the Far Right'.

30. The PPF was over represented in those areas of Lyon defined by Jean-Luc Pinol as 'working class'. See Pinol: *Espace social et espace politique*, p 108.

31. For example, Me Pierre Dufès, whose relatives were involved in the engineering industry; Louis Allaix, whose father was a member of the Chamber of Commerce, and Jean Pila, member of a family of silk traders, also present in the Chamber of Commerce.

32. Engineers/senior managers: 3.7 per cent in the Fédération Républicaine, 8.7 per cent in the PSF and 6.9 per cent in the PPF, compared to 2.1 per cent in the population as a whole

33. Boltanski, Luc: *The Making of a Class. Cadres in French Society* (Cambridge, 1987); Kolboom, Ingo: 'Patronat et cadres: la contribution patronale à la formation du groupe des cadres', *Mouvement social* 99 (1982), pp 71-95; Maurice, Marc: 'L'évolution du travail et du syndicalisme chez les cadres', *Mouvement social*, 61 (1967), pp 47-64.

34. AN: BB[18] 3063, 29 June, 1937

35. Chaix: *Les lauriers du lac de Constance*, pp 9-11; CJS: 516 40733 Dossier Beugras-Célor

36. Boltanski: *The Making of a Class*, pp 76-7; in *L'Attaque*, 27 November, 1937, Buffière wrote that because of the surplus of technicians, many had been forced either to accept famine wages or to resign themselves to abandon their lengthy training by changing jobs.

37. See *Le Nouvelliste* 17 September, 1936 on the 'Sovietization' of the Rhodiaceta factory
38. *L'Attaque*, 20 November 1937, 8 January, 15 April, 1938
39. *L'Attaque*, 2 October 1937; CJR: 1420[1]. Similarly, Louis Senti, whose parents were shopkeepers, had left school at 14. He became head of department for a large publishing firm, then south eastern representative of the F. Belge pencil manufacturers.
40. CJR: 1576
41. Passmore: 'The Right and the Extreme Right', pp 362-3
42. *L'Attaque*, 8 January 1938
43. Passmore, 'The Right and the Extreme Right', pp 166-238
44. AN: BB[18] 3063, 8 and 10 October, 1937. See also *Le Nouvelliste*, 30 June, 1937 for further accounts of this practice
45. ADR: *dossier élections cantonales de 1937*, 7, 8, 9 October, 1937; *Lyon Républicain* and *Nouvelliste*, 10-12 October, 1937. A young worker was killed by a volley of shots fired from their vehicles by the departing PSF.
46. *L'Attaque*, 7 August, 1937
47. CJR:1454
48. *L'Attaque*, 24 July 1937; 21 August 1937
49. *L'Attaque*, 12 February 1938
50. *L'Attaque*, May, 1936
51. *L'Attaque*, 5 February and 9 April 1938
52. *L'Attaque*, 5 November 1938
53. *L'Attaque*, 26 June 1937. This conception of nationalism as ultimately rooted in reason rather than sentiment clearly owed something to Charles Maurras.
54. *L'Attaque*, 18 October 1937
55. *L'Attaque*, 28 August 1937
56. *L'Attaque*, 12 June 1937. Similar ideas informed 1920s fascist movements. See Koos, Cheryl: 'The Family, Gender and the Development of Fascism: The Case of Antoine Rédier and the Légion' (Unpublished conference paper, 1996)
57. *L'Attaque*, 26 March 1938
58. *L'Attaque*, 15 January 1938
59. Chaix: *Les lauriers du lac de Constance*; Chaix: *Juliette, Chemin des Cérisiers*
60. *L'Attaque*, 15 January 1938. The reference to the 'aridity' of the PPF press from the female point of view betrays the assumption that rational political argument is not the forte of women.
61. *L'Attaque*, 15 January 1938
62. *L'Attaque*, 15 January 1938
63. *L'Attaque*, 25 December 1937
64. Thanks to Claire Gorrara for explaining this reference to me.
65. *L'Attaque*, 12 February 1938

66.   *L'Attaque*, 5 February 1938. (The article is signed 'Alberte')
67.   *L'Attaque*, 5 February 1938
68.   *L'Attaque*, 5 February 1938
69.   *L'Attaque*, 2 April 1938
70.   *L'Attaque*, 22 January 1938
71.   *L'Attaque*, 12 February 1938
72.   *L'Attaque*, 7 May 1938
73.   This is a matter for further research. It is likely, however, that the existence of women's sections within the PPF and PSF was related to the beginnings of a female presence within the professions and particularly 'para-professions' such as social work. On social work see Reynolds, Siân: *France Between the Wars. Gender and Politics* (London, 1996).
74.   In other words, this is as a critique of the approach to gender, from a one-sided reading of Joan Scott's *Gender and the Politics of History* (New York, 1988), which reduces history to the monotonous recounting of the 'power-knowledge complexes' that 'constitute' women. See also Behhabib, Seyla: 'Feminism and the Question of Postmodernism', in *The Polity Reader in Gender Studies* (1994)
75.   *L'Attaque*, 18 October 1937
76.   *L'Attaque*, 18 October 1937
77.   *L'Attaque*, 7 January and 4 March 1939
78.   *L'Attaque*, 9 April 1938.
79.   *L'Attaque*, 18 October 1937
80.   *L'Attaque*, 2 October,1937; 23 October 1937 on the 40 hour law
81.   ADR: 4m 236, 22 December 1937
82.   *Le Nouvelliste*, 7 July 1937 for the attitudes of building industry employers.
83.   AN: BB[18] 3121, 28 July, 1938; *L'Attaque*, 8 and 15 October 1938; *Le Nouvelliste* 10 and 16 July 1938 for PPF activity in the Borie dispute
84.   *L'Attaque*, 30 April 1938.
85.   CJS: 516 4073[3] Dossier Beugras-Célor
86.   CJR: 1294
87.   CJR: 1294
88.   *L'Attaque*, 7 August 1937
89.   *L'Attaque*, 5 November 1938
90.   *L'Attaque*, 15 January 1938
91.   Soucy: *French Fascism*, pp 248-9
92.   *L'Attaque*, 7 August 1937
93.   *L'Attaque*, 1 November 1936 on the place of the 'cadres' in the corporation
94.   CJR: 1294
95.   *L'Attaque*, 7 January 1939
96.   *L'Attaque*, 14 January 1939
97.   ADR: 4m 263, 29 July, 1937; *L'Attaque*, 21 August 1937
98.   AN: F[2] 2667; *Le Nouvelliste*, 16-18 December 1936
99.   The two regional party conferences were by invitation only

100. Machefer, Philippe: 'L'Union de droits, le PSF, et le Front de la liberté, 1936-7', *Revue d'histoire moderne et contemporaine*, 17 (1970), pp 112-26. Irvine, William D.: *French Conservatism in Crisis. The Republican Federation of France in the 1930s* (1979), pp 127-58; *L'Union Républicaine du Sud-Est* 23 May, 6 June 1937 for Perret's views on the proposed Front. Béguet, Bruno: 'Comportements politiques et structures sociales. Le Parti Social Français et la Fédération Républicaine à Lyon, 1936-1939', (Mémoire de maîtrise, Lyon II, 1988), p 63.

101. Burrin: *La dérive fasciste*, pp 291-300

102. *L'Attaque*, 12 June, 6 November 193

103. *L'Attaque*, 13 November 1937

104. *L'Attaque*, 7 August, 2 October, 25 December, 1937

105. *Union Républicaine*, 27 February, 1938; *L'Attaque*, 26 February, 1938, *Volontaire '36*, 4 March, 1938; ADR 4m 236, 22 February, 1938

106. AN: CJS, 514 4703[1]

107. *L'Attaque*, 21 August 1937; Chauvy, pp 174-6

11. A BROAD CHURCH: FRENCH CATHOLICS AND NATIONAL-SOCIALIST GERMANY

Kay Chadwick

In the preface to his 1936 text *L'évangile de la force. Le visage de la jeunesse du Troisième Reich*, the right-wing Catholic writer Robert d'Harcourt summarized his view that in National Socialism 'the youth of Germany have been given a "false God".'[1] In his 1937 text *La gerbe des forces. Nouvelle Allemagne*, Alphonse de Châteaubriant, another right-wing Catholic writer, defined the National Socialists as 'l'apparition humaine d'un recommencement de l'oeuvre de Dieu.'[2] Such different comments from two representative Catholic writers of similar background demand explanation. The purpose of this chapter is to assess a range of French Catholic responses to German National Socialism, from those whose reservation and condemnation was matched by their opposition to communism, to those whose Catholicism motivated a prewar sympathy for National Socialism which, in a few extreme cases, resulted in wartime collaboration with Hitler's Germany.

Before 1940

On 30 January 1933, Adolf Hitler became Chancellor of Germany. In September 1933, he signed a Concordat with the Vatican which recognized the German Catholic Church's right to operate as an educational provider and to act in a pastoral capacity, but which obliged the Church to give up its social, political and professional organizations. In France, there was some evidence of concern over the nature of the Concordat and what this meant in terms of both the potential impact of National Socialism and the status of the Church. For example, the non-confessional newspaper *Le Temps*, writing in response to the Concordat, commented that, 'loin de pouvoir influencer le régime hitlérien, la religion catholique va devoir combattre celui-ci, qui est une nouvelle religion.'[3] Religious imagery abounds in the accounts of National Socialism written in the second half of the 1930s by sympathetic French visitors to Germany (many of whom would go on to collaborate with Germany during the Occupation), as illustrated by the men of the newspaper *Je Suis Partout*. Pierre-Antoine Cousteau, for example, wrote of 'tout un peuple qui prie dans une gigantesque cathédrale païenne', while Robert Brasillach described Germany as 'la cathédrale de lumière' and National Socialism as 'cette religion nouvelle', suggesting that 'qui ne voit pas dans la consécration des drapeaux l'analogue de la consécration du pain, une sorte de sacrement allemand, risque fort de ne rien comprendre à l'hitlérisme.'[4]

Many French Catholic writers and intellectuals were disturbed by National Socialism's quasi-religious aspects, much as they denounced the godlessness of communism, and reacted strongly in the face of such images. For example, the Catholic Personalist groups of the 1930s called for a spiritual revolution, termed a *nouvelle chrétienté*, to counter the crisis of modern civilization which they believed was rooted in the individualist and totalitarian (fascist or communist) regimes of the day and accorded inappropriate priority to the temporal above the spiritual. The November 1933 edition of the Personalist publication *L'Ordre Nouveau* included an open letter to Hitler in which the Personalists attacked National Socialism for its 'fausse référence à une primauté du spirituel dont "vous ne connaissez que les reflets, les imitations, les ersatz"',[5] while fascism in general was condemned in a December 1933 special number of the review *Esprit* for its 'pseudo-valeurs spirituelles fascistes'.[6] Definition of National Socialism as a false religion featured also in other Catholic-inspired publications of the later 1930s, most notably after the publication of the March 1937 papal encyclical on the situation of the Church in Germany, *Mit brennender Sorge*.[7] For example, following the 1938 Munich agreement, *Le Voltigeur Français*, a review in the spirit of *Esprit*, proclaimed that cooperation with Nazism represented 'un esclavage spirituel et matériel' and that France must 'rester humain'. The Jesuit review *Études* condemned the inhuman and anti-Christian nature of totalitarianism, targeting both the 'sans-Dieu du communisme' and the 'faux-dieux du national-socialisme'. And the Dominican *La Vie Intellectuelle* attacked the Third Reich's 'paganization' of Christian festivals and its substitution of racism for religion. Denunciation of National Socialism also featured in the conservative Catholic press, such as *La Croix* and *L'Echo de Paris*, the latter also fuelled at least in part by its long-standing Germanophobia.[8] Moreover, the influential Catholic thinker Jacques

Maritain, the acknowledged authority behind the theory of the *primauté du spirituel* at the heart of *nouvelle chrétienté*, was also manifestly concerned by the situation of the Church in Germany, defining the Concordat as an example of 'les formes de totalitarisme qui prétend protéger Dieu' but which, in reality, represented 'un retour offensif de l'antichristianisme et de l'athéisme ouverts'.[9]

In the mid 1930s, fear and condemnation of National Socialism was exceeded by a Catholic obsession with communism as the absolute evil. Catholic anti-communism flourished in 1930s France, nourished particularly by the internal experience of the Popular Front. Some liberal Catholics saw the Blum government's campaign against the social ills of poverty, unemployment and injustice as not dissimilar to the Church's programme of Catholic Social Action, thereby activating a debate on the potential for cooperation between Catholics, socialists and communists. And a minority of left-wing French Catholics (including those linked to the journal *Terre Nouvelle*, the *organe des chrétiens révolutionnaires*) reacted positively to the Communist leader Maurice Thorez's *main tendue*, first proffered to Catholics in 1936.[10] However, conservative Catholics feared that the arrival of the Popular Front in power would revitalize secular-clerical conflict in France, and conservative Catholic newspapers such as *L'Echo de Paris* and *La France Catholique*, both variously linked to Castelnau's right-wing Fédération Nationale Catholique (FNC) movement, presented the Popular Front's 1936 election victory as 'un accident et une duperie',[11] a communist threat which surpassed the Nazi threat since 'à la différence du danger nazi, le danger communiste apparaît intérieur à la France.'[12] In the eyes of Pius XI, communism undoubtedly represented the greatest danger to Catholicism. The Pope had already written in his 1931 encyclical *Quadragesimo anno* that 'là où il a pris le pouvoir, [le communisme] se montre sauvage et inhumain', emphazising its 'nature impie et injuste';[13] and Catholic anti-communism received further papal expression in the equally denunciatory 1937 encyclical *Divini redemptoris*, which described communism as a 'pseudo-idéal' and condemned 'le nouvel Evangile que le communisme bolchevique et athée prétend annoncer au monde, comme un message de salut et de rédemption.'[14]

Although clearly obsessed with communism, the Catholic Church was not unaware of the potential threat simultaneously posed by National Socialism, especially given Germany's violation of the 1933 Concordat and her attempted subordination of universal religion to a 'religion' of the state. Germany was hostile to religion on the grounds of its power and influence, and many Catholics clearly feared that Hitler's goal was the suppression of Christianity. The papal encyclical *Mit brennender Sorge*, written in response to these events and published just a few days before *Divini redemptoris*, caused significant front-page comment in the French Catholic press. No doubt prompted by the Pope's comment that 'seuls des esprits superficiels peuvent tomber dans l'erreur qui consiste à parler d'un Dieu national, d'une religion nationale [...] dans les frontières d'un seul peuple',[15] some publications chose to extend the papal condemnation of Germany into a debate on the doctrine of National Socialism itself and its potential as a new religion. But, significantly, in 1937 the French confessional press devoted more column space to a discussion of the content of *Divini redemptoris* than to *Mit brennender Sorge*, thereby underlining the Catholic preoccupation with communism.[16]

So, despite the definite emphasis on anti-communism in the mid 1930s, there is no doubt that there also existed a considerable background of Catholic concern, papal condemnation and popular fear of National-Socialist Germany, which was variously perceived as overly nationalistic, excessively revolutionary, basically pseudo-spiritual and even anti-Christian. And yet, against this background, a few Catholics chose openly and fervently to support Hitler and his regime. Intransigent Catholic anti-revolutionary sentiment and inherent anti-communism meant that most conservative Catholics were suspicious of the Popular Front and feared the rise of communism. But while most opposed communism with Catholicism, a few turned to National Socialism as a lesser evil, on the basis of 'Hitler plutôt que le bolchevisme'.[17]

For these Catholics, National Socialism represented a system of defence in the face of the communist threat. Their numbers included men like Jean Guiraud, a sympathiser of the FNC, joint editor of *La Croix* from 1929 to 1939, for whose readers he represented 'la véritable défense du catholicisme'.[18] A virulent anti-communist, he publicly proclaimed 'tout plutôt que le communisme, tout, même l'hitlérisme'.[19] Mention must also be made of Louis Bertrand, an enthusiastic visitor to Nuremberg in 1935 and author of *Hitler* (1936), and a man credited with the pronouncement 'Hitler est notre seule planche de salut contre les bolchevistes et le communisme.'[20] Bertrand's nationalism underscored his belief that cooperation with Germany would not entail the subjugation of France. National Socialism was simply an expression of the fatherland's defence of freedom and France could learn much from the example of Germany's struggle against domination by communism, itself heavily influenced by international Jewry. Bertrand saw the shadow of communism everywhere he looked, and his extreme fear of this one ideology no doubt veiled his eyes to the true nature of National Socialism, especially with regard to the regime's antisemitism. Robert d'Harcourt, himself a right-wing Catholic anti-communist, repeatedly warned Bertrand of the aggressive nature of National Socialism, writing on one occasion that 'nous pouvions tendre la main à l'Allemagne de 1920. Nous ne pouvons aujourd'hui hélas que montrer le poing à celle de 1934.'[21] But such comments fell on deaf ears, for Bertrand maintained his position at least until 1939, the date of his final correspondence with d'Harcourt. Interestingly, despite their prewar sympathy for National Socialism, after 1940 neither Guiraud nor Bertrand became committed active collaborators with the German occupier. Guiraud resigned from *La Croix* in order to devote his time to historical research; and, following the unauthorized German republication of his text *Hitler* in 1942, Bertrand distanced himself from his work, writing that, 'sa brochure datait de 1936 et ne correspondait plus à la situation actuelle.'[22]

The most striking example of Catholic commitment to National-Socialist Germany before 1940 is the writer Alphonse de Châteaubriant, whose intransigent Catholic roots predisposed him to anti-communism, like many others, but whose dissatisfaction with popular, institutional Catholicism set in progress an individual religious quest which stemmed from his conviction of the need for spiritual regeneration (or a *nouvelle chrétienté*), and which, in his case, resulted in an unconventional definition of National Socialism in Christian terms, unique in the period before 1940. For Châteaubriant, National Socialism was not a lesser evil than Communism but a positive Christian response to the contemporary crisis of civilisation, one manifestation of which was, of course, the Popular Front in France. With communism considered a force for dechristianization and National Socialism perceived as anti-communist, Châteaubriant adopted a neat but questionable logic which interpreted National Socialism as the counter-force of communism, and therefore as a force for rechristianization. He advocated complete spiritual renewal through the rediscovery and reactivation of early medieval values as exemplified during the Gallo-Germanic Empire of the 'divine right' ruler Charlemagne (742-814). His 1937 essay *La gerbe des forces. Nouvelle Allemagne* revealed that National-Socialist Germany matched his Christian requirements: the nation was founded, he believed, on the primacy of the spiritual, while the National Socialists were defined as an elite group of reborn heroic warrior-crusaders, governed by Hitler, a spiritually guided Charlemagne-type ruler. Germany represented the potential for a new unified Frankish Christian Europe in which the French would play a significant role associated with the Germans on the grounds of race, and which would be 'purified' by the removal of the 'inferior' and 'unworthy' communists and Jews. With that end in mind, Châteaubriant promulgated racism and supported National Socialism because he was a Christian and not because he upheld some form of fascist ideal. Châteaubriant's commitment to a policy of alliance with Germany can, in fact, be traced back to the First World War: he was not 'converted' to National Socialism during his exploratory visits of 1935 and 1936, but rather used his account of those visits to give direct expression to his long-standing commitment and to detail his desired form of cooperation between France and Germany. Before 1940, Châteaubriant was a collaborator in waiting.

1940 Onwards

Following the defeat of France after nine months of the Second World War, Hitler's forces entered Paris on 14 June 1940. Inevitably, all in France were principally concerned with the nature of the relationship with the occupier, and, in Vichy, Philippe Pétain, a First World War hero, was accorded full governmental powers on 10 July 1940 'in the name of stabilizing the situation and establishing a *modus vivendi* with Germany.'[23] Pétain was swiftly and widely regarded as France's 'providential man', a description employed by Mgr Caillot, Bishop of Grenoble, as early as 23 June 1940 (but an epithet by no means restricted to Catholics),[24] both because of his meeting with Hitler at Montoire, which found favour with many keen to establish a working relationship with the occupier, and because of the programme of *révolution nationale*, through which Vichy came to represent a 'rallying point for all those who reviled and feared the Popular Front and everything it stood for.'[25] Under the slogan *travail, famille, patrie*, the *révolution nationale* aimed to combat decadence and disorder, and to promote tradition, order and anti-republican values.[26] Catholic attraction to the *révolution nationale* was immediate and deepened throughout 1940, largely because of its reactionary programme. Many Catholic leaders had been quick to root the defeat of France in 1940 in the 'godless' Third Republic, and saw in Vichy a form of revenge of authoritarianism against republicanism and secularism, as well as an opportunity for France to rediscover her Christian potential, even to 'refaire une chrétienté',[27] and for the Church to recover its lost privileges. Pétain's popular image as the 'saviour' of France was sustained by the French Catholic Church which not only adopted Vichy's slogan as its own with the words 'ces trois mots sont les nôtres',[28] but also participated in the maintenance of the 'cult of Pétain', which was much more markedly accepted by French Catholics than Protestants, even holding religious services to celebrate Pétain's visits to towns in the southern zone. Cardinal Gerlier's famous Lyon proclamation of November 1940 that 'Pétain c'est la France, et la France, aujourd'hui, c'est Pétain' summarized well Pétain's popularity with Catholics at this time, suggesting that he was the very symbol of Catholic France. And when, in July 1941, the Church proclaimed its stance as one of 'loyalisme sans inféodation au pouvoir établi', the mass of Catholics supported their Church's attitude, no doubt confirmed in their opinion by the Vatican's endorsement of the regime.[29] Adulation of Pétain, then, was widespread, and clerical and lay Catholics alike clung to Vichy. However, Catholic support for Vichy was not matched by a similar enthusiasm for the German occupier. Given Hitler's response to Catholicism at home, it is not surprising that Germany's occupation of France was viewed by the Church with a degree of suspicion and reserve, a climate which was broadly maintained throughout the war; indeed, Church activities were consistently and closely monitored by the occupier, and clerics suspected of involvement in 'resistance' were increasingly subjected to harassment or deportation.[30]

Nevertheless, despite Germany's hostility to religion, a minority of French Catholics did openly favour collaboration, prompted to act by a range of phobias and beliefs (none of which was exclusive to Catholics) including Anglophobia or a certain presumption that Germany and France together formed the ideal partnership of equals to lead Europe into the future. However, in line with those Catholics who reacted positively to National Socialism before 1940, they acted principally through anti-communism, especially following the Soviet Union's entry into the Second World War on 22 June 1941 and the subsequent creation on 7 July 1941 of the Légion des Volontaires Français contre le Bolchevisme (LVF), whose members fought in Russia for the German cause and to which some Catholics gravitated. Many clerics supported Vichy, but few were 'manifestly guilty of advocating or practising collaborationism', in the sense of wholehearted militant commitment to National-Socialist Germany and its doctrine.[31] However, a few characters can be identified, including such prominent and striking clerics as Cardinal Alfred Baudrillart, the aged rector of the Institut Catholique de Paris, a former sympathiser of the nationalist Action Française (AF) movement and zealous Germanophobe, who promoted collaboration with Germany from 1940; the self-styled Mgr Jean Mayol de Lupé, a veteran of the Great War, who became chaplain-general to the LVF; and Mgr Henri Dutoit, Bishop of Arras, who wrote a pastoral letter advocating collaboration in the post-Montoire period and who has been described as 'the only diocesan bishop that could really have been said to have "collaborated".'[32]

Baudrillart's 'conversion' to National Socialism is particularly striking. His long-standing Germanophobia was rooted in his interpretation of history, focusing especially on the Franco-German conflicts begun in 1870 and 1914, and he was no less hostile to Hitler and National-Socialist Germany in 1939. Hitler was 'un monstre peu ordinaire' who had duped both Daladier and Chamberlain at Munich; his annexation of Bohemia and Moravia in 1939 is described as 'la conquête pure et simple; le droit de la force';[33] and National Socialism itself is defined as 'une barbarie renouvelée du paganisme'.[34] But Baudrillart's horror of communism, alongside his Anglophobia and sympathy for Pétain, finally outweighed his Germanophobia and in November 1940 his post-Montoire pro-collaboration declaration was published in Châteaubriant's collaborationist newspaper La Gerbe.[35] Motivated by his anti-communism, Baudrillart saw the war against Russia as a new crusade, at a time when 'le monde chrétien et civilisé se dresse dans un élan formidable pour défendre et sauver notre antique société chrétienne en péril de bolchevisation, c'est-à-dire en péril de mort.'[36] Germany's action represented a noble enterprise which was 'susceptible de délivrer la France, l'Europe, le monde, des chimères les plus dangereuses, d'établir entre les peuples une sainte fraternité renouvelée du Moyen Age.'[37] And his commitment to the creation and activity of the LVF was unequivocal, lauding its members as 'les meilleurs fils de France, l'illustration agissante de la France du Moyen Age' and concluding that 'ces légionnaires sont les croisés du vingtième siècle; que leurs armes soient bénies! Le tombeau du Christ sera délivré.'[38]

Such statements elicited a range of responses from French Catholics: expressions of admiration and support came from the Catholic university system, for which Baudrillart worked, as well as from some members of the Catholic hierarchy, such as Mgr Duparc (Bishop of Quimper), Mgr Marmottin (Bishop of Reims) and Mgr Valeri (the Papal Nuncio to Vichy). But many other Catholics, both clerical and lay, were more reticent: Cardinal Suhard (Archbishop of Paris) visited Baudrillart the day after his declaration in La Gerbe, indicating that he would have preferred him to make a statement 'excluant complètement la collaboration religieuse avec le nazisme'; and Baudrillart received numerous letters from lower clergy and lay Catholics which ranged in tone from disappointment through reproach to condemnation and insult.[39] Baudrillart was never directly condemned by Rome, although many judged him to be on the verge of senility. Moreover, after his death in November 1942 at the age of 83, the

French episcopacy displayed 'an extraordinary show of solidarity, some 30 bishops attending the requiem mass in Notre Dame.'[40]

The case of Mgr Mayol de Lupé bears some similarities to that of Baudrillart, since he was also a veteran of the First World War and a committed crusader against communism, although in his case and despite his advancing years (he was 67 in 1940), he played an active role through his position as chaplain-general to the LVF. This role of 'prélat botté' was allegedly offered him by Otto Abetz, German ambassador to France during the Occupation and whom Mayol de Lupé had met in Germany in 1938, and he is said to have accepted the post 'sans aucun déplaisir et même avec le plus vif plaisir, aimant l'action et sans doute la guerre qui en est la forme la plus rude et la plus enivrante.'[41] Active in the field, Mayol de Lupé rode and fought alongside the LVF troops, his uniform decorated with both the rosette of the French Légion d'honneur, which he gained in 1938, and the German Iron Cross, won on the Russian front in 1942. Dressed in German uniform, his photograph even appeared on the front page of the German newspaper *Signal* in October 1943.[42] His commitment to Germany's 'crusade' against Russia was complete—he allegedly ended each Sunday mass celebrated with the LVF in the field with the words 'Heil Hitler! Et pieux dimanche, mes fils!'—and his belief in a German victory remained steadfast, even when defeat loomed in 1945.[43] Judged and sentenced to 20 years' hard labour in May 1947, he was freed after four years and died in 1956 at the age of 83.[44]

Mgr Dutoit, Bishop of Arras, shared Baudrillart and Mayol de Lupé's fervent anti-communism, and, like most Catholics, had reviled the Popular Front and welcomed its demise in 1938 as an opportunity for France to effect a *redressement*. Following the declaration of war in September 1939, he displayed no hesitation in defining the conflict as 'une véritable croisade pour le salut de la civilisation chrétienne' but considered Germany to be the aggressor, believing that her action represented 'la renaissance de l'éternel danger allemand et aussi la perversion de la civilisation chrétienne qu'il [Dutoit] prétendait défendre contre l'autre danger, le communisme.'[45] However, loyal to Pétain and the Vichy regime as the established authority in France from July 1940, Dutoit effected 'un curieux phénomène d'occultation'[46] following Pétain's post-Montoire declaration, erasing all criticism of Hitler and Nazi neo-paganism from his discourse and henceforward promoting collaboration. In a pastoral letter dated 22 December 1940, Dutoit justified a policy of collaboration with Germany on the grounds that 'le Maréchal est l'autorité légitime: donc nous devons lui obéir en tout.'[47] For Dutoit, Pétain's announcement on 30

November 1940 that 'j'entre aujourd'hui dans la voie de la collaboration'[48] required all of France to do the same. He argued that the word *collaborer* had been misunderstood, stating that 'la collaboration suppose une libre et loyale volonté d'entente' rather than the subjugation of one country by another. He continued in similar vein, writing that:

> Je collabore: donc je ne suis pas l'esclave à qui l'on interdit toute initiative de parole et d'action et qui n'est bon qu'à enregistrer des ordres. Je collabore: donc j'ai le droit d'apporter une pensée personnelle et un effort original à l'oeuvre commune; je puis dire non et je puis dire mieux.

Not surprisingly, the Germans capitalized on Dutoit's letter, although many diocesan priests refused to read the text out from their pulpits[49] and, with few exceptions, the Catholic response to Dutoit consisted of 'critiques et remonstrances'.[50] Even though Catholic theology states that 'une autorité légitime peut parfois donner des ordres qui ne sont plus conformes à la morale' and that, in such instances, 'il faut obéir à Dieu plutôt qu'aux hommes',[51] Dutoit was incapable of political indifference. He maintained his attitude throughout the war, his steadfast and unreserved commitment to Vichy and collaboration setting him apart from the Church's official position of 'loyalisme sans inféodation au pouvoir établi' which it held from July 1941.

A small number of lay Catholics held influential ministerial positions particularly during the first two years of the Vichy regime, including Raphaël Alibert, a devout Catholic convert who headed the ministry of justice in the early months of the Vichy regime, and Xavier Vallat, who ran the Commissariat Général aux Questions Juives (CGQJ) from its creation in March 1941 until May 1942. However, as the Occupation progressed their numbers diminished and, by May 1942, few Catholics remained in post.[52] Moreover, most Catholics at Vichy acted on the basis of *collaboration d'état*, that is 'collaboration with Germany for reasons of state', while very few can be charged with *collaborationnisme* 'in the sense of an openly desired cooperation with and imitation of the German regime.'[53] The exception is Philippe Henriot, a committed member of the Catholic nationalist right, evidenced by his prewar links with the FNC, who on 6 January 1944 was appointed Vichy's Minister of Information and Propaganda. In 1936, General de Castelnau, leader of the FNC, described Henriot as 'un défenseur ardent de la religion, de la famille et de la société'.[54] In the mid 1930s, Henriot's anti-republican prejudices made him a natural opponent of the Popular Front in France and supporter of

Franco's nationalists in Spain, prejudices confirmed by the 1940 defeat of France. Henriot was soon a committed Pétainist, and, despite his initial hesitation, gradually developed into one of the most enthusiastic propagandists for collaboration. Like so many others, his commitment to Germany was rooted in his anti-communism: he saw his mission as nothing less than the reconciliation of National Socialism and the Church, alongside the union of France and Germany, 'the natural corollary to [which] was the fight against bolshevism as the enemy of Christianity.'[55] During his time as Minister for Information, Henriot broadcast twice daily on Radio Vichy, repeatedly and eloquently attacking all those he considered lukewarm in their attitude to collaboration and calling on all good Catholics to support the German cause in the fight against communism. He even demanded that Catholics submit to the duty of obedience to the state on the grounds that Christ's teaching was one of submission, thereby effectively challenging those in the Church who increasingly deplored Vichy's submission to Germany and argued that such matters of conscience negated the Catholic duty of loyalty to the state.[56] There is no doubt that Henriot's broadcasts were influential, attracting a large and diverse audience. This made him an obvious target for the Resistance, who eventually assassinated him on 28 June 1944.

Outside Vichy, other lay Catholics held significant positions within collaborationist organizations, including Marcel Bucard, who headed the Franciste movement which had been founded in 1933 and claimed to represent Christian piety; the now infamous Paul Touvier, a member of Joseph Darnand's notorious Milice, created in January 1943, which attracted a distinctly Catholic element; and Châteaubriant, whose prewar commitment to Germany was traced earlier, and who, during the Occupation, was owner-director of the collaborationist newspaper *La Gerbe*, director of the *Groupe Collaboration* and who was also involved in both the Milice and the LVF.

A collaborator in waiting before 1940, Châteaubriant immediately became a collaborator in practice once the Occupation began. His was a collaboration of conviction, based on his interpretation of the war as a 'croisade de salut',[57] in which both the Germans and the LVF legionaries were seen as crusaders, and on his belief that Hitler's actions would reunify Catholic Europe as a single empire as had existed under Charlemagne. In his interpretation of National Socialism the universal far outweighed the temporal: the contemporary campaign against Russia was nothing less than the incarnation of the eternal ideological battle between Christianity and atheism, of which he had written in apocalyptic terms in *La gerbe des forces*. Collaboration with Germany in that struggle would bring about his desired end of the rechristianization and regeneration of the contemporary world, this through the establishment of what he saw as a strong, heroic and militant Christianity, which is also revealed to be elitist and racist in inspiration and activity. The Second World War, then, was not so much a war in itself, but rather one battle in the long-standing war for Christian strength and unity, and hence against the despiritualization caused, as he believed, by individualism and materialism. It is this reasoning which led him to conclude that 'c'est parce que je suis chrétien que je suis allé au national-socialisme, parce que le national-socialisme reconstituait l'homme.'[58] Châteaubriant's brand of Christianity may not have evolved alongside that of the Catholic Church, but his attitude to the world and his proposed programme for regeneration through collaboration with Germany nonetheless came out of his interpretation of Catholicism. Châteaubriant believed in the validity of his vision and his ideals to the end: his rejection of National Socialism as the incarnation of his desired *nouvelle chrétienté* after Germany's defeat in 1945 did not result from any realization of its true nature and activity, but stemmed from his conclusion that Germany had failed to live up to his personal expectations. He left France in July 1944 and died in exile in Austria in 1951 at the age of 74, three years after a French court had sentenced him to death for his wartime activities.

Conclusion

From 1933 to 1945, many French Catholics were as opposed to National Socialism as they were to communism, and very few openly and wholeheartedly collaborated with the German occupier. Those who did were motivated by a range of phobias but principally by their anti-communism, some believing that Hitler's Germany was in some way a 'Christian' regime which could successfully combat communism, others accepting that National Socialism was simply a lesser evil. Historical analysis has often chosen to dismiss these men on the grounds of an alleged political and religious naivety and instability: both Dutoit and Mayol de Lupé have been deemed politically 'naive';[59] Mayol de Lupé has been labelled 'une victime de son trop grand coeur' for his willingness to accept the chaplaincy of the LVF;[60] Baudrillart has been dismissed on the grounds that 'il avait très mal vieilli' with the result that he was unable to place his phobias in any sort of perspective;[61] and Châteaubriant has been dismissed for his 'quasi-mystical, if not crackpot, vision of Nazism'.[62] Although evidently *ultraminoritaire* in their response to National-Socialist Germany, the men studied here should not be lightly dismissed: indeed, their cases serve to reveal Catholicism as a 'broad church', since where some from the same soil evolved to the far left, these men evolved to the far right and even to an endorsement of National Socialism. Their significance lies in the fact that they prove that 'Catholicism', albeit often in an unorthodox form, can lead to collaboration.

Notes

1. Lindenburg, Daniel: 'French Intellectuals and a German Europe: An Aspect of Collaboration', in J. Jennings, ed: *Intellectuals in Twentieth-Century France. Mandarins and Samurais* (London, 1993), p 155

2. Châteaubriant, Alphonse de: *La gerbe des forces. Nouvelle Allemagne* (Paris, 1937), p 161

3. Ponson, Christian: 'L'information sur le nazisme dans la presse catholique française entre 1933 et 1938', in X. de Montclos, ed: *Eglises et chrétiens dans la deuxième guerre mondiale. La France* (Lyon, 1982), p 20

4. Dioudonnat, Pierre-Marie: *Je Suis Partout, 1930-44. Les maurrassiens devant la tentation fasciste* (Paris, 1973), p 158; Brasillach, Robert: *Notre avant-guerre* (Paris, 1981, 3rd edn), pp 277, 282, 285

5. Loubet del Bayle, Jean-Louis: *Les non-conformistes des années 30. Une tentative de renouvellement de la pensée politique française* (Paris, 1969), p 309

6. Winock, Michel: *Histoire politique de la revue 'Esprit', 1930-1950* (Paris, 1975), p 82

7. Pius XI: *Mit brennender Sorge* (Paris, 1989)

8. Christophe, Paul: *1939-1940. Les catholiques devant la guerre* (Paris, 1989), pp 53-7

9. Maritain, Jacques: *Humanisme intégral. Problèmes temporels et spirituels d'une nouvelle chrétienté* (Paris, 1936)

10. *Terre nouvelle* was added to the Index, the Vatican's list of prohibited publications, in July 1936.

11. See Rémond, René: 'Les catholiques et le Front Populaire, 1936-1937', *Archives de sociologie des religions*, 10 (1960), pp 63-9; and Christophe, Paul: *1936. Les catholiques et le Front Populaire* (Paris, 1986).

12. Ponson: 'L'information sur le nazisme', p 22

13. Pius XI: *Quadragesimo anno* (Paris, 1989), pp 88-9

14. Pius XI: *Divini redemptoris* (Paris, 1989), pp 9, 13

15. Pius XI: *Mit brennender Sorge*, p 10

16. Ponson: 'L'information sur le nazisme', pp 22, 31

17. Christophe: *Les catholiques devant la guerre*, p 43

18. Christophe: *Les catholiques devant la guerre*, p 45

19. Guiraud, Jean: 'Le sabotage de l'Alsace-Lorraine par les communistes', *La Croix*, 13 October 1936

20. Bertrand, Louis: *Hitler* (Paris, 1936). Bertrand's alleged pronouncement on Hitler was reported to Cardinal Alfred Baudrillart by Robert d'Harcourt. See Alfred Baudrillart, *Carnets*, Archives de l'Institut Catholique de Paris: MS 6667, 21 January 1939, p 54.

21. Cited in Christophe: *Les catholiques devant la guerre*, p 49

22. Christophe: *Les catholiques devant la guerre*, p 50

23. Larkin, Maurice: *France since the Popular Front. Government and People, 1936-1986* (Oxford, 1988), p 83

24. Duquesne, Jacques: *Les catholiques français sous l'occupation* (Paris, 1986, 2nd edn), p 45

25. McMillan, James F.: *Twentieth-Century France. Politics and Society, 1898-1991* (London, 1992), p 136

26. For the text of Pétain's 11 October 1940 speech announcing the aims of the *révolution nationale*, see G. Jaray, ed: *Le maréchal Pétain. Paroles aux français, messages et écrits, 1934-1941* (Lyon, 1941), pp 78-88.

27. Duquesne: *Les catholiques français sous l'occupation*, p 68

28. Duquesne: *Les catholiques français sous l'occupation*, p 48

29. Duquesne: *Les catholiques français sous l'occupation*, pp 61-5, 54. For an excellent summary of Catholic attitudes to Vichy, see Halls, William D.: *Politics, Society and Christianity in Vichy France* (Oxford, 1995).

30. Halls, William D.: 'French Christians and the German Occupation', in G. Hirschfeld and P. Marsh, eds: *Collaboration in France. Politics and Culture during the Nazi Occupation, 1940-1944* (Oxford, 1989), pp 72-91

31. Halls: *Politics, Society and Christianity in Vichy France*, p 361

32. Halls: *Politics, Society and Christianity in Vichy France*, p 363

33. Christophe: *Les catholiques devant la guerre*, pp 62-4

34. Halls: *Politics, Society and Christianity in Vichy France*, p 361

35. Baudrillart, Alfred: 'Choisir, vouloir, obéir: ce que pense un prince de l'église de la collaboration allemande', *La Gerbe*, 21 November 1940, p 1. Baudrillart had read and admired Châteaubriant's *La gerbe des forces* in July 1940 and welcomed Montoire as the concrete representation of Châteaubriant's ideas. See Christophe: *Les catholiques devant la guerre*, pp 71-2.

36. Duquesne: *Les catholiques français sous l'occupation*, p 167

37. Lefèvre, Eric and Mabire, Jean: *La LVF* (Paris, 1985), p 241

38. Duquesne: *Les catholiques français sous l'occupation*, pp 167-8

39. For details of Catholic attitudes to Baudrillart, see Christophe: *Les catholiques devant la guerre*, pp 79-94

40. Halls: *Politics, Society and Christianity in Vichy France*, p 363

41. Amouroux, Henri: *La grande histoire des français sous l'occupation*, (Paris, 1976-93) vol 3, p 275

42. Amouroux: *La grande histoire des français sous l'occupation*, vol 3, p 311

43. Halls: *Politics, Society and Christianity in Vichy France*, p 350

44. Tournoux, Jean-Raymond: *Le royaume d'Otto, France 1939-1945. Ceux*

qui ont choisi l'Allemagne (Paris, 1982), p 353

45. Claude, Hubert: 'L'évêque, le maréchal, la collaboration, 1940-1945', *Revue d'histoire de la deuxième guerre mondiale*, 135 (1984), pp 53-4

46. Claude: 'L'évêque, le maréchal, la collaboration', p 54

47. Dutoit's pastoral letter is reproduced in Claude: 'L'évêque, le maréchal, la collaboration', pp 58-62

48. For the full text of Pétain's announcement, see Jaray, ed: *Le maréchal Pétain. Paroles aux français*, pp 89-91

49. Halls: *Politics, Society and Christianity in Vichy France*, p 363

50. Claude: 'L'évêque, le maréchal, la collaboration', p 62

51. Claude: 'L'évêque, le maréchal, la collaboration', p 85

52. For details of Catholic ministers at Vichy, see Atkin, Nicholas: '*Ralliés* and *Résistants*: Catholics in Vichy France, 1940-1944', in C.K. Chadwick, ed: *Catholicism, Politics and Society in Twentieth-Century France* (Liverpool, forthcoming).

53. This distinction between *collaboration d'état* and *collaborationnisme* is detailed in Hoffmann, Stanley: 'Collaborationism in France during World War II', *Journal of Modern History*, 40 (1968), pp 376-7.

54. Duquesne: *Les catholiques français sous l'occupation*, p 170

55. Halls: *Politics, Society and Christianity in Vichy France*, p 355

56. Henriot, Philippe: 'Théologie et mobilisation', *Editoriaux*, 9 May 1944, pp 2-3. On Henriot, see also Kedward, Roderick: 'The Vichy of the Other Philippe', in Hirschfeld and Marsh, eds: *Collaboration in France*, pp 32-46.

57. Châteaubriant, Alphonse de: 'Pourquoi je parlerai dimanche au Vel d'Hiv', *Le Cri du Peuple*, 29 January 1942, p 3

58. Châteaubriant, Alphonse de: *Cahiers, 1906-1951* (Paris,1955), pp 212-3. The entry is dated November 1942.

59. Halls: *Politics, Society and Christianity in Vichy France*, pp 363, 350

60. Amouroux: *La grande histoire des français sous l'occupation*, p 275

61. Duquesne: *Les catholiques français sous l'occupation*, p 167 and Christophe: *Les catholiques devant la guerre*, p 90

62. Pryce-Jones, David: *Paris in the Third Reich. A History of the German Occupation, 1940-1944* (London, 1981), p 51

12. SEXING THE SUBJECT: WOMEN AND THE FRENCH RIGHT, 1938-58

Miranda Pollard

Did French women have a special relationship with the right from the end of the Third through to the beginning of the Fifth Republic? The vast historiography on the right gives us few answers and little material from which to begin an analysis. Studies of 'la droite' and 'les hommes de droite' have rendered women invisible. But is right-wing political discourse a sexless, genderless subject?

In this chapter, I will not be attempting a comprehensive survey of the right's politics or attitudes to women, nor indeed of women's experience of rightist politics. Rather, I want to sketch out some more abstract themes, to problematize briefly the whole subject of women and right-wing politics and of how we incorporate women into political history. The apparent absence of women both in the political discourse of the right and in its historiography suggests an imperative re-envisioning of our subject. In these volatile years, 1938-58, we know French 'droitiste' women existed, had conservative or counter-revolutionary opinions, negotiated their public and private lives with quiet or often noisily, explicit articulations of political interest, ranging from active involvement in campaigns to have women 'return to the home' in the 1930s, enthusiastic support for Pétain and Vichy, pro-nationalist Resistance and Gaullism, electoral support for the Mouvement Républicain Populaire (MPR), anti-communism and colonialism in the 1940s and 1950s.

Of course, in no way do I wish to argue that French women were *a priori* right wing. On the contrary, the significance of French feminism, the history of women in the French Resistance and the labour movement, suggests that women were extraordinarily active on the left. Rather, I want to argue that women are never purely absent: their material or symbolic presence or erasure tells us as much about the political discourse or history

231

being constructed, as it does about what 'happened'. History and politics *are* intrinsically engendered, and only a critical rethinking of the process whereby political and historical subjects are (de)sexed or constituted as masculine (universal/neutral) or feminine (particular/subjective) can explain the apparent 'absence' of a subject we know to be present.

The three elements of this topic—women, the right, politics—are dynamic, in flux and highly contextual. Their meanings are never static or fixed. As feminist historians and theorists have shown in the last two decades, 'women' do not represent a transparent, self-evident category. Women were not an historical or material constituency utterly distinct from men. Nor are they always silenced or invisibilized. Their histories, crisscrossed by class, ethnic and geographic differences, as well as by *political differences*, must be told not as parallel to 'mainstream' history, but as always already within and constitutive of that history—in the same way that gender is integral to subaltern or colonial history, for example.

Similarly, 'the right' is not a single phenomenon, but instead a fluid admixture of conservative ideologies, not containable within the strict limits of self-professed (or other-denounced) right or extreme right orthodoxies. As Sirinelli and Vigne point out in their introduction to *Histoire des droites en France*, one is obliged to analyse the different levels of existence of right-wing politics:

> Les droites existent: d'une part, dans l'autoperception des acteurs politiques, c'est-à-dire les Français eux-mêmes; d'autre part, dans les mots du débat civique et de la mémoire collective; enfin, dans la production savante, qui, le plus souvent, a entériné cette autoperception et confirmé le sens de ces mots.[1]

The right potentially comprises the self-representation of French *women* themselves, political discourse and collective memory about women, and, finally, scholarship/intellectual discourse which authorizes the very subject—right-wing women, the right and women, and/or antifeminism. Could these various women-centred elements alter our traditional analyses? Although the authors of this massive three volume history do not seem to concur, this could provides a starting point at least for looking at women and the right. But as Richard Golsan and Melanie Hawthorne point out, the representation of women in this *Histoires des droites* is 'woefully inadequate'.[2]

Looking at antifeminism may provide some clues. I define antifeminism not anachronistically as a conscious movement *against* women, but rather as a broad ideology which rested on presumptions of woman's 'otherness', her essential or 'natural' subordination. As I have argued elsewhere,[3] French antifeminism in this period found unique support, institutionally and ideologically, on the French right.[4] The right, in the most catholic, inclusive use of the term, encompassing moderates and fascists, royalists and republicans, committed itself to 'a certain France', an imagined community, in Benedict Anderson's terms, which could not be envisaged outside of or without the imagery of sexed citizens. The French right (broadly) did have a common discourse on women, a discourse that was intensely antifeminist and intensely *political*.

In a post-Foucaultean world, this epistemological shift from 'high politics' to politics as *power*, is not entirely innocent. Changing masculinist political history will require more than an empirical corrective (or 'political correctness'). To alter the fundamental terms of masculinist representations, the conceptual limits of the subject itself must be re-examined.

For example, in the late 1940s and 50s, when French political pre-occupations centred on decolonization, constitutional reforms and economic reconstruction, women seem peculiarly absent, lost and invisible. The standard political histories covering the Fourth Republic tend to mention women not at all or only briefly in the context of female suffrage.[5] One might argue that this simply reproduces the coverage of contemporary newspapers. Women were almost totally absent from the 'news', from the political pages of *Le Figaro*, for example, even as they were, in these years, all over its back pages—the pages that advertized the delights of the new consumer products, like washing machines, cookers, blenders and coffee grinders.

Yet far from what we might believe, the immediate post-war years are profoundly significant for gender politics. Beyond the debates about how women were using their vote or how complicitous they were in their own subordination, we need to look at the subterranean currents of antifeminist reaction, the subtle shifting of antifeminist discourse away from a direct attack on equality (of citizens, between the sexes) to a reamplification of arguments of sexual difference and natural sexual complementarity, to a marked sexing of citizens by virtue of essential/natural characteristics. The search for a new relationship between France and the colonies, between France and the world, and between French citizens and their execu-tive/legislative body—the 'news' that *was* in *Le Figaro* or the *Journal Officiel* or our standard histories—was paralleled by and articulated through the discourse of a new relationship between women and (male) society. Fraught by years of social/sexual anxieties, marked by institutional reforms and socio-economic changes, the right invested in a quiet antifeminism in the postwar years. Women could be encouraged to embrace and defend their identity of 'woman'—*la femme au foyer* or *la femme française*—even as the imagery of an essential, feminine France could symbolize the vulnerability of France as a whole.

Indeed, the very language of domesticity and appropriate feminine activity became entangled in the *political* crises of the moment as Kristin Ross demonstrates in her study of post-war French modernization, *Fast Cars, Clean Bodies*. Torture in Algeria represents a violent form of national housecleaning, 'distorted, in that French *men*, who would never lift a finger to do housework at home in France, are put to work in the homes of Algerians.' The target of military action is the 'inhabitant', the Algerian 'at home', so that the normal identity of civilian/combattant is inverted.[6] Conquering the feminized body of Algeria, and mobilizing Algerian women, as Frantz Fanon argued in *A Dying Colonialism*—and as the filmmaker, Pontecorvo, graphically showed in *The Battle of Algiers* —was at the heart of the war. Algeria unveiled was Algeria rendered properly French (and dominated, 'subjected') because properly feminine. Materially and symbolically, women uniquely represented the specific horrors of this struggle.

In the *hexagone*, a discourse of sexual difference was more in evidence than ever, not only because of postwar consumerism, which required and addressed female subjects, but, arguably, because the anxieties raised by the Fourth Republic's instability, demanded a 'commonsensical' reassertion of 'core' French culture. In the face of rapid Americanization, anticommunism, decolonization, political and economic uncertainty, appeals to the eternal values of French civilization and nature multiplied.[7]

'Nature', the realm of the ahistorical and biological (therefore irrefutable?), was critical to this discourse. For example, in a review of *The Second Sex*, written in 1949, *Le Figaro Littéraire*'s critic noted that Madame de Beauvoir was 'obsessed' with male supremacy and female humiliation:

> Comment lui faire comprendre que c'est au bout du don de soi que sont les enrichissements infinis? Et en ce sens la femme, vouée par sa nature a plus de don que l'homme, est plus grande créancière que lui de ces richesses qui sont quelques chose de sacré. C'est que révère, au delà de toute galanterie, ce culte de la femme qui est l'honneur de notre civilisation, et que Madame de Beauvoir voudrait démolir. Il ne sert à rien de lui dire. Les mots même que j'emploie ici, elle les met au ban de son vocabulaire. La nature? Allons

donc! 'Dans la collectivité humaine rien n'est naturel; entre autres la femme est un produit élaboré par la civilisation'.[8]

This attempt at the destruction of *Woman* by a woman scholar is, according to this reviewer, particularly repugnant. It flies in the face of common sense:

> Il suffirait, après tout, ces gros livres refermés, de rencontrer un couple d'amoureux et de ceuillir un rayon de la lumière qu'échangent leurs regards.

De Beauvoir is effectively, if all too revealingly, dismissed as an embittered bluestocking, a loveless and profoundly un-French, unnatural (read 'unfeminine') person.

This attack prefectly encapsulated some of the key themes which merit analysis in any discussion of rightist antifeminism in these years: the appeal to nature (in particular a natural 'femininity'); the idealization of maternalism and 'love'; the consolidation of a commonsensical ideology of heterosexuality; the institutionalization of 'sexual difference'; and, most importantly, the sense that French civilization and 'order' depend on the endorsement of these values. The right did not have an exclusive hold on these values. But, in this period, the right most conspicuously and successfully mobilized them as *political values*. From the closing days of the Third Republic through Vichy and the Fourth Republic, the right was able to promote a certain vision of women, family and social order that served both to legitimate its own policies and to further its claims to be *politically* greater than the sum of any one party position. Promoting order and stability were synonymous with supporting French *grandeur*; both relied on conceptions of how things really were and should be, where people really belonged, and what were the essential, *natural* elements of human hierarchy. The right's interest in women and sexual difference did not stem from some intrinsic misogyny or antifeminism; rather anti-feminism was produced within the discourse of rightist politics generally. Desire for order, stability and 'natural' hierarchy, produced and sustained multiple intersecting discourses: of gender, nation and race, for example. These discourses were not ethereal or 'merely prescriptive' phenomena. Defining women, fixing and containing the meaning of femininity and/or family, for example, was an everyday political process, which found its articulation in a spectrum of ideological and material activities—from welfare policies to strikes, from colonialism to consumerism.

As Joan Scott argues in her study of French feminists and the Rights of

Man, *Only Paradoxes to Offer*, 'debates about gender typically invoked "nature" to explain the differences between the sexes, but they sought to establish these differences definitively by legal means. By a kind of circular logic a presumed essence of men and women became the justification for laws and policies when, in fact, this essence (historically and contextually variable) was only the effect of those laws and policies.' She continues:

> This was the case with citizenship in France. From the Revolution of 1789 until 1944, citizens were men. The exclusion of women was variously attributed to the weaknesses of their bodies and minds, to physical divisions of labor which made women fit only for reproduction and domesticity, and to emotional susceptibilities that drove them either to sexual excess or to religious fanaticism. For each of these reasons, however, the ultimate authority invoked was 'nature'. And nature was a difficult authority to challenge.[9]

The invocation of 'nature' became all the more pressing when socio-economic crisis and direct political challenges threatened to bring unpalatable changes. The anxieties and fears of French conservatives in the interwar years have been well documented. In *Civilization Without Sexes*, Mary Louise Roberts, for example, details the complex process by which French society articulated these anxieties through and around gender.

With the Third Republic already deep in crisis, and post Popular Front reaction politically consolidating itself in a rightwards drift, 1938 provides an important 'transition' year. Feminist historians rightly mark 1938 as a breakthrough as the year in which married women were finally given some legal recognition of this modern status (by the Law of 18 February on the legal capacity of the married woman). The wife would now be allowed to obtain a passport and an identity card, to sign a contact or choose a profession, to open a bank account or accept an inheritance in her own right.

The spokesman for the Commission de Législation Civile et Criminelle, René Renoult, argued that these proposals were designed to give the 'married woman a situation which the 1804 Code did not wish to accord her but which is in perfect harmony with current mores' and to the 'situation which she has won for herself in modern society.'[10] The impact of modernity and current mores was precisely what worried conservatives. Giving a married woman equality involved a disruption of the fundamental hierarchy of the family. Georges Pernot, Senator and President of the Fédération des Associations de Familles Nombreuses de France asserted that the 'tradition of the French family was respect for the authority of the father of the family' and that 'it is necessary to uphold the tradition that provides the strength and stability of our homes.'[11] In place of the defunct Article 213 of the Civil Code which read 'the husband owes protection to the wife, the wife obedience to her husband', Pernot put forward an amendment stating 'the husband, head of the family has the choice of place of residence of the household.' This specific version of reform had been vigorously pursued by the Catholic feminist organization, the *Union Féminine Civique et Sociale* (UFCS) since 1930.[12] The UFCS argued that the Renoult proposals sought the 'greatest possible autonomy' for the individuals involved, but that the UFCS wanted 'a stronger family unit' which respected individual rights. The law would in their view 'suppress the necessary idea of hierarchy, of coordination by authority ... We do not recognize the total independence of the wife, such as that shown by the free choice of a profession, a choice which could even entail a separate domicile, since normally the wife, the mother, should not work outside the home and the husband, the father, should provide for the needs of the household.'[13]

Pernot argued that all societies needed a power of 'decision'. If fathers still had legal responsibility for their wife and children, they had to retain ultimate authority. The Law of 18 February 1938 operated squarely on the principle of '*the interest of the household or the family*' even as it allowed for an apparent emancipatory step.[14] Pernot's interest in the questions was illustrative of a rightist preoccupation.

Pernot's speech to the Senate in January also demanded action on the issues of family and population, an intervention that led to the passing of the 1939 *Code de la Famille*. Maintaining that his speech on the future of the French family was above partisan quarrels, having 'absolutely no political character', Pernot delivered an impassioned plea for urgent government action in favour of large families.[15] Pernot had two explicit targets: one the halting of the rural exodus (which he believed had been exacerbated by the introduction of the 40 hour week), the other the return of women to the home. Drawing attention to the fact that 8 million women were working, he deplored women's 'abandoning' of the family home, which after the rural exodus was the principal cause of depopulation. The payment of a premium for women to stay at home would not only help the family, it would reduce unemployment. He then drew attention to the disproportionate contribution made by large families to national defence and emphasised that those who assured the life of the country should at least be given justice. Pernot claimed that, 'if the government wishes to undertake this policy with courage, it will have behind it the unanimity of Parliament and the unanimity of the country, for all of us share the deep conviction that we will not achieve the health of the nation except by a return to the old virtues of the family.'

This speech gave a forceful summary of the natalist-familialist program, which graphically drew together all the interwar presumptions and prejudices about women's proper social place. It also demonstrated the backward looking tendencies of conservative thought into which this program fitted, the desire for the return to the 'old virtues' which was to reemerge so dramatically in Pétainism. In the political discourse of this one right-wing activist, Georges Pernot, women were not stepping out into a modernist new age but were, rather, being re-captured in the rush to save France from imminent catastrophe.

Pernot, briefly Minister for the Family (in the last cabinet of the Third Republic), was a family association militant who remained active under Vichy. Gauging the shape of antifeminist politics under Vichy does not simply mean following the path of one individual or group, but rather looking at the policies and propaganda of the regime.[16] We can, even in a brief snapshot, spot the gender politics in the French State's devotion to *travail, famille, patrie*. As Pétain declared, 'the new regime is founded on the natural group: family, commune and corporation and the stronger these groups are, the stronger the state is too.' Pétainism encapsulated nineteenth-century right-wing organicist social philosophy:

> the right of families is in effect prior to and above that of individuals. The family is the essential cell; it is the very basis of the social structure; it is on (the family) that we must build; if it gives way, all is lost; if it holds, everything can be saved.[17]

This new moral order, explicitly antithetical to the supposed materialism and individualism of the Republic, promoted family, authority and hierarchy as sacred political values. The unspoken assumption of this traditional conservatism was the need to mobilize citizen-subjects in their appropriate place, to assert difference over equality, authority over democracy. Woman's place was not simply in the home, but more importantly within the orbit of patriarchal authority—a subordinate subject—recognized as crucial to the common good, but nonetheless subordinate, marked as 'other'. This woman/wife/mother was a potent panacea to the ills of defeated France. Even more than for individual laws or policies against women, Vichy stands out as a political regime that wanted to reify and institutionalize sexual difference.

Robert Nye has argued in *Masculinity and Male Codes of Honor in Modern France* that French society seems to have a 'particular bias in favour of biological sex as a primordial category of being' persisting into the contemporary era. The two decades (1938-58) appear as a very specific historical enactment of this bias. Nothing was inevitable or preordained, for example, about the initiatives of 1938, or 1940 (when married women's employment in the public sector was prohibited), or 1944 with the so-called 'granting' of female suffrage. The terms and the context of each of these initiatives must be separately examined (and at greater length than I have here). But each was intimately connected to the right's vision of social order and politics.

Pronatalism, for example, shows us both the tenacity of the links between reproduction and national grandeur, which is strongest on the right but extends to the Parti Communiste Français (PCF), and the hidden, but unshakeable, centrality of women to the political discourse of reconstruction. Promoting the family and advocating population growth created a bridge from 1919 to 1945, from Clemenceau to Daladier via Pétain to de Gaulle. Clemenceau claimed in 1919 that the Treaty of Versailles would be useless if France turned her back on large families; Reynaud claimed in 1937 that France was beaten because of the demographic factor; Pétain announced that France had been beaten in 1940 because of 'too few children'; and, in 1945, de Gaulle demanded 12 million 'beaux bébés' for liberated France. Women were not directly spoken of or to, in these political speeches; their role in reconstruction was presumed. At stake is how certain political processes (for example, economic growth, paternalism, pronatalism) are depoliticized via the mobilization of women (that must remain largely implicit) and a 'naturalization' of sexual difference (that paradoxically creates social unity and political consensus).

Women may not be spoken of explicitly, but may be central to certain political agendas. The mother tongue, maternal identity, racial health, female fertility and female sexuality are all readily political issues. Antisemitism, eugenics and racism crucially depended on women as sexed-subjects.[18] While gender was often repressed in the urgency or 'unity' of the national vision, it could also move centre stage. The right's propaganda on women, as Francine Muel-Dreyfus points out in *Vichy et l'éternel féminin*, was refocused on women with the shift of state patronage to previously marginal groups. If the *Union Française pour la Défense de la Race* asserted in 1943, 'Nous avons tout perdu. Notre seul trésor national est désormais notre race', their message was clear: biology was to be destiny for French citizens in the New Order.[19]

Familialism reveals somewhat different priorities and interests. Under Vichy the concern which Pernot had articulated with diminishing patriarchal authority was given a new spin, and new urgency. For example, in a book entitled *L'ordre familial en marche*, a family movement activist declared in 1944:

> There are not two heads of the family which would divide the family. Neither is there a head of the family and a deputy head. The responsibilities of the man and the woman are of a different nature, as are the qualities that they both bring to the service of the family.
>
> As long as one distinguishes between the job of authority and that of education, the head and the heart, one will realize that neither replaces the other but that the support of the man and woman is vital for the family.[20]

Defeat had 'proved' the devastating consequences of a lack of hierarchy and discipline. The circumstances of the Occupation themselves made order and authority more necessary than ever. In the new France, both men and women had to know their place, forestall the dangers of blurred boundaries and social/sexual disorder. 'Women's occupations are not less important to the public good than men's', declared an advocate of private schools in 1941, 'because they have a house to manage, a husband to make happy and children to bring up well.' Women were especially critical in a symbolically castrated France. They occupied a unique metaphorical and material space, given the restrictions of the Armistice and the absence of the POWs:

> The woman's place is at the center and the heart of the home. If she does not occupy this place, the national revolution ... will be finished ... In a crisis one conscripts citizens. The crisis exists. It is serious. It will only be overcome if we conscript wives and mothers ... this conscription will not be compulsory but instead a voluntary call resolutely undertaken.[21]

This reactionary vision was not just quaint rhetoric. Largely unchallenged, except by the Communist Party—which refused to concede the political terrain to the right and Vichy—this political discourse was continuously used because, at some level, despite all the obvious, terrible failings of the regime, it worked. Home, love of family, recognition between spouses—these images worked to suggest that Vichy could speak for French people in intimate ways, and to reassure men and women that a certain known set of social relationships were secure in a world that was terrifyingly insecure.

The vision of sexual harmony which Vichy offered—the panacea to the anxieties of the interwar years—was not an empty allusion, even when articulated in the most unusual of circumstances and by the most unlikely spokesman for sexual difference and traditional sexual values. The last and ultra-collaborationist Vichy Minister of Education, Abel Bonnard, more associated with the profascist Paris right than the traditionalist Vichy right, waxed lyrical to French students on Joan of Arc Day, 1942:

> Young men of a renewed France, you must show constant respect to young girls who represent the new springtime of France. Leave behind in the sad and loathsome disorder of our past, leave behind in an outdated society, that inappropriate promiscuity where too often our youth degraded themselves. Instead let there be between our young French girls and young French boys that open and cheerful friendship without prudery or ambiguities, [the friendship] that excludes all illicit familiarity and which does not allow any love other than that which unites a couple faithfully.[22]

Bonnard, days before the Allies landed, when the French State had almost ceased to exist, wrote with similar enthusiasm about the glories of Vichy's domestic science educational program to his colleague, Philippe Renaudin, the Commissaire Général à la Famille. The date is 3 June 1944:

> I personally attach the greatest importance to this project: domestic instruction is meant to make those who receive it perfectly qualified to fulfil their role of wives and mothers; capable of bringing to family life the skills that not only make it better ordered ... but also make it more gentle and more sweet. In contrast to past education, so abstract and so indifferent to whether it applied to girls or to boys, not really suiting one or the other, this [education] will become the preparation for an occupation and for life which all true education should be.[23]

The fact that Bonnard, with all the gossip about his pederastic proclivities, should have extolled sexual difference or separate spheres in this way, is not simply a sham. (Nor indeed is his individual motivation my prime concern.) In June 1944, the government was still looking to the business of addressing its subjects through the discourse of sexed citizens. Order, sweetness, love, romance, family and domesticity were social virtues with direct political implications.

Explicitly or implicitly, in a variety of ways, 'women' were being brought back to 'nature', women were being enlisted to regenerate France or to ward off the perils of an undifferentiated sexless future, that threatened by Gide or Beauvoir, the Third or Fourth Republic.

In a front page article entitled, 'Une certaine droite', published in April 1958 by *Le Figaro*, André Siegfried noted that, 'Vichy undoubtedly represented the most reactionary of any regime in French history.' Although accepting that France needed a right, Siegfried wondered how one could know what sort of right. Rejecting the excesses of the far right, Siegfried asserts that they certainly do not represent 'le fonds du pays, dont le sentiment national, sous réserve de quelque zenophobie, semble être sain.' In the imaginary of 'le fonds du pays', women have an integrative and often articulated place. 'Le fonds du pays' is the healthy, homely France which we know exists (apparently beyond or regardless of the politics of Pétain or de Gaulle, Bidault or Poujade, Bousquet or Le Pen.) Is the absence of women in such political commentary—an absence that is replicated in most of our political histories—not evidence of the very success of the right's discourse on women? The significance of gender is precisely in its ability to recede from view or to be thrust into the limelight, to frame and make comprehensible the political changes of the moment, to appear beyond or above politics.

This leaves us with the job of sorting out how women as a category get mobilized and adressed in given historical situations. But it also reminds us that there is no simple phenomenon—the right—with a hermetically sealed agenda, antifeminism in this case. Tracing the appeal and entrapments of antifeminism may require further unravelling the very fabric of all political ideologies which speak *to* and *for* sexed subject-citizens.

Notes

1. Sirinelli, Jean-François and Vigne, Eric, 'Introduction générale', in J.-F. Sirinelli, ed: *Histoire des droites en France* (Paris, 1992), vol 1, p x
2. Hawthorne, Melani and Golson, Richard J, 'Righting Gendered Writing: A Bibliographic Essay', in *Gender and Fascism in France* (Hanover/London, 1997), p 175
3. My argument is developed at length in my *The Reign of Virtue. Mobilizing Gender in Vichy France, 1940-1944* (Chicago, forthcoming)
4. Antifeminism does not 'belong' to any French political group exclusively. We have only to think of the Jacobins or of Proudhon to realize that there is no necessary corollary between the left and feminism, or the right and antifeminism. Indeed, I would contest the notion that antifemism, broadly defined, is even the exclusive property of men (left or right). The defence of sexual essentialism, of inequality or 'difference', like the advocacy of separate spheres or a natural feminine/masculine binarism can be

forwarded, indeed clung to, as vociferously by women as men, although usually not with the same consequences. Sexism, misogyny, feminism and antifeminism exist and proliferate in multiple, complex ways across the spectrum of French political life, serving to unite, as much as distinguish, many (odd) political positions.

5.   For example, Rioux, Jean-Pierre: *The Fourth Republic, 1944-1958* (Cambridge, 1987); Williams, Philip: *Politics in Postwar France* (London, 1955); and Elgey, Georgette: *La république des illusions* (Paris, 1965).

6.   Ross, Kristin: *Fast Cars, Clean Bodies. Decolinization and the Reordering of the French Body* (London, 1995), p 110

7.   A fascinating account of French reaction to American influence can be found in Kuisel, Richard: *Seducing the French. The Dilemma of Americanization* (1993). Despite the promise of its title, this study does not investigate the gendered discourses of French anti-Americanism.

8.   Cited in Laubier, Claire ed: *The Condition of Women in France, 1945 to the Present. A Documentary Anthology* (London, 1990), p 22

9.   Scott, Joan: *Only Paradoxes to Offer* (Harvard, 1996)

10. Projet de loi portant modification des textes de Code Civil rélatifs à la capacité de la femme mariée. Sénat, séance du 19 mars 1937. In: *Journal Officiel, Débats Parlementaires* (*JO*), 20 mars 1937

11. Sénat, séance du 8 décembre 1936, *JO*, p 1565. Pernot, a fervent Catholic, was also honorary president of the Ligue pour le Vote Familial. He served later on the Haut Comité de la Population and was to become Minister of the Family in the last government of the Third Republic. See Pollard: *The Reign of Virtue.*

12. In 1930,the UFCS established its own study group on reform of the Civil Code which included A. Rouast, professeur de droit (Paris). The UFCS debated the issue at its 1931 congress. See UFCS: *La femme et la réforme du code civil* (Paris, 1937).

13. *La femme et la réforme du code civil*, p 12

14. Loi du 19 février 1938 portant modification des textes du Code Civil rélatifs à la capacité de la femme mariée: *JO*, 19 février 1938.

15. Pernot rejected both defeatist passivity at the demographic crisis and short-term politics. The family vote, reform of the tax code, improved housing, priority in public service recruitment for members of large families and finally the creation of an appropriate moral climate, were all familiar remedies. Pernot's entire speech is reproduced in 'Interpellation de M Georges Pernot devant le Sénat, le 8 janvier 1938'. In: *Pour la vie*, mars 1957, pp 88-103. The Senate intervention was made possible with the cooperation of the President Camille Chautemps, himself a member of a family association. See Talmy, Robert: *Histoire du mouvement familial*, p 225.

16. See Pollard: *The Reign of Virtue*

17. Pétain, Philippe, 'La politique social de l'avenir', in *Revue des deux*

mondes, September 1940

18. The most concise argument for this interconnectedness remains Bock, Gisel, 'Racism and Sexism in Nazi Germany: Motherhood, Compulsory Sterilization and the State', in Bridenthal ed: *When Biology Became Destiny* (New York, 1984).

19. Muel-Dreyfus, Françoise: *Vichy et l'éternel féminine* (Paris, 1996), p 354

20. Maxime, H.:*L'ordre familial en marche* (1944), p 67

21. Association des Parents des Ecoles Libres (APEL): *L'éducation des filles* (1941)

22. Bonnard, Abel: 'Jeunes gens de France', in his *Les messages de M Abel Bonnard* (1942), contained in AN: 2 AG 570

23. AN: F^{17} 13347, Bonnard to Renaudin, 3 juin 1944

13. THE INTERNAL DYNAMICS OF GAULLISM, 1958-69

Jonathan Watson

Some might consider an assessment of Gaullist ideology during the 1960s a foolhardy enterprise. After all, most commentators refuse to accept that Gaullism has ever been an ideology. Contemporary observers[1] were dismissive of the phenomenon, describing Gaullism as no more than a tenure of supreme power by General de Gaulle, backed by a team of unwaveringly loyal subordinates. Frédéric Grendel, a contemporary journalist, claimed in one Gaullist publication that, 'Dans gaullisme, il y a de Gaulle (Charles de). Le reste est silence.'[2] Political scientists have accepted this view,[3] generally endorsing Stanley Hoffmann's claim that Gaullism was charac-terized by 'ideological emptiness'.[4] Even those who do concede some ideological content to Gaullism usually intepret it primarily in terms of the actions and beliefs of Charles de Gaulle.[5] 'Le gaullisme, c'est d'abord, bien entendu, la pensée politique du général telle qu'elle ressort de ses écrits, ses messages, ses discours', wrote one French commentator.[6] The few historians to have tackled the subject up to now have not significantly deviated from this view.[7]

The object of this essay is to explain why this view of Gaullism is fundamentally flawed. Gaullism cannot be reduced to the achievements of its founder. It will look beyond 'the last great Frenchman'[8] to examine the importance of individual Gaullists, assessing their contribution to Gaullist ideology and considering the implications of their views and actions. In this way, a more complete view of the complex and flexible doctrine of Gaullism emerges. De Gaulle, despite the strength of vision that consti-tuted so powerful a part of his charismatic personality, never produced a specific or coherent political statement. It was the task of the Gaullist *party* to produce a practical policy agenda. In so doing, Gaullist politicians inevitably contributed to a definition of Gaullism. The monolithic, authori-tarian construct described by René Rémond,[9] who insisted that Gaullism represented a modern form of Bonapartism, is an over-simplification. The contributions of de Gaulle's associates and supporters must be taken into account.

The Union pour la Nouvelle République, 1958-59

In most accounts of the 1960s, it is usually argued that the sole reason for the existence of the Gaullist party, the Union pour la Nouvelle République (UNR)—which later fused with the Union Démocratique du Travail (UDT) after the legislative elections of 1962 to form the UNR-UDT before becoming the Union des Démocrates pour la République (UDR) in 1967—was purely to provide President de Gaulle with the parliamentary support he needed to ensure a veneer of democratic respectability.[10] Utterly lacking in initiative and vision, Gaullists contented themselves with uncritical approval of all the General did. As one analyst wrote, 'Pour que de Gaulle soit tout, il fallait qu'elle ne soit rien.' [11]

In many ways, this was the impression the Gaullists created. In 1958, the newly-constituted UNR gave the prestigious name of de Gaulle a prominent place in the party's statement of aims, and referred to it 10 times in the model election address suggested to candidates.[12] The slogan which appeared most frequently on campaign posters was 'UNR=DE GAULLE'. Alain Peyrefitte, standing for the first time as a candidate in the November legislative elections, was advised by the local party official to base his campaign around the phrase: 'Je suis pour de Gaulle et de Gaulle est pour moi'[13] and informed by Roger Frey, the party's general secretary at the time, that the UNR needed deputies who would be ready to follow de Gaulle with 'corpse-like obedience'.[14]

Such a comment reveals a great deal about the kind of behaviour that was initially expected of Gaullists. After the election victory, Albin Chalandon, Frey's successor as general secretary of the UNR, described the main role of the party in its first newsletter as the provision of unconditional support for de Gaulle and his government 'pour tous les problèmes qui mettent en jeu l'intérêt national et dans lesquels la personnalité du chef de l'Etat se trouve engagée.'[15] Later in the same year, at the opening meeting of the party's national council, he appeared to exclude any possibility of positive contributions by Gaullists by arguing that de Gaulle had no responsibilities towards the UNR—'nous sommes sa chose et il n'est pas la nôtre',[16] was his claim. Michel Debré, de Gaulle's Prime Minister between 1959 and 1962, echoed this in a speech to the party's central committee, and insisted that Gaullists should keep quiet about the Gaullist government's shortcomings, commenting, 'il faut critiquer ses adversaires, il ne faut point critiquer ses amis.'[17]

This imperative was felt to be particularly relevant for those who represented Gaullism in parliament. A report on the role of UNR deputies, written by prominent party member Michel Habib-Deloncle for the first of the party's parliamentary study days held in April 1959, argued that they could in no circumstances disassociate themselves from de Gaulle's policies. 'Toute tentative de cet ordre serait une imposture et une trahison', he remarked.[18] Habib-Deloncle made a similar point at the party's Bordeaux assises in November of the same year, pointing out that, since Gaullist deputies owed their electoral sucess to their support for the General, it was their civic duty not to betray their electors by revoking this support. On the contrary, their function was to focus on the government's achievements, ready to campaign for a further five-year mandate.[19]

Given such statements, it is easy to see why Gaullists aroused so much criticism for 'unthinkingly' supporting the General, and why Gaullism was seen as little more than a 'culte du chef', an authoritarian ideology in which loyal troops venerated a great leader. The satirical journal *Le Canard Enchaîné* regularly referred to the Gaullists as 'les godillots du Général', de Gaull's infantry.[20]

Yet throughout de Gaulle's time as President, and particularly in 1959, considerable efforts were made by individuals within the party actively to contribute to the governing process. Although the party's official discourse did stress the fidelity of the party to de Gaulle and contrasted the stability this afforded the country with the chaotic ministerial merry-go-round of the Fourth Republic, those within the UNR were keen to fulfil a less passive role.

First among these was Albin Chalandon himself. Although he was careful to underline the fact that the UNR supported de Gaulle, he also felt that it should maintain a certain degree of independence. As he argued in the internal party newsletter, accepting the main policy options proposed by de Gaulle '*n'implique pas pour autant* l'abdication de la personnalité politique de l'Union.'[21]

On the contrary, he argued that it was the duty of the Gaullist party to assert itself, to propose policy ideas to the government and to press for their adoption: 'il est bon que s'exprime une tendance collective de notre Union, et que celle-ci essaie de faire prévaloir ses vues.'[22] Roger Frey, speaking at the Théâtre des Ambassadeurs in Paris had already made a similar point: the constitution of the Fifth Republic indicated that the President should perform the role of an arbiter. For him to do this, there had to be distinctive choices for him to make: '... pour qu'il y ait un arbitre, il faut *des thèses en présence* ... ' The UNR thus had to have 'conceptions personnelles et précises'.[23] Bertrand Flornoy, at the 1959 parliamentary study days, had followed this lead by arguing that the UNR should have its own independent approach 'afin d'apparaître comme un mouvement original intrinsèquement libre, face au pouvoir exécutif.'[24]

The practical meaning of these ideas had already become apparent. In December 1958, immediately after the legislative elections, Chalandon presented a report on economic policy to the UNR central committee. The text was published in full in the internal bulletin for the newly elected UNR deputies.[25] In the preface to this work, it was asserted that even if not all of the measures Chalandon had proposed had been accepted by the government, the analysis it contained of the economic situation, especially the pressing need for fiscal reform, was still held to be valid.[26] Chalandon disagreed with the government's insistence on austerity and judged the current priority to be stimulating growth.[27]

Remarkably, the secretary-general did not confine his critique to the party's internal publications. In a declaration to the press at the end of 1958, he refused to endorse the government's economic policy, stressing instead the differences of opinion between the party and the government. The UNR, due to its belief in governmental stability, would not withhold its support altogether, but would continue to use its influence to press the government to avoid crises, to achieve full employment, and to ensure that the burden of progress would not fall on one particular social group.[28]

Nor were the party's criticisms limited to economic policy. When the government announced the abolition of pensions for war veterans, the communiqué issued by the secretariat of the UNR noted the measure's offensive 'sécheresse administrative' and promised that in the future the Gaullists would press for measures which took more account of veterans' rights and needs.[29] Evidently, although the government could generally rely on the support of the UNR, it could by no means expect docility.

Meanwhile, the proliferation of press articles, in which the Gaullist party criticized the government it professed to support with such loyalty, continued. In February 1959, the *UNR Bulletin de Presse* published an article entitled 'L'UNR veut une vraie relance économique'. With reference to Chalandon's report of December 1958, the author of the article pointed out that the government's plans did not conform to the wishes of the party, which would have preferred more emphasis on stimulating production rather than on reducing consumption. In fact, the article declared, the public had the UNR to thank for the modification of the measures, which went too far too quickly and had rightly been opposed.[30]

In this way, the UNR showed itself to be an active influence on government decisions.

In the handbook for party candidates of the March 1959 municipal elections, in which the UNR again disassociated itself from the austerity programme, it was asserted that, 'L'Union se réserve le droit de continuer à proposer ses solutions propres.'[31] Chalandon showed this was not an empty promise when later the same year he published the conclusions of a round-table meeting he had convened to study France's economic situation. In this discussion, he complained that the administration's modernization plan was unambitious and that it contributed nothing to the agricultural sector,[32] comments which were repeated the following month in an interview with *Les Echos*, an economic daily.[33]

Prime Minister Debré had already shown himself to be annoyed by such arguments, which he regarded as characteristic of the undisciplined parties of the hated Fourth Republic. In a television broadcast of March 1959, he reminded critics that economic recovery took time.[34] However, this did not prevent Chalandon from writing to Debré in June 1959 on behalf of the UNR central committee to criticize the government's position and to demand closer links between the executive and the party. Gaullists had just learnt from newspapers that the government had decided to increase child benefit. This letter came after several angry meetings of the central committee which, in May for example, had unanimously condemned the subordinate position the government wished to force upon the UNR, a problem which Chalandon sought to highlight in his speech to the meeting of the party's National Council at the end of July.[35]

The Bordeaux Assises: November 1959

It was evident that, in the minds of many, there was no incompatibility between supporting de Gaulle and criticizing a government he had formed. Initially, however, the UNR's attempt to give itself the right to independent views was frustrated by its own internal divisions over the Algerian question. Some of those within the UNR, who encouraged the party to maintain its own identity, were people such as Jacques Soustelle and Léon Delbecque, whose main concern was keeping Algeria French. Categorical refusal to grant the territory its independence was the policy they intended to see the party adopt.[36] For de Gaulle, this would have represented an intolerable restriction on his position at a time when he was attempting to negotiate an end to a conflict which had threatened to generate civil war in France.

At the Bordeaux assises, Jacques Chaban-Delmas argued that problems such as Algeria, foreign policy, defence and the French Community were so vital to national security that the party should not expect to have any influence on government policy in these areas. They should constitute the President's *domaine réservé*.[37] Soustelle was opposed to this, but his resolution expressing a commitment to the maintenance of French sovereignty in Algeria was rejected; and soon afterwards de Gaulle removed him from the government and the party leadership expelled him from the UNR. In a letter to Debré, he expressed regret that the UNR seemed to be becoming the party of unthinking loyalty to one individual: '... si l'on veut faire de l'UNR une machinerie insensible, d'où la réflexion soit bannie et où l'obédience passive tienne lieu de pensée, il est bien évident que je n'y ai plus ma place.'[38] Debré's reply was uncompromising, arguing that, 'L'UNR n'a de valeur, l'UNR n'a de sens, l'UNR n'a de légitimité que dans la mesure où son action épouse *totalement* les directives politiques du général de Gaulle.'[39]

The 1959 congress thus marked the temporary eclipse of Chalandon's attempt to impose his own interpretation of what Gaullist ideology should mean. He was replaced as general secretary of the party by Jacques Richard, who was less interested in encouraging an active role for the Gaullists; this enabled Prime Minister Debré to assert himself as the effective leader of the UNR and thus identify it more completely with the government. Richard argued that the Gaullists should support de Gaulle's government and not seek to influence it; in his speech to the party's second assises in 1961, he argued that Gaullists should be proud of their unconditional support for de Gaulle. According to him this was 'un *certificat de gaullisme* puisque le premier devoir du gaulliste est de tout mettre en oeuvre pour aider le président de la Cinquième République et le défendre contre ses ennemis.'[40]

Once the trauma of the Algerian conflict was over, however, the Gaullist party began once again to define a role for itself independently of de Gaulle. Outside the *domaine réservé* as defined by Chaban-Delmas, the Gaullists still had considerable room for manoeuvre.

The UNR-UDT, 1962-1967

After 1962, Gaullism may be defined in terms of the ideology elaborated by the party's new secretary-general, Jacques Baumel, and the activities of the Gaullist deputies who put Baumel's ideas into action. For while he outlined a coherent definition of Gaullism without reference to de Gaulle, the parliamentary party refused merely to accept instructions from above. The status of the leader lost its importance as Gaullism, emboldened by a second election victory in November 1962, envisaged life after the death of its founder. Although the Gaullist party did not seek to undermine the authority of the government, or completely disassociate itself from its actions in the manner of the parties of the Fourth Republic, its members did not allow themselves simply to be manipulated by those in power.

For Jacques Baumel, Gaullism was much more than the thoughts of de Gaulle. It inaugurated a new kind of politics. France in the twentieth century, he argued, had had enough of ideology.[41] French people did not want politicians endlessly to debate matters of principle, as had been the case under the Fourth Republic. Such discussions were dismissed as 'absurd rituals'.[42] The function of Gaullist deputies was to take speedily the right decisions that would ensure the material prosperity of the nation.[43] The real issues of the 1960s were, according to him, 'problèmes de gestion, de réalisations *précises*, de plans concrets.'[44] The core concepts of Gaullism were cohesion, modernity and efficiency.[45] It was neither 'right wing' nor 'left wing'—such distinctions were out of date.[46] The regime of the Fifth Republic was the triumph of 'the democracy of management'.[47] Sound administration and technical knowledge were more important to French power than great oratory, impressive though this had been in the old days.

In using such language, Baumel was following the example set by Chalandon in the first year of the UNR's existence; he too had stressed the importance of practical problem-solving ability above doctrinal purity.[48] As we have seen, however, scope for party initiative had been limited by the need for unity in the face of the Algerian crisis.

But once this had been settled, no such restrictions needed to apply. Baumel articulated a practical definition of Gaullism in which Charles de Gaulle figured only as the temporary guarantee of the state authority that had been lacking in previous republics, and thus as the necessary corrective for certain defects and inadequacies of French political behaviour. However, the existence of state authority need not entail blind obedience to its decisions, as the activities of the Gaullist deputies after 1962 proceeded to illustrate.

The Gaullist Parliamentary Party, 1962-69

As the new party journal *La Nation* pointed out, Baumel's ideas did not mean that Gaullists should concern themselves purely with 'la gestion des affaires courantes'.[49] They should also exert an active influence on Gaullist policy. Already, the previous year, this same publication had included an article by a prominent Gaullist deputy criticizing the Fourth five-year plan.[50] The journal further highlighted the UNR parliamentary amendments to the plan, many of which had been accepted by the government.[51] The Gaullist party could, in this way, show itself to have an identity distinct from that of the government and maintain its own freedom of action.

La Nation constantly pointed out that although government policy should be defended against the opposition, the parliamentary party 'n'est pas pour autant dispensée de faire preuve d'esprit critique et d'apporter ses suggestions et ses critiques.'[52] On many occasions, the journal enthusiastically pointed out that delegations of deputies were received by the Prime Minister at Matignon to express the view of the party.[53] In this way, the collaboration between the administration and the Gaullist party was seen to be active. Furthermore, members were invited to lunches with the Prime Minister; the parliamentary party had an annual weekend meeting outside Paris, attended by members of the government; and, as in all legislatures, there were informal contacts in the lobbies and at meals and receptions.[54]

Contrary to the belief of their opponents, and that of many historians since the 1960s, Gaullist deputies did not tamely acquiesce in all government policy. Bills were frequently altered to satisfy Gaullist criticism, sometimes before they reached parliament, like the great Agriculture Act of 1962, and sometimes in the house itself, as with a bill on car insurance which arrived there in 1966. Many ministers consulted the party in advance of legislation. As the Gaullist deputy René Sanson argued in 1966, 'Avant qu'un projet de loi ... soit déposée, le minstre compétent vient l'exposer aux membres de sa majorité. Si le ministre et la majorité n'arrivent pas à un accord, il est de pratique courante que le premier minstre vienne à son tour à la réunion pour tenter d'arbitrer les points de divergence. Lorsque la conciliation se révèle impossible, il arrive au gouvernement de retirer son projet de loi.'[55]

Indeed this made sense, for after 1962 Gaullists dominated almost all the important positions on the Assembly's standing committees, and a minister who neglected to discuss matters with the chairman or *rapporteur* would find him making trouble on the floor of the house. Gaullist spokesmen frequently took the lead in criticism, such as future minister André Fanton when he obliged the government to produce more money for the victims of Organisation de l'Armée Secrète (OAS) bombings in 1963.

In some cases, a substantial compromise could be obtained, such as when Joël Le Theule and the defence committee reshaped the military service bill in 1965. Every year it was Gaullist *rapporteurs*, such as Alexandre Sanguinetti,[56] who brought forward the most informed, incisive and damaging criticisms of the budget. On other occasions, the committee representative would express the disquiet of the house as a whole, an unease which was further demonstrated through the threatened defection by the allies of the UNR-UDT within the parliamentary majority—the Républicains Indépendants.

Gaullist deputies did not simply react to the measures that were presented to them. Through their specialized study groups, they became actively involved in drafting policy. These groups were the party equivalent of the National Assembly parliamentary committees. Each one normally included all the Gaullist deputies belonging to the corresponding committee in the Assembly, and by July 1968, it had become compulsory for every Gaullist deputy to belong to at least one permanent study group.[57] The groups represented a unique opportunity to make a contribution to government policy, and it was one that Gaullists did not neglect.[58]

The agricultural study group was the most active. Its members kept in regular contact with the major interests in their field,[59] invited their spokesmen for hearings, kept in touch with *rapporteurs* of parliamentary commissions in charge of important projects,[60] questioned the minister Edgard Pisani on his proposals,[61] and sometimes promoted bills of their own. On one occasion, they persuaded the party to sponsor a private members' bill on contracts for farmers' supplies or products, which passed into law in 1964. The labour study group also inspired an important government bill to increase the powers of works committees in factories.[62]

The negative role of the study groups could be equally important, for they could mobilize party opinion against a measure as well as in favour of one. Thus the agriculture group in 1964 forced Pisani to withdraw the bill reforming land law which conservatives feared as a potential threat to property. The sub-committee on fiscal policy succeeded in delaying and modifying the bill introducing the value-added tax—a warning the government should have heeded more than it did when, two years later, after revising details to appease the sub-committee but without making sufficient effort to prepare the parliamentary ground, it finally brought the unfortunate measure before the Assembly.[63]

The most direct means of bringing pressure to bear on the government was, of course, by making a speech in the Assembly. During debates, the Gaullists frequently reiterated their commitment to making critical but constructive comments on government measures. In the debate on education reform in May 1965, which saw many Gaullists speak out against government proposals, the minister concerned, Christian Fouchet, in his reply to all the speakers in the debate, noted that: 'Certains appartenant à la majorité n'ont pas ménagé leurs critiques au projet et c'est tout à fait normal.'[64] One deputy remarked during a debate on overseas territories in 1967 that, 'l'appartenance à la majorité ne peut conduire à cacher ce que l'on sait ni ce que l'on pense.'[65] The majority's support for ministers was not an excuse for inactivity. As Achille Peretti, a future minister, pointed out during a debate on the education budget in 1964: 'C'est justement ce soutien qui m'impose le devoir de dire ce qui ne va pas encore, tout en me réjouissant de ce qui va déjà mieux.'[66]

The relationship between the Gaullist deputies and the government they supported never became an oppositional one. But the Gaullist insistence upon their right to contribute to government ensured that it was at least co-operative. The discipline respected at the final vote on a measure did not preclude the possibility of preliminary discussion, as was illustrated by the preparation of the 1968 Higher Education Act. The Gaullist deputies set up a working group to study reform and its point of view was put forward by the party secretary to the Prime Minister Maurice Couve de Murville, the Minister of Education Edgar Faure, and former Prime Minister Georges Pompidou. This meeting made it clear to Faure that the Gaullists did not have the same view of the reform as he did, and so he arranged a three-hour meeting with all the deputies in which he reassured them that he was not a partisan of politicization of the universities, nor would he be asking the government to use the package vote on the debate in the Assembly.[67]

When the proposed bill was presented to the Gaullist study group, its approval was made subject to many significant amendments, thus initiating further negotiations between minister and deputies. When the bill was finally debated in full session, many Gaullists, including former ministers, abstained.[68] The editorial of *La Nation* noted with satisfaction the degree of collaboration which had been achieved, arguing that the anxieties of loyal supporters had been taken into account without endangering the spirit of the bill.[69] This clearly illustrates the Gaullist attitude towards participation in the articulation of policy.

The Gaullists could exercise discreet but effective influence on the government. They could get bills introduced, like the amnesty for political offenders which the minster refused in November 1964 and presented in December; or modified before their introduction, like the Agriculture Act of 1962 or the bill to regulate broadcasting; or amended in the house itself, like the pensions code, the value-added tax, the state security court bill, or the agriculture acts; or postponed, like the conscientious objection bill; or withdrawn and improved, like the measure for settling refugees from North Africa; or cancelled, like the proposed land law reform. As such activity went on behind closed doors, only when a major public row occurred, as over the value-added tax in December 1965 where electoral panic in the majority forced an important government retreat,[70] did commentators observe that deputies still counted for a good deal. Much the same happened over death duties in 1968.[71]

Gaullism, then, must be recognised as an active parliamentary force. Although they gained the reputation of 'godillots', they did succeed in being an active influence in the governing process. It was really the fact that Gaullists found ministers more readily made concessions in private preliminary talks or in committee discussion than in the glare of public debate that created the false impression that they never examined government policy.

Conclusion

This brief summary of some of the activities and views of Gaullist politicians during the 1960s has sought to show that Gaullism was not the monolithic ideology described by opponents and political scientists. The Gaullists' concern was to define a viable role for themselves which was more than hero-worship of de Gaulle and yet which did not sacrifice stability to dynamism. In so doing, they abandoned the anti-party and anti-parliamentary aspects of Gaullism which had dominated the Rassemblement du Peuple Français (RPF). Proper consideration of the party administration's attempts to produce a coherent ideology and of the active influence exerted by Gaullist deputies on de Gaulle's government reveals that Gaullism was an ideology more closely related to Orleanism than Bonapartism.[72] The Gaullists realized that Gaullism could not survive on the basis of de Gaulle's prestige alone and gave it a doctrine and method of action which ensured its survival after the General's departure from office in 1969. In this way, they reinvigorated the French parliamentary tradition. It is now time that historians give them more credit for this achievement.

Notes

1. 'Mais où est le gaullisme?' asked André Chêneboit in *Le Monde*, 2 December 1958. See, also, 'Clarus' in *Capital*, 28 April 1964; André Weil-Curiel in *Le Monde*, 21 July 1966; and Philippe Viannay in *Combat*, 11 September 1968. Opposition leaders were even more hostile, describing the Gaullist regime either as a modern form of absolutist monarchy or as neo-fascism; see, for example, Mitterrand, François: *Le coup d'état permanent* (Paris, 1964) and Duclos, Jacques: *De Napoléon III à de Gaulle* (Paris, 1964).

2. *Notre République*, 7 February 1964

3. See, for example, Pickles, Dorothy: *The Government and Politics of France* (London, 1972), vol. 1, p 214.

4. Hoffmann, Stanley and Hoffmann, Inge: 'De Gaulle as Political Artist', in S. Hoffmann: *Decline or Renewal? France since the 1930s* (New York, 1974), p 217

5. See, for example, Hartley, Anthony: *Gaullism. The Rise and Fall of a Political Movement* (London, 1972); Touchard, Jean: *Le gaullisme* (Paris,1978); Frears, John: *Political Parties and Elections in the French Fifth Republic* (London, 1977).

6. Petitfils, Jean-Christian: *Le gaullisme* (Paris, 1977), p 6. See, too, Charlot, Jean: 'Le gaullisme', in J.-F. Sirinelli, ed: *Histoire des droites en France* (Paris, 1992) vol 1, p. 654: 'Pour définir le "gaullisme", autant partir de son inventeur, le général de Gaulle.'

7. See, for example, McMillan, James: *Twentieth Century France* (London,1992), p 164; Berstein, Serge: 'De Gaulle and Gaullism in the Fifth Republic', in H.Gough and J.Horne, eds: *De Gaulle and Twentieth Century France* (London, 1994), p 113.

8. This is the title of a recent biography of de Gaulle by Charles Williams, published by Abacus in 1993.

9. Rémond, René: *Les droites en France* (Paris, 1982). This hugely influential book has dominated contemporary thinking on the French right.

10. Wright, Derek: *The Government and Politics of France* (London, 1989, 3rd edn) pp 190-1; Williams, Philip and Harrison, Martin: *De Gaulle's Republic* (London, 1961), p 217; Hayward, Jack: *The One and Indivisible French Republic* (London, 1983), p 15; Larkin, Maurice: *France since the Popular Front* (Oxford, 1988), p 295; Stevens, Anne: *The Government and Politics of France* (London, 1992), p 226; Pickles, *Government and Politics*, p 213; and Berstein: 'De Gaulle and Gaullism', p 119.

11. *Le Monde*, 7-8 October 1973

12. See Charlot, Jean: *Le gaullisme* (Paris, 1970), pp 88-92.

13. Peyrefittette, Alain: *C'était de Gaulle* (Paris, 1994), p 39

14. 'Perinde ac cadaver', the Latin phrase used by Jesuits to describe the nature of their loyalty to the Pope. Frey used military as well as religious imagery:

'Nous n'avons pas besoin de cavaliers caracolants, mais de piétaille impavide sous la mitraille ... N'oubliez pas que la discipline fait la force des armées.' Peyrefitte: *C'était de Gaulle*, p 38.

15. *UNR Bulletin de Presse*, no 1, 26 February 1959, p 1
16. *UNR Bulletin de Presse*, special edition, 6 November 1959
17. Michel Debré, speech to the central committee, 2 July 1962, Orsay Palace, Paris; printed in the candidates' handbook for the legislative elections, November 1962.
18. *UNR Bulletin de Presse*, special edition on the Journées parlementaires d'Asnières, 15 May 1959
19. Michel Habib-Deloncle: 'Rôle de l'UNR dans la Ve République', *Courrier de la Nouvelle République*, no 7, November 1959
20. See, for example, the edition for 28 November 1958
21. *UNR Bulletin de Presse*, 26 February 1959, p 1. My italics.
22. *Courrier de la Nouvelle République*, March 1959, p 3
23. Roger Frey, speech at the Théâtre des Ambassadeurs, Paris, 1959
24. Bertrand Flornoy, report on 'Les partis politiques classiques et l'Union', *UNR Bulletin de Presse*, special edition on the Journées parlementaires d'Asnières, 15 May 1959, pp 6-7
25. Albin Chalandon, report presented to the UNR central committee, 15 December 1958, *Documentations et informations parlementaires*, February 1959, 17 pp
26. Chalandon: *Documentations et informations*, p 1
27. Chalandon: *Documentations et informations*, p 1
28. General circular no 3, issued by the UNR secretariat, Paris, 31 December 1958
29. Communiqué issued by the UNR secretariat, Paris, 20 February 1959
30. *UNR Bulletin de Presse*, 26 February 1959
31. UNR candidates' handbook for the municipal elections, March 1959, Economic and Financial affairs, A 3
32. UNR candidates' handbook for the municipal elections, March 1959, Economic and Financial affairs, A 3, p 7
33. *Les Echos*, 22 June 1959
34. *L'année politique*, 1959, p36
35. *Le Courrier de la Nouvelle République*, August-September 1959, p 10
36. In 1955, Soustelle had founded his own organization to secure this end, the *Union pour le Salut et le Renouveau de l'Algérie Française*
37. *Le Courrier de la Nouvelle République*, special edition, November 1959
38. Soustelle, Jacques: *L'espérance trahie* (Paris, 1962), p 171
39. Soustelle: *L'espérance*, p 166
40. Jacques Richard, second assises nationales, Strasbourg 17-19 March 1961
41. Speech to local party members at Bourges, reported in *La Nation*, 15 February 1965
42. *La Nation*, 9 October 1964

43. *La Nation,* 11 March 1963
44. *Notre République,* 18 October 1963. My italics.
45. Speech given by Baumel to the assises of the UNR-UDT Federation of the Seine, reported in *La Nation,* 28 October 1963
46. Baumel's address to local party secretaries in Paris, reported in *La Nation,* no 215, 21 January 1963
47. As opposed to 'le régime de la parole qui nous paralysait hier.' Speech made by Baumel at Lyon, reported in *La Nation,* 10 February 1964.
48. *UNR Bulletin de Presse,* 26 February 1959, p 2: '(L'UNR) fait table rase des idéologies parce qu'elles sont dépassées et paralysantes, pour envisager tous les problèmes avec un esprit ouvert.'
49. *La Nation,* 7 October 1963
50. *La Nation,* 28 May 1962
51. *La Nation,* 25 June 1962
52. *La Nation,* 27-8 April 1963. See, too, the edition of 30 May 1963: 'notre rôle ne constitue pas, en défendant la politique du gouvernement, à prétendre que sa politique économique est toujours et en tous points la meilleure.'
53. *La Nation,* 21 March 1963. Pompidou received a delegation of UNR-UDT deputies to discuss the miners' strike. Alain Peyrefitte, who was present at the meeting, describes the delegation as 'hargneuse'. Peyrefitte: *C'était de Gaulle,* p 556. Another delegation, sent to seek aid for the motor industry, was reported on 14 October 1964.
54. Williams, Philip: *The French Parliament, 1959-1967* (London, 1968), p 103
55. *Le Monde,* 4 October 1966
56. See, for example, the report on defence policy he presented to the 1963 UNR-UDT assises, held at Nice, reported in *La Nation,* 23-24 November 1963.
57. Article 18 of the new statutes adopted by the parliamentary group in July 1968. Membership of the specialized study groups had been optional in preceding legislatures.
58. A circular issued by the secretariat of the party, dated 4 January 1963, indicates the importance of this feature to those involved in organising the GES: 'Il ne vous échappera pas, l'intérêt que présenteront de la sorte les réunions des groupes d'études spécialisés du fait qu'y seront confrontés les points de vue du gouvernement et les députés UNR-UDT sur le problème en cause.' *Information et documents,* 30 April 1963
59. In October 1963, for example, the group received M de Cafarelli, president of FNSEA. *Informations et documents,* 31 October 1963
60. Philippe Rivain, *rapporteur* of the finance commission, came to defend the agriculture budget in October 1963. *Informations et documents,* 31 October 1963
61. On 15 January 1964, for example, they asked him about the European

agreements signed the previous month (*Informations et documents*, January 1964), and in February 1965 Pisani was asked about the Brussels negotiations (*Informations et documents*, February-March 1965).

62. *Informations et documents*, May 1965

63. Williams: *The French Parliament*, p. 93.

64. *Journal Officiel (JO)*, 18 May 1965, p 1442. *La Nation* noted the following day that, 'Certes, personne ne s'attendait à des approbations unanimes... aucune réforme de cet ordre n'est absolument parfaite.'

65. *JO*, 2 November 1967, p 4345

66. *JO*, 29 October 1964, p 4136

67. *Le Monde*, 19 September 1968. See also *La Nation*, 18 September 1968, for the Gaullist party's point of view.

68. *Le Monde*, 11 October 1968

69. *La Nation*, 2 October 1968

70. Williams: *The French Parliament*, pp. 93-5

71. Williams, Philip: *Politics and Society* (London, 1971), p 220

72. Even Rémond admitted this when he said, 'La pensée profonde du général de Gaulle, qui n'est pas toujours aisée à saisir, n'est pas tout le gaullisme: le gaullisme, comme fait d'opinion, déborde largement son inspiration initiale.' Rémond: *Les droites*, p. 314.

14. NEITHER RIGHT NOR LEFT? TOWARDS AN INTEGRATED ANALYSIS OF THE FRONT NATIONAL

Jim Wolfreys

This chapter will address the problematic question of how to define the Front National (FN). The majority of French historians and political scientists who have attempted to interpret the FN have identified it as part of a specifically French tradition of authoritarian populism, distinct from fascism, which rises to challenge the political establishment in times of crisis. This current, baptised national-populism, has been variously embodied over the years by Boulangism, the interwar leagues and Poujadism.[1] However, in a study published in 1995, Pascal Perrineau noted a significant difference between the FN and its precursors. Whereas these earlier movements had proved themselves to be little more than a flash in the pan, Le Pen's organization had set down roots in French society, had established itself at every electoral level, and had thus signalled an end to the extreme right's tendency to produce transitory phenomena.[2]

Perrineau's comments are indicative of a general shift in attitude towards the electoral fortunes of the FN. Throughout the 1980s, the Front's performances in most elections were greeted with expressions of shock and surprise. Indeed, the consensual response to FN progress at the polls during the 1980s can be characterized as one of permanent surprise as Le Pen's organization persistently confounded the widespread view that it would follow precedents 'in which the extreme right-wing parties inflate themselves like bullfrogs before blowing up in their own contradictions.'[3] Thus, 13 years after its first significant election successes, the Front is now recognized as having broken with precedent. Curiously, this has not yet produced a revision of the broadly held definition of the FN as a national-populist organization.

The Front is accordingly regarded as the latest manifestation of an extreme right-wing tradition which flares up every so often, like a fever on the French body politic, only to fade away as quickly as it has surfaced. The only difference, and it is a fairly fundamental difference, is that while most of these *fièvres hexagonales*[4] have died out within a couple of years, the FN has become a fixture of French political life and has established itself as a major political force in France. What I intend to show is that the definition, or rather the description, of the FN as a national-populist organization is misleading and inaccurate, and that the use of this epithet is a product of the failure by French historians to recognise fascism as a component part of the right in France. This chapter examines exactly what is meant by national-populism, before placing the term within the broader context of the debate over the nature of French fascism. The final section argues that studies which approach the doctrine of the Front National in isolation tell us little about the organization as a whole.

What is National-Populism?

This term was introduced to discussion of the FN by Pierre-André Taguieff[5] and Michel Winock and has gradually become common currency, accepted even by members of the Front National.[7] Its widespread use has done little to clarify its meaning. Indeed, it is the vagueness, rather than the accuracy, of the term which explains its acceptance.

According to Taguieff, national-populism is ostensibly republican. It aims to rally all classes against existing elites; it is resolute in its defence of the nation, the family and private property against both internal and external foes; it is plebiscitary; it is authoritarian; and it is economically liberal. Despite his fierce attacks on those who use labels such as fascism as little more than terms of abuse, Taguieff's own terminology proves scarcely more helpful. Although he provides an excellent analysis of the explicit features of the FN programme as it stood in 1986, his definition of national-populism is tautological: the doctrine of national-populism is the doctrine of the Front National, which is a national-populist party. No generic explanation of the term is offered. Taguieff argues that the cross-class appeal of Frontist national-populism sets it apart from Poujadism and compares Lepenism to Thatcherism and Reaganism, an analogy which, he believes, can 'hardly be disputed'.[8] All three are linked by an authoritarian populism which seeks to use a strong state to demolish the structures of social democracy, and to replace the post-war consensus with a new one, based on economic liberalism and the revival of nationalism. No explanation is offered as to why the characteristics listed are more akin to national-populism than to fascism.

For Michel Winock, Taguieff's label is a reformulation of Le Pen's own claim that the FN is part of a 'popular, social and national' right. Winock places it in an historical context. National-populism, in a celebrated article, thus emerges as *'une vieille histoire'*.[9] It first surfaced between the Boulanger crisis and the Dreyfus Affair in the form of a new right which opposed official conservatism and mobilized the masses, including sections of the left, around a handful of demagogic slogans. This right was social, in that it was for the small man against the big; national, in that it opposed its own tribal egoism to the abstractions of the humanist tradition; and popular, in its pioneering use of techniques of political propaganda which fitted the new era of mass society.

National-populist discourse, Winock claims, is based on three central affirmations:

1) Decadence is prevalent. Like Drumont, Barrès and Drieu La Rochelle, Le Pen uses pathological images to convey the idea that the fabric of society is decomposing.

2) The use of scapegoats. This 'diabolic causality' is present in Boulanger's attacks on the political elite, in Drumont's antisemitism, in the xenophobia of the far right in the 1930s and today in Le Pen's attacks on immigrants.

3) The saviour is at hand. National-populism is based on the identification of a man of providence who will lead the nation out of decadence.

This comparison between Le Pen and the revolutionary right has no frame of reference other than discourse. As such, it provides a useful insight into the FN's cultural influences, but is a long way from proving affiliation to a political tradition. Indeed, all the evidence used by Winock to identify the FN as national-populist (the references to decadence, the use of scapegoats, the appeal to a saviour figure) could equally be used to identify the FN as fascist, always assuming, that is, that such a method of reasoning were acceptable.

The most comprehensive attempt to assess the relationship between national-populism and fascism has been made by Pierre Milza. He likens the situation in which the FN has emerged not to the *situation de détresse* which accompanied the rise of Mussolini and Hitler in 1920-21 and 1931-

33, but to periods of sweeping change which affected the whole of society, periods in which bourgeois values were challenged by traditionalism. The present crisis of French society is therefore comparable to the late nineteenth century, the interwar years, and the 1950s. The FN represents the reaction of those resisting the accelerated movement of history and its remedies are taken from 'the old panoply of a national-populism of which fascism *à la française* was merely one example, and which has been successively embodied in Bonapartism, Boulangism, anti-Dreyfusism, the "revolutionary right" of the early twentieth century, the nationalist leagues and, later, Poujadism.'[10]

According to Milza, the Front National differs from fascism in the following ways. First, in terms of its structure and activity, the FN cannot be considered a revolutionary organization. Fascist organizations want to turn society upside down, set up a totalitarian regime and create a new order based on a repudiation of traditional ethics. The Front's 30,000 members, however, do not constitute a mass party. The FN is not armed, hierarchical, fanatically devoted to its leader, or militarily organized. Admittedly, some of the Front's founder members remain active; and, along with younger extremists, they form a reserve force, not averse to violence, which could be quickly mobilized in the event of a political radicalization. Yet these elements represent a minority, and are closely controlled by the leadership. Moreover, the organization as a whole is now dominated by a young cadre who joined the Front in the late 1970s and during the 1980s.

Second, the FN's aims are not fascist. The FN is firmly anchored on the right, whereas fascism, and particularly French fascism, resisted being labelled 'right' or 'left' and sought a third way between capitalism and collectivism. In seeking to unite the nation, fascism effaces differences between individuals and social classes, setting out on the path towards totalitarianism. Le Pen, far from wanting totalitarianism, states that he wants the individual to blossom and only conceives of a strong state as a framework in which the natural organs of society (families, religious communities, businesses) can develop in harmony. This opposition between fascism's desire to construct society in its own image and the FN's desire for mediation between the individual and the state is, for Milza, fundamental in setting the FN apart from what he terms 'totalitarian fascism'.

National-populist at its core, the FN has inherited elements from all the historic traditions of the French extreme right. These elements, Milza argues, include its obsession with decadence, its use of scapegoats, its appeal to heroes and saviour figures, and its critique of the *classe politique*. From the counter-revolutionary syncretism of Vichy, the FN has developed its conception of the state, the idea of a natural order, the desire for a compromise between authority and freedoms (as opposed to abstract 'freedom') and the desire to restore natural communities (the family, the region, the crafts, etc.) Like the Vichy regime, which embraced technocracy, the FN proposes to end France's decline while welcoming modernity, in the shape of Le Pen's supposed Reaganism.

The Front National is, therefore, seen as part of an extremely broad tradition which has resurfaced at various crisis points in French history and is characterized by antisemitism, demagogic populism, anti-intellectualism and the defence of the 'little man' against the corruption and decadence of the establishment. Although Milza considers fascism to be part of this tradition, the FN, despite having been a fascist organization for the first decade of its existence, can no longer be considered one.[11] The transformation of the Front took place at the end of the 1970s when revolutionary nationalist elements left the organization and Le Pen, who has always been part of the non-fascist national-populist tradition, surrounded himself with Solidarists, national-Catholics, and Nouvelle Droitistes. The adoption of economic liberalism was a key element in this 'national-populist turn'[12] and was more than simply an opportunist attempt by the FN to modernize its programme by embracing fashionable ideas. Economic liberalism thus becomes a defining feature of the FN's national-populism, aligning it with the Reaganite, rather than the fascist, model.

There are a number of problems with this analysis. As suggested earlier, the FN's status as a major political player, with deep roots in French society, and over a decade on the national political stage behind it, set the organization apart from Boulangism, Poujadism, and other passing 'fevers'. The Front's 1993 programme, with its stringent critique of free-market economics, undermines the comparisons with Reaganism. Furthermore, the Front's latest slogan, and the title of its most recent publication, *Ni droite, ni gauche: français!* also belies Milza's rather dubious claim that the FN's insistence that it is on the right sets it apart from fascism.

The national-populist school denies the complexity of the FN phenomenon at the expense of a convenient historical parallel. This reductionism is like a concertina, contracting to produce a rigid set of criteria to distinguish fascism from national-populism and then expanding to include a myriad of diverse organizations under the national-populist umbrella. There is no sense of a strategy at work on the extreme right, no account taken of the conscious process of development whereby aspects of radical nationalism, secreted into political life over the decades, have been filtered and modified and adapted to present conditions. Ultimately the term is so broad, applied to movements as diverse as the Parti Populaire Français (PPF) and the Ligue de la Patrie Française, as to be almost meaningless. In this respect, it is clearly a description, and as such is as useful as any other label, be it far right, nationalist, populist, extremist, dangerous, all of which are equally vague and none of which tell us anything in particular about the Front National.

Fascism and National-Populism

The principal weakness in the national-populist argument is that it blurs the distinctions between surface features and fundamental elements of the FN. This weakness is a feature of the debate over the nature of French fascism, a debate which has greatly influenced attempts to define Le Pen's organization. Since the war, studies of the extreme right have been dominated by a consensus view[13] which regards French fascism as virtually non-existent.[14] Fascist influence during the interwar period has been seen, in much the same way as the Occupation, as an imported phenomenon. For René Rémond, the most influential of consensus historians, fascist organizations which did exist were marginal, while other, more significant movements merely took on the surface characteristics of fascism in the spirit of the age.[15] France was preserved from fascism by the solidity of the republican tradition and the presence of an indigenous right-wing conservative authoritarianism which weakened the appeal of more extreme alternatives.

The consensus school has interpreted fascism as a radical, left-leaning, anti-capitalist phenomenon with significant proletarian support, and has based its arguments on a comparison between the French interwar leagues and various features of fascist regimes,[16] notably expansionism and totalitarianism. This largely disqualifies the French far right from identification with fascism, for the simple reason that it never seized power.

A number of non-French historians have challenged this consensus. Studies by Ernst Nolte and Zeev Sternhell have indicated that France, far from being immune to fascism, incubated its own proto-fascist tradition. Sternhell has convincingly argued that the anti-democratic, anti-capitalist and xenophobic nationalist leagues of the late nineteenth century were the precursors of fascism. Less persuasive are his claims that fascism possesses a rounded ideology, the product of a convergence between socialism and nationalism. Sternhell chooses not to offer a definition of fascism, but produces instead an abstract checklist of themes, such as antisemitism, anti-democracy and anti-capitalism, which, paradoxically, confirms the consensus thesis of French fascism's marginalization: those groups which comply with Sternhell's checklist, such as the Cercle Proudhon, the Faisceau and Marcel Déat's neo-socialists, were never mass organizations. The principal parties of the interwar extreme right, Doriot's Parti Populaire Français and Colonel de la Roque's Croix de Feu/Parti Social Français (PSF), scarcely get a mention.

Sternhell's contribution to the debate was roundly condemned, largely for debunking the myth of French republicanism's inviolability. Less ideologically motivated critics, however, highlighted serious flaws in his methodology. In seeking out the 'pure' ideology of fascism, Sternhell was guilty of producing a history of ideas[17] which greatly exaggerated the role of the left in the development of the phenomenon[18] while neglecting the influence of external circumstances. As a result, Sternhell had identified similarities between various groups and individuals and fascism based on abstract, theoretical characteristics and not much else. As Edward Tannenbaum remarked, merely observing that two successive things are similar does not mean that there is a direct link between them. Furthermore, 'to assert such a connection without empirical evidence is a logical fallacy: *post hoc, ergo propter hoc*. And to use the similarities as the evidence is to argue in a circle.'[19]

This debate, and its methodology, has clearly had an impact on analyses of the Front National. The widespread acceptance, after Sternhell's intervention, that the roots of fascism are also French, has given greater pertinence to the debate over whether Le Pen's organization represents a resurgence of fascism. The national-populist label can be seen as a response to Sternhell in that it recognizes the significance, in particular, of the antisemitic leagues of the late nineteenth century and their influence on later movements, including the FN. However, although studies of the FN have been forced to acknowledge the existence of a fascist current in France between the wars, the national-populist school can be seen as a new variant of the old consensus, which has inherited flaws from both Rémond and Sternhell.

These flaws are fourfold. First, comparisons between the FN and fascism are based on a set of rigid criteria derived from the study of fully fledged fascist regimes, although the FN is a movement not a regime. Second, the FN is located within the national-populist tradition on the basis of naive discourse analysis rather than empirical evidence relating to the organization's structure, aims and origins. Where reference to these factors is made, it is often misleading and inaccurate. Little distinction is made between programmatic elements of FN discourse and the organization's doctrine. Consequently, pronouncements by the FN leadership are often taken at face value and used as evidence of the organization's acceptance of democracy.

Third, apart from a few vague references to 'the difficult gestation of post-industrial society'[20] and 'post-materialism',[21] studies of the FN make little attempt to situate the FN within the context of post-war society. The effect of both the Second World War and the Algerian War on the development of the extreme right, creating the need to advance in a more covert and less agitational fashion, are overlooked. Ample empirical evidence which shows the FN to have been built by activists seeking to adapt fascism to a modern context is dismissed with reference to the 'national-populist turn'. This manoeuvre exaggerates the significance of the Front's espousal of economic liberalism and places great importance on the supposed moderation of individuals recruited to the Front at the time of the organization's electoral breakthrough. The 'original sin' approach to the Front, which focuses exclusively on the extremist origins of the organization in order to pin the label of fascism onto the FN, is therefore turned on its head—the FN cannot be fascist because many of its new cadre have never belonged to overtly revolutionary nationalist groups. In reality, such trenchant distinctions between supposedly extremist and moderate elements within the Front have been shown to be over simplistic. Many of the apparently moderate figures in the FN leadership are simply the most sophisticated exponents of the strategy outlined by the organization's revolutionary nationalist founders in 1972.[22]

Finally, the view that economic conservatism and fascism are incompatible has been undermined by recent studies of the extreme right in France.[23] Doriot's PPF was, for most historians[24] the only authentic mass fascist party to have developed in France, yet, as Robert Soucy has demonstrated, both the PPF and de La Roque's PSF were economically conservative. In *Refaire la France* (1938) Doriot called for measures to combat the might of trusts and monopolies and to protect and strengthen the private sector, in particular small businesses. 'Individual profit remains the motor of production,' Doriot claimed,[25] in terms which the Front National was to repeat almost word for word in its 1984 manifesto. Of course, there is nothing new in fascist organizations avoiding overtly anti-capitalist rhetoric: even Mussolini expressed his fidelity to the principles of Manchester liberalism.

Towards an Integrated Analysis

A meaningful comparison between different forms of fascist and extreme right-wing movements, as opposed to regimes, should locate specific features of both their ideology and structure within a given context. In order to make such a comparison, a set of minimum shared characteristics of fascism can be established. Fascist ideology is based on the following principles: it is anti-democratic, anti-egalitarian and hierarchical; it seeks to replace existing elites; its nationalism is based on the exclusion of enemies (notably the left) and portrays the national community as a victim and as the source of moral regeneration; its vision of the state is authoritarian, and privileges the community over the individual. Where fascism differs from other reactionary movements is in its attempt to build an independent mass movement. This movement, organized hierarchically around the leadership principle, seeks to mobilize on a large scale and possesses the capacity to make violent, if necessary armed, interventions. Some fascist movements adopt the rhetoric of racial supremacy and antisemitism, but these, like anti-capitalism,[26] are not fundamental characteristics of fascism. With this in mind, the remainder of the chapter will sketch an outline of the FN's fascist credentials with regard to its organizational structure and doctrine.

The FN: A Mass Party

In terms of the organization's structure and activity, we see that the differences between Doriot's mass fascist party and Le Pen's national-populist movement are far from conclusive. As Milza points out, the PPF, in numerical terms, was no more marginal than Mussolini's Partito Nazionale Fascista (PNF) in late 1920,[27] and scarcely differs in size from the Front National. Estimates of PPF membership range from 15,000 activists to between 50,000 and 100,000 members.[28] Milza himself gives a figure of 30,000 for FN membership in 1987, and 60,000 in 1993. The organization itself claims 100,000.

Aside from these statistical comparisons is the fact that the PPF and the FN both share, as a defining feature, the desire to build an independent mass movement. (Milza, bizarrely, does not compare FN membership with the PPF but with the Rassemblement pour la République [RPR]). The FN's desire to build an extra-parliamentary base is evident in its efforts to infiltrate professional associations and trade unions. Le Pen even employed two veterans of the PPF, Victor Barthélemy, Doriot's former general secretary, and André Dufraisse, who joined Doriot in the fight for a Nazi Europe as a member of the Légion des Volontaires Français contre le Bolchevisme (LVF), to oversee the creation of internal structures for the FN.[29] The Front's attempts to establish a network of satellite organizations on the Doriotist model have resulted in the formation of over a dozen FN affiliated groups in industry, banking, the health service, education, the civil service, and most notably in the police and in the transport industry.

The PPF, like the FN, was conscious of the dangers of appearing aligned to the Nazi model. During the 1930s, the PPF had neither an official party uniform, nor a paramilitary organization. Although the FN is not officially armed, a culture of weaponry pervades the movement. At a very general level, this culture is expressed in Le Pen's speeches which contain off-hand remarks about the efficiency of particular weapons, and speak of the FN as an 'army in civilian clothes'.[30] Elsewhere, this culture can be found in the adverts for pistols carried by *National Hebdo,* and in the simple fact that it is not considered unusual for FN members to own guns, or unacceptable to carry them on demonstrations.[31] More concretely, this culture was tragically visible during the 1995 presidential election campaign, when three FN members, all armed, broke off from putting up posters of Le Pen to attack a group of rappers. One of them, a 17 year-old youth from the Comoro islands, was shot in the back and killed. FN Chairman Bruno Mégret argued that the shooting was a legitimate act of self-defence.[32].

This culture is channelled into the structure of the FN via the Cercle National des Combattants (CNC) and the Cercle National des Gens d'Armes (CNGA). The CNC claims 5,000 active combatants, happy to enjoy 'their civic right', and 300 *Cadets,* for whom 'physical, moral and patriotic training' is provided. The CNGA organizes among the police force and the army. Its role, as laid out by Bernard Lefèvre, former member of the Comité de Salut Public set up by rebel army officers in Algiers in 1958, is 'to defend the Common Good of the nation as soon as there is a threat from beyond its borders or from within the country.' This threat, posed by France's rising immigrant population, barbaric foreign cultures and the 'mondialist economico-financial conglomerate' may one day require the *Gens d'Armes* to 'take on the mission of the last resort'.[33]

Many of Milza's claims with regard to the structure of the FN reveal themselves to be factually incorrect. The FN, like the PPF, is indeed hierarchically organized and proclaims itself so. The organization's internal structure, a 'human pyramid',[34] is based on the rigid subordination of each element of the organization's apparatus to the unassailable discipline of the hierarchical party *nomenclature*: leader, general secretary, national secretary, regional secretary, departmental secretary, branch secretary. This subordination is made explicit in the instructions laid down by the general secretary's office to the membership which insist on the sovereign status of 'the hierarchical decision'.[35]

The FN and Democracy

Milza claims that the FN belongs to a Christian humanist tradition and cites the Front's acceptance of pluralism and parliamentary democracy, and the absence of bellicosity from FN propaganda, as fundamental differences between fascist national-populism and national-populism *ordinaire*. These distinctions are somewhat undermined by Milza's own analysis of the fascist PPF which, as he points out, not only repudiated the label of fascism before the war, but lacked an expansionist programme and was ready to accept a role in a Nazi Europe. Furthermore, while it is true that an important part of the FN's membership is made up of Bernard Antony's Catholic integralists, the extent to which this current may be considered 'humanist' is debatable. The close ties which Antony's antisemitic Christian-Solidarity has forged with reactionary Catholic groups in the Lebanon, Indo-China, Croatia and Lithuania, along with the Nicaraguan Contras and the upper echelons of the ruling ARENA party in El Salvador, beg the question as to how rigorous an interpretation of the term 'Christian humanist' Milza intends. Certainly, as far as Antony is concerned, the regular slaughter of Catholic priests by government death squads in El Salvador have not harmed relations with the regime.[36]

As regards totalitarianism, Milza himself provides a fitting rebuttal to his own insistence that this is a defining feature of a fascist movement: 'To say, for example, that certain elements of the French ultra-right are not fascist, or do not carry the seeds of fascism, simply because their discourse is neither "revolutionary" nor "totalitarian" is to forget rather quickly that totalitarianism, if it is present in the mass ritual of the first stage of fascism, only appears in the institutional practice and the speech of the charismatic leader after taking power.'[37] Milza, eager to point out the specificity of French fascism, and generally anxious to distinguish between fascism as a movement and fascism as a regime, fails to do so with regard to the FN.

The Front's attitude to democracy is a key element in assessing the nature of the FN. Many commentators are clearly convinced that Le Pen's claim to be a 'Churchillian democrat' (a supporter of democracy in the absence of anything better) is a sufficient endorsement of the parliamentary process. Evidence exists to challenge this view. The organization's founders made plain that the FN's attitude to democracy was strategic rather than principled. The Front National was formed in 1972 on the initiative of a small group of revolutionary activists seeking to escape from small-scale activity and build a mass base through engaging in electoral activity. The emphasis on electoralism for purely tactical reasons has been a constant feature of dialogue between the FN leadership and its members from 1972 to the present day, an attitude best summed up by Le Pen in October 1982, when he told delegates at the party's *assisses nationales* in Nice that, 'We must be respectful of legality while it exists.' Such declarations are consistent with Le Pen's unequivocal support for the Franco regime;[38] his reaction to the Chilean coup, when he argued that if a similar situation arose in France the army would have a right and a duty to follow Pinochet's lead;[39] and his claim that the apartheid regime in South Africa was democratic, since 'the definition of democracy is not restricted simply to the exercise of the right to vote.'[40] More recently, Le Pen warned that the 'wormeaten structures of our system' would collapse and that, like the extreme left, the Front National should prepare for revolution.[41]

Conclusion

Explanations of political movements based on historical parallels cannot be made with reference to discourse alone and must be set in a more rigorous framework, accompanied by empirical evidence relating to the structure and origins of the organizations concerned. In the case of the Front National. No historical parallel is entirely accurate, largely because the post-war extreme right has been forced to adapt to an environment which differs considerably from that which incubated fascist organizations in the interwar years.

If comparisons are to be made, therefore, a number of important considerations must be taken into account, relating to the context within which the FN is operating, which differs significantly from that which helped shape far-right organizations between the wars. Whereas the First World War brought fascist organizations into the open and the crash of 1929 accelerated their development, the Second World War and the recession have had the opposite effect. The defeat of Nazi Germany meant that fascists could no longer advance under that name or openly identify with the ideas and organizational structure associated with fascism. If it was fashionable in the 1930s for right-wing organizations to dress up in fascist clothes, post-war fascists were obliged to shed these clothes. Euphemism and disguise were the essential elements which the FN and its founders brought to the extreme right. Furthermore, the relative stabil-ity of capitalist society in the post-war period imposed a long-term perspective on fascist groups while the current economic recession, longer in duration but less profound in impact, gives fascism a longer time span in which to grow. In concrete terms, these factors are reflected in the FN's organizational form (FN members do not parade around in uniforms or in armed units), and in its propaganda, which eschews the rhetoric of racial supremacy and emphasizes cultural difference and the defence of national identity, and does not openly advocate the overthrow of capitalism, the smashing of the left or the establishment of a corporate state.

An integrated analysis of the Front National, which relates program-matic and doctrinal elements to the overall process of the organization's development and activity, shows Le Pen's FN to be much more than simply a resurgence of an old historical tradition: it is a new kind of organization which has given a modern and sophisticated form to fascism.

In terms of its ideology, the Front shares its core values with fascism: behind the organization's ambiguous identification with democracy is a leadership which favours authoritarian government; which is anti-egalitarian;[42] which seeks to replace 'the corrupted oligarchies' with 'the authentic elites rooted in our people';[43] whose nationalism portrays France as a victim (of immigration, of mondialism, of abortion policies, etc.) and is based on the exclusion of enemies (la préférence nationale); and whose vision of the state is unequivocally authoritarian with regard to social policy.[44] With regard to economic policy, the Front's espousal of popular capitalism rather than corporatism is a product of strategic decisions made during the organization's incubation period, but also of the current debate over the relationship between the state and the market. The recent revision of its economic liberalism and the shift towards protectionism could presage further modifications of the economic role which the FN envisages for the state. Finally, the Front, despite its economically liberal rhetoric, regards the individual as subordinate to the national community. For the FN, the individual is a meaningless abstraction, no more than a transient phenomenon, given a past, or heritage, by the nation, and a future, or genetic continuity, by the family.[45]

The organization's origins are clearly fascist. The formation of the Front National was a result of a conscious reshaping of fascism by self-proclaimed revolutionary activists during the 1960s. Studies which refer to the departure of some, but by no means all, of these elements from the

Front in the late 1970s, ignore the fact that the basic structure of the organization remained the same, allowing revolutionary nationalists to operate as part of the FN's network of parallel organizations. These structures, inspired by the PPF model, allow the Front to combine unofficial and official activities and to infiltrate sections of society ranging from trade unions to chambers of commerce.

The aim of the Front is the construction of a mass organization. Its electoral successes over the past twelve years have proven the FN's capacity for mobilizing widely, picking up support from those thrown into difficulties by recession and retaining a sizeable and loyal hard core.[46] The organization's strategy of federation, reflected in the structure of the FN, has allowed it to achieve what no other organization of the French extreme right has achieved before. The Front has united all the diverse tendencies of the extreme right, from conservatives to ultras, Catholic integralists and royalists to pagans and fascists, behind a single leader in a nationally organized federation. This federation, reflecting the circumstances in which it has developed, represents the most advanced contemporary form of fascism. The Front, therefore, shares a core of basic characteristics with interwar fascism, and possesses others in embryonic form. Above all it boasts durability, consistently proving reports of its demise to be exaggerated, and flexibility, carrying with it the potential for metamorphosis.

Notes

1.   See especially the articles by Taguieff, Pierre-André: 'La rhétorique du national-populisme. Les règles élémentaires de la propagande xénophobe', *Cahiers Bernard Lazare*, June-July 1994; 'La rhétorique du national-populisme', *Mots*, October 1984; 'La doctrine du national-populisme en France', *Etudes*, January 1986. See too Milza, Pierre: *Fascisme français* (Paris, 1987); Winock, Michel: *Nationalisme, antisémitisme et fascisme en France* (Paris, 1990); Wiervioka, Michel: 'Les bases du national-populisme', *Le Débat*, September/October 1990; Buzzi, Paul: 'Le Front National entre national-populisme et extrémisme de droite', *Regards sur l'actualité*, March 1991; and Perrineau, Pascal: 'L'electorat à reconquérir', in D.Martin-Castelnau, ed: *Combattre le Front National* (Paris, 1995).
2.   Perrineau: 'L'electorat à reconquèrir'
3.   Webster, Paul: *The Guardian*, 24 March 1992
4.   Winock, Michel: *La fièvre hexagonale* (Paris, 1987)
5.   Taguieff: 'La rhétorique du national-populisme'
6.   Michel Winock writing in *Le Monde*, 12 June 1987.
7.   Birenbaum, Guy: *Le Front National en politique* (Paris, 1992)
8.   Taguieff: 'La doctrine du national-populisme en France', p 46

9.   Michel Winock writing in *Le Monde*, 12 June 1987.
10. Milza: *Fascisme français*, pp 421-3
11. Milza: *Fascisme français*, pp 423-4
12. Camus, Jean-Yves: 'Origine et formation du Front National, 1972-1981', in N. Mayer and P. Perrineau, eds: *Le Front National à découvert* (Paris, 1989) p 31, and Buzzi: 'Le Front National entre national-populisme et extrémisme de droite', p 37
13. See especially Irvine, William D.: 'Fascism in France and the Strange Case of the Croix de Feu', *Journal of Modern History*, 63/2 (1991), pp 271-95
14. See notably Rémond, René: *Les droites en France* (Paris, 1982); Plumyène, Jean and Lasierra, Raymond: *Les fascismes français* (Paris, 1963); and Burrin, Philippe: 'La France dans le champ magnétique des fascismes', *Le Débat*, November 1984
15. Rémond: *Les droites*
16. Dobry, Michel: 'Février 1934 et la découverte de l'allergie de la société française à la "révolution fasciste"', *Revue française de sociologie*, (July/December 1989), pp 518-520
17. See Winock, Michel: 'Fascisme à la française ou fascisme introuvable?' *Le Débat*, May 1983.
18. See Julliard, Jacques: 'Sur un fascisme imaginaire: à propos d'un livre de Zeev Sternhell', *Annales ESC*, 39/4 (1984), pp 849-59
19. Tannenbaum, Edward R.: 'Review of Zeev Sternhell, *Maurice Barrès et le nationalisme français* (Paris, 1972) and Robert Soucy, *Fascism in France. The Case of Maurice Barrès* (Berkeley and Los Angeles, 1972)', in *The American Historical Review*, 78/5 (1973), p 1479
20. See Winock: *Nationalisme, antisémitisme et fascisme*
21. See Perrineau, Pascal: 'Le Front National: 1972-1992', in M.Winock: *Histoire de l'extrême droite en France* (Paris, 1993).
22. See Fysh, Peter and Wolfreys, Jim: 'Le Pen, the National Front and the Extreme Right in France', *Parliamentary Affairs*, 45 (July 1992), pp 309-26.
23. Notably Irvine: 'Fascism in France', and Soucy, Robert: *French Fascism. The Second Wave, 1933-1939* (Yale, 1995)
24. Rémond: *Les droites en France,* and Milza: *Fascisme français*
25. Doriot quoted in Soucy, Robert: 'The Nature of Fascism in France', *The Journal of Contemporary History*, 1 (1966), pp 37-8
26. Jenkins, Brian: 'Robert Soucy and the "Second Wave" of French fascism', *Modern and Contemporary France*, 4/2 (1996), pp 193-208
27. Milza, *Fascisme français*, p 441
28. Wolf, Dieter: *Doriot* (Paris, 1969), and Brunet, Jean-Paul: *Jacques Doriot. Du communisme au fascisme* (Paris, 1986)
29. Konopnicki, Guy: *Les filières noires* (Paris, 1996), Lorien, Joseph, Criton, Karl and Dumont, Serge: *Le système Le Pen* (Antwerp, 1985)
30. *Le Monde*, 2 November 1982

31. Tristan, Anne: *Au Front* (Paris, 1987)
32. *Le Monde*, 24 February 1995
33. *Le Glaive*, no 1
34. *Le Guide du Responsable*, no 1, p 93
35. *Le Guide du Responsable*, no 1, p 69
36. Camus, Jean-Yves and Monzat, René: *Les droites nationales et radicales en France* (Paris, 1992)
37. Milza: *Fascisme français*, p 53
38. *Le National*, October 1976
39. *La Croix*, September 1973
40. *Le Monde*, 8 May 1987
41. *Le Monde*, 17 September 1996
42. Front National: *Militer au Front* (Paris, 1991), p 8
43. *Nos Valeurs* (internal FN document, Paris, 1989), p 12
44. Wolfreys, Jim: 'An Iron Hand in a Velvet Glove: The Programme of the French Front National', *Parliamentary Affairs*, 46 (July 1993), pp 415-29
45. Taguieff: 'La doctrine du national-populisme', p 39
46. Mayer, Nonna and Perrineau, Pascal: 'La puissance et le rejet ou le lepénisme dans l'opinion', in *SOFRES. L'état de l'opinion 1993* (Paris, 1993), pp 69-71

15. YOU *CAN* POUR NEW WINE INTO OLD BOTTLES: THE FRENCH RIGHT SINCE 1958[1]

Charles Hauss

Most of the chapters in this volume have painted a picture of the right that emphasizes its anti-republican and often violent nature. To use an expression from the American left of my youth, from 1789 onwards, the right was largely 'outside the system'.

The events covered in this chapter, from the creation of the Fifth Republic until the present, mark an important break with that long-standing image of the French right. Since then, the largest conservative parties have not just been inside the system, but have also defined how it is structured and what most of the state's major public policy initiatives have been. Far from being revolutionary or even reactionary, the mainstream right has become the establishment. Even those parts of the right that hark back to the xenophobia, racism, and anti-republicanism of earlier regimes have taken giant steps toward respectability, if not moderation.

In short, to use but one of the many clichés about French politics, the experience of the French right under the Fifth Republic suggests that you can pour new political wine into old bottles. The present chapter seeks to illustrate this process in three stages, beginning with the most obvious and least controversial.

First, the transformation of the right is easiest to see for the Gaullists and their allies. De Gaulle's return to power in 1958, the creation of the Fifth Republic, and the formation of the various Gaullist parties and their allies represented the blending of the traditional anti-republican right with republican conservatism that has forced the revolutionary right into the most marginal position it has occupied in the twentieth century.

Second, this development also overtakes the right-wing critics of the Gaullists, most notably the Front National (FN) which has established itself as a major force in electoral politics since the mid 1980s. To be sure, the

277

FN has violent and anti-system roots, and it still has its share of violent and anti-system right-wingers today. But the key point is that its supporters are every bit as marginalized as Derek Becon or Alf Garnett in Britain or David Duke and Archie Bunker in the USA.

Third, and hardest to document empirically, are signs that the very meanings of the terms 'left' and 'right' are up for 'political grabs'. In France, as in Britain or the USA, widespread public dissatisfaction with both politics and politicians has led to a growing alienation manifested in part in a rejection of traditional labels such as left and right, evidence of which can be seen in recent waves of strikes and a sharp rise in the number of abstentions in elections for all public offices. Nonetheless, those uncertainties do not seem to be a precursor to the kind of violent and anti-system right that most other chapters in this book have charted.

Before proceeding to the argument itself, I wish to make two things clear. First, while I think the preponderance of evidence lies in these three directions, not all of it does. For example, perfectly plausible cases have been made, especially about the challenge the FN poses for French democracy.[2] It may well be that I have overstated how moderate all elements of the right have become. If so, that should not keep the reader from seeing the sharp contrasts between what has to be seen as a relatively tame right of the 1960s onward and the more disruptive activities of the like of Action Française or the Boulangists. Second, what follows should not be read as some sort of self-serving homage to the brilliance of the right. This author, in fact, is personally very much on the left and, if anything, rues the fact that it has not been anywhere near as effective in revitalizing itself over this same time period.

The Gaullist Synthesis[3]

The Status Quo Ante

Though few realized it at the time, most of the anti-system right was fated for an unceremonious end once General Charles de Gaulle returned to power in 1958. The prospect of yet another humiliating defeat four years after Dien Bien Phu and the loss of Algeria led many of the million or more white settlers onto the streets in that euphemistically named overseas department. Though the historical record is still rather murky, all the signs suggest that the soldiers and settlers were supported by right-wing plotters from the hexagon most of whom clamoured for General de Gaulle's return to power. In the longer run, most of them were hoping for some sort of non-republican regime. Less than five years later, those hopes and expectations had been dashed.

To see the full implications of this, it is important to recall how dire the situation seemed in the mid- to late-1950s in ways that evoked Trotsky's quip that 'repeated history' produces both tragedy and farce. France lost in 1940 for many reasons. At the top of any list of those causes would be its *immobiliste* party system and the stagnant parliamentary system it produced, which failed to provide the country with effective governance.[4] *Faute de mieux*, France in 1946 returned to what Philip Williams called 'crisis and compromise' at a time when it needed effective governance more than ever.[5]

The consequences make for depressing reading. A host of problems at home and abroad went unsolved. There was so much alienation from and disinterest in political life that while virtually all the 1956 intake into the army could name the winner of the *tour de France*, next to none could identify the prime minister. France modernized so little from the 1920s into the 1950s that Georges Simenon could write his Maigret mysteries, setting them in an unchanged and unchanging Paris.

All this did little to calm right-wing hostility to the Republic. Despite the shame of Vichy, centre-right parties quickly regained their place in political life, winning nearly a sixth of the vote as early as 1951. Meanwhile, Gaullists, Poujadistes, and others on the far right also did well at the polls and, more ominously, still had a disruptive presence in the streets.

The fragmentation of partisan political life and the menace from the extra-parliamentary right continued to grow as the Fourth Republic's woes mounted. It was in its last legislative elections in 1956 that the Poujadistes scored their breakthrough, among other things sending the young Jean-Marie Le Pen to parliament. Meanwhile, as crisis followed crisis, Gaullists and others kept taking verbal and not so verbal potshots at the regime that seemed so old and fragile a mere decade after its creation.

Le treize mai

The twin revolution in Algeria took the Fourth Republic out of its misery and seemed to portend a less democratic future more congenial to the far right. Stung by the humiliating defeat in Vietnam, most French politicians and military leaders vowed to act more decisively and effectively when the Front de Libération Nationale (FLN) took up arms against Paris in 1954.

For good or ill, they failed to live up to their word. The naming of the moderate Pierre Pflimlin as Prime Minister-Designate in spring 1958 proved to be the last straw for many *colons* in Algeria, right-wing politicians and voters, and soldiers. On 13 May 1958, a second revolt broke out in Algiers, this one pitting white settlers and their military supporters against the Republic.

To cut a long and complicated story short, by the end of the month, the Fourth Republic politicians had to beg de Gaulle to take over the government. The general demanded and got extraordinary powers to revise (and, in fact, actually rewrite) the constitution, creating the Fifth Republic.

While anyone reading these pages will know what happened, it is important to stress that all sorts of outcomes were possible, and few observers at the time expected a viable democratic regime dominated by the first stable majority coalition in history. Indeed, most on the centre and left at least expected de Gaulle to become the most recent in a string of what Stanley Hoffmann called heroic and (in practice) dictatorial leaders of a Bonapartist bent.[6] After all, de Gaulle came from anything but good republican stock. He had spent the years after he first left power in 1946 taking potshots at the Fourth Republic from his retirement home in Colombey-les-Deux-Eglises. Shortly after becoming premier in 1958, he made his famous and ambiguous statement of *je vous ai compris* while visiting Algeria which many understood to mean that he was pro-army and *colon*.

De Gaulle's Impact

By the mid 1960s, de Gaulle and his supporters transformed the shape of French politics, which, among other things, included marginalizing the far right more than anyone could have dreamed possible in the 1950s. De Gaulle used to talk about the need for France to 'marry its century'. For our purposes here, he also succeeded in getting the right to marry democracy.[7]

Early on, his Republic was dogged by criticisms about its strong and, after 1962, directly elected president, its overcentralization, and the weakness of its parliament. However, it did not take long for the doubts about de Gaulle's personal commitment to democratic politics to disappear. In particular, de Gaulle's handling of Algeria was a first and powerful sign that he had no intentions of operating outside the framework of liberal democratic institutions.

It is important to remember that there was an active and strong far right at the time. Plans for a military coup were underway when the Fourth Republic's parliamentary leaders called on de Gaulle. The shift toward negotiations with the Algerian revolutionaries strengthened the far right whose many sects kept laying plans for the next coup. De Gaulle himself was the subject of as many as 30 assassination attempts, most of which were organized by the former soldiers of the Organisation de l'Armée Secrète (OAS) who wanted to wreak vengeance on the man they thought had sold the country out over Algeria. And there certainly were people in de Gaulle's own entourage who had something less than wholly democratic credentials.

For the purposes of this essay, the most important of de Gaulle's accomplishments was the creation of the Gaullist party which was the dominant force in France's first stable parliamentary majority elected in 1962, and has dominated the centre-right ever since.[8] De Gaulle despised political parties which he felt had been a major reason for France's woes under the Third and Fourth Republics. On the other hand, Georges Pompidou and some of his other lieutenants understood from the beginning that the General, his successors and his regime would need strong electoral support. Thus the moribund Gaullist political party was revived and strengthened.

De Gaulle had disbanded the original Rassemblement du Peuple Français (RPF) after it failed to win the 1951 election and some of its leaders demonstrated a willingness to cooperate in forming governing coalitions in the republic he was committed to destroying. As a result, the Gaullists virtually had to rebuild their grass roots organization from scratch. In 1958, they only managed to put together a motley collection of people who came from all over the political map. It included some former socialists and even some of the right-wingers who would be on the barricades trying to overthrow the new republic once de Gaulle decided to grant Algerian independence. Many, too, were opportunists who were eager to claim the Gaullist mantle if it would help them get or stay in parliament.

Over the next few years, however, Pompidou and his confederates turned the Gaullist party into a modern political machine. People from the far right either moderated their views or left the movement. The few 'hard' right-wingers who remained, for example Charles Pasqua today, have rarely occupied positions of much influence either in the party or the governments the Gaullists formed. Instead, a good third of the members of parliament, and an even larger proportion of its most important leaders, were recruited not from the *ministrables* of the Fourth Republic but from the upper ranks of the civil service. Others moved up the ranks through the Gaullist party hierarchy and, most notably, were all beholden to the

Pompidou machine for their careers.

In short, since the early 1960s, the Gaullist party has been dominated by centre-right politicians who occupy roughly the same space on the political spectrum as the German Christlich-Demokratische Union (CDU). Despite a flurry of interest in the market under the first cohabitation government (1986-88), there has not been a Gaullist equivalent of either the Thatcherite fixation on privatisation or the American religious right's obsession with abortion and other 'moral' issues.

The Gaullists have become what the late Otto Kirchheimer called a 'catch-all' party.[9] Ideology matters little. The RPR and its centre-right allies seek to win elections by literally trying to catch people from all major social, economic, and political groups. Campaigns are run primarily on television rather than by legions of ideologically committed militants.

Most importantly of all, the Gaullists all but wiped out the far right electorally for the better part of a quarter century. In the 1965 presidential election, Jean-Louis Tixier-Vignancour, who had made a name himself defending prominent Vichy government collaborators, won only 5 per cent of the vote. Other far right candidates fared even worse until the emergence of the National Front in the mid 1980s.

The anti-democratic right did not disappear. Organizations such as Ordre Nouveau had a visible presence in most cities and universities, especially in the law faculties. Other groups engaged in sabotage campaigns, such as the bombing of supermarkets. And, of course, the OAS was a major thorn in the Republic's side until de Gaulle had to court General Massu and then free General Salan and its other jailed leaders in May 1968.

Nonetheless, within a few short years, the far right—which, it will be recalled, had come very close to seizing power in 1958— became as weak as it had ever been since the Revolution of 1789. One simply has to look at leaders like Jacques Chirac or Alain Juppé to see how far toward the centre the French right has moved in the last forty years. Chirac's brusque and impatient nature has earned him to nickname of *le bulldozer,* but that's a far cry from what one might have said about right wing politicians of his parents' or grandparents' generation.

The National Front

At this point, the sceptical reader could well counter with the claim that the Gaullists and their allies are not where the right-wing 'action' is in France today. That is the province of Le Pen's FN which offers an entirely different and more menacing alternative and which reflects considerable continuity with the movements covered in early chapters.

At first glance, such arguments make sense. The FN does take what have to be regarded as all but explicitly racist and antisemitic positions which bring to mind the neo-fascist and neo-Nazi movements of earlier generations. Along those lines, the BBC World Service's Jonathan Marcus, states early in his book on the FN:

> It was established by the leadership of France's most important postwar neo-fascist organisation, Ordre Nouveau. Its aim was to create a movement that would bring together the disparate and often feuding families of the extreme right to amplify their message ... The Front was also to be a 'front' organisation in the literal sense, providing a respectable political facade, behind which the more traditional activist and street politics of the far right would continue.[10]

Emphasizing those origins and the occasional violence associated with the FN—for example, the fatal attack following one of its rallies between the two *tours* of the 1995 presidential election campaign and the often racist actions of the municipalities it controls—misses the most important historical development of Le Pen's movement. It, too, has made its peace with a republican regime.

The FN was formed in 1972 as the electoral arm of Ordre Nouveau and other far-right groups, all of which had clear links to many of the organizations discussed in earlier chapters. As long as the FN defined itself that way, it enjoyed little or no popular support.

Its breakthrough, chronicled in *Table 1*, reflects the remarkable success the FN has more recently enjoyed and, especially, the impact of the surprisingly charismatic Le Pen. As a 28 year old, he had been elected to parliament as a Poujadiste in 1956 and was re-elected two years later after having served as a *para* in Algeria. His opposition to de Gaulle and his pro-independence policy for Algeria undoubtedly cost Le Pen his seat in 1962.

He rallied early to the new FN and by the mid 1970s had became its most visible leader. A windfall inheritance and a failed assassination attempt in 1976 led him and his aide, Bruno Mégret, to try and soften the party's image, although the anti-Europeanism and racism was only partially disguised. The party's breakthrough came as a result of this change which enabled the FN to appeal to a wide cross-section of the electorate and not just the fanatical anti-republicans of the far right. Its first

notable success came in the 1983 municipal election in the dreary city of
Dreux, west of Paris, where its candidates won nearly 20 per cent of the
vote and where the first FN officials took seats on a municipal council.[11]

Table 1: Votes for the Front National Since 1986

Year	Type of election	Per cent of the popular vote
1986	legislative	9.9
1988	presidential	14.4
1988	legislative	9.8
1993	legislative	12.4
1995	presidential	15.2

Source: Hauss, Charles: *Comparative Politics. Domestic Responses to
Global Challenges* (St Paul, 1997, 2nd edn), pp. 128, 129, 132

It cannot be denied that Le Pen and his party adopt nationalistic, racist,
antisemitic, and anti-European positions that most people who read these
pages will find reprehensible. As Harvey Simmons most notably stresses
in his recent book on the FN, its rhetoric is as 'bad' as one sees anywhere
in the industrialized world today. What sets the FN apart from the parties
and sects considered elsewhere in this book is a commitment to 'working
within the system'. To be sure, the party has its share of thugs and others
who would prefer taking it dramatically rightward. Yet the polling
evidence is clear that any such move would cost the party dear in the
elections and could reduce its share of the vote to the minuscule levels won
by far-right candidates and parties in the 1960s and 1970s.

Unlike the groups covered in most of the early chapters of the present
volume, the FN has attracted remarkably broad-based and loyal support,
though the polling evidence is sketchier on the latter point. As *Table 2*
shows, the party does draw disproportionately from small shopkeepers and
others who have traditionally supported the far right. However, it also does
extremely well among manual workers and the poorly educated, including
(though *Table 2* does not show it) in areas that have recently voted heavily
communist.

Table 2:A Statistical Profile of Le Pen Voters in 1988

Category	Per cent of total population	Per cent Le Pen voters
Men	47	57
Less than baccalaureat	55	62
Live in cities <100,000	36	45
Shopkeepers	7	10
Blue collar workers	24	29

Source: Hauss, Charles: *Beyond Confrontation. Transforming the New World Order* (Westport, 1996) p 79. Adapted from Mayer, Nona and Perrineau, Pascal: 'Why Do They Vote for Le Pen?' *European Journal of Political Research*, 22 (1992), pp 123-141

The most compelling bit of evidence from *Table 2* is how much the FN's electorate resembles the voting population as a whole, and we know from other polling data that does not probe these questions, that there is next to no support for anti-system political parties or movements of any sort. While there is plenty of alienation from politicians and parties in France today, there is no reason to believe that it is more likely to manifest itself in insurrectionary politics than in Britain, the USA or Germany. Put simply, the French equivalents of German skinheads or the American militias are politically isolated, and the signs are that they will stay that way.

The FN is a serious and potentially very powerful force in French political life. Although the electoral system has virtually frozen it out of parliament with the exception of 1986 when a form of proportional representation was used, it has done well in all other kinds of elections. In particular, it has won control of four municipalities in southern France since the presidential election of 1995, and some polls showed it, rather than the Socialists, as the leading threat to the Gaullists for the 1998 parliamentary balloting. (In the event, the elections were held in 1997, and the Gaullists suffered atthe hands of the Socialists.)

There is little chance of the FN coming to power on its own, and the major centre-right parties have been reluctant to work with it even at the local levels. Nonetheless, there is little evidence that the party envisages fundamental constitutional change, anti-republican or otherwise.

To be sure, FN elected officials have engaged in what can only be considered reprehensible behavior, for example banning local libraries in the cities they control from buying left-wing books and periodicals or instituting a 'national preference' scheme that would amount to a sort of reverse positive discrimination for native-born French men and women. But that is a far cry from the kind of anti-system behavior we came to expect from their predecessors, including the very organizations that gave rise to the FN in the 1970s. Indeed, the rising star of the party, Bruno Mégret (whose wife was elected mayor of Vitrolles as his stand-in in February 1997) is widely seen as the leader most committed to shedding its street-fighting and anti-democratic past.

Again, consider the opinions of Jonathan Marcus on Mégret and the implications of the FN's victory at Vitrolles. From his (and my) perspective, Mégret represents all that is despicable about the far right, including veiled support for the Nazis and doubts about whether the Holocaust ever happened. But Marcus goes on to note:

> For all its success, the Front still exists within a political ghetto. Its national share of the vote appears stuck at a little less than the 15 per cent won by Le Pen in last year's presidential race. It can influence the political agenda. But it will not win power alone. Mégret has judged that for the Front to make a broad appeal to conservative voters it must move away from the strident, abusive tone of Le Pen. His aim is to take control of a party of protest and make it a party of government.[12]

I do not want to appear too pollyannish here. I am not trying to understate how awful the FN's rhetoric is or how objectionable its policies in those four municipalities have been. Rather, I believe that Le Pen's movement currently poses no threat to French democracy and that any further growth on its part will require even further moderation of its goals.

What is Left of the Right

The right is by far the dominant force in French politics having been in power on its own for 25 and sharing governmental control with the Socialists for four more of the first 39 years since de Gaulle came out of his 'retirement'. However, that does not mean it is particularly healthy, let alone showing signs of returning to the kinds of anti-system thought or action discussed in earlier chapters in this volume. Thus, if the third and most ambiguous piece of the argument presented here is correct, we may not only have seen the end of the anti-system right as a viable force in French politics, but we have now entered a period in which the very definitions of such terms as left and right no longer have any meaning.

As in so many industrialized democracies today, the right is not doing well so much because of its own strengths, but because of the far greater problems facing the left. In the French case, the failure of the Socialist Party to solve (m)any of the domestic problems it inherited in 1981 and its U-turn in the face of international economic pressures two years later threw the left into crisis long before the end of the Cold War. The collapse of communism and the *de facto* end of any sort of radical democratic socialism as a viable rallying point have sapped the left of much of what it used to offer voters. Former Prime Minister Michel Rocard has frequently spoken of the need for a 'big bang' to recreate the French left. Despite attempts at reform led by Lionel Jospin in the Parti Socialiste (PS) or efforts by Bernard Kouchner and others to form a new political party, nothing approaching the reforms of British New Labour, let alone a big bang, seem to be looming on the horizon.

In other words, the French right has been winning more by default than as a result of its own effective appeals or popular candidates. As noted earlier, neither the Gaullists nor their allies have been able to push through the kinds of sweeping reforms associated with Ronald Reagan, Margaret Thatcher, or Newt Gingrich. Instead, the most recent centre-right government has been characterized by its marked inability to pare back the welfare state and other domestic programmes to make the budgetary savings that will be required for France to join the European Monetary Union when and if it happens. French foreign policy under Chirac has been even more moderate, if by moderate we mean bringing it more into line with the European norm. Thus France has been one of the strongest supporters of further European union, has taken strong steps toward integrating its troops into NATO, and has even floated the possibility of joint German-French management of the *force de frappe*. In sum, the French right is probably less distinctive and, literally, less right wing, than any of its counterparts in the other major industrialized democracies.

On top of that, the French—in common with almost every other nation in Europe—are divided by issues of race and European integration that show only the faintest echoes of the kind of politics we saw before 1958. It is true that the far right has historically played on racial and nationalistic themes. It is true that both have fuelled the growth of the Front National and, occasionally, candidates from other far-right rganizations. But, for the reasons discussed earlier, there does seem to be a strong psychological firewall that keeps even strong opposition to current policy or leaders from turning into the anti-system protest of earlier generations.

One can certainly go too far in stressing cultural explanations of specific events or even trends. Nonetheless, the limited polling data and more anecdotal research of leading journalists suggest that French voters are as much at peace with their regime as they have ever been. Indeed, one of the most remarkable trends is that support for the Fifth Republic has not dropped at all despite the many policy problems it has faced, especially since the OPEC oil embargo and the end of *les trentes glorieuses.*

Perhaps most important of all for the long term, a series of polls and less systematic soundings of public opinion have shown that the very terms left and right no longer matter much to most voters, especially younger ones.[13] *Table 3*, for instance, shows an increasing number of people who felt that the terms left and right had become out of date. Similarly, *Table 4* shows that on all but two issues, a majority of the voters questioned in one 1993 survey found little or no difference between left and right.

Table 3: The Meaning of Left and Right (1)

Per cent stating that the terms left and right were still meaningful

Year	Still meaningful	Out of date
1981	43	33
1993	33	55

Source: Duhamel, Olivier and Jaffré, Jérôme: 'Un paysage politique dévasté,' in O. Duhamel and J. Jaffré, eds: *L'état de l'opinion 1993* (Paris, 1993) p 12

Tables 4:The Meaning of Left and Right (2)

In a 1993 SOFRES poll, the per cent answering that there was little difference (rather than a lot) between the right and left was:

Issue	Per cent
National defence	47
Foreign policy	47
Economic policy	52
Fight against crime	55
European integration	55
Suburban problems	55
Education	57
Social welfare and security	65
Fight against unemployment	77

Source: Duhamel, Olivier and Jaffré, Jérôme: 'L'abécédaire de l'opinion', in Duhamel and Jaffré, eds: *L'état de l'opinion 1993*, p. 223

For 30 years, political scientists have been talking about the *marais*, a sizable group of essentially apolitical voters who place themselves in the middle but for whom that—or any political self-definition—means virtually nothing.[14] The sketchier recent evidence, though, goes further in pointing to a relatively large group of voters who are politically engaged but find the politicians and policies of the established parties *passé*, at best. Thus, as *Table 5* shows, we have seen a marked shift in the percentage of voters supporting 'outside the system' parties over the last 20 years.

Table 5: The Decline of the Mainstream Parties

	1978	1986	1993
Mainstream parties	74	56	45
Non-mainstream parties	7	19	20
Abstentions/spoiled ballots	19	25	35

Source: Adapted from Mény, Yves: 'The Reconstruction and De-construction of the French Party System', in G. Flynn, ed: *Remaking the Hexagon. The New France in the New Europe* (Boulder, 1995)

Some observers find it tempting to read signs of an incipient, major anti-systemic protest lurking in these data. What such analyses fail to note is that for virtually all French men and women, the anger and alienation only go so far. However little they may think of today's parties and politicians, virtually no one is willing to question the basic institutions and practices of the Fifth Republic. For the first time in French history, almost everyone from all but the most extreme leftist to the most reactionary rightist accepts the political rules of the game which puts powerful, if hard to specify, limits on what any protest movement can hope to accomplish.

Another Cliché Bites the Dust?

One thing we political scientists should have learned from historians by now is that it never makes sense to say that 'x' will never happen. There have been too many 'x's' in the last 10 to 20 years for us to rule anything out politically.

Nonetheless, the shifts discussed in this chapter and the stark contrast between it and the rest of this volume suggests that 1958 may have been as important a turning point in French history as 1789. If so, it may well be time to shed one of those enduring clichés about France—*plus ça change, plus c'est la même chose*.

If the argument made here is even close to correct, 1958 marked one of those major watersheds in French history which also forms a sharp line of demarcation between the normal concerns of historians and political scientists. On the basis of listening to and now reading the papers that form the rest of this book, that may not be a good thing for us academics since it will make interdisciplinary work all the more difficult. On the other hand, there should be no question that it is good for France, which, of course, is far more important...

Notes

1.   I should like to dedicate this chapter to the memory of Peter Morris. Though long an admirer of his work, our brief friendship only began at the conference that led to this volume. This was to have been his chapter, but the illness that tragically ended his life made that impossible, and that task fell onto my shoulders. Peter's insight, grace and wit inluenced my writing for years from afar and my life as a visiting scholar in the United Kingdom for but a few months. The ideas that follow are as much his as mine. The essay was completed before President Chirac unexpectedly called the parliamentary elections in 1997.

2.   On this issue, see the latest and most comprehensive analysis of the Front National, Simmons, Harvey G.: *The French National Front. The Extremist Challenge to Democracy* (Boulder, 1996).

3.   This section draws heavily on my *Politics in Gaullist France. Coping with Chaos* (Westport, 1991).

4.   These are, of course, familiar themes. For an overview see Cobban, Alfred: *A History of Modern France* (New York, 1966), vol 3, or Thomson, David: *French Democracy* (Oxford, 1969).

5.   Williams, Philip: *Crisis and Compromise. Politics in the Fourth Republic* (Hamden, 1964)

6.   Hoffmann, Stanley: *Change and Renewal* (New York, 1969) and his 'Heroic Leadership: The Case of Modern France', in L.Edinger, ed: *Political Leadership in Industrialized Societies* (New York, 1967), pp 108-54

7.   On the long-term impact of the Gaullists as a governing and electoral force, see Knapp, Andrew: *Gaullism since de Gaulle* (Aldershot, 1994) and the rest of the voluminous literature on the subject, most of which is cited in Knapp's volume, the most comprehensive source on this subject.

8.   The Gaullist party went by a number of names. In fact, it changed its name before each election until Jacques Chirac and his colleagues renamed it the Ralliement pour la République (RPR) which it has been since the mid 1970s. To minimize possible confusion, I have used the generic term Gaullist throughout this essay even though it was never one of the party's

formal names.

9.   Kircheimar, Otto: 'The Transformation of the Western Party Systems', in
      M.Weiner and J.LaPalombara, eds: *Political Parties and Political
      Development* (Princeton, 1966), pp 166-200
10.   Marcus, Jonathan: *The National Front and French Politics. The Resistible
      Rise of Jean-Marie Le Pen* (London, 1995), p 12
11.   Gaspard, Françoise: *A Small Town in France* (Cambridge, Mass., 1995)
12.   Marcus, Jonathan: 'The Long March of Bruno Mégret', *New Statesman*, 14
      February 1997, p 26
13.   See the delightful in-depth study of about 60 voters coordinated by
      Mossuz- Lavau, Jeanine: *Les français et la politique* (Paris, 1994)
14.   Deutsch, Lindon and Weill: *Les familles politiques en France* (Paris, 1966)
      and Pierce, Roy and Converse, Philip: *The Politics of Representation in
      France* (Cambridge, Mass., 1986)

16. TOWARDS A SIXTH REPUBLIC? JEAN-MARIE LE PEN AND THE 2002 ELECTIONS

Nicholas Atkin and Frank Tallett

'Etat de choc.'[1] 'Le cauchemar Le Pen.'[2] 'La blessure'.[3] 'Séisme.'[4] 'Démolition.'[5] 'Non'.[6]

These were some of the headlines in the French political press in the aftermath of the first round of the presidential elections of 21 April 2002 in which the Front National (FN) leader scored some 16.95 per cent of the vote pipping the mainstream Socialist candidate Lionel Jospin who managed 16.12 per cent, thus putting the extreme right candidate into the second round run-off with the incumbent president Jacques Chirac, who garnered a scarcely resounding 19.71 per cent. Having broken into the mainstream of French politics after the left's overwhelming victory in 1981—in the 1984 European elections, the FN won 11.2 per cent of votes cast—the party appeared to some to be on the brink of attaining what it had always threatened, the transformation of its modest success in local, parliamentary and European elections into victory on the national stage by securing the most glittering of political prizes, the presidency. It also seemed to have bounced back from the internal divisions of 1999 when Bruno Mégret, the spokesperson of the traditionalist and integrist wing of the FN, broke away, eventually to found the Mouvement National Républicain (MNR). In April 2002, Mégret came twelfth in the list of 16 presidential candidates, managing a meagre 2.35 per cent.

To many commentators, April 2002 was a return to the crisis politics de Gaulle's Fifth republic had been designed to avert, and which had characterised the earlier Third and Fourth Republics, both of which had witnessed shocks linked to the emergence of the far right: Boulanger; Dreyfus; the Stavisky scandal; June 1940; and Poujade. Both *Le Monde* and *L'Express* outlined a chilling foretaste of what a Le Pen presidency might mean: a huge expansion of the prison population; restoration of the death penalty and the franc; an end to abortion; the curtailment of women's rights; expulsion of immigrants; renegotiation of France's international treaty arrangements; in sum, the establishment of an autocratic police state cut off from the rest of Europe.[7] To make matters worse, the flowering of the far right in France seemed to be part of a more general shift to the extremes, marked by the success of Jorg Haider's Freedom Party in Austria, the Italian Alliance Nationale, Belgium's Vlaams Blok and Pim Fortuyn's List in Holland. Small wonder that committed liberal democrats throughout the world raised their voices in horror. Within Germany, the Social Democrat foreign minister Joschka Fischer called the result of 21 April 'alarming' while Neil Kinnock, the EU Commissioner and former leader of the British Labour party, described it as 'a great dirty rock in the European political pool', an opinion shared by Tony Blair. Their concerns were perhaps best summarised by the intervention of the Polish premier, the left-leaning Leszek Miller, who labelled Le Pen as a real threat to the European Union.[8]

The purpose of this essay is not to proffer a definition of the politics of the FN. Arguments as to whether it is a continuation of the Bonapartist, Legitimist or Orleanist traditions, or whether it represents a new phenomenon in the history of the far right, have been rehearsed more than adequately in the essays by Jim Wolfreys and Chip Hauss in the present volume, as well as in the works of Jean-Yves Camus, Nonna Mayer and Renaud Dély, to name but a few.[9] It is instead to consider whether the performance of Le Pen and his party in 2002, in both the presidential and parliamentary elections, is nothing more than a blip or if it constitutes a truly seismic shift which poses a real threat to liberal democracy. In this context, it must also be asked whether there is a fundamental malaise at the heart of the Fifth Republic which has allowed Le Pen to come so close to securing power. Commentators are speaking of the 'parenthesis' of the regime as if it had already passed.[10] The threats from without, including globalisation, immigration and European integration, appear to be stretching the constitutional structures of the Fifth in such a way that it is struggling to cope with internal matters. Should the regime disintegrate into crisis, it can only be believed that the FN will exploit this for whatever it is worth.

While many media commentators in both France and elsewhere were deeply unsettled by Le Pen's first round 'victory', cooler heads recognised that the result was not out of line with previous performances. In 1988, he secured 4,375,894 votes; in 1995, 4,570,000; and in 2002, nearly 4.8 million. Moreover, there was an appreciation that he had little chance of defeating Chirac in the second round face-off, as indeed proved to be the case. On 5 May, the FN leader mobilised 5,525,907 votes (17.79 per cent) against the incumbent president's 25,540,874 votes (82.21 per cent). Taking advantage of the political situation, Chirac moved quickly to initiate parliamentary elections in which the Gaullist-orientated Union pour la Majorité Présidentielle (UMP) secured over 40 per cent of the popular vote, thus securing a comfortable majority in the 577-seat parliament. While the Socialist party was ousted from office, there were few crumbs for comfort for the FN, its share of the vote down to 11.2 per cent in the first round, similar to performances in the 1990s, but unable to sustain the momentum of seven weeks earlier.

Even allowing for the way in which the anti-Le Pen vote rallied behind Chirac in the presidential run-off, the above statistics suggest that the FN may well have reached a plateau in its appeal, unable to move beyond the successes of the 1990s when it captured the mayoralties of Toulon, Orange and Marignane. As in the past, the majority of Le Pen's support came from men; 20 per cent of all males voted for the far right leader as opposed to 14 per cent of women.[11] Nor were there any great surprises in the patterns of regional strength. FN heartlands have long included those areas subject to insecurity: fear of crime; fear of unemployment; and fear of immigrants. So it was that Le Pen gained more than 20 per cent of the popular votes in the following regions: the Nord; Picardy, Champagne; Alsace-Lorraine; Franche-Comté; Provence; the Côte d'Azur; and Languedoc-Roussillon. Crudely described, these areas form an arc along the eastern border and Mediterranean coastline. Political scientists have frequently spoken of a Caen-Montpellier dividing line in which the western half of France is less susceptible to FN propaganda.[12] It will not go unnoticed that, in very general terms, the most urbanised regions are located in the east; in the more rural districts of the west, it has proved difficult to manufacture a single issue such as fear of foreigners around which to coalesce support. Another constant apparent in 2002 was the momentum built up among the 'have nots'. Typical of a party which in 1995 only won the support of 9 per cent of those with a higher education qualification, Le Pen outscored his rivals among the unemployed (38 per cent of all votes) and blue-collar workers (26.1 per cent of all votes). This might give support to Mégret's argument that the FN should make greater efforts to tap into mainstream conservative sympathies, but as others have stressed we should not perhaps dwell overly on the demographics of FN support.[13] As already stressed, fear has been the common currency of

Lepénisme and this is a theme which plays well with all social and regional groupings.

Yet if Le Pen's support in April 2002 reached a plateau, what remains disturbing and depressing is the way in which he was able to influence the agenda for debate. The focus was shifted from the legacy of the Jospin government, in particular the credibility of the thirty-five hour week, to the issues of crime, unemployment, big business, anti-Europeanism and, inevitably, immigration. Like other far right movements in France, the FN has never been a single-issue party, but has been singularly successful in placing so many issues under the banner of 'race', a process termed 'ethnisation de l'insécurité'.[14] On one level, this has disrupted moves towards greater integration, especially of the so-called *beurs*, those French nationals born of Algerian parents. An example of this has been the fortunes of the French national football team. In 1996 Le Pen had mocked the chances of the squad led by the talented midfielder Zinedine Zidane, originally the son of Algerian immigrants to Marseilles, pronouncing that it was 'artificial to bring in foreign players and call them the French team', adding that they did not know the words of the *Marseillaise*.[15] Two years later, on 12 July, the French victory in the World Cup produced a celebration of France's multi-cultural traditions, epitomised in such slogans as 'tricolore et multicolore' and 'black-blanc-beur'. Not everyone, however, was convinced, and a mood persisted that only those outsiders prepared to be assimilated into French culture were to be tolerated. As the FN's *Cinquante Propositions sur l'immigration* made clear, it was primarily those of European origin, generally Catholic and with French blood in their veins, who were acceptable as French citizens.[16] This was the language that Pétain, Maurras and Vallat would have understood, and which had flowed through Vichy's early legislation on citizenship.

Another way in which Le Pen's presidential campaign, together with his previous electioneering, set the agenda was to drive all parties into the adoption of tough rhetoric and policies on race. When elected in 1995, Chirac extended the discriminatory legislation first introduced under his premiership in 1986 by the interior minister Charles Pasqua. In 1997, the Debré law compelled citizens to notify the authorities of foreigners staying on their premises. It was a ridiculous piece of legislation, and one which the Socialists promised to repeal on their parliamentary triumph later that year, only to find that public opinion was against them. Although the left had earlier rallied to the cause of *SOS Racisme* and its local counterpart, *Alerte Orange*, and although left-wing voters fell behind Chirac in the second round of the presidential vote in 2002, there was no escaping the fact that Le Pen, with his talk of French identity being 'mutilated', had succeeded in legimating a particular type of discourse over race in which politicians have been frightened of appearing 'soft', preventing any proper debate and undermining any sustained moves towards multi-ethnic integration and positive discrimination.[17] It remains the case that there are no *beurs* in the Senate, nor among the 36,000 mayors. Yet sooner than address this issue, the mainstream conservatives continue to press for more restrictive measures in this area. Thus Jean de Belot, editor of the conservative *Le Figaro*, predicted, 'Chirac should more further towards the right. He will have to address the problems that Mr Le Pen has raised. One isn't supposed to say it—but France does have a problem with immigration and this is something Mr Chirac will have to do something about.'[18]

If Le Pen has succeeded in legitimating a particular mode of speaking on race, he has also succeeded in legitimating the FN as *the* party of protest. Notwithstanding the outcry that greeted his success in the first round, there is not denying that he drew votes from all those who believed they had a grievance. 'La France d'en bas' either ignored the ballot box altogether or used the FN as the receptacle for their *vote de doléance*. Should they have drawn up their own *cahiers*, in the manner of 1788-9, these would have listed an opposition to the faceless bureaucrats of Brussels and Strasbourg, the unfamiliarity of the euro, their alienation from the political elites, the fear of crime, unemployment and poverty, and their profound mistrust of 'outsiders'.[19] While these voters did not necessarily expect, nor even wish for a Le Pen victory, they were concerned to give a kick to the system, not always an indicator of the good health of a liberal democracy. For his part, Le Pen has encouraged such malcontents not just by rehearsing his familiar laments about immigration and Europe, but also by altering FN policy in a fairly pragmatic and unashamed way. For instance, the earlier stress on free-market economics, an admiration for Thatcher and Reagan, has given way to the championing of 'préférence nationale' which would give priority to French citizens in respect of employment, social security payments, medical assistance and state support for small businesses. At the time of this chapter going to press there were suggestions that the youngest of Le Pen's daughters, Marine, was seeking to dilute the FN's hard-line position on Europe, bringing it into line with the populist approach favoured by far-right parties in Austria and Holland.[20] While some elements of the FN have never been altogether sure whether the movement should remain a party of protest, Le Pen himself has never had any doubts that it should seek power and the April results have done nothing to dent his unbridled ambition and unwavering confidence.

The chief casualties of the confirmation of the FN as *the* protest party have been the Greens and the Communists. The former—riddled by internal divisions, split over their attidue towards the left and with certain of their environmentalist policies stolen by the FN—could never hope to gain a substantial following in the presidential elections, but in the ensuing parliamentary campaign they saw their share of seats down from 7 to 2. As to the Communists, already struggling with long-term decline, they fared so poorly in April that they did not even cross the threshold which would have entitled them to repayment of their election expenses. The fact that there were three Trotskyist candidates hardly helped the cause. As *Libération* pointed out, the crisis of identity on the left has helped the right in much the same way as divisions on the left in Italy have assisted the populist Berlusconi.[21] The Communists did better in June, retaining the 20 or so deputies needed to comprise a parliamentary bloc though their leader, Robert Hue, lost his own constituency. On becoming leader of the PCF in 1994, after the resignation of the unreconstructed Stalinist Georges Marchais, Hue had promised to repulse the FN onslaught; in 2002 his dream seems in tatters. As the historian Marc Lazar has observed, Hue's fate has been to play the part of a Gorbachev—to have opened the archives, to have renounced Stalinism, to have made contact with intellectuals—only for his vision of social democracy to fail.[22]

Jospin's fate has been to emulate that of Pierre Mendès-France, to have been a fundamentally decent man who failed to connect with the concerns of the voters. He had anticipated from the onset that he would be in the second-round run-off with Chirac and grossly underestimated the challenge from the far right, relying too heavily on opinion polls which were ultimately misleading. Whereas Le Pen spoke the language of *le métallo*, Jospin hesitated to speak of *les travailleurs*; whereas Le Pen embraced the working classes, Jospin appeared to be surrounded by elitist intellectuals; whereas Le Pen appropriated *La Marseillaise*, Jospin vaunted the merits of the European union; whereas Le Pen denounced weekly car burnings by 'yobs' from immigrant ghettos, Jospin alluded to 'incivilities' caused by 'youths'; whereas Le Pen happily revealed his anti-Semitism, Jospin believed that to address such matters was to descend to the level of gutter politics; whereas Le Pen's electioneering was its usual crude sloganeering, Jospin hesitated and failed to use the media to its full potential; whereas Le Pen's campaign was clear from the outset, Jospin's was anything but (he himself ordered various last-minute alterations to the manifesto); whereas Le Pen blasted the record of the government, Jospin failed to play up the very real achievements of his premiership. It proved to be an unequal contest, but should not have been, and it has plunged the French left into another round of despair and soul-searching, made worse by having to vote for Chirac in order to deny Le Pen. That the Parti Socialiste (PS) may bounce back is evidenced in the reconstruction previously undertaken by Mitterrand after 1965 and Rocard in 1988, but the left must take responsibility for failing to rally around Jospin when he took over the leadership in 1995.

If Jospin conducted a torpid presidential campaign, he has received further criticism for his silence after defeat. It was only after the intervention of the PS secretary Françoise Hollande, that he issued a four-line fax urging French men and women to vote for democracy, albeit without mentioning the name of Chirac.[23] While this could be interpreted as pique, there was some measure of truth in Jospin's belief that the incumbent president had opened the way for extremism. We have already noted how the Gaullist response to the flourishing of the far right was to move politics towards this end of the political spectrum and not to condemn in outright terms the unashamed racism of Le Pen's supporters. In the campaign itself, Chirac was mechanical and uninspirational, living up to his image as 'resident of the Republic' rather than 'president of the Republic'. Even his adherents were dismayed at the small turn-outs at his rallies and the obvious lack of enthusiasm. The decision to put the focus of his campaign on 'security' almost certainly played into the hands of Le Pen. As Serge July remarked in *Libération*, 'On this ground [security], Le Pen was the best, much better even than Chirac and naturally better than Jospin without having to make the slightest effort. Security eclipsed every other subject, every other consideration.'[24] In the event, the slight increase in the FN presidential vote, compared to 1995, appears to have come predominantly from disaffected Chiracians. It was not just his role in the electoral campaign which told against him, but the record of his *septennat*, which had failed to provide direction and grandeur. The allegations of corruption dating back to when he was mayor of Paris, which would have almost certainly have led Chirac into the dock had he not won in May, further damaged his own prestige and that of his office. As many disaffected socialists chanted after April, 'votez escroc, pas fascho' (vote for a crook, rather than a fascist').[25] In these circumstances, it is perhaps fitting that the presidential term should have been recently reduced to five years, but it was Chirac's inertia which had persuaded many of the logic of this move, including the former president Giscard d'Estaing.

It is too early to know whether the confirmation of Chirac as president, the ensuing parliamentary triumph of the UMP and the premiership of Jean-Pierre Raffarin, who promises the politics of austerity, will heal the divisions within the democratic right. Up until the April elections, this was seriously divided between its many factions, notably those fronted by François Bayrou, Charles Pasqua and Alain Madelin. What is certain is that April 2002 was a hollow victory for Chirac, something he himself more or less admitted. On the morning after, he acknowledged, 'Our parties are ridiculed. They are ineffectual. The system has become powerless. We have grave responsibilities.'[26] As his more far-sighted supporters added, 'We do not know who has won, but we know who has lost.'[27] The obvious answer is, of course, the Socialists. Yet what of the Fifth Republic itself? Given that the FN has repeatedly called for a Sixth Republic, is it the case that the Le Pen vote has paved the way for a change of regime?

That the Fifth is not in a good state of health cannot be doubted. It has recently endured several misfortunes, some of which it has brought upon itself. The inability of politicians to establish 'transmission belts' with the people, to move outside of their ivory towers and understand the popular pulsebeat, has produced a general apathy towards politics, most vividly expressed in the number of abstentions, although these have not reached the levels recorded in Britain. This has long been a problem for the Republic, especially in parliamentary and regional elections, and has been notably marked in such areas as the Nord and Alsace, localities suffering from economic retrenchment. Yet the April 2002 election set a new low in turn-out in presidential voting, at 27.83 per cent abstentions, compared to 20.3 per cent in 1995 and 15.9 per cent in 1988, 14.1 per cent in 1981 and 12.7 per cent in 1974.[28] In this respect, it could be argued that the media fuelled this malaise by failing to highlight the differences between Jospin and Chirac. This blurring has, above all, been facilitated by the process of *cohabitation*, a phenomenon which has constantly divided public opinion. As *Libération* commented, five years of *cohabitation* gave the impression that the script for the election had been written in advance and that Chirac and Jospin were guaranteed to carry on in government regardless.[29] This undoubtedly led many on the right to express their disappointment by voting for Le Pen; and for those on the left to abstain, or to vote for one of the extreme leftist challengers, 'une gauche de gauche' as Pierre Bourdieu noted.[30] Not that politicians themselves have helped their cause. Voters have long empathised with Le Pen's claims that their leaders are fundamentally corrupt. When de Gaulle founded the Fifth Republic, he was quick to call upon experts and tech-nocrats, notably the graduates of the Ecole Nationale d'Adminstration (ENA), a process that has continued with men and women holding ever-multiplying portfolios in local and national government, as well as in the worlds of commerce and business. This has inevitably led to a clash of interests and, in certain instances, the temptations have proved too great. The past ten years have seen a steady succession of politicians charged in the courts with corruption: for instance, the prominent RPR men François Léotard, Maurice Arreckx, and Jacques Médecin of the Independents. While a majority of these scandals have involved the right, the left has not been exempt, witness the case of Pierre Bérégovoy, Laurent Fabius, Bernard Tapie and, most crucially, Mitterrand himself.

Le Pen has also been able to throw mud at the Fifth Republic thanks to a growing feeling that those in charge are no longer in control of the country's destiny. Here, the principal culprits are threefold. First, Le Pen has been able to exploit a growing Euroscepticism prevalent among the public, albeit not among the elites. This has not just been the familiar lament about faceless bureaucrats, but a wider anxiety that France is in danger of losing its identity and independence as Europe grows in size, the euro is implemented, voting procedures are amended, the Common Agricultural Policy is reviewed, a deflationary economic policy is pur-sued and Germany remains overbearing. The second aspect, closely tied to the first, has been the influx of immigrants both from within the com-munity and from former colonial possessions. One of the reasons why the Maastricht vote of September 1992 was so finely balanced (51 per cent for, 49 per cent against) was the fear that 'non-French' candidates could occupy public office, not that this has happened to any great extent. Le Pen, however, would argue that foreigners have brought their un-fathomable quarrels into France, in particular the quarrels which divide Islamic fundamentalists and Zionists in the Middle East. The final factor, one which is not unique to France, is the threat of globalisation, that is the takeover of French culture and economic autonomy by multinationals, often Anglo-Saxon in background, which are unanswerable to elected governments.[31] To be fair, globalisation threatens the elites just as much as it does the popular classes, though their respective perceptions of the phenomenon vary. Yet it is the men and women in the street who often feel most helpless. Like Poujade before him, Le Pen has always been the purported champion of the 'little man' in the struggle for economic survival, a decent standard of living and the maintenance an untainted French identity.

Viewed from this broader perspective, it may be argued that the show-ing of Le Pen in the April 2002 elections is a symptom of the systemic weaknesses within the Fifth Republic and not the cause of its malaise. When de Gaulle established the regime in the period 1958-62, the consti-tutional structures were vital and reinforced the power of the state whose destinies were very much in the hands of its president and a cadre of elites drawn from the commercial, academic, industrial and bureaucratic matrix. What has happened, especially over the past two decades, is that socio-economic changes, characterised by globalisation, multi-ethnicity, information technology and the end of the Cold War, have produced a dysfunction between the state and its elites and the increasingly amor-phous population. Multi-national corporations or Brussels take decisions which previously would have been the province of local notables, pre-fects, deputies or the president. In this situation, charismatic politicians offering apparent panaceas come to the fore. Le Pen, with his demand for a renegotiation of Maastricht, his demands for 'France for the French', his desire to implement compulsory repatriation and to see off the malign influence of American culture, is merely the latest, albeit the most suc-cessful, in a long line of individuals, the majority of whom have sprung from the right: Boulanger; de la Rocque; Pétain; and Poujade. In the past, such men and their movements have been damaging to the mainstream right, as has been true of the FN which split the Rassemblement pour la République (RPR), forcing it into unsavoury local pacts and compelling it to adopt hardline policies which disturbed the fundamental faith in democracy. What was so damaging in April 2002 was the harm which the FN was able to inflict on the Socialists although, again, the left failed to heed the warning signs.

It is perhaps reassuring that, although France has had a propensity to turn to national savours at moments of crisis and to accord them extensive powers, this has happened only rarely and in times of grave emergency: Bonaparte in 1799; Pétain in 1940; and de Gaulle in 1958. Although there is a general sense of insecurity at the moment, and Le Pen is able to capitalise on this, there is no counter-revolution, no Nazi menace and no Algeria. Nor does he enjoy the same stature as these other figures; his record as paratrooper in Algeria has not played prominently in his appeal. None of this, however, is cause for complacency. What consequences might have resulted had the attempt of the neo-Nazi Maxime Brunerie to assassinate the President on 14 July been successful must remain specula-tive. This could have led to a rallying around the Republic, or it might have precipitated a crisis of nerve in which a constitutional melt-down became a possibilitiy. That the Fifth Republic is a regime in trouble is not in doubt, and if it is to offset the extreme right-wing threat it must deal with the problems that provide Le Pen with his opportunity. This involves a fundamental rethinking of its structures so as to promote integration, to rid the system of corruption and to reduce the power of the adminstrative elites. As the distinguished historian of France Stephen Kaplan has observed, to speak of April 2002 as a 'seismic shift' is over the top, excessive and 'very French', but the crisis is real and will not go away.[32]

Notes

We are grateful to our colleague, Joël Félix, for his comments on an earlier draft of this paper.

1.   *Le Point*, 25 April 2002.
2.   *L'Express*, 2-8 May 2002.
3.   *Le Monde*, 23 April 2002.
4.   *Le Parisien*, 22 April 2002.
5.   *Le Figaro*, 23 April 2002.
6.   *Libération*, 22 April 2002.
7.   *Le Monde*, 28-29 April 2002 and *L'Express*, 2-8 May 2002.
8.   Quotations from BBC News online, www.news.bbc.co.uk, 22 April 2002.
9.   See Camus, Jean-Yves: *Le Front National. Histoire et analyses* (Paris, 1996); Mayer, Nonna: *Ces Français qui votent FN* (Paris, 1999); and Dély, Renaud: *Histoire secrète du Front National* (Paris, 1999).
10. See the forthcoming article by Vinen, Richard: 'The parenthesis of the Fifth Republic', in the Oxford History of France, edited by James F. McMillan. We are grateful to the author for an early sight of this piece.
11. *The Observer*, 28 April 2002.
12. See Camus, Jean-Yves: *Le Front National* (Toulouse, 1998), pp 42-3.
13. See Vaughan, M.: 'The Extreme Right in France: *Lepénisme* or the Politics of Fear', in L. Cheles, R. Ferguson & M. Vaughan eds: *Neo-Fascism in Europe* (London, 1991), p 226.
14. Christophe Barbier writing in *L'Express*, 28 May 2002.
15. Quoted in Gildea, Robert: *France since 1945* (Oxford, 2002, 2nd ed), pp 176-7.
16. Camus, *Front National*, pp 40-1.
17. *Nouvel Observateur*, 2 May 2002.
18. BBC News online interview, www.news.bbc.co.uk, Monday 6 May 2002.
19. See Matthieu Crossandeau and Sophie des Désarts, 'Voyage en Nouvelle-lepénie', *Nouvel Observateur*, 2 May 2002.
20. *The Independent on Sunday*, 20 October 2002.
21. *Libération*, 22 April 2002.
22. 'Gauche: union à géométrie variable', *L'Express*, 2-8 May 2002.

23. The fax is reproduced on the front page of *Libération*, 27-28 April 2002.
24. Serge July writing in *Libération*, 22 April 2002.
25. *The Observer*, 28 April 2002.
26. Quoted in *L'Express*, 2-8 May 2002.
27. *Ibid.*
28. Figures from *Le Point*, 25 April 2002.
29. *Libération*, 22 April 2002.
30. *Ibid.*
31. See especially Gordon, Philip: *The French Challenge. Adapting to Globalisation* (New York, 2000).
32. Stephen Kaplan writing in *L'Express*, 2-8 May 2002.

INDEX